1991

THE
POLITICAL
ECONOMY
OF
CONTEMPORARY
EGYPT

Edited by
Ibrahim M. Oweiss

Center for Contemporary Arab Studies
Georgetown University
Washington, DC 20057

Tel.: (202) 687-5793
Fax: (202) 687-1431

Published by Center for Contemporary Arab Studies,
Georgetown University, Washington, DC

Library of Congress Cataloging-in-Publication Data

The Political Economy of Contemporary Egypt/edited
by Ibrahim M. Oweiss
    p.   cm.
Includes index.

ISBN 0-932568-20-3 (cloth). —ISBN 0-932568-21-1 (pbk.)
    1. Egypt—Economic conditions—1952-
2. Egypt—Economic policy.   3. Egypt—Politics and
government—1952-   . I. Oweiss, Ibrahim M.
II. Georgetown University. Center for Contemporary Arab
Studies.
HC830.P63 1990
338.962'009'045—dc20   90-15057

CONTENTS

Part 3: Epilogue

ACKNOWLEDGEMENTS

It is a pleasure to acknowledge the contributions of the authors of this volume and the efforts of all of those who participated in one way or another in the symposium that led to it.

The book originated with a decision by the Executive Committee of the Center for Contemporary Arab Studies of Georgetown University to devote its annual symposium in 1988 to the study of Egypt. Members of the Center's Executive Committee are Halim Barakat, Michael C. Hudson, Ibrahim Ibrahim, Peter F. Krogh, Ibrahim M. Oweiss, John Ruedy, Hisham Sharabi, Barbara Stowasser, Seth Tillman and Judith Tucker. The Center's Steering Committee was cochaired by Michael C. Hudson and Ibrahim M. Oweiss, assisted by several colleagues, the Center's staff and many student volunteers. The symposium benefited from the leadership and participation of Dr. Peter F. Krogh, Dean of the School of Foreign Service. The Center's public affairs administrative officer at the time, Marisa Tamari, ran the conference with skill and devotion. Michael Baker, then the Center's assistant director, spared no effort to ensure the symposium's success.

In the process of converting the symposium proceedings into a book, several persons lent valuable support. I would like to express appreciation to Charles Issawi, Said El-Naggar and Yusif A. Sayigh, who read part of the economic section, as well as others who acted as referees and wish to remain anonymous, in line with publishing conventions. Without the continuous and meticulous work of Michael Simpson, the Center's Director of Publications, the volume could not have appeared in its present form.

Generous support for the publication of the book was provided by a private fund created in honor of Dr. Constantine K. Zurayk, who is a former CCAS Visiting Scholar and longtime friend of the Center, and by the School of Foreign Service's Father Edmund A. Walsh Fund, administered by Dr. Charles E. Pirtle, Associate Dean of the School of Foreign Service.

Finally, I would like to express my personal appreciation to the

Egyptian students in Cairo, Alexandria, Tanta, Assiut and Aswan who ably assisted me as researchers in the survey of the economic behavior of Egyptian households whose results are reported in my study in this volume.

Ibrahim M. Oweiss
Center for Contemporary Arab Studies

PREFACE

Most books on recent political and economic developments in Egypt deal with either the Nasser or the Sadat periods. This volume examines the aftermath of both. Its focus is the economic and political systems and problems of contemporary Egypt. The contributors engage in surveys and analyses of the present situation, its difficulties and opportunities. Many also look to the future, with a variety of suggestions as to how a country in Egypt's situation can surmount its daunting problems.

All but one of the contributions to the book originated in a symposium organized by the Center for Contemporary Arab Studies in 1988 on the critical decisions facing Egypt. The book includes articles derived from those papers whose principal subject was the political economy of Egypt. Most have been revised and updated with the intention of making the volume a cohesive book and not merely a record of conference proceedings.

By the end of the 1980s, Egypt faced crises in virtually all economic sectors. Problems of low productivity and poor economic management were compounded by the adverse social effects of large population growth rates, high inflation and massive urban overcrowding. Overshadowing Egypt's future plans lay the problems of servicing a massive foreign debt. Despite this, most contributors to the part of this book dealing with the Egyptian economy argue that there are economic options available to Egypt that could ameliorate its situation.

The article by Ibrahim Oweiss, the editor of the book, offers a comprehensive overview of the situation of the Egyptian economy. It deals with the performance of different sectors, giving particular attention to agriculture, and analyzes the problems of income maldistribution, unemployment, inflation, the underground economy, the budget and balance of payments deficits, investment commitments, the housing shortage, bureaucratic mismanagement and the decline in marginal productivity.

One of the notable features of the contribution by Dr. Oweiss is its development of a new methodology for dealing with the problem of estimating the size of an "informal" or underground economy—a methodology which seems to be widely applicable to the study of other Third World countries. In Egypt, as in many other countries, official macroeconomic statistics are clearly defective. Yet because bank records are maintained accurately, it is possible to obtain estimates of the total bank savings deposits of the population. By matching these estimates with the results of survey research showing the propensity to save of a stratified random sample of Egyptians, it is possible to estimate the real total income of the population. Using this method, Dr. Oweiss concludes that the "informal" economy alone has a value greater than the entire national income reported in the official statistics. This in turn presents policy-makers with the challenge of integrating the informal economy into the formal economy, which would enable the cash flowing in it to be used for long-term investment, and allow the government to tap it for taxes and revenues.

A major decision facing any Egyptian government is the role to be played by the state in the economy. Said El Naggar examines the scope and performance of public enterprises, especially in industry, transportation and utilities, citing the available statistics on the deficits, budgetary burdens, rates of return, and contribution to exports of these enterprises. He argues that "the present system is too costly," and Egypt can no longer afford it now that it lacks oil revenues and remittances on the scale of the 1970s. He sketches a plan for an economy in which public enterprises control important natural resources, major communications and utilities, and important industries in which private entrepreneurs are unwilling to invest. On the other hand, privatization is recommended in other areas, in which activities are typically better handled by private enterprises. "Privatization," he argues, "would reduce the burden on the national budget, eliminate a major source of waste and inflation, and make a positive contribution to the balance of payments position."

Fouad Sultan looks specifically at the problem of inadequate production, which cuts across all sectors. Arguing that Egypt produces at a level well beneath its capacity, and that its principal problems lie in the system of management and poor financing arrangements and credit facilities, he maintains that greater privatization would encourage more effective management and a larger and more developed capital market.

For much of the 1970s and early 1980s, Egypt's economy was assisted greatly by remittances from Egyptians living abroad and by foreign aid and loans. These sources of finance became increasingly problematic in the mid and late 1980s as the oil recession resulted in the repatriation of Egyptian workers and the accumulation of debt requiring servicing. In her article, Ann Lesch outlines the importance of labor migration for the Egyptian economy. In evaluating the effects of migration, she examines both the patterns of expenditure of money from migrants and the evolution of an Egyptian government policy on the issues raised by labor migration.

The issues of aid and indebtedness that overshadow the country are the focus of three articles. While their authors approach the subject from significantly different perspectives, they agree that the US aid policy has not been optimal for the Egyptian economy. Heba Handoussa's critical review of the aid policy argues that while mutual cooperation between Egypt and the US has resulted in many benefits, "the combination of poor economic management and the disproportionately high emphasis of US aid on military expenditure, and infrastructural projects, as well as the anti-public sector bias of the aid policy, have contributed to the misallocation of the country's scarce resources." She argues that a higher priority should have been allocated to industrial and agricultural expansion, and that a more favorable trade policy to Egypt by the United States would also have benefitted the country.

In the only contribution to this volume that did not originate in a contribution to the Center's symposium on Egypt, Denis Sullivan expresses a similar concern to that of Dr. Handoussa: why has aid not been more effective? Dr. Sullivan, however, focuses on a different dimension of the problem:

> . . . primary attention should . . . be directed toward a problem that is common to virtually all political and economic systems, whether in more developed or less developed countries, in socialist or capitalist economies. The problem is one of bureaucratic and political struggles inherent in the policy-making process. Bureaucracies and other political units compete for power to make or, at least, to influence policy. This competition is found not only *between* bureaucracies but also *within* them. Such competition is enough to cause numerous problems when it is engaged in by one government or political system. But when another government becomes involved, as in the case of a foreign donor, then the problems are not just doubled but increase exponentially.

He examines how political factors and competition between ministries or different government agencies can affect the allocation of aid and thwart efforts to allocate it in pursuit of a rational economic policy. Through on-the-spot research in Egypt, Dr. Sullivan was able to observe first-hand the bureaucratic competition that arose among Egyptian government departments over aid decisions, and differences between American institutions such as USAID and the US Embassy in Cairo over the priorities of aid allocation. His article suggests that bureaucratic and administrative reform is a prerequisite for effective aid planning.

Delwin Roy examines the problem of Egypt's indebtedness to the United States and other countries. His article is both an attempt to summarize the extent and composition of the debt and to look toward the future and a number of new options for dealing with the problem. Emphasizing that the current level of debt is an impediment to future Egyptian economic growth, he offers a number of recommendations, including the suggestion that the United States should offer Egypt a two-year moratorium on debt interest and principal repayments for past US economic aid in exchange for an Egyptian commitment to undertake fundamental economic reforms.

The section on the Egyptian economy concludes with an overview by Charles Issawi, which places the current problems in historic perspective. While outlining the failures of Egyptian policy, Dr. Issawi also points to some developments that hold out glimmers of opportunity in the future, notably the rapid increase in Egyptian educated manpower.

In the decades following the 1952 Nasserist revolution, Egypt was one of the most politically stable states of the Middle East. Paradoxically, its swing from a socialist economy and strong links with the Soviet Union under Nasser to the pro-Western political and economic policies of Sadat and Mubarak highlighted an inherent stability in its political system, which was able to absorb these fundamental ideological changes without serious civil conflict. The contributors to the section on Egyptian politics examine the bases of contemporary Egyptian politics, investigate the rise of Islamic fundamentalism and increased sectarianism in Egypt, analyze the liberalization process, and evaluate the implications for the Egyptian government of the continuing lack of a peaceful solution to the Palestinian problem.

Raymond Hinnebusch and Robert Bianchi examine different aspects of Egypt's contemporary political system. Dr. Hinnebusch analyzes the development of the Egyptian state since the Nasser period, and identifies key features of the "post-populist state" under the presidency of Mubarak: presidential "monarchy," pluralization and the burden of powerful political and economic constraints. He argues that the Egyptian parliament is almost exclusively a preserve of the bourgeoisie, and that the mass public has not been incorporated into the political system; indeed, "mass indifference has in part been bought by the regime's eschewing of a frontal assault on food subsidies, the surest catalyst of class conflict and political mobilization." (p. 202) Dr. Hinnebusch notes the striking capacity of the post-1952 state "to survive in spite of intense pressures and constraints."

Robert Bianchi investigates a feature of Egyptian political life that has become more prominent with liberalization: the toleration of a diverse and heterogeneous set of interest groups. He suggests that Mubarak is likely to view democratization as a means of involving politically active segments of the population in the tough decisions that face Egypt, and points out that "the diversity of political organization and the volatility of public opinion in Egypt today make repression far more costly and risky than expanding the modest experiments with 'corporatist democracy' that were initiated by Sadat."

One of the most important developments in Egyptian political life has been the Islamic revival. In his analysis of the recent growth in the importance of the Islamic movement in Egypt, Moustapha K. El-Sayyed identifies the different components of the movement, contrasting its mainstream and radical trends. As Dr. El-Sayyed points out, the Islamic revival cannot be treated merely as a political development, since its presence has been felt in the social and economic fields, through the establishment of Islamic economic enterprises and the provision of educational and social services.

The central demand of the Islamic movements is the introduction of *shari'a* law. In an article on Egypt's juridical system, Enid Hill examines the tensions between a number of Egyptian laws and codes and the prescriptions of the *shari'a*. Particular attention is given to the state's response in the 1970s and 1980s as the Islamic movement gathered strength and the government itself promoted a firm commitment to Muslim piety as part of state ideology.

Religious revivalism has not been limited to Egypt's Muslim majority. As Amira Sonbol points out, there has been an increased tendency among Copts to define their identity in religious terms. While the origins of Coptic revivalism can be dated to the beginning of this century, the recent Islamic revival has also been a major factor stimulating similar sentiments among Copts. Dr. Sonbol notes that, although both Muslims and Copts face similar social problems, frustrations arising from these have a significant potential to generate intersectarian conflict.

Faced by such a variety of problems, will it be possible for the recent liberalization moves in Egypt to lead to a stable democracy? Afaf Lutfi al-Sayyid Marsot identifies a number of recent developments in Egypt that would normally be favorable to democracy, such as the independence of the judiciary and the opportunity for voters to choose between different political parties. On the other hand, she points out, a major problem arises from the lack of mass participation and a lack of faith among many sectors of the population that the present electoral system will improve their situation. Her article surveys a number of different institutions and groups on which the prospects for democracy depend: the army, parliament, the judiciary, professional organizations, the bureaucracy and the religious establishment. Ultimately, she suggests, successful democratization will depend on economic improvement and the healthier political climate that would be created in the area if the Palestine problem were resolved.

Egypt's policy on the Palestine issue is addressed by Ibrahim Ibrahim, who examines the tension between public support for the *intifada* in Egypt and the unsuccessful attempts of the Egyptian government to arrange meaningful Israeli-Palestinian negotiations. Despite the efforts of the Egyptian government to find a compromise acceptable to Israel, no progress has been made toward a solution. If there is no shift in Israel's policy of hostility to Palestinian self-determination and its refusal to talk to the PLO, Dr. Ibrahim predicts a serious threat to peaceful relations between Egypt and Israel, and to the United States policy "which depends upon maintaining both Egypt and Israel as allies."

In the final section of the book, one of Egypt's elder statesmen, Ashraf Ghorbal, Egypt's former ambassador to the United States, looks to the future. Citing three major obstacles to Egypt's development—population growth, productivity, and the bureaucracy—Ghorbal outlines some measures that might address the problems. With regard to the future of peace in the Middle East, he cautions that while "peace with Israel is here to stay," Israel's policy in the occupied territories is an obstacle to future progress, and he suggests that Israel's "true friends should now dissuade her from her present repressive policies."

The publications program of the Center for Contemporary Arab Studies deals with major developments and issues facing the Arab world, and the different regions within it. Its books typically consist of essays by a number of authors providing concise information and relevant analyses of important subjects. *The Political Economy of Contemporary Egypt* is the latest addition to the Center's edited collections, whose subjects include the Palestine issue, the Islamic revival, the Lebanese conflict, the challenges facing the Arab world in the next decade, contemporary North Africa, and the resources of the Arab world.

MICHAEL SIMPSON
Director of Publications
Center for Contemporary Arab Studies

PART 1: THE EGYPTIAN ECONOMY

1 EGYPT'S ECONOMY: THE PRESSING ISSUES

Ibrahim M. Oweiss

Introduction

After the tribes of the Prophet Moses suffered from a lack of food in the desert, God sent down quail while water sprang out of the rocks, according to Surat Al-Baqara of the Holy Quran. Verse 61 relates that they still complained, "Oh Moses, we cannot endure one kind of food all the time. So beseech thy God to produce for us what the earth grows, its herbs and cucumbers, its garlic, lentils and onions." He said, "Will you exchange the better for a lesser . . . go land in Egypt and you shall find what you want."

While Egypt of the past was recognized as a land of plentiful variety of agricultural products and abundance of food, it is currently heavily dependent on imports of wheat, flour and other products to feed its people. This would not in itself constitute an economic problem if Egypt's exports could pay for its imports of food. However, its exports lag behind its imports and the gap between them keeps widening over time.

The complicated and interrelated sets of economic problems facing Egypt's economy go beyond inadequate agricultural production and balance of payments deficits. In spite of recent efforts to ameliorate Egypt's economy, these problems have compounded in the last twenty-five years. They include a population explosion, high rates of open and disguised unemployment, a crushing debt service burden, high rates of inflation, substantial budget deficits, widespread price-cost distortions, low productivity and acute external imbalances.

It is not the purpose of this study to examine the economics of every sector. The purpose of this study is to analyze inhibiting factors that are crippling Egypt's economic growth and are hindering its long-promised take-off stage. For a more accurate assessment of Egypt's economic situation, the study also estimates the country's vast informal economy on the basis of a savings function derived from a direct questionnaire survey of 500 Egyptian households conducted in December 1988. This survey found Egypt's informal economy to be even larger than the country's officially announced national income. The present study also indicates that before Egypt's

3

open-door policy in 1974 and after twenty-two years of Nasser's socialism, the maldistribution of income in Egypt was worse than that in three capitalist nations, the United Kingdom, Japan, and even the United States of America.

Other estimates made in this study are for the following parameters: (1) Egypt's rate of unemployment; (2) Egypt's foreign exchange earnings during 1980-87; and (3) Egypt's housing shortage as of 1990. A new term, "rentalism," is introduced to indicate and to analyze the economic consequences of government control of property rents since Nasser's regime.

Egypt's Economic Accomplishments in the 1980s

During the political campaign for the presidency of Egypt and prior to the re-election of President Mubarak for another six-year term, the January 1988 issue of *al-Ahram al-Iqtisadi* made a detailed list of economic accomplishments and financial reforms undertaken during his first term.

From 1981 to 1986, agricultural land increased from 5.7 to 6.3 million feddans; the number of factories more than doubled; oil production increased by 40 percent; the number of harbors increased from four to seven capable of handling 19.1 million tons of merchandise, in comparison to only 1.8 million tons in 1981; the road network increased from 26,000 to 42,000 kilometers; the number of trucks more than doubled; the number of telephone lines increased more than two-and-a-half times; electric generation increased from 18 billion kilowatt/hours to 45 billion. As a result, electricity, which had been connected to 5.2 million homes in 1981, was connected to 8.2 in 1986; and townships supplied by fresh water increased from 4200 to 4500 towns. Furthermore, to encourage tourism, hotel construction increased by 20 percent, while new modern facilities increased airport capabilities more than threefold.

Even though the above figures represented real growth in the sectors mentioned, they are by no means indicators of per capita real growth because of the substantial increase in Egypt's population. The performance of the economy should not be measured by such partial indicators as the number of bridges built or the kilowatt capacity installed. It can only be measured by macroeconomic indicators such as the growth of real per capita gross domestic product, the reduction in the rate of unemployment, the level of price stability and improvement in the external balance. In the *al-Ahram al-Iqtisadi* study, all figures denominated in Egyptian pounds are misleading because of the failure to adjust them to take into account the official rate of inflation. In Table 1, a comparison of the *al-Ahram al-Iqtisadi* statistics with statistics adjusted by myself to reflect a reasonable 20 percent annual rate of inflation reveal the opposite of what the study presented. Columns 1 and 2 were quoted from the study of *al-Ahram al-Iqtisadi,* while column 3 shows my adjusted figures for the year 1986. It is, therefore, apparent that *al-Ahram al-Iqtisadi's* monetary comparisons of Egypt's economic performance in 1986 vis-a-vis 1981 were inaccurate, misleading and highly inflated. In fact, the performance of the Egyptian economy on all counts during the period 1981 to 1986 left much to be desired.

TABLE 1
Egypt's Economic Performance, 1981-86
(in Egyptian pounds)

Item	Col. 1 1981	Col. 2 1986	Col. 3 1986 in 1981 prices
Bank deposits (bn. E.P.)	8.5	23.7	7.95
Expenditures per household (E.P.)	1964	2701	906
Investments per household (E.P.)	688	883	296
Public sector investments (bn. E.P.)	10	17	5.7
Exports of industrial products (mn. E.P.)	396	853	286
Agricultural production (bn. E.P.)	5.6	11.5	3.9
Pensions (mn. E.P.)	530	1572	527

Population

Even if we take into consideration the real growth of some of its infrastructure, Egypt's economy is seriously affected by a population growth outstripping many economic gains. Given the existing constraints of an inhabited area of only 34,000 square kilometers out of a total area of one million square kilometers, Egypt's high birth rate, coupled with a high but declining death rate, make it one of the most densely populated countries in the world. Based on an area of only 214.2 square miles, my estimate of Cairo's density in 1990 was 42,000 inhabitants per square mile, the highest in the world.[1]

It is worth noting that Egypt's population increased fourfold in the nineteenth century, from 2.5 million in 1800 to 10 million in 1900.[2] By comparison, another fourfold increase materialized in the first three quarters of the twentieth century.[3] While Egypt's population was in excess of 54 million inhabitants in 1990, its annual growth rate ranged between 2.8 and 3.0 percent, one of the highest in the world. In the midst of this population explosion, Egyptians are living under intolerable conditions of overcrowdedness in the narrow band of Egypt's habitable area of 3.4 percent, the remainder of its territory being predominantly desert. In spite of the existence of a Supreme Council on Population headed by the President of Egypt, no systematic or effective population policy is being adopted. In 1956, a program for a workable birth control policy likely to achieve effective results within fifteen years was presented to President Nasser, according to the unpublished memoirs of his Minister of Finance, Abdul-Galil al-Imari. Nasser refrained, however, from taking any measure to curb Egypt's high population growth because, in my opinion, he feared fighting two difficult uphill battles at the same time—income redistribution, which was then a priority, and the curbing of people's right to have children. A well-known verse of the Quran states that money and offspring are the two ornaments of life. Nasser was taking away money with his socialist income redistribution policies; he could not have politically afforded to curb the people's right to have children as well.

With the shrinkage of the per capita area under cultivation, the need to import food increases while the ability to export agricultural products is reduced. An increase in exports is necessary for the service and payment of Egypt's foreign debt. With high rates of population growth, the same pressures apply to the production levels of industry and of other sectors in which the satisfaction of internal needs will have to be at the expense of exports. Furthermore, with an acute shortage of housing, an annual increase of one and a half million inhabitants compounds an already critical situation, as the lack of shelter could also be politically destabilizing. In addition to the problem of limited resources and a depleted infrastructure, pressures are mounting because the high population growth rates have not been matched by either new discoveries of natural resources or an increase in marginal productivity. In spite of strenuous efforts to conquer the desert in an attempt to cultivate parts of it and in spite of the establishment of cities such as the "Sixth-of-October," "Tenth-of-Ramadan," and "Sadat," there is neither a realistic plan for the establishment of sufficient new cities, nor is there a known break-through in technology which could substantially increase production. Without a full commitment of the Egyptian government to the implementation of a comprehensive population program, including punitive measures against families with more than two children in the form of deprivation of subsidies to which they would have been otherwise entitled, the pessimistic outlook of Thomas Malthus in his *Essay on The Principle of Population* (1798) may be applicable to Egypt. The intolerable population situation threatens to worsen, as more than 40 percent of the inhabitants are less than fourteen years of age.[4]

Agriculture

In contrast to the more than fivefold increase in its population since the beginning of the twentieth century, Egypt's cultivated land has increased by no more than one fifth during the same period. Agricultural production per capita has declined both because of a declining land-to-labor ratio, and because of a host of other factors. For example, the policy of taxing the agricultural sector by pricing export crops, such as cotton and rice, at levels well below international prices for the purpose of raising public revenue, has resulted in a serious weakening of incentives. Other factors which have adversely affected agricultural production in Egypt include: (a) price/cost distortion in relative prices, such as wheat prices compared to those of clover or other such agricultural commodities which are not subject to strict government control or equally subsidized; (b) the system of forced delivery of underpriced crops; (c) the lack of competition among the public-sector companies which have monopolized the supply of seeds, fertilizers, pesticides and credit; (d) complete government monopsony in the purchase of principal crops such as cotton from farmers; and (e) the monopoly by the Egyptian government of the marketing of such products.

Per capita agricultural production has, therefore, declined while imports of food have been on the rise. As Egypt imports most of its needs of wheat and flour from abroad, the call for food security has arisen. The Specialized National Councils, an advisory institution to the President of Egypt which has included top experienced talents such as former ministers Abdul-Galil al-Imari, Ali al-Graitli, Ibrahim Hilmi Abdul-Rahman, Fuad Kamil Hussein, Hamid al-Sayih, Mustafa al-Gabali and others, formed a Council of Production and Economic Affairs. In its report to the President of Egypt, the Council issued its call for food security through an expansion in the areas under cultivation for food production, an increase in the productivity of the existing cultivated areas and an expansion of new arable lands. In evaluating Egypt's system of trade agreements, the Council had also called for an improvement in the existing inefficient system of exporting agricultural products. The final recommendation included the development of exports from the non-agricultural sectors and an attempt to increase foreign exchange earnings from tourism and exports of processed industrial products.[5] The Council's report outlined in detail the means of achieving the goals it spelled out without neglecting the theory of comparative advantage.

Unfortunately, such studies and recommendations are seldom taken into account in the Egyptian decision-making apparatus. In most cases, ministers are either busy promoting their own political ambitions or are preoccupied with ensuring their continuation in the cabinet. They tend to be engaged in bureaucratic matters which could easily be delegated to subordinates. With a few remarkable exceptions, the majority of Egyptian ministers since the time of Nasser's regime have had no time to think of an innovative approach to problems they are facing or to plan a strategy for implementation and follow-up. In certain instances a minister may be reluctant to adopt a certain valuable idea for fear that he might be replaced by whoever recommended it in the first place.

The failure to carry out structural reform in agriculture, however, is only partly a matter of overburdened, overambitious or overcautious ministers. The main reasons are fiscal and ideological. When President Mubarak came to power in 1981, he was constantly reminded by the then Prime Minister, Fuad Muhieddin, and other top officials, of the political disturbances of January 1977 (known as the food riots), which might, they argued, be repeated if any policy for a structural reform was proposed. After being commissioned by the President, two prominent Egyptian economists, Abdul-Galil al-Imari and Ali al-Graitli made recommendations for structural reforms of the country's economy in December 1981, but Mohieddin convinced the President that the proposals were politically destabilizing and kept the report in an inactive file. Ironically, the Prime Minister did not disagree with the findings, particularly with the need to allow for gradual increases in prices of subsidized items. However, it was decided to go about it indirectly and, hopefully, in an unnoticeable manner. For example, the contents of gas containers sold to Egyptian household were reduced while the same price was charged! From time to time, train riders are confronted with a sudden steep rise in the price of train tickets without any prior announcement. The one piaster loaf of bread was reduced in weight and worsened in quality when the two piaster loaf was introduced in the market. The same method was applied when the current five piaster loaf replaced all others.

In spite of efforts for Egypt's industrialization since the 1930s, the agricultural sector still remains important to the country's economy, as is evident from figures provided in Table 2.

TABLE 2
Egypt's Economy by Sector, 1986-87

Sector	% of GDP	% of Employment
Agriculture	21%	33%
Industry	19%	14%
Construction	4%	6%
Services	56%	47%

Sources: The statistics are calculated from Egypt, Central Agency for Public Mobilization and Statistics (CAPMAS), *Statistical Yearbook* (Cairo, 1988), p. 234; National Bank of Egypt, *Economic Bulletin,* Vol. XL, No. 1, 2, Cairo, 1987.

It should be noted, however, that if the service sector is divided into its constituent sub-sectors — transportation, communication and storage; Suez Canal; trade, finance and insurance; foreign trade; housing; tourism; and other services — agriculture ranks first both in terms of its contribution to Gross Domestic Product (GDP) and in terms of employment. Furthermore, almost half of Egypt's industrial production is based on agricultural output.[6] In addition, many items of the service and export sectors revolve around agricultural production. Egypt's exports of cotton still remain one of its major sources of foreign exchange, as shown below. In spite of its relative importance to Egypt's economy, agriculture has deteriorated, as has been shown in Table 1 and other studies.[7] This decline in Egyptian agriculture runs counter to a historical trend. In the nineteenth century, in the time of Muhammad Ali, the cultivated area increased by 33 percent, from three million feddans in 1813 to four million in 1852, and the water resources of the River Nile were more efficiently utilized than ever. By 1900, the overall cultivated land had increased to 5.3 million feddans.[8] With the near quadrupling of cotton prices resulting from shortages in the world market caused by the American Civil War,

Egyptian export prices of cotton increased from 12 riyals per kantar in 1860 to 45 in 1864.[9] In realizing their comparative advantage, Egyptian farmers allocated the bulk of their land to the cultivation of cotton. Cotton remained the backbone of the Egyptian economy as well as the main source of Egypt's foreign exchange earnings until the 1960s.

Egypt's cultivated land has increased by no more than 19 percent in the twentieth century, in spite of the construction of the Aswan Dam in 1902 and the Aswan High Dam in 1970. Notwithstanding this, Egypt has been producing a variety of agricultural products, mainly cotton, maize, wheat, berseem, beans, barley, rice, sugar cane and onions. Indeed, the foreign exchange earnings from the exports of cotton until the 1950s were in excess of the country's needs to pay for its imports. The Egyptian balance of payments was favorable, while the Egyptian pound, whose value was freely determined in world markets, was exchanged at 1.02 pounds sterling or $5.00 dollars in the 1940s.

One of the major developments in Egypt's agricultural system after the Nasser revolution was the implementation of the Land Reform Law of 1952, which placed a ceiling on the size of individual ownership, expropriated and redistributed land in excess of the statutory

TABLE 3
Structure of Land Ownership in Egypt (1952-1965)

Size	1952 % Ownership	1952 % Land	1965 % Ownership	1965 % Land
Less than 5 feddans	94.3%	35.5%	95.1%	57.1%
5-10	2.8%	8.8%	2.4%	9.5%
10-20	1.8%	10.7%	1.3%	8.2%
20-50	0.7%	10.9%	0.9%	12.6%
50-100	0.2%	7.2%	0.2%	6.1%
100-200	0.1%	7.3%	0.1%	6.5%
200 or more	0.1%	19.6%	—	—
TOTAL	100%	100%	100%	100%

Source: The above percentages were calculated from Robert Mabro, *The Egyptian Economy 1952-1972* (Oxford: Clarendon Press, 1974), p. 73. Official data at the Ministry of Agriculture in Giza were made available to the author to check the above figures. In 1952, before the Law, there were 2,801,000 landowners, while the total land area was 5,984,000 feddans. In 1965, there were 3,191,000 land owners while total land was 6,462,000 feddans.

maximum to landless peasants (as shown in Table 3), fixed land rent at seven times the amount of land tax, and abolished the right of the landlord to terminate tenancy, making tenancy perpetual so that it would pass from one generation to the next. Finally, Egypt's land reform legislation organized all agricultural producers in so-called cooperatives which are, in effect, public sector companies with a monopoly of the marketing of the principal crops and the supply of seeds and basic inputs.

One of the favorable outcomes of the 1952 Land Reform Law was a reduction in the inequality of land distribution. It does not, however, seem to have significantly affected the inequality of income distribution, in spite of Nasser's socialism, as is shown in even more detail below. Furthermore, the Law created built-in rigidities, such as the fixing of land rents at seven times land taxes, which have been kept at the same level ever since. It also guaranteed permanent tenancy. As the real value of rent became negligible over time due to an average rate of inflation of 20 percent annually, a tenant could afford to pay rent indefinitely with a minimum amount of work. Lack of incentives and mismanagement led to the deterioration of the single most important sector of the Egyptian economy. In the early 1970s, Bent Hansen candidly summarized the situation in the following statement:

Rents on land (but not land prices) were fixed by the land reform of 1952 on the basis of tax assessments from 1949, and have not been changed since [and still had not been changed by the date this book was published]. Immediately after the breakdown of the Korean boom, the official maximum rents were probably in line with what free market rents would have been, but since then a large gap has grown between official [fixed] rents and hypothetical "market rents." Moreover, the relative rents on different lots of land are becoming increasingly out of line with relative marginal-value productivities because of changes in water supply, patterns of production, land improvements, and the like. As a result, absentee landowners (who still own substantial areas, albeit in smaller plots) have become increasingly uninterested in making land improvements; this may have been offset, however, by government efforts and greater efforts by tenants who have obtained more secure and longer-lasting terms of tenure. Probably the most serious allocation effect of the fixed rents is that there is no longer any mechanism (aside from the black market) to ensure that the most competent people cultivate the land.[10]

Without an overall reconsideration of the built-in rigidities that the Egyptian government has created over the years and without adoption of a program to implement structural reform, the agricultural sector is likely to stagnate even further in the future. Before an expensive program of expanding agriculture in Egypt's deserts is launched — given the very limited capital the country has — a priority has to be given to raising the economic efficiency of the six million feddans under cultivation. In his study of Egypt's agricultural sector, while referring to the country's productivity in agriculture measured by output per hectare, Richard Adams concluded that

> The Egyptian rate of growth in output per hectare for major food crops far exceeded that of 36 other developing nations [before Nasser's Revolution, in the period 1948-1952]. However, after 1963-67 Egypt's rate of yield growth for major food crops dropped sharply, while that of the average of the 36 other developing countries rose considerably. Between the periods 1963-67 and 1978-82 the 36 developing countries averaged a much higher rate of growth in output per hectare than Egypt.[11]

No wonder Egypt is heavily dependent on food imports, especially from the United States.

Income Distribution

Due to distortions created by the worsening of income distribution in Egypt, particularly after Sadat's open-door policy, conspicuous consumption rose sharply and merchant trading increased, while investment and growth in production lagged behind. Even before Sadat's open-door policy, inequality of income distribution in Egypt had turned out to be worse than in the capitalistic nations of France, England, Israel, Japan or the United States of America. This was the case in spite of Egypt's 1952 Land Reform Law (later amended to put an upper limit of no more than 50 feddans on land ownership), and in spite of Nasser's socialism, taxation, and rent controls. While there are methodological problems with cross-country comparisons of income distribution, it may serve a purpose to compare figures for income distribution in Egypt prior to its open-door policy in 1974 with those in other nations (Table 4).

In analyzing the data, it can be observed that the households in the upper 20 percent of income brackets had almost half of Egypt's national income, while in other capitalistic nations their share was approximately 40 percent. The richest 10 percent of Egypt's house-holds had one third of the country's income, in comparison to less than one quarter in the case of England, France and even the United States.

TABLE 4
Percentage Share of Household Income, 1974

Country	Lowest 20%	Second 20%	Third 20%	Fourth 20%	Highest 20%	Highest 10%
Egypt	5.8%	10.7%	14.7%	20.8%	48.0%	33.2%
France	5.5%	11.5%	17.1%	23.7%	42.2%	26.4%
England	7.0%	11.5%	17.0%	24.8%	39.7%	23.4%
Japan	8.7%	13.2%	17.5%	23.1%	37.5%	22.4%
Israel	6.0%	12.0%	17.7%	24.4%	39.9%	22.6%
USA	5.3%	11.9%	17.9%	25.0%	39.9%	23.3%

Source: The World Bank, *World Development Report, 1989* (New York: Oxford University Press, 1989), pp. 222-23.

While it may be argued that income maldistribution in many Third World countries is worse than that of the capitalistic nations, it would have been reasonable to expect Egypt to be different since it had adopted socialism as its economic system since its 1952 Revolution.

It is difficult to assess the maldistribution of income in Egypt during the 1980s because of the growth of an unaccountable informal economy in which earnings are neither taxable nor invested but rather lavishly spent on weddings and luxurious items, or otherwise saved or invested abroad. However, inequality in Egypt's income distribution has certainly worsened in comparison to 1974 as a result of Sadat's open-door policy.

An Estimate of Egypt's Informal Economy

Several studies have been conducted on the nature and extent of the informal economy. Henry (1978)[12] called it "the hidden economy," but Portes and Sassen-Koob (1987)[13] preferred the phrase "the underground economy." Gershuny (1978)[14] used the term "self-service economy," and Feige (1979)[15] chose the "irregular economy," while Hansen (1981)[16] used yet another phrase, "the border economy." All of the above terms and other similar ones, such as "off-the-books economy," mean more or less the same phenomenon. The phrase "informal economy" has become the most widely used. Among the many definitions offered in this regard is the following by Castells and Portes: "The informal economy is . . . a process of income generation characterized by one central feature: it is unregulated by institutions of society, in a legal and social environment in which similar activities are regulated."[17] Even though such a definition may seem appropriate, the use of the word "process" may give an ambiguous meaning to the phenomenon of informal economy.

I define the informal economy as that which encompasses all economic activities unknown to established authorities — or unadmitted by them even if known — and all incomes generated thereof but not reported to the government and not included in the country's national income accounts. The total of such incomes may be referred to as the "informal income." Furthermore, a labor market operating without the knowledge of the authorities and without adherence to existing laws and regulations may be called "the informal labor market." Similar terms apply to capital markets and to all other informal economic activities.

It should be noted, however, that all sources of informal income are not necessarily illegal. An informal income may be lawfully earned, such as that derived from certain cash payments to physicians, lawyers, tutors, plumbers, mechanics, nightclub operators or otherwise obtained from unreported remittances. In addition to these legal sources of an informal economy, there are other illegal sources such as trading in illegal drugs and unlawful black market transactions in commodities or in foreign currencies. Whether the source of an informal income is lawful or unlawful, the act of concealing it from the authorities is in itself illegal. Moreover, there may be different reasons for not reporting a legally-earned income to the authorities such as an attempt to evade taxes or a fear of confiscation, sequestration and/or nationalization of an economic activity, or any other precautionary purpose.

To estimate an informal economy, Gutmann (1979), for example, [compared] the ratio of outstanding currency to demand deposits in 1978 with the average for the years 1937 to 1941, a period when underground activities were assumed to be close to zero. Increases in the ratio were imputed to growth in these activities. On the basis of this method, Gutmann estimated that the informal economy represented about 10 percent of the currently measured Gross

National Product, or $177 billion, in 1978. This approach has been employed with variations by other authors. Spitznas (1981) applied Gutmann's formula to the Second Federal Reserve District, which includes New York City, and estimated the city's underground economy at $16.2 billion in 1978. He also estimated that these activities had been growing rapidly.[18]

Gutmann's methodology has led to a wide range of estimates of the informal economy in industrialized societies, despite the criticism by Castells and Portes that there is no assurance that the base period had no informal economy. It does not, however, appear to be appropriate for Egypt.

In my attempt to evaluate Egypt's informal economy, I did not rely on official figures for my estimation. A questionnaire was devised for a stratified random sample of five hundred households in Egypt in December 1988 in an effort to estimate first the ratio of income that Egyptians are accustomed to allocating for savings. It should be noted that the sample is indicative of aggregate savings, as a large number of Egyptian households have a zero or even negative rate of savings.

With an estimate of a savings ratio (s), and with an estimate of total savings (S), I then estimated Egypt's Gross National Product (GNP) in 1987.

The result of the sample indicates with 95 percent statistical confidence that the savings ratio in Egypt is somewhere between 9 and 11 percent of income. This result was found to be significantly different from the 19.9 percent which was derived from applying regression analysis to a thirteen-year time series of published official data as shown in Appendix 1. It would have been inconceivable for Egypt to have a savings ratio of 19.9 percent in 1987, at a time when a country such as the United States, with a much higher per capita income than Egypt, only had a savings ratio of 12.4 percent (gross saving was $566.4 billion out of a Gross National Product of $4486.2 billion).[19] Even in applying regression analysis to the case of the United States for the same period of thirteen years, the savings ratio was found not to be significantly different from that based only on the figures for 1987.

The estimates are consistent with that of Robert Mabro, whose analysis of the data for the period 1952 to 1970 concluded that Egypt's savings ratio is between 9 and 14 percent.[20] Such a contrast —between results obtained from primary data and those derived statistically from published official data—should not be surprising.

Official data on Egypt's savings and national income do not reflect the actual performance of the country's economy. As total savings (S) in Egypt are unknown I attempted to estimate them in spite of institutional and cultural difficulties. Since certain financial institutions, such as the Islamic capital investment companies, do not report actual deposits of savings to Egypt's Central Bank in spite of their significance, the official figures on national savings are definitely unrealistic. Furthermore, Egyptians save in many different forms, some of which cannot be fully accounted for, such as hoarding in the form of cash or else in the form of gold, jewelry or other such objects bought with the intention of "saving" for possible future sale for investment or needed expenditures. Thus, actual total saving is undoubtedly more than any recorded or estimated figures.

The methodology I used to estimate Egypt's aggregate saving was based on the following premises. First, official figures for savings are to be avoided. I found out that these turned out to be only the sum of net sales of savings certificates[21] in addition to post office savings deposits. By mid-1987, net sales of savings certificates amounted to E.P. (Egyptian pounds) 3.1 billion,[22] while the post office saving deposits were half a billion Egyptian pounds,[23] the total of which represented the official figure for Egypt's total saving (S)! Second, I used the published figures of time deposits in banks as a relatively more reliable base for (S) since all of those among the stratified sample of 500 who had savings defined their time deposits as savings. Third, I estimated savings deposited with non-bank institutions, mainly the Islamic capital investment companies, since they are not a fully integrated part of Egypt's banking system. As there was no access to the accounts of the twelve major Islamic capital investment companies, I used an estimated figure of the total dividends of E.P. 2.5 billion they distributed in 1987 (d), which was given unofficially by Egypt's Central Bank, as the numerator in the following equation:

$$d \text{ (estimated)/total deposits (unknown)} = \text{Annual yield}$$

Since the annual yield was advertised by the Islamic investment companies as ranging between 20 percent and 25 percent, I conservatively took the lower percentage of 20 percent to estimate the unknown total deposits made with such institutions, which turned out to be in the neighborhood of ten billion Egyptian pounds.

My estimate of the total deposits with the Islamic capital investment companies is conservative in comparison to other estimates. *Al-Ahram al-Iqtisadi,* for example, estimated deposits at the two largest of them, Al-Rayan and Al-Saad Islamic Investment Companies, at E.P. 11.7 billion in 1987.[24] Muhammad Dowaidar provides two estimates of the total deposits with the Islamic capital investments companies, between E.P. 5 and 14 billion, or between E.P. 13 and 48 billion.[25] Furthermore, some of those deposits were made by Egyptians working abroad and denominated in US dollars, as well as in other major European currencies. Whatever the amounts of money deposited with the Islamic capital investment companies may have been, the fact remains that they were substantial, even though such institutions were not under any banking supervision or control (as shown in Appendix 2).

Assuming that the E.P. 10 billion in total deposits with those companies were the result of accumulated savings over their period of expansion of five years, a conservative estimate of E.P. 2 billion may be regarded as annual savings deposited with those institutions.

In 1987, therefore, Egypt's total saving (S) can be estimated at E.P. 10.3 billion, representing the sum of time deposits with the country's banking system of E.P. 8.3 billion[26] plus the savings deposited with the Islamic capital investment companies of E.P. 2 billion.

Using the saving ratio (s) derived above, which was found to have been in the range of 9-11 percent, and given the estimated (S) at E.P. 10.3 billion, my estimate of Egypt's national income in 1987 would be somewhere between E.P. 94 and 114 billion.

Even if the lower limit of E.P. 94 billion is to be considered, then Egypt's informal economy in 1987 may be estimated at a minimum as E.P. 50 billion, i.e., the difference between the E.P. 94 billion figure and the official one of only E.P. 44 billion. In other words, Egypt's national income in reality was at least more than double the official estimate in 1987.

Regardless of how the above estimates reflect Egypt's economy, my conservative approach indicates the existence of a substantial informal economy in the country, which complicates the implementation of structural economic reforms.

With an informal economy even larger than Egypt's reported national income, it can be presumed that the income maldistribution of the country is even worse than that shown in the available statistics. The wealth and most of the purchasing power are highly concentrated in the hands of a small percentage of the country's population, while the majority live under extremely tight budgetary conditions, where basic needs cannot be met among the poor and middle class alike. The dilemma of policy makers becomes apparent whenever they wish to implement a policy of structural reform which necessitates a rise in prices, bringing further economic hardships to the majority of Egyptians, as this could lead to frustrations, riots and political instability. Yet, in the absence of any reform, economic problems keep worsening at a compounded rate, while rates of inflation keep increasing because of a decline in productivity, an increase in the government's printing of money, the substantial purchasing power concentrated in the hands of the few, and the high rates of growth in Egypt's population.

Egypt's Contemporary Economic Problems

Apart from the complicated issue of population, Egypt's contemporary economic problems may be classified under three main headings: (1) external economic factors, (2) internal economic factors, and (3) government policies, laws and regulations.

The exogenous, or external, economic factors which have compounded Egypt's economic problems in recent years can be attributed to the decline in the main sources of its foreign exchange earnings since 1983, when the price of oil was substantially reduced, declining to less than $10.00 a barrel in 1986. With the subsequent economic recession in major Arab oil-exporting nations, there was a decline in the remittances of the three million Egyptians working in those countries, which constituted the highest source of foreign exchange earnings for the country. The relative contributions of sources of Egypt's foreign exchange earnings are shown in Table 5.

TABLE 5
Egypt's Principal Sources of Foreign Exchange
(Percentages)

Years	Remit-tances	Oil Exports	Suez Canal	Tourism Revenues	Cotton Exports	Total %	Total ($bn)
1980/81	40.4	36.8	10.5	7.9	4.4	100	6.3
1981/82	31.4	42.7	14.2	7.1	4.6	100	5.4
1982/83	43.7	34.9	12.6	4.6	4.2	100	6.4
1983/84	49.4	30.0	11.4	3.9	5.3	100	7.2
1984/85	45.9	32.3	11.0	5.8	5.0	100	6.7
1985/86	42.4	33.0	14.3	5.0	4.9	100	6.1
1986/87	27.1	12.6	31.5	20.6	8.2	100	3.1

Source: National Bank of Egypt, *Economic Bulletin,* Vol. XL, Nos. 1, 2 (Cairo, 1987), p. 33. See also Appendix 3.

There are, however, other sources of foreign exchange not listed in Table 5. They are classified as (a) other food and raw materials (onions, potatoes and oranges), (b) semi-finished goods and (c) finished goods.

TABLE 6
Other Sources of Egypt's Foreign Exchange
(In millions of US dollars)

Year	(a)	(b)	(c)
1980/81	104.6	208.8	151.8
1981/82	104.4	225.9	155.3
1982/83	134.8	168.5	148.1
1983/84	155.4	176.7	208.7
1984/85	140.0	200.0	253.8
1985/86	132.2	177.3	223.7
1986/87	117.5	274.1	305.3

Source: National Bank of Egypt, *Economic Bulletin,* Vol. XXXX-No. 3 (Cairo, 1987), pp. 210-13.

If the figures for (a), (b) and (c) are added to the last column in Table 5, we get the total foreign exchange earnings in billions of dollars consecutively in the years above as follows: 6.8, 5.9, 6.9, 7.7, 7.3, 6.6 and 3.8, adding up to $45.0 billion for the seven-year period.

It is to be noted that, with the drop in the price of oil in 1986, the relative contributions of remittances and oil exports were significantly reduced, while the absolute amount of Egypt's total foreign exchange earnings dropped by about three billion dollars. After 1987, however, as the price of oil rose, the Egyptian government decided to increase both the production and the export of crude and refined oil.

The inability of Egypt to control external factors affecting its economy makes structural internal economic reforms imperative. Domestic economic problems at present include the rise in both disguised and open unemployment, low productivity, high rates of inflation, government deficit financing, unaffordable subsidy programs, deficits in the balance of payments, accumulated public debt, the lack of adequate domestic investments, the acute shortage in housing, price disequilibria and, in general, low rates of real economic growth, often even leading to negative per capita real growth rates.

Unemployment

According to official statistics, there were more than two million Egyptians unemployed in 1986 out of a labor force of 13.7 million,[27] representing a rate of unemployment in the neighborhood of 15 percent. My estimates indicate, however, that there were 2.8 million unemployed while the labor force was 14.5 million, representing an unemployment rate in excess of 19 percent in 1986. Since half of Egypt's population, according to published official age distribution data, are of labor force age, I used the figure of 24.2 million Egyptians of both sexes as the basis for estimating the size of the labor force. Traditionally, however, approximately 20 percent of females are in the labor force. Thus my estimate of Egypt's labor force in 1986 was 12.1 million males plus 2.4 million females, representing a total of 14.5 million, of whom 11.7 million[28] were employed, according to official statistics. The remaining 2.8 million can thus be estimated to have been unemployed.

This estimate represents only those who were unemployed and does not take account of underemployment. Many work places in the Egyptian government and public sector companies are staffed with people beyond work needs, and some employees on the payroll have little or no work at all. This phenomenon of disguised unemployment has increased over time because of Nasser's unemployment act, which obligated the government to provide employment to all. As labor offices assign people to vacancies on the basis of "first listed, first served," a backlist of more than five years of university graduates is still awaiting employment.

Inflation

The official rates of inflation are downwardly biased because of the rigidity in prices of certain items, as in the case of subsidized goods and fixed rents which enter in the consumer basket when prices are compared from one year to another. Inflation rates as measured by consumer price indices (CPI) are shown in Table 7.

The average annual rate of inflation computed from the above statistics is approximately 16 percent. In previous research I estimated Egypt's annual rate of inflation at 23 percent,[29] which is in line with most estimates of the World Bank. Even if we take a conservative estimate of 20 percent, this rate of inflation imposes an unbearable burden on the majority of Egyptians who are poor, and even those in the middle class.

TABLE 7
Egypt's Consumer Price Indices
(1966/67 = 100)

Year	Urban	Rural
1976	164.2	187.8
1977	185.1	206.7
1978	205.6	234.2
1979	226.0	248.7
1980	272.7	311.0
1981	301.2	353.4
1982	345.8	402.8
1983	401.4	523.6
1984	469.9	565.5
1985	554.3	646.4
1986	708.8	795.8
1987	829.7 (June)	843.7 (May)

Source: National Bank of Egypt, *Economic Bulletin,* Vol. XXXX, No. 3 (Cairo, 1987), pp. 204-205.

While there are other economic, social and political implications of such high rates of inflation, it is important to assess the root causes of Egypt's substantial increase in its consumer price index. One of the main sources of inflationary pressure in Egypt is the high budget deficit and the way it is financed. In the most recent estimate by the International Monetary Fund, Egypt's budget deficit was about 17 percent of the country's Gross Domestic Product (GDP). Roughly half of this deficit is financed by borrowing from the public or from publicly-owned institutions such as pension funds and social security funds. The other half, amounting to eight to ten percent of GDP, is financed by printing money. This monetized part of the budget deficit is the main cause of inflation. The government's policy of excessive printing of money is shown in Table 8.

While the monetized part of the budget deficit is the major source of the "demand-pull" inflation in Egypt, other sources include (1) imported inflation, which is becoming increasingly important following depreciations of the Egyptian pound; and (2) the raising of the price of principal commodities to reflect the increasing cost of labor and other inputs. These fuel the flame of "cost-push" inflation. The decline in marginal productivity is a further cause of inflation.

TABLE 8
Egypt's Currency in Circulation (M)
(Billions of Egyptian Pounds)

Year	M	Year	M
1976	1.4	1982	7.0
1977	1.7	1983	7.9
1978	2.2	1984	8.8
1979	2.7	1985	9.3
1980	4.7	1986	8.7
1981	6.0	1987	9.3

Source: National Bank of Egypt, *Economic Bulletin,* Vol. XXXX, No. 3 (Cairo, 1987), p. 200.

Budget Deficit

As the government has not been able to track down the vast untaxable underground economy, its total public revenues have increased modestly from E.P. 8.3 billion in 1981/82 to E.P. 13.5 in 1986/87. Its expenditures meanwhile have increased from E.P. 13.2 billion to E.P. 22.2 billion. The overall budget deficits have therefore increased from E.P. 4.9 billion to E.P. 8.7 billion during the same period. It should be noted, however, that there was a slight reduction in the budget deficit from E.P. 8.8 billion in 1985/86 to E.P. 8.7 billion in 1986/87. Furthermore, the relative burden of the budget deficit as a percentage of the country's national income, even though still high, has been reduced from 23.5 percent in 1981/82 to 19.9 percent in 1986/87. Most of Egypt's budget deficit, however, was internally financed by its banking system, social security surplus, development bonds, savings certificates, postal savings, government bonds for public sector companies, and by the printing of money, the total of which covered up to 83 percent of the deficit. The remaining 17 percent was foreign-financed from credit facilities for the development plan (mainly project loans), grants for the development plan, cash and commodity loans such as PL 480 and other US loans and grants, and European and Japanese loans and grants.[30]

In summary, the three methods of financing the budget deficit in Egypt are (1) borrowing from the public and savings institutions, which is essentially non-inflationary although it crowds out private investment; (2) borrowing from the banking system through the printing press, which is highly inflationary; and, (3) foreign borrowing, which is non-inflationary but creates external debt with far-reaching implications for the balance of payments position and the prospects of economic growth.

Two of the most prominent and internationally respected Egyptian economists, Abdul-Galil al-Imari and Ali al-Graitli, have concluded that the root cause of Egypt's economic problems is deficit financing. Having been commissioned by President Mubarak to present a study on Egypt's structural reform, they presented an important document to him in December 1981, which is summarized in Appendix 4. According to them:

Since the mid-1960s, Egypt has been facing serious economic problems to which inadequate attention has been paid, since Egypt's policy-makers were engaged in matters of war and peace. Since that time, the State has pursued a policy of deficit financing from Egypt's banking system, as expenditures exceeded revenues. . . . As a result, inflation prevailed and was even compounded by a continuous rise of international prices since the 1970s. In order to reduce the burden of inflationary pressure, the state resorted to a policy of subsidization for which appropriations have been increasing year after year. In 1981/82, government expenditures for subsidies were in excess of 2 billion Egyptian pounds in comparison with only 9 million Egyptian pounds at the beginning of the 1960s, when only three basic commodities were subsidized.

The total amount of direct and indirect subsidies had, however, been substantially increased, at times reaching more than 26 percent of Egypt's published national income (as was the case in 1985). It is worth noting that studies made by the Specialized National Councils in Cairo, an advisory institution to Egypt's President, and others have all concluded that the benefits to the poor of the subsidies are minimal, and that most of the benefits are reaped by those who can afford to pay full market prices. Apparently, no more than 15 percent of the total amount of subsidies reaches those whose income bracket is the lowest quintile. Because of the misallocation of resources resulting from inefficient yet expensive subsidy programs, the Specialized National Councils proposed the replacement of the existing system by one of outright and direct payments to the needy. The idea was called "Ganih al-da'am" or the subsidy-pound. It was calculated that not only would the subsidy-pound system have been less costly than the existing subsidy program, but that its burden could be gradually reduced over time.

Balance of Payments Deficit

Turning to Egypt's balance of payments, the current account deficit rose from $3.5 billion in 1981/82 to $5.3 billion in 1985/86, after which it declined to $3.8 billion in 1986/87. After taking consideration of the capital account, however, with its direct investments and official capital grants, the overall balance of payments deficit in 1986/87 was $2 billion.[31] Several factors have led to chronic deficits in Egypt's balance of payments. One of the main causes was Nasser's policy of industrialization, which was geared towards import substitution—even if it turned out that the domestically produced commodity was more costly than the imported one—rather than export-oriented. Highly inefficient industries were thus established with no regard to considerations of comparative advantage. Other factors contributing to Egypt's chronic balance-of-payments deficit included: (1) Excessive borrowing to finance current consumption on projects with low or zero or even a negative rate of return; (2) Cost overruns; (3) The failure of the export industries to improve their competitiveness; (4) A highly restrictive trade policy which supported waste and inefficiency. Egypt's balance of payments may, however, ameliorate in the 1990s because of an expected increase in tourism and its related industries, in addition to an expected rise in the price of oil by the mid-1990s.

As a result of accumulated deficits in both Egypt's balance of payments and its government budget, and as a result of excessive borrowing from abroad in the period 1980 to 1982, public debt increased exponentially and reached a level in excess of the official figure of Egypt's Gross National Product (GNP) as shown in Table 9.

TABLE 9
Egypt's Macro-Economic Data & Foreign Debt, 1987
(1987; Figures are in billion US dollars)

Debt	GNP	Goods & Services Exports	Imports	International Reserves
40	34	11.7	15.3	2.6

Source: The World Bank, *World Debt Tables* (Washington, DC: 1988-89), p. 118.

Debt thus constituted 117.6 percent of GNP in 1987; it totalled 343.1 percent of exports. Egypt's international reserves only totalled 6.3 percent of its debt.

It is important to note that the policy of excessive borrowing occurred at the time of Egypt's highest levels of foreign exchange earnings. This period was characterized by an unprecedented high price of oil at $34.00 a barrel, high earnings and a surge in the remittances of Egyptians working in Arab oil-exporting countries, high Suez Canal earnings due to an unprecedented traffic of oil tankers, and an increase in revenues from tourism. Instead of retiring some of Egypt's public debt in the early 1980s, or using part of the country's foreign exchange earnings in investments to broaden and strengthen the base of productive capacity and create new jobs, the Egyptian government chose to increase Egypt's borrowing from abroad. Furthermore, an insignificant percentage of the amounts borrowed from abroad and of the unprecedented accumulation of foreign exchange was allocated to investments and capital deepening, while the lion's share was diverted to consumption expenditures and trading activities. The outcome of such a policy was manifold: the beginning of uncontrolled inflationary pressures, the vast expansion of Egypt's informal economy, increased inequality in income distribution, and a level of public debt beyond Egypt's ability to repay.

As Egypt's foreign debt exceeds the published figures of the country's national income, and as international interest rates are still high, the debt service burden accounts for an exceedingly high proportion of export earnings. There is a need to bring this burden in line with the country's payment capacity if the Egyptian economy is to grow at acceptable rates.

As a result of low per capita income, Egypt's national savings seem to be insufficient to cope with the investments needed for accelerated growth. Despite a vast informal economy and cash obtained from overseas by Egyptians working in Arab oil-exporting countries, savings institutions have failed to attract as many funds as they could, with the exception of the Islamic capital investment companies. The main reason has been the ceiling of 13 percent interest imposed by government regulations at a time when the annual rate of inflation was in excess of 20 percent. Although some Egyptians may be subject to a "money illusion," which makes them accept a monetary return for their deposits, others are aware that if they deposit their money under the above conditions, they lose from a negative real rate of interest (–7%). In its negotiations with the Egyptian government, the International Monetary Fund proposed in its economic reform package an increase in interest rates. Interestingly, Islamic investment companies got around the ceiling on interest rates imposed by the government. Their announced policy is that interest paid on deposits is usury and, therefore, any such payment is against Islam. Instead, they have paid 20 to 25 percent of their deposits annually in the form of dividends, thus attracting over ten billion Egyptian pounds from depositors in a span of less than five years.

Inadequate Investment Expenditures

Investment expenditures were negatively affected by the enactment of Nasser's socialist laws in 1961, and the natural response of capital owners in adopting a wait-and-see attitude while part of their money went into an underground economy. The Egyptian treasury subsequently suffered from having to finance a meaningless war in Yemen in the early 1960s. Nasser's military defeat in June 1967 resulted in a major blow to the economy following the Israeli invasion and occupation of Sinai, with all of its mineral and petroleum resources. All of these developments left insufficient resources for badly needed investments and capital replacement of Egypt's ailing and depleted infrastructure.

New nationalistic sentiments arose after the 1973 October War, when the Egyptian armed forces successfully crossed the Suez Canal, destroyed the fortified Israeli Barlev line, and recaptured part of the territories occupied since 1967. With the advent of Sadat's new open-door policy in 1974, Egyptian and other Arab investors responded positively with increased investments. A significant reversal of the pattern of investment expenditures ensued as Arab governments, institutions and individuals participated in Egypt's quest for accelerated growth. In 1976, the governments of Kuwait, Qatar, Saudi Arabia and the United Arab Emirates established GODE, the Gulf Organization for the Development of Egypt. Its entire two billion dollar package was disbursed to Egypt in 1977.[32] By the end of 1986, the Islamic Development Bank, Abu Dhabi Fund, OPEC Fund, Saudi Fund, Arab Fund for Economic and Social Development and the Kuwait Fund for Arab Economic Development had contributed a total of $773 million in finance for investment projects, of which 85 percent was contributed by the last three institutions.[33] Out of the total E.P. 7.3 billion invested in Egypt up to mid-1987 under the provisions of Law 43 of 1974 Concerning Investment of Arab and Foreign Funds and the Free Zones, 18 percent were contributed by Arab countries in contrast with only 5.3 percent from the United States, 6.1 percent from the countries of the European Community, and 5.6 percent from all other countries. The major portion of 65 percent was contributed by Egyptians, as is shown in Table 10.

TABLE 10
Capital of Projects Approved up to June 30, 1987
(In billion Egyptian pounds)

Items	Total (E.P.bn.)	Egypt %	Other Arab Countries %	USA %	Europe %	Others %
Inside Egypt						
Industry	2.5	72.0	9.0	5.5	8.5	5.0
Finance	1.7	70.3	19.4	1.3	6.2	2.8
Agriculture	0.4	76.0	14.0	1.0	3.0	6.0
Construction	0.7	87.7	9.1	0.7	1.5	1.0
Services	1.1	56.0	17.0	14.0	5.0	8.0
Sub-total	6.4	70.3	13.7	5.1	6.3	4.6
In Free Zones						
Public Zones	0.2	51.0	14.6	10.0	10.5	14.0
Private Zones	0.7	24.0	58.0	5.0	3.0	10.0
Sub-total	0.9	31.0	47.0	6.0	5.0	11.0
TOTAL	7.3	65.0	18.0	5.3	6.1	5.6

Source: Data were obtained from the General Authority for Investment and Free Zones in Cairo.

It should be noted that the above official data should be treated with caution as they were obtained from adding up total capital earmarked for projects approved by the General Authority for Investment and Free Zones (GAIFZ) as submitted by investors, whether or not projects have actually been completed. Furthermore, while capital in foreign currency was E.P. 7.3 billion, total investment costs were nearly double the amount at E.P. 14.3 billion. According to information obtained from GAIFZ, only 53.4 percent of the investment projects have started activity while 17.9 percent are under implementation and the remaining 28.7 percent are still on the drawing board.

Law 43 of 1974 with its later amendments in 1977, and Law 230 of July 1989, provided generous tax exemptions and other privileges to individuals and institutions, with the main purpose of attracting them to invest in Egypt. The 1989 law has extended the privileges and tax exemptions to investors even though such generous preferentials are by no means sufficient to attract foreign investments. Indeed, even without such generous privileges as those granted by the Egyptian law, foreign investments would be attracted by streamlining bureaucratic procedures, a commitment not to pass new laws and regulations with a retroactive effect, and a conducive environment for investment. The Egyptian government was clearly informed of these needs in 1978, when I pointed them out in my capacity as the Chief of the Egyptian Economic Mission to the United States in New York.[34]

In spite of the negative aspects of Egypt's open-door policy and economic legislation under Sadat's regime, there were also positive aspects, as annual economic growth rates increased from an average of 5.4 percent in the period 1967-73 to 7.8 percent in 1974-81.[35]

As a percentage of Egypt's Gross National Product, investment started a downward trend after 1981, when it was 6.4 percent, declining to 5.2 percent by 1984.[36] This development took place for several reasons.

In the first place, the relative share allocated by the government to investment has been reduced because of the mounting pressures caused by an increase in other expenditures to finance a variety of programs, such as those of subsidies for consumer goods and services. In the meantime, the Egyptian government is unable to tap the country's vast informal economy for taxation and for increased revenues. It does not seem that the Egyptian government will be able to substantially cut other expenditures in order to increase appropriations for investment. It is reluctant to undertake a thoroughgoing economic structural reform for fear of possible political instability. However, with accumulated budget deficits ever since the mid-1950s which have been increasing at an accelerated rate (particularly in the 1980s), the Egyptian government will have no other alternative but gradually to adjust its expenditures in order to allow for an increase in investment. For the first time since the early 1950s, the overall budget deficit was reduced in 1986/87 by E.P. 136 million from its 1985/86 level of E.P. 8843 million.[37]

In the second place, the investments of Egypt's private sector did not increase to a level compatible with its capabilities. After Sadat's assassination on October 6, 1981, investors adopted a cautious strategy until Mubarak's economic orientation was known. While the new President announced a policy of unequivocal support and encouragement of private sector activities, his regime adopted restrictive measures in the course of its attempt to reduce economic exploitation and to fight corruption. If such tasks had been left to Egypt's courts and its legal system, there would have been no adverse effects on the majority of the country's business community. Special Emergency Laws which were retained throughout the 1980s created a duality of Egypt's legal system incompatible with the country's quest for confidence in long-term commitments for investments.

In addition to Egypt's legal prosecuting system, Special Emergency Laws continued a practice inherited from the Sadat regime of having a dual prosecutor's position known as the Socialist General Prosecutor, whose actions generated a cautious attitude on the part of investors. With the continuation of Egypt's Special Emergency Laws and Egyptian bureaucratic practices, in addition to the government's favoritism toward public sector companies, an overall set of negative signals was sent to investors. Such an environment is not conducive to the commitment of considerable amounts of capital for long-term industrial projects or for an accelerated increase in investments. Not surprisingly, there is now a vast informal economy in Egypt, while a significant portion of money is spent on unnecessary luxury items and lavish consumption, or hoarded, or spent, saved or invested abroad. While there is no official information regarding the flight of capital from Egypt, I believe that it is sizable. The noticeable excess demand for US dollars in Egypt's black market is indicative of the flight of capital from the country.

"Rentalism" and the Housing Shortage

The housing shortage has been created not only by the above-mentioned obstacles to investments but also by a complicated system of laws and regulations pertaining to rents which, in the final analysis, have led to a lop-sided and inefficient pricing structure. Price distortions have resulted from the control of rents both for land and housing, and from control of the price of subsidized goods and services in a situation where other prices are determined by the forces of supply and demand. For example, under the rent control system, the monthly rent for a seven-bedroom apartment with high ceilings, marble floors and spacious halls in the best districts in Alexandria or Cairo can be the equivalent of the price of one watermelon or seven Egyptian pounds ($2.50), if the house was originally rented in 1943 (with the difference that the seven Egyptian pounds were equal to $35 or one ounce of gold at that time). In 1989, an ounce of gold was approximately equal to one thousand two hundred Egyptian pounds.

The legislation recorded in Appendix 5 froze rents at the level which prevailed some thirty or forty years ago, with no adjustment whatsoever for inflation, while giving the tenants the right to stay in the rented premises along with their offspring or whoever occupies them so long as the rent is paid, unless or until the premises are unfit to live in.

For lack of any terminology describing such a system, I propose the term "rentalism," which may be defined as the system in which a tenant owns the right to stay for a fixed, low rent and the offspring or whoever is the occupier retains that right until the end of the lifetime of the premises.

Along with taxation and subsidies, rentalism was initially used as a means of income redistribution through an indirect transfer of money from landlords to tenants. Whatever the reasons for rentalism, it led to one of the most serious economic problems that Egypt is currently facing—an acute shortage of rental housing. This shortage has been compounded over the years as the government has not had the financial ability to fill the needed gap in spite of its large construction programs.

Based on an average household of 4.9 individuals,[38] and with fifty-four million Egyptians in 1990 representing eleven million households each in need of shelter, I estimated the existing shortage in housing units by subtracting the seven million existing units from eleven million. Moreover with an increase of one and a half million inhabitants each year, there will be an added need for another 300,000 housing units annually. At the existing construction rate of 200,000 annually, the housing shortage can never be eliminated but will get even worse in the future. If the same rates continue, the housing shortage is expected to reach at least five million units by the turn of this century.

The shortage, however, may substantially exceed the above estimates because of the rapid depreciation of existing buildings due to the lack of incentives on the part of property owners to undertake even necessary replacements and minimum care, as rents are absurdly low.

The acute housing shortage in Egypt has led to a rush to own or rent additional apartments, that are kept closed, for future use. It has been customary for the financially able or the lucky persons who rent or own more than one apartment to keep other rented or owned housing units closed until their children get married, even when the children are still in their infancy. Units can also be kept for use for vacations if they are in a different city. The phenomenon of closed and unused apartments has begun to appear in rural areas of Egypt, as well as urban areas.

Rentalism led to a price distortion between rented properties and freehold ones. If two adjacent buildings identical in terms of area, height and all other specifications are compared, and one is occupied by tenants while the other is vacant, the latter can be sold in the market place at a price five to ten times the price of the former, depending upon their location. An acre of agricultural land with no one renting it may be sold at two or three times the price of an adjacent acre rented to someone. Furthermore, a vacant lot with no construction on it can be much more expensive than an adjacent lot of equal size with an existing building on it with several rented apartments. The anomaly arising from strict rent control on the one hand and free market sale value on the other has led to further distortions in this sector. So long as rentalism continues, the disparity in the pricing of rented versus unrented properties will grow substantially — even more than before — as the real value of Egypt's limited supply of urban land is increasing at a compounded rate. As a result, there is an unfair discrimination against the wealth of real estate owners whose properties are rented out.

There is no incentive to maintain buildings even for those proprietors who can financially afford such expenditures. It is undoubtedly in their economic interests for their buildings to become unsafe through neglect so that they can be legally demolished. Vacant lots can then be utilized more economically than before or can be sold with a phenomenal capital gain.

From the above analysis it may be concluded that the housing shortage is one of the most serious problems that Egypt is currently facing. In theory it is conceivable that some benefit will be obtained from it. With a lack of housing along with other such factors as current high rates of unemployment, it can be argued that there might be a reversal of the high rate of Egypt's birth rate and the encouragement of emigration. So far, however, the impact on the birth rate has been negligible. As for emigration from Egypt, there are only very limited opportunities available to young Egyptians who wish to settle permanently in the USA, Canada, Australia and other nations in Europe. While there are more than three million Egyptians working in Arab oil-exporting nations, their stay is only temporary because, with few exceptions, Arab countries do not allow the permanent settlement of foreign workers. With no appreciable effect so far on Egypt's birth rate or on migration from the country, the acute housing shortage remains a threat to social and political equilibrium. Overcrowdedness in apartments has created a variety of social problems and crimes[39] in addition to its negative effect on the overall productivity of the country and also on hygiene and sanitary conditions. In the meanwhile, the lack of adequate housing for the majority of young Egyptians, who are also faced with an unemployment rate of at least 19 percent, leads to frustration, hopelessness, possible mass disturbances and political instability.

Obviously, the current status quo is untenable. To improve the situation, there are only three possible options, in addition to an increase in housing construction by the government: (1) To encourage the private sector to increase its investments in housing construction, or, (2) To pursue a less efficient system by socializing Egypt's housing sector in its entirety so that at least the existing buildings may be properly maintained and their lifetime can be extended, or, (3) a combination of both. Due to the government's problem of bureaucracy and its budget deficits, and for other cultural and practical considerations, the last two options may be ruled out. The only viable solution to Egypt's acute shortage in housing is, therefore, the first option, yet it cannot be achieved without a gradual elimination of rent control. The phasing out of rentalism over a specific period of time is a necessary condition for a long-term solution to one of the most pressing problems that Egypt is currently facing.

Government Bureaucracy

As in the case of the housing laws which led to the current acute shortage in shelter, several other laws and regulations have created myriad economic imbalances and problems. With the decision to move quickly along the road of industrialization, the Egyptian government interfered in the relationship between the prices of industrial products and those of agricultural goods. Bent Hansen has candidly observed that "There has been a clear tendency to let the terms of trade of agriculture deteriorate as a means of financing industrialization. . . . Before World War II, fertilizers were imported duty free. Although this policy was dictated by the wishes of landlords, it obviously had positive allocation effects. Since the 1950s the government has sold fertilizers to peasants at prices generally above import prices, probably as a device to tax agriculture."[40] As the sole purchaser, the government of Egypt also established the rule of buying cotton from its growers at a price less than that of world markets as a means of raising public revenue.

Bureaucratic inefficiency, a characteristic of governments, especially in the Third World, has had negative effects on the country's economy. Ironically, the system of long bureaucratic procedures requiring several approvals, signatures, stamps and the like for the simplest government authorization was established by the British authorities upon their military occupation of Egypt in 1882. The system has remained in place ever since in spite of all attempts to overhaul it. In a major policy speech on November 11, 1989, President Mubarak acknowledged and bitterly criticized Egypt's suffocating bureaucracy, "which seeks to make the easy difficult and the possible impossible."[41]

A case study of a tourist project of Arab Misr Investment Company in Cairo reveals that it required 18 different steps to obtain the final licence needed to operate, as shown in Appendix 6. It is little wonder that it took five years after the full completion of the project for the licence to be issued. During that period all capital and investment expenditures were frozen, as there were no returns for a closed-down project. Meanwhile, there were financial obligations to banks on the borrowed money, in addition to the depreciation of capital assets and the payment of all financial obligations throughout the long-awaited period for the necessary final licence. Financial hardships to investors, some of whom were small investors committing the savings of a lifetime, crippled the company financially, prevented it from further expansion and investment, and finally forced it to close down.

Because of the problems of bureaucracy, several other projects have not been completed after their start. A feasibility study of a project might rely heavily on certain privileges allowable under existing regulations, such as duty free imported machinery for the project allowable under the open-door policy and the issuance of Law 43 in 1974. However, during project construction in the early 1980s, companies were faced by an unmanageable situation when the government reversed its position and decided to impose a heavy duty retroactively on the imported machinery for an already approved project which had not yet been completed. Through such unexpected actions, some projects were forced to declare bankruptcy, or at least stop short of completion after having spent all of their paid capital, as well as all sums of money borrowed from banks. No estimates have actually been made of the total of such sunk capital but it is believed among the accountants whom I have interviewed to be more than ten billion Egyptian pounds.

Some Egyptian and private companies, therefore, have devoted their activities to short-term trade, reaping high cash profits that have largely been diverted to an expanding informal economy. These high cash profits have often been hoarded in the form of cash or jewelry, or spent on unnecessary luxuries, lavish consumption, or otherwise invested or saved abroad. The effects of Egypt's inefficient bureaucracy were limited when the role of the government in the economy was small. With Nasser's move towards more centralization, which meant more consolidation of government power and centralization of decision making, the role of Egypt's government in the economy was substantially increased, particularly after the 1961 socialist laws. Under these laws private companies, such as Mahalla al-Kubra, Kafr al-Dawar Textile Companies and others, which were efficient and able to compete in world markets with high quality products, became public sector companies under the control and management of an inefficient bureaucracy. Even some of those public sector companies that show profits in their published annual budget are in fact operating at a loss, once an allowance is made for subsidized inputs such as energy, raw material and others, for which the companies do not pay the actual economic cost. As a result, in the 1980s, there has been a call for the denationalization or privatization of Egypt's public sector companies.

In fairness, there have been good managerial talents in charge of some of the public sector companies. Unfortunately, they have often been caught in a cobweb of bureaucratic procedures and an overlapping of conflicting jurisdictions among several different ministries. Their capabilities are not properly utilized. Constraints on their action and limits on their budget have prevented Egypt from taking advantage of the world's substantial technical progress since the 1950s. After almost forty years of assembling cars in Egypt, the industry has not been able thus far to produce a fully manufactured Egyptian car. In comparison, South Korea, which had almost the same economic and demographic characteristics as Egypt in 1952, has successfully been able to penetrate world markets, even those of the United States, with its inexpensive Hyundai, a fully manufactured Korean car.

The Root Cause of Egypt's Contemporary Economic Difficulties

There has been a decline in per capita real income in Egypt throughout the period 1983-87. During this period, the rate of increase of real GNP, according to official data, was one percent per annum[42] while the population growth rate averaged 2.9 percent.[43] This meant an annual decline in per-capita income by 1.9 percent in spite of the amelioration of some of Egypt's infrastructure during the period. Some economic progress in 1989 may, however, lead to an agreement with the International Monetary Fund as a prerequisite for the possible rescheduling of Egypt's foreign debt and the continuation of US aid.

In analyzing data on the Egyptian economy I have concluded, contrary to the views of al-Imari and al-Graitli, that the financing of the budget deficit was not the root cause of Egypt's contemporary economic difficulties. Rather, it was the result of the government's mismanagement of economic problems. However, it has worsened real economic conditions, as it has been a major source of inflation.

The results of my research on the root causes of the internal economic problems in Egypt indicate that the single most important factor has been a steady decline in productivity in comparison to other nations.[44] With the exception of the first phase of Egypt's open-door policy in the period 1975-1980, I observed a continuous decline in the marginal productivity of Egyptian labor since the mid-1950s. A decline in marginal productivity led to further deterioration in Egypt's balance of payments and a further deficit in the government's budget and has pushed inflation in an upward spiral.

Concluding Remarks

Egypt's economic reforms will have to be part of a long-term strategy covering ten to fifteen years, during which time there should be no stop-gap measures or short-term remedies which could obstruct long-run structural reform. In addition to an implementation of new medical technologies in the field of family planning, there must be a full state commitment to a reduction of the current high birth rate. Disincentive measures may be used, such as the removal of subsidies and other benefits after a second or third child is born. As to the root cause of internal economic problems in Egypt, namely the decline in marginal productivity, a policy for reform goes beyond what any government by itself can do. In recognizing these serious problems, some recommendations have urged efforts to increase managerial abilities or to reform educational and training systems.[45] Others have called for an overhauling of all emergency laws and regulations and of existing labor laws to provide more effective incentives for talented and highly productive workers. Furthermore, it has been argued that either a substantial reform of Egypt's ailing public sector be made, or else a systematic policy of privatization be implemented.[46] As a start, it may be recommended that shares of ownership of public companies be given to talented and highly productive workers as a bonus and an incentive be provided by the end of every budget year to increase marginal productivity.

There exists, however, a vicious circle of cause and effect that may have led to the deterioration of Egypt's marginal productivity. The reasons include over-crowdedness, the lack of adequate housing, hardships in public transportation, poor or crippled management and the existing labor laws which led to a system in which the inefficient is subsidized through equal earnings, treatment and opportunity while the efficient is penalized by the absence of adequate recognition, compensation and promotion.

In my opinion, a reform of the decline in marginal productivity is a national issue in which the state can only play a role by initiating a new system including incentives and disincentives for labor as well as an effective and continuous public awareness program. A change in people's attitudes toward increased marginal productivity will have to include a deepening of their sense of belonging through more active political participation and the removal of existing political impediments currently obstructing the freedom of choice of people's representatives in Egypt's Peoples' Assembly. The requirement inserted by Nasser in Egypt's constitution that no less than 50 percent of the parliament should have a working-class or peasant background should be removed. After all, Nasser himself declared that "In my opinion, this clause [the amendment providing for the 50 percent] will be discontinued. The clause is temporary until we pass through the current transitional period, after which we will give up our control over elections and stop saying 'this group is workers' and 'this group is peasants, etc.' In fact, our country is the only country to have adopted such a principle."[47] Overall political reforms which enable greater political participation will safeguard each individual's basic human rights. They may also have a positive effect on the people's attitude toward increased productivity by encouraging them to accept temporary hardships accompanying structural economic reforms. There is no doubt that some progress has been made in this context in recent years under Mubarak's regime.

The process of political liberalization and reinforcement of democratic institutions are necessary conditions for generating an atmosphere of confidence and long-term political stability.[48] These, in turn, could encourage capital owners who have invested in Egypt's vast and expanding underground economy to invest in long-term projects in the country. As the role of an economically efficient private sector is increased in an environment of competition, marginal productivity will necessarily increase. Otherwise, a continuation of the status quo—low productivity and an increase in population—will undoubtedly make Egypt more dependent than ever before on outside sources.

While economic assistance to Egypt from Arab countries, the US and other industrial nations is sizable, it should not be regarded as a continuous flow in the future. Even if it does, there is an economic and/or political price tag to it. Currently, Egypt is the second largest recipient of US aid after Israel, yet this aid was the consequence of the signing of the Camp David accords with Israel and the continuation of that treaty. The vulnerability of foreign economic assistance to Egypt and its possible discontinuation in the future leave no choice for Egypt other than to devise a consistent policy for self-reliance through increased productivity.

Among badly needed reforms are a restructuring of Egypt's public administration to minimize the crippling conflicts of jurisdictions and authority among different ministries, a series of continuous training and retraining programs, and an amelioration of the educational system, especially those parts of it which develop managerial capabilities. The proposal to reward highly productive and talented innovative workers with an equity share in the capital of the public sector companies in which they work could be an added incentive to increased productivity.

As a policy of liberalization of both political and economic spheres is the only viable alternative for a meaningful economic reform, it has to be consistently pursued with vigor. Rentalism should be gradually abolished over a period of ten to fifteen years. Emergency special laws for security purposes should be canceled as a means of generating an atmosphere conducive to attracting money now circulating in Egypt's informal economy for long-term investments. Furthermore, the current costly subsidy system, which has been a failure in helping the poor,[49] has to be totally eliminated and replaced with another that is less costly but more directly geared to helping the poor through such means as food stamps or direct cash payment according to need. With a reduction in subsidy expenditures and with a comprehensive overhaul of Egypt's tax system, the government's budget deficit could be substantially reduced. Every attempt should be made to rest public revenue on a solid base of progressive income tax, which would also serve as a means of reducing the current and eventually unsustainable degree of income maldistribution.

Export-oriented industrialization should be encouraged as a means of identifying the country's comparative advantage, as well as a way to reduce its balance-of-payments deficits. An analysis of a subset of import-competing industries in Egypt found them to be mainly operating at an economic loss or producing at a far lower level than their capacity. While such losses may in some cases be justified on the basis of non-quantifiable national security considerations, in others there is no justification for the continued depletion of the country's limited economic resources, which could be better utilized and more efficiently allocated. Other than their generally known economic advantages, such as efficiency in allocating limited resources, export-oriented industries would also be attractive because of the increase in the size of export markets resulting from recent moves towards regional economic integration. For example, Egypt, Iraq, Jordan and Yemen formed the Arab Cooperation Council on February 16, 1989.[50] Historically, the benefits of Egypt's integration with other Arab countries were analyzed by Charles Issawi as far back as 1954.[51]

Egypt can overcome most of its economic problems in the long run if it can identify its comparative advantages not only in its reservoir of special human talents but also in such fields as tourism, which has been barely utilized in spite of the country's world-wide unique features, and agriculture. Tourism, for example, had witnessed substantial progress by the end of the 1980s because of a strong policy against red tape and inefficiency. The Ministry of Tourism established direct links to several inland airports in Egypt for foreign carriers at a time when the only two international airports were in Cairo and in Alexandria. In the agricultural sector, a removal of rent and price controls while retaining the 1952 law of land reform is a necessary but not sufficient condition for expanding the agricultural output from the existing six million cultivated feddans. Special emphasis should be placed on sound pricing policies, while there should be no bias against agriculture in favor of industrialization. In the meanwhile, a scientific utilization of underground water reservoirs in Egypt's vast deserts to expand the area under cultivation should be pursued on the basis of cost-benefit economic principles.

In spite of the multiplicity and complexity of economic problems that Egypt is currently facing, there is room for optimism so long as there are possible solutions. Benign neglect of problems will only complicate them more. Solutions become much more difficult with the passage of time. If there is no firm commitment by the state to a reduction of the current high birth rates, and if the pace of economic reforms is too slow to be fundamentally corrective of the accumulated problems of the past, pessimism and alarm will be justified.

Notes

1. Even though outdated, an excellent description of Cairo was presented by John Waterbury in *Egypt, Burdens of the Past/Options for the Future* (Bloomington: Indiana University Press, 1978), pp. 125-44. The problems of overcrowding and pollution in metropolitan Cairo that are presented in the book have compounded as the city's population has nearly doubled since 1977. In 1990, Cairo's population was in excess of thirteen million inhabitants. On December 28, 1984 at the conference on "Egypt: The Year 2000," held at the Arab League in Cairo by the Association of Egyptian-American Scholars, it was revealed that lead pollution had reached one of the highest and most critical levels in the world in downtown Cairo. Lead pollution, which does not usually rise above four feet from the ground, could cause cancer and mental retardation among children. In his article in *The New York Times* (March 26, 1990), Alan Cowell reported that noise pollution in Cairo is "ten times higher than recommended by international health and safety regulations" and that close to two thirds of the city's inhabitants "use pills or other sedatives to get to sleep." Such factors have undoubtedly led to external diseconomies and have adversely affected productivity.

2. A. E. Crouchley, *The Economic Development of Modern Egypt* (London: Longman, Green, 1938), p. 256.

3. Central Agency for Public Mobilization and Statistics (CAPMAS), *Statistical Yearbook* (Cairo, 1988), p. 24.

4. *Ibid.*, p. 18.

5. The Presidency of the Republic, *The Report of the Council of Production and Economic Affairs, Magazine of the Specialized National Councils,* No. 6, Cairo (January 1979, in Arabic).

6. Alan Richards, "The Agricultural Crisis in Egypt," *Journal of Development Studies,* Vol. 22 (1986), p. 303.

7. See Elias H. Tuma, *Economic and Political Change in the Middle East* (Palo Alto: Pacific Books, 1987), p. 109; and John Waterbury, *Egypt Under Nasser and Sadat* (Princeton: Princeton University Press, 1986), p. 203.

8. *Ibid.*

9. *Ibid.*, p. 263.

10. Bent Hansen, "Economic Development in Egypt," in Charles A. Cooper and Sidney A. Alexander (editors), *Economic Development and Population Growth in the Middle East* (New York: American Elsevier Publishing Co., 1972), pp. 82-83.

11. Richard H. Adams, Jr., *Development and Social Change in Rural Egypt* (Syracuse: Syracuse University Press, 1986), p. 21.

12. S. Henry, *The Hidden Economy* (London: Martin Robertson, 1978).

13. A. Portes and S. Sassen-Koob, "Making it Underground: Comparative Material on the Urban Informal Sector in Western Market Economies," *American Journal of Sociology,* No. 93 (1987), pp. 30-61.

14. J. I. Gershuny, *After Industrial Society? The Emerging Self-service Economy* (Atlantic Highlands, New Jersey: Humanities Press, 1978).

15. E. L. Feige, "How Big is the Irregular Economy?" *Challenge,* No. 22 (1979), pp. 5-13.

16. N. Hansen, *The Border Economy* (Austin: University of Texas Press, 1981).

17. Manuel Castells and Alejandro Portes, "World Underneath: The Origins, Dynamics and Effects of the Informal Economy," in A. Portes, M. Castells and L. Benton (editors),

40   Ibrahim M. Oweiss

The Informal Economy: Studies in Advanced and Less Developed Countries (Baltimore: The Johns Hopkins University Press, 1979), p. 12.

18. *Ibid.*, p. 20.

19. Council of Economic Advisors, *Economic Report of the President* (Washington, DC: US Printing Office, 1988), p. 280.

20. Robert Mabro, *The Egyptian Economy 1952-1972* (Oxford: Clarendon Press, 1974), p. 182.

21. For the different forms of Egypt's saving certificates, which started in 1965, see Mona Issa al-Ayouti, "Financial Flows and The Role of Financial Intermediaries in the Egyptian Economy in the Period 1975-1981," Ph.D. Dissertation, Faculty of Economics and Political Science, Cairo University, 1985, p. 177.

22. National Bank of Egypt, *Economic Bulletin,* Vol. XXXX, No. 3 (Cairo, 1987), p. 188.

23. *Ibid.*, p. 201.

24. David Butter, "Egyptian Banking and Finance," *Middle East Economic Digest,* June 3, 1988, p. 92.

25. Muhammad Dowaidar, "Capital Investment Companies in the Egyptian Economy," *L'Egypte Contemporaine,* Vol. 80, No. 415-416 (January and April 1989), p. 12.

26. National Bank of Egypt, *op. cit.*, p. 193.

27. CAPMAS, *op. cit.*, p. 23.

28. *Ibid.*

29. Ibrahim M. Oweiss, "Egypt: Strategic, Economic and Political Assessment," in Robert A. Kilmarx and Yonah Alexander (editors), *Business and the Middle East: Threats and Prospects* (New York: Pergamon Press, 1982), p. 63.

30. Data were obtained directly from Egypt's Ministry of Finance in Cairo.

31. Data were obtained directly from Egypt's Central Bank in Cairo.

32. Ibrahim M. Oweiss, *op. cit.*, p. 71.

33. Arab Fund for Economic and Social Development, Coordination Secretariat, *Financing Operations as of 31/12/1986* (Kuwait, 1987).

34. "A different opinion was voiced during a seminar on Egypt sponsored by the National Foreign Trade Council on September 29, 1978. In a luncheon conversation, Dr. Ibrahim Oweiss, Director of the Egyptian Economic Mission, asked the eight representatives of multinational firms present at the table whether foreign investors will be much more disposed to invest in Egypt now that the political uncertainties had largely been settled with the Camp David accords. The business representatives each stated that he thought not; while the political factor is important, foreign investors might not move forward eagerly until the other serious environmental obstacles are taken care of. I concur in the latter view. The resolution of the regional political difficulties is a necessary but not sufficient condition for attracting much more foreign investment to Egypt." See David William Carr, *Foreign Investment and Development in Egypt* (New York: Praeger Publishers, 1979), pp. 93-94.

35. Ibrahim M. Oweiss, "Egypt's Open-Door Policy: An Economic Assessment," *The Columbia Journal of World Business,* Vol. XXIII, No. 1 (Spring 1988).

36. National Bank of Egypt, *op. cit.*, p. 153.

37. Data were obtained from the Ministry of Finance in Cairo.

38. CAPMAS, *Population, Housing and Establishment Census, 1986* (Cairo, 1987), p. 9.

39. It is not surprising that one of Egypt's most prestigious research institutions, the National Center for Social and Criminology Studies, devoted its lengthy seventh volume to the subject of housing under the supervision of Dr. Mustafa al-Hifnawi. The volume was published in Arabic in Cairo in 1985.

40. Bent Hansen, *op. cit.*, p. 83.

41. American Mideast Business Association (New York), *Bulletin of American Mideast Business,* Vol. XX, No. 10 (December 1, 1989), p. 1.

42. The annual rate of increase of Egypt's Gross National Product has been calculated from the source for statistics provided in Appendix 3.

43. The annual rate of increase in Egypt's population was calculated from Table 1-15 in CAPMAS, *Statistical Yearbook 1952-1987* (Cairo, 1987), p. 24.

44. Charles Issawi, *Egypt in Revolution: An Economic Analysis* (London: Oxford University Press, 1963), pp. 180-83.

45. Ibrahim Shihata, *A Program for Tomorrow: Challenges to and Prospects of the Egyptian Economy in a Dynamic World* (Cairo: Dar al-Shuruq, 1987), pp. 38, 40-43, 59-62 (in Arabic).

46. Said El-Naggar (editor), *Privatization and Structural Adjustment in the Arab Countries* (Washington, DC: International Monetary Fund, 1989). See in particular Said El-Naggar, "Privatization and Structural Adjustment: The Basic Issues," pp. 1-17; Ibrahim Hilmi Abdul-Rahman and Muhammad Sultan Abu Ali, "Role of the Public and Private Sectors with Special Reference to Privatization: The Case of Egypt," pp. 141-81; Abdul-Aziz Higazi, "Comment," pp. 182-88.

47. Nasser's statement was made on March 20, 1967 and quoted in *al-Ahram* on March 21, 1967. It was quoted again in an article written by Ambassador Issam al-Din Hawwas, "The Forgotten Dimension in the Case of the Restructuring of the Egyptian Individual," *Al-Ahram*, June 5, 1987.

48. Issam al-Din Hawwas, *A Strategy for the Restructuring of the Egyptian Human Being* (Cairo: General Egyptian Book Publishers Authority, 1980) (in Arabic).

49. The Presidency of Egypt, *op. cit.*, pp. 221-33. See also another point of view in Karima Korayem, "Distributing Disposable Income and the Impact of Eliminating Food Subsidies in Egypt," *Cairo Papers in Social Science*, Vol. 5, Monograph 2 (April 1982). See also the same author's *The Impact of Economic Adjustment Policies on the Vulnerable Families and Children in Egypt*, A Report Prepared for The Third World Forum, Middle East Office, and the United Nations Children's Fund (UNICEF), Cairo 1987. In the two studies there are estimates based on field work and econometric modeling.

50. Muhammad Wahby, "The Arab Cooperation Council," *American-Arab Affairs*, No. 28 (Spring 1989), pp. 60-67.

51. Charles Issawi, *op. cit.*, pp. 255-57.

Appendix 1
Egypt's Savings Ratio

Year	Y	S	Year	Y	S
1974/75	12,583	306	1981/82	21,709	3,319
1975/76	13,827	1,632	1982/83	23,408	4,984
1976/77	15,195	2,005	1983/84	25,285	4,960
1977/78	16,926	2,074	1984/85	25,445	3,948
1978/79	18,121	2,269	1985/86	25,689	2,842
1979/80	19,203	2,364	1986/87	26,292	1,945
1980/81	20,931	3,002			

Y = Egypt's Gross National Product (GNP)
S = Egypt's National Savings
Figures are in million Egyptian pounds at 1981/82 constant prices.
Source: Data were obtained directly from Egypt's Ministry of Planning in Cairo.

Based on the above figures, the following savings function was derived through regression analysis:

Savings ratio (s) = 19.9%

The regression equation statistics, based on 13 observations, with National Savings as the dependent variable, were:

Variable	Coefficient	Std. Error	t	2-tail sig.
Constant	−1313.1229	1211.3773	−1.0839916	0.302
GNP	0.1992359	0.0580589	3.4316136	0.006

R-squared = .517; R-squared (adj.) = .473; Durbin-Watson stat. = 0.667; log likelihood = −106.63; F = 11.77597

Appendix 2
Islamic Capital Investment Companies

The *Sharikat Tawzif al-Amwal al-Islamiyah* are known in the English language as "Islamic capital investment companies" (ICIC). They should, however, be differentiated from the other phenomenon of "Islamic banking," which started with one bank in 1970 and grew to more than 100 by the mid-1980s. Both groups claim that they adhere to Islamic law (*shari'a*) in which usury (*riba*) is forbidden and is interpreted as synonymous with interest rates. Their practice, therefore, is based on the concepts of *mudaraba,*[1] *musharaka*[2] and similar ideas.

Whereas Islamic banking is governed by strict central bank regulations and Islamic banks have become recognized as national and international institutions, the ICIC were established as companies without supervision by any central monetary authority. In Egypt, the ICIC were started in the late 1970s more or less by money exchange dealers in the outlawed black market of foreign currencies (mainly the US dollar).

Duwaidar has divided the development of ICIC into three distinctive stages:

The first stage lasted from 1978, when the first ICIC was established, until 1983. In this stage, money-exchange dealers conducted their business through the banking system, especially in private and joint-venture banks, by opening foreign-currency denominated accounts which were used to finance the growing import sector.

The second stage may be identified as lasting from July 1983 to January 1985, during which time the Ministry of Economy tried to freeze the bank accounts of 55 major money-exchange dealers. To circumvent the Ministry's action, they resorted to forming their own companies, through which they have directly attracted the savings of Egyptians, including those working in the rich Arab-oil exporting countries.

The third stage may be seen as starting in January 1985. By November 1987, the number of ICIC had substantially increased to about 180.[3] They had successfully mobilized unprecedented amounts of savings deposits totalling between $10 and $14 billion.[4]

The achievement of the ICIC in collecting such massive amounts in a short period of time was not only due to an ability to capitalize on deep-rooted religious convictions, but also because of their campaign announcing rates of return on deposits ranging from 20 to

25 percent annually. They accepted deposits either in the form of cash or in gold or other jewelry. At the beginning, the ICIC were able to distribute such high and unmatchable rates of return from the accumulated amounts of new deposits. Such an inflated balloon was bound to burst. In November 1987, when some depositors were not paid by one of the largest ICIC, the Egyptian government had to intervene. It issued Law 146 in 1988 with the purpose of safeguarding the interests of Egyptian depositors in the ICIC. Even though the collapse of some of the ICIC and the deposits of millions of Egyptians invested in them constituted a major political and financial problem in the country, the Egyptian government is still attempting to find some means through which the money deposited in them can be returned to its owners. It does not seem that the government will be able to track down the assets of the ICIC, especially since a major part of them was transferred out of Egypt.

Notes

1. *Mudaraba,* meaning speculation, is based on a contractual agreement for profit-sharing between an Islamic financial institution providing 100 percent of the capital of a venture and an entrepreneur managing the venture.

2. *Musharaka,* meaning partnership, is based on a contractual agreement for capital sharing in a venture between an Islamic financial institution and an entrepreneur managing the venture. In this case, profits and losses are distributed according to relative equity sharing in the venture's capital.

3. A list of the Islamic capital investment companies, with information regarding the amounts deposited with them, was published in Cairo in *October,* No. 627 (October 30, 1988) and No. 634 (December 18, 1988).

4. Duwaidar, *op. cit.,* pp. 11-12.

Appendix 3

In calculating the last column in Table 5, the following statistics have been used:

Year	Suez Canal Dues (in million EP)
1980/81	546.3
1981/82	636.2
1982/83	669.6
1983/84	681.8
1984/85	609.8
1985/86	719.8
1986/87	803.6

Source: National Bank of Egypt, *Economic Bulletin,* Vol. XXXX, No. 3 (Cairo 1987), p. 198. The last column is based on the percentages provided in Table 5, and the official accounting method at that time of equating the US dollar to 0.83 Egyptian pounds (EP).

Appendix 4

Summary of the Report "Egypt's Major Economic Problems" by Abdul-Galil al-Imari and Ali al-Graitli, presented to President Mubarak in December 1981

The most important problems facing Egypt are described in the report as the population increase, the housing problem, the neglect of public utilities, the shortage in agricultural production, especially food, the shortage in technical and skilled labor, the neglect of small and medium industries, and contradictory economic goals.

While Egypt's resources had increased in recent years, as a result of petroleum revenues, remittances from Egyptians working abroad, tourism and Suez Canal earnings, there was no guarantee that they would continue. Therefore, they should not be used for consumption, but rather for productive investment. The report stresses the importance of self-dependence and a reconsideration of the following basic economic policies:

First: Policies on consumption, and family and private savings.

Second: Policies on investment in the public sector as well as private and joint investment.

Third: Foreign trade and balance of payments policies.

Fourth: The foreign exchange market and prevailing foreign exchange rates.

Sacrifices had to be made to bring about economic reforms. While the poor should not be further burdened beyond their means, sacrifices should be shared by the rich and middle-income levels.

The Reconsideration of Basic Economic Policies

1. *Consumption and Family and Private Saving Policies*

A. *Private Consumption:* For economic stability, national consumption should be less than national production in order to achieve a savings ratio of between 20 percent and 25 percent. In order to achieve a goal of allocating 25 percent of GNP for investment, increased savings are necessary. A decrease in the rate of increase in private consumption and the provision of incentives for increased savings can be achieved through the following: (a) an increase in the prices of luxury and semi-luxury commodities to the levels prevailing in international markets and an increase in custom duties, production fees and consumption fees imposed on them; (b) an end to extravagant publicity for such commodities; (c) a decrease in the rate of increase of consumption of necessities through a stage-by-stage reduction in subsidies which will lead to an increase in their prices. The use of the price tool to decrease consumption should be an economic priority.

It is necessary to take a political decision to convince people of the necessity of reducing subsidies, and also to ensure that the needy do not suffer by (a) keeping the standard of living of persons with limited incomes unaffected, by a continuation of some subsidies in the short run; (b) the cancellation of subsidies on all commodities over a period of five years, accompanied by an increase of wages and pensions of persons with a limited income.

An example of extravagant private consumption is extravagance in wedding parties and funerals. A tax of 100 percent of the bill of wedding parties is suggested.

B. *A Reduction in Public Expenditures:* Defense appropriations should be fixed; the rate of increase in expenditures of governmental services should be reduced.

2. *Investment policies*

A. *Egypt's Public Sector:* (1) The management of each public sector company should be free to determine the prices of output of commodities and services, and to choose and employ what they need from the factors of production: labor, capital and materials; (2) The structure of public sector companies should be changed to provide them with autonomy; (3) Companies which are unable to turn their losses into profits should be liquidated; (4) Commodity stocks should be investigated; and (5) Policies pertaining to wages and incentives should be reconsidered.

B. *Private and Joint Investments:* It was noted that published investment statistics are exaggerated, while investments by Egyptian nationals turned out to be greater than those by all foreigners. Most such investments are capital-intensive, while conditions in Egypt would have been better served with labor-intensive industries. Finally, some of the objectives of Law 43 have not been realized. It is, therefore, proposed that: (1) Tax and customs exemptions should be confined to investments producing essential commodities and those located in remote areas as well as industries which export a portion of their production (at least 25 percent); and (2) There should be an immediate reconsideration of the Free Zone in Port Said, because of the problem of smuggling.

3. *Foreign Trade and the Balance of Payments*

Imports have been increasing at higher rates (20-25 percent annually). It is, therefore, proposed: (a) To adopt policies aimed at reducing the rates of inflation and increase in income which have caused the increase in the demand for imports; (b) To increase customs taxes on luxury commodities, and to cancel customs exemptions; (c) To use the idle capacity in public sector companies to increase exports.

Appendix 5
Special Emergency Rent Laws

1. *After World War II and prior to Nasser's 1952 Revolution*
    Law 121 of 1947 established the relationship between owners and tenants, except for the determination of rent. However, a rent ceiling was imposed for premises constructed before Jan. 1, 1944 and contracts signed after May 1, 1941, with possible incremental increases. Rents for all premises constructed after January 1, 1944 were to be freely determined through the law of supply and demand. The law gave the right to owners not to renew a contract once it expired.

2. *After the 1952 Revolution*
    1. *Law 199 of 1952* reduced rents by 15 percent on all premises constructed after January 1, 1944 and before September 18, 1952 while maintaining the fixed rents on those constructed before January 1, 1944 at the 1943 level.
    2. *Law 55 of 1958* reduced rents by 20 percent on all premises constructed since June 12, 1958.
    3. *Law 168 of 1961* reduced rents by 20 percent on all premises constructed since June 12, 1958.
    All the above three laws were amendments to Law 121 of 1947.
    4. *Law 7 of 1965* further reduced existing rents by 20 percent.

The following is a list of other laws pertaining to housing that were enacted following the 1952 revolution: 159, 196 and 657 of 1953; 453, 577, 605, 656 and 712 of 1954; 222 and 564 of 1955; 27, 66, 127, 140, 259, 317, 344, 353, 371 and 372 of 1956; 33 and 80 of 1957; 230 of 1959; 169, 178 and 1968 of 1961; 12, 45, 46, 71, 93, 147 and 157 of 1962, 15 of 1963; 6, 55, 100, and 139 of 1964; 7 and 24 of 1965; 1, 29 and 36 of 1966; 38 of 1967; 52 of 1969; 68 of 1970; 1, 3 and 59 of 1973; 62 and 63 of 1974; 109 of 1975; 84, 106 and 107 of 1976; 49 and 71 of 1977; 27 and 57 of 1978; 59 of 1979; and 14, 135, 136 and 143 of 1981.

Appendix 6
Steps Required to Establish a Tourist Project in Cairo

A. *District Government*
   1. Approval of District Security.
   2. Approval of the District Planning Committee.
   3. Approval of the District General Committee.
   4. Approval of the District People's Local Council.
   5. Approval of the President of the Local District Government.

B. *Cairo Government*
   1. Licenses Department.
   2. Office of the Undersecretary of the Ministry.
   3. Planning Committee.
   4. Security Committee.
   5. Undersecretary of the Ministry of Housing prepares a report to the People's Local Council at the government of the city of Cairo.
   6. Approval of the Planning Committee of the People's Local Council.
   7. Approval of the Security Committee of the People's Local Council.
   8. Approval of the People's Local Council, which usually meets once a month.
   9. Approval of the Executive Council.
   10. Approval of the Governor of Cairo.
   11. Deputy Governor of Cairo informs Department for the Encouragement of Tourism.
   12. Department for the Encouragement of Tourism informs the Department of Licenses at the Ministry of Tourism.
   13. Undersecretary of the Ministry of Tourism issues the final license.

2 PROSPECTS AND PROBLEMS OF PRIVATIZATION

Said El-Naggar

The recent decline in income from petroleum and workers' remittances has substantially reduced the total resources available to the Egyptian economy. The result is a serious deficit in the balance of payments, which calls for adjustment at both the macroeconomic and structural levels. As part of structural adjustment, privatization would significantly improve the productivity of labor and capital.

The case for privatization in Egypt rests on two bases: the first is the size of the public sector, and the second its performance.

Since nationalization in the early sixties, the public sector has accounted for much economic activity. It covers a wide range of sectors and sub-sectors in industry, foreign trade, banking, insurance, construction, transport, and so on.

The dominant position of the public sector was not seriously challenged by the open-door policy—commonly known as *infitah*—launched by President Sadat in the mid-seventies. One of the basic objectives of the open-door policy was to reduce the role of the public sector in favor of the private sector. The policy succeeded in attracting some Arab and foreign investments and in encouraging domestic private enterprise. However, in terms of total economic activity, the impact of the *infitah* policy remains limited. Compared to other developing countries, Egypt ranks among the highest as regards the relative importance of the public sector. Currently, the sector accounts for 70 percent of total investments, 80 percent of manufactured exports, and 55 percent of Gross Domestic Product.

A large, inefficient public sector had a negative impact on the Egyptian economy. This was reflected in a slowdown of growth, a poor export performance, a heavy external debt, a widening food gap, and an unhealthy dependence on foreign assistance. Admittedly, there are other factors besides the public sector that affect the performance of the Egyptian economy. Reference may be made in particular to macroeconomic imbalances, pervasive price and cost distortions and an unfavorable external environment. Nevertheless, the public sector remains of major importance. Moreover, distortions and imbalances are not independent of the public sector.

It is often argued that the public sector should not be judged solely on the grounds of efficiency. According to this argument, the role of the public sector in bringing about a redistribution of income in favor of the poor is no less important. However, upon closer examination, it can be shown that the income redistribution argument is groundless. The impact of the public sector on income distribution cannot be determined on the basis of selling a few goods and services at subsidized prices. Consideration has to be taken of inflation caused by deficits in the public sector. It is recognized that inflation has a significantly regressive impact on income distribution which could easily wipe out any benefits that might be derived from subsidized prices. Moreover, the pricing system as an instrument for income redistribution is inefficient. It is excessively wasteful and there are other more efficient methods for achieving the same goals.

Under these circumstances, the scope of the public and private sectors must be redefined. The public sector will continue to play an important role in the Egyptian economy. There are four identifiable areas where public enterprises should continue to operate: control over important natural resources such as petroleum and the Suez Canal, natural monopolies, the existence of substantial externalities, and activities where the scale of capital requirements and/or high technology exceed the capability of the private sector. Continuation of public enterprises in these areas serves specific and identifiable needs. But government involvement in other activities falling presently under the purview of the public sector serves no particular purpose. These include such activities as grocery and department stores, bakeries, flour mills, printing, bookshops, newspaper and magazine publishing, advertising, hotels, travel agencies, contracting, and so on. Privatization of these activities can only benefit the performance of the Egyptian economy, since they are currently heavy money losers, and constitute a drag on the economy and a drain of public funds.

Privatization runs against the interests of powerful pressure groups. It takes a strong commitment by the political leadership to overcome vested interests and break the inertia of the present system. The challenge facing the political leadership is to resolve the conflict between short-term expediency and long-term viability, between sectional and national interests.

Privatization will have a better chance of success if it anticipates obstacles and pitfalls and tries to overcome them. In addition to divestiture, it should be broadly interpreted to include privatization of management as distinct from ownership, partial conversion to private ownership, and the removal of regulations impeding competition with the private sector. Privatization in this broad sense could be made to accommodate the great differences among many enterprises in the public sector. It should go hand in hand with the development of the capital market, avoid concentration of wealth, and ensure wide popular participation in the ownership of national assets. The burden of reform should not fall on the work force in companies subject to privatization. Provisions will have to be made for the participation of workers and employees in ownership, the compensation of those who will be laid off, and the reassignment and retraining of redundant labor. The formulation and implementation of the privatization program should be entrusted to a special entity established for that purpose.

Background

Recent developments in the global economic environment have adversely affected the Egyptian economy. The most serious development was the sharp decline in the price of oil. Since the mid-seventies, oil exports have been a major source of foreign exchange earnings. With the collapse in oil prices in early 1986, Egypt's earnings from this source declined by nearly 50 percent. The problem was aggravated by a similar decline in workers' remittances—another major source of foreign exchange receipts. The falling income from these two sources resulted in a decline exceeding 30 percent of total current foreign exchange receipts.

As a result of these developments, Egypt has to cope with substantial deficits in the balance of payments. Under the circumstances, adjustment is inevitable. A recent standby arrangement with the International Monetary Fund included policy measures designed to reduce external deficits to sustainable levels. Most of these measures, however, are directed at macroeconomic imbalances such as the budget deficit, the excess money and credit supply, and the over-valuation of the Egyptian pound.

It is hoped that the stabilization program covered by the standby arrangement will bring about a viable balance of payments position. However, IMF-supported programs are essentially short-term. While short-term equilibrium is crucial, it does not answer the long-term problems of the Egyptian economy. This raises the question of structural adjustment, which affects the productivity of labor and capital. Structural adjustment covers many aspects of development policy. In the case of Egypt, one of the most important needs is to eliminate price and cost distortions. This is a pervasive phenomenon, since prices and costs in Egypt do not reflect the real scarcity of resources.

The waste resulting from such distortions is substantial. Another important element in structural adjustment is the inefficiency of the public sector, which has been one of the major preoccupations of the Egyptian government. Recognizing that the performance of the public sector leaves much to be desired, the government has introduced reform measures more than once. The last 25 years witnessed at least three major reorganizations of the public sector, the last of which was introduced by Law 97 in 1983. The reform focuses on the division of authority and responsibility between the operating units on the one hand and higher levels of control on the other. There is no indication, however, that the most recent attempt at reform is faring better than its predecessors.

The persistence of poor performance despite strenuous efforts for reform is causing developing countries to explore alternative approaches. In the last few years, interest has surged in privatization as an effective tool in dealing with the problems of the public sector. The privatization drive is visible in countries as diverse in their history, background, and level of development as Jamaica, Bangladesh, Chile, Togo, Brazil, Turkey, Malaysia, Pakistan, Sri Lanka, East European countries, China, and many industrial countries, notably Britain, France, Australia, and New Zealand.[1]

Size of the Public Sector

One of the most critical decisions facing the Egyptian government over the next few years is determining the relative role of the public and private sectors. At present, the Egyptian economy is dominated by the public sector. This situation has existed since the nationalizations of the early sixties. Following nationalization in July 1961, the public sector emerged as the dominant force in a wide range of activities. Most of the manufacturing sector went to the government. The same is true of mining, foreign trade, banking and insurance, construction, public utilities, transport, and numerous firms in other sectors. The private sector was reduced to a subsidiary role. Central planning displaced market forces as the driving force for modernization and development. "Few developing countries other than those that are professedly Marxist ever cut so deeply into their private sectors as Egypt."[2]

A major exception to the takeover by the public sector was agriculture, where ownership of land continued to be in private hands. However, the agricultural sector was subject to many government restrictions. Moreover, the marketing of principal crops as well as the supply of essential inputs such as fertilizers, pesticides, and agricultural credit were monopolized by public enterprises.

The open-door policy—commonly known as *infitah*—launched by President Sadat in the mid-seventies represented a major departure from the socialist philosophy of the early sixties. Its purpose was to initiate a new development strategy based on export-oriented policies, a more important role for the private sector, foreign investment, and market forces. According to the October Working Paper, which laid the foundation of the open-door policy:

> The public sector played a crucial role in Egypt's past development, but experience revealed some shortcomings. In particular, the sector suffered from an excess of bureaucracy, and some of the activities that were "annexed" were not compatible with the public sector's mission and should have been left to the private sector. . . . Reorientation was required to rid the sector of obstructions and increase its efficiency. In the future, the public sector would concentrate on carrying out the plan . . . undertaking basic projects that other sectors would not or could not take up . . .[3]

The thrust of the October Working Paper was to diminish the scope of the public sector. There was no attempt, however, to privatize certain public sector activities. The basic strategy was to provide incentives and inducements for the private sector on the assumption that it would eventually dominate the Egyptian economy and reduce the public sector to a secondary role. The results of the open-door policy show the limitations of such a strategy. Due to the variety of incentives offered in Law 43 of 1974, amended by Law 32 of 1977, the open-door policy was able to attract Arab and foreign investment and to push domestic private enterprise forward. This, however, has not changed the fundamental character of the economy, which is still dominated by the public sector. During the 1975 to 1985 period, total investments under Law 43 were less than 7 billion Egyptian pounds, which represent a small fraction of total public investments over the same period.

The open-door policy notwithstanding, the public sector still accounts for more than 55 percent of the Gross Domestic Product, 70 percent of total investment, and 80 percent of total manufactured exports. Compared to other developing countries, Egypt ranks among the highest as regards the relative importance of the public sector.

Performance of the Public Sector

Given the size and scope of the public sector, its efficiency has become a major determinant of the overall performance of the Egyptian economy. The question has been a subject of several studies by the World Bank. All came to the conclusion that the performance of the public sector was inadequate. Performance was measured by five indicators: overall deficits, impact on the national budget, rate of return, impact on the balance of payments, and international competitiveness.

This discussion of the five indicators draws heavily on data in *Egypt: Review of the Finances of the Decentralized Public Sector*, Vol. I (March 1987). The study examines the operations of 360 public companies and 37 economic authorities over the decade 1973 to 1983/84. It covers all activities except enterprises in the financial sector.[4]

Overall Deficits

In this section, public enterprises will be viewed as including public companies and economic authorities, but excluding the so-called service authorities which do not constitute separate entities and carry out essentially governmental functions in such fields as health, education, research, and so on.

Overall surplus or deficit is defined as the difference between total revenue and total expenditure. Neither revenue nor expenditure statistics take account of subsidies received from the government or profits transferred to the government. Moreover, public enterprises, like private enterprises, are supposed to be self-supporting and able to cover both their current and capital expenditures. Thus, the overall surplus or deficit represents the net result of the operations after covering current as well as capital expenditures. At the same time, revenue is defined in gross terms so that it is not reduced by the amount of depreciation allowance.[5]

Table 1 shows that during 1973 to 1983/84 public companies, as distinct from economic authorities, realized a surplus on their current operations, which declined from 8 percent of the GDP in 1973 to less than 4 percent in 1983/84. However, if account is taken of capital expenditure, public companies would show a persistent deficit ranging from about 3 percent of the GDP in 1973 to nearly 7 percent in 1983/84.

As for the economic authorities, the overall picture depends on whether the Petroleum and Suez Canal Authorities are included. These two authorities are major sources of surplus, and their inclusion

TABLE 1
Overall Balance of Public Enterprises
(As Percentage of GDP)

	1973	1977	1979	1980-81	1981-82	1982-83	1983-84
Public Companies							
Current	7.94	9.10	8.22	6.12	3.77	3.85	3.88
Capital Expenditures	-10.73	-15.28	-13.25	-13.27	-12.39	-11.30	-10.81
Overall Balance	-2.79	-6.18	-5.03	-7.15	-8.62	-7.45	-6.93
Economic Authorities							
Current	2.94	-1.59	-1.49	-1.56	-4.08	-1.24	-1.53
Capital Expenditures	-3.40	-5.23	-5.86	-5.47	-4.58	-6.00	-5.62
Overall Balance	-0.46	-6.82	-7.35	-7.03	-8.66	-7.24	-7.15

Note: Economic Authorities in this table exclude those for Petroleum and the Suez Canal.
Source: Central Agency for Public Mobilization and Statistics (CAPMAS), Ministry of Finance, and estimates of the International Bank for Reconstruction and Development (IBRD).

would obscure the real performance of other economic authorities. According to Table 1, economic authorities, apart from those responsible for Petroleum and for the Suez Canal, are persistent losers even on their current operations.

If the Petroleum and Suez Canal authorities are included, the economic authorities would show a surplus on their current operations, which averaged about 6 percent of GDP from 1980 to 1984. However, if both current and capital accounts are considered, the surplus would become a deficit of about 2 percent over the same period.

Combining both the public companies and economic authorities, including those for Petroleum and the Suez Canal, the picture that emerges is far from reassuring. Public enterprises of both types recorded overall deficits throughout the period under consideration. The magnitude of deficits was over 8 percent of GDP in 1983-84, having increased from less than 4 percent at the beginning of the period.

Impact on the National Budget

The overall deficit of public enterprises was partly financed from the national budget, partly from the banking system, and partly by direct borrowing from abroad. Concentrating on the part which is financed from the national budget, it becomes clear that the fiscal burden has been quite substantial. The fiscal burden is defined as the net transfer of resources from the national budget to public enterprises. It takes into account the actual payment of subsidies by the treasury as well as profits transferred to the treasury (Table 2).

Table 2 calls for some observations. It is revealing that the fiscal burden of public enterprise accounts for about one-third of the total budget deficit. Since the budget deficit represents anywhere between 15 and 20 percent of GDP, the net fiscal burden of public enterprises ranges between 5 and 6 percent of GDP.[6] In some years, however, the net transfer was well over 6 percent. This is a heavy burden indeed, even by the standards prevailing in Third World countries.

There are reasons to believe that the fiscal burden of public enterprises may be even higher than these figures suggest. The calculations underlying Table 2 account only for open subsidies as reflected in the state budget. They do not account for implicit subsidies such as those connected with foreign exchange allocations at less than market rates. Moreover, the losses incurred by the public authorities under the Ministry of Supply are not included in these calculations. These losses are substantial and would significantly affect the calculations. Finally, much of the period under review was

TABLE 2
Budgetary Burden of Public Enterprises
(As Percentage of GDP)

	1973	1977	1979	1980-81	1981-82	1982-83	1983-84
Public Companies	1.20	4.17	6.35	6.17	4.48	4.70	4.13
Economic Authorities	2.51	2.10	2.42	-5.94	-0.23	2.07	1.40
Total Burden	3.71	6.27	8.77	0.23	4.25	6.77	5.54
Fiscal Deficit	14.70	16.90	26.90	15.80	25.30	20.60	20.20
Total Burden as % of National Fiscal Deficit	25.31	37.00	32.47	1.47	16.80	32.89	30.20

Note: A negative sign indicates a net transfer from public enterprises to the national budget.
Source: CAPMAS, Ministry of Finance and IBRD estimates

exceptionally prosperous, following the increase of income from oil
and workers' remittances. The slowdown of economic activities under
1983-84—the last year covered by the table—probably had a negative
impact on the financial position of public enterprises.

Comparison with other Developing Countries

It is interesting to compare public enterprises in Egypt with those of
other developing countries. Table 3 provides data on the overall
deficit of public enterprises in twenty developing countries. Between
1974 and 1977, the overall deficit of public enterprises in Egypt stood
at 9.8 percent, the highest in the table. The ratio of deficit in Egypt

TABLE 3
Overall Balances of Public Enterprises
in Selected Developing Countries
(As Percent of GDP)

Country	1974-77	1978-80
Egypt	−9.8	−9.3
Turkey	−8.3	−9.7
India	−6.9	−6.8
Venezuela	−6.3	−5.9
Mali	−5.9	−2.7
Peru	−5.2	−1.8
Mexico	−4.9	−4.6
Jamaica	−4.5	−4.0
Bolivia	−4.5	n.a.
Argentina	−4.3	−3.4
Tanzania	−3.9	n.a.
Barbados	−2.8	−3.4
Bahamas	−2.7	−2.1
Malawi	−2.5	−3.5
Guatemala	−1.9	−2.7
Paraguay	−1.7	−1.0
Chile	−1.2	−0.7
Colombia	−1.2	−0.5
Uruguay	−0.3	−1.1
Costa Rica	n.a.	−4.4

Note: A negative sign means a deficit.
Source: Robert Floyd et al., *Public Enterprises in Mixed Economies* (Washington, DC: International Monetary Fund, 1984).

as a percent of GDP was more than double the corresponding ratio in 14 countries and more than 50 percent higher than the rest, except Turkey. Between 1978 and 1980 the picture was not significantly different although Egypt ranked second after Turkey, with a deficit ratio of 9.3 percent.

Table 4 compares the situation in sixteen developing countries with respect to the net fiscal burden of public enterprises. Again, Egypt ranked high in terms of the fiscal burden caused by deficits of public enterprises. In 1974-77 the ratio of deficit to GDP was exceeded only by India and Tanzania. In 1978-80 Egypt's was the highest among sixteen countries.

TABLE 4
Budgetary Burden as Percent of GDP

Country	1974/77	1978/80
India	5.2	5.5
Tanzania	5.0	n.a.
Egypt	4.75	5.7
Barbados	3.8	n.a.
Bahamas	3.0	2.0
Turkey	2.3	3.5
Venezuela	2.3	−0.6
Malawi	2.2	1.8
Mexico	2.1	2.9
Jamaica	1.9	3.9
Guatemala	1.5	1.9
Peru	1.0	0.4
Uruguay	0.5	0.6
Chile	0.2	−2.5
Colombia	0.1	0.3
Bolivia	−0.4	3.8

Note: A negative sign implies a positive impact on the budget.
Source: Robert Floyd et al., *op. cit.*

Rate of Return

Another indicator of the financial performance of public enterprises is the rate of return. In order to evaluate whether a given rate of return is high or low, it is important to relate it to a reference value. Since the rate of return measures the ratio between net revenue and the value of capital stock, it should reflect the relative scarcity of capital.

Egypt has abundant labor and limited capital resources compared with most other developing countries. Accordingly, one would expect capital to earn relatively high rates of return, as in principle interest rates measure scarcity of capital. This measure, however, is vitiated by a high rate of inflation which presently runs at about 20 percent per annum. Due to inflation, there is a divergence between nominal and real rates of interest. Presently, the nominal long-term rate of interest ranges between 12 and 16 percent, which means a negative real interest rate. Consequently, current levels of nominal interest rates fail to reflect the true scarcity of capital. Evidently, real interest rates should be positive. For the sake of argument a nominal interest rate of 14 percent is taken as the reference value, which is slightly higher than the rate paid by the government on investment certificates.[7]

TABLE 5
Rates of Return in Public Sector Companies
(Percentages)

	1973	1977	1979	1980/81	1981/82	1982/83	1983/84
Net Rate of Return (book-value capital)	9.02	11.14	9.37	7.69	4.49	4.64	4.77
Net Rate of Return (revalued capital)	5.25	5.88	5.52	4.30	2.18	1.99	1.71

Source: CAPMAS, IBRD Estimates.

Table 5 gives the net rates of return in public sector companies on the basis of the book value of capital, as well as on the basis of revalued assets. The former is largely an accounting concept. In the present context it is of limited significance. By understating the replacement value of assets, it grossly overstates the rates of return. A more relevant concept is the rate of return on revalued assets, which takes into account the impact of inflation on replacement value. Table 5 clearly shows that the net rate of return in public companies is unacceptably low. Beginning 1981-82 it stood at around 2 percent, which is only one-seventh of the reference value under Egyptian conditions. Before that, it hovered around 5 percent. No less significant is that it has shown a deteriorating trend throughout the period. It steadily declined from over 5 percent in 1973 to less than 2 percent in 1983-84. This declining trend is also noted in the rate of return on book value capital.

The rate of return in the economic authorities is not shown in Table 5. According to World Bank estimates, it was negative, if the Petroleum and Suez Canal Authorities are excluded. The main authorities showing a negative rate of return were the Egyptian Railways, Cairo and Alexandria Transport Authorities, and Cairo and Alexandria Water and Sewage Authorities. Although the Electricity Authority earned a positive rate of return on revalued assets, it was less than 3 percent in 1984-85.

The position of public enterprises in the industrial sector was described in a World Bank study:

> The main finding is that the financial performance of the public industrial enterprises has been unacceptably poor and has been deteriorating at a rapid pace. An indication of the extent of the deterioration is that, in 1974, about 23 percent of the firms under the Ministry of Industry suffered operational losses, whereas in 1980/81, the figure was 57 percent. It appears that this number increased further in 1982/83. The rapid deterioration in financial performance despite increases in physical output implies a growing dependence of public enterprises on budgetary support.[8]

Impact on the Balance of Payments

During the last ten years Egypt experienced a rapid increase in external indebtedness. There are various estimates of foreign debt, as a result of differences of definition and coverage. The size of foreign debt depends on whether it includes military debts, short-term obligations (i.e., debts of less than one year maturity), and the extent to which it includes foreign currency obligations to residents. A further source of discrepancy is the estimation of foreign debts which are not reported through the Debt Reporting System of the World Bank. Since the IBRD World Debt Tables cover mainly debts reported through the Debt Reporting System, they tend to underestimate the magnitude of external indebtedness. The most recent estimate puts Egypt's foreign debt in June 1986 at about $40 billion, including both civilian and military debt as well as short-term obligations and the net foreign currency exposure of the banking system. Much of this debt was incurred at a time of high interest rates. Consequently, the debts carried a debt service burden which amounted, before rescheduling, to over 35 percent of current foreign exchange receipts. Rescheduling agreements are estimated to have reduced this ratio to a much more manageable proportion of 17 percent in 1986-87 and a projected 10 percent in 1987-88. As expected, the public sector accounts for most of the foreign debt—upward of 90 percent. But the public sector includes the central government as well as service authorities, in addition to the public companies and economic authorities which are the focus of the present study. Unfortunately, there is no breakdown of public sector by different entities. According to World Bank estimates, public enterprises (i.e., public companies plus economic authorities) account for about half the total public sector debt. Considering, however, that a high proportion of foreign borrowing dealt with the financing of major infrastructure projects, the figure of 50 percent may be on the high side. A conservative estimate would probably put the share of public enterprises (excluding those in the financial and defense sectors) at about one-third of the total public sector debt. This means that external indebtedness caused by public enterprises stood at about $13 billion in June 1986. Most of these debts were contracted by public enterprises other than the Petroleum and Suez Canal Authorities. The debt service burden attributed to the external debts of these enterprises is estimated at about $1.2 billion per annum from 1984 to 1986.

TABLE 6
Development of Exports by Public Enterprises
(In Million US $, Current Prices)

	1977	1981-82	1984-85
Total Public Enterprises	1,243	5,356	5,279
of which: Petroleum	187	3,329	2,891
Suez Canal	—	909	897
Exports Excluding Petroleum and Suez Canal	1,056	1,118	1,491

Note: Exports include goods and non-factor services.
Oil exports exclude share of foreign oil companies.

It is important to know the extent to which such a magnitude of external borrowing and debt service burden was matched by a corresponding growth of exports. Between 1974 and 1983-84 exports by public enterprises grew by an annual rate of 16 percent. Much of the growth, however, was due to petroleum and the Suez Canal. If these are excluded, export receipts of public enterprises other than petroleum and the Suez Canal would amount to about $1.5 billion in 1984-85, implying an average annual rate of export growth of 3.5 percent, and a debt service ratio of nearly 80 percent. At the same time the foreign exchange needs of the enterprises for imports of raw materials, intermediate products, and capital equipment ran at approximately $4.5 billion per annum. Compared to net export earnings (i.e., net of debt service payments) of only $300 million, this means that public enterprises other than the Petroleum and Suez Authorities imposed a net annual burden on the balance of payments of more than $4 billion or more than 40 percent of total current foreign exchange receipts.

International Competitiveness

The poor export performance of public enterprises reflects weak competitiveness in international markets. Several factors are involved. There is first the macroeconomic framework within which these enterprises operate. For most of the period under consideration, the Egyptian pound was significantly overvalued in relation to the currencies of principal trading partners. Overvaluation made the domestic market more profitable than export markets. As such, it acted as a major disincentive to exports. The recent devaluation of the pound, in addition to allowing exporters to retain all or most of their foreign exchange receipts, has contributed to the improvement of the situation. However, according to IMF analysis, the real effective exchange rate still contains a certain measure of overvaluation. This is explained by the fact that the rate of inflation in Egypt continues to be significantly higher than in the principal trading partners.

Aside from overvaluation of the currency, export performance has been seriously affected by the high degree of protection accorded to domestic industries. The average rate of tariff is well above that for most developing countries. For many finished products, it goes as high as 200 percent. In addition, there is a list of imports which is completely banned. While some of these imports belong to the category of "luxury" goods which have no counterpart in domestic production, a good number are banned because there is enough domestic production to satisfy local demand. At the same time, quantitative restrictions are widely resorted to through direct controls and rationing of foreign exchange. As a consequence, domestic producers have been largely sheltered against foreign competition.

The restrictive character of trade policy is accentuated by a high degree of tariff escalation. In Egypt, as in many developing countries, tariff rates tend to increase with the increase in the degree of processing. Raw materials are typically admitted free of import duties. Intermediate products are subject to higher rates. But tariff rates reach their highest levels when applied to goods in the final stages of production. As a result of tariff escalation, the effective rate of protection, measuring the protection of value added, is significantly higher than nominal rates stated in the tariff schedule. In many branches of the manufacturing industry, the effective rate of protection is several times the nominal rate.

Exchange and trade policies affect the international competitiveness of both the public and the private sector. There are, however, certain factors which are peculiar to the public sector. The first relates to the organization of the public sector. Public enterprises are organized by sectors. Enterprises producing the same product are grouped under a single public authority which is responsible for coordination among the different units. Often the coordinating function includes fixing the quantities to be produced as well as the prices at which they are to be sold. The system does not permit much competition among firms belonging to the same sector or sub-sector. The absence of effective competition in the domestic market translates into weak export performance at the international level.

The second and perhaps the most important factor affecting international competitiveness is the efficiency of investment. The public sector controls as much as 70 percent of total investment. That was the proportion of public investment in the Five-Year Plan, 1982-83 to 1986-87. In the current Five-Year Plan, from 1987-88 to 1991-92, it is planned to reduce the ratio to 60 percent. Evidently, international competitiveness will depend largely on how public investments are allocated among various economic activities in line with comparative advantage. But comparative advantages cannot be determined on the basis of money costs and prices which do not reflect the real opportunity cost of resources. In both industry and agriculture, tariffs, taxes, subsidies, price and quantity controls make product prices and input prices imperfect measures of economic opportunity costs. In addition, government intervention in the markets for capital and labor introduces further divergences between market prices and economic or shadow prices. The World Bank carried out a detailed investigation of efficiency of investment in the industrial sector. Efficiency was measured in terms of domestic resource cost ratio (DRC) in a sample of 70 firms in the public sector and 24 firms in the private sector covering twelve major industrial groups. The basic idea in domestic cost ratios is to avoid distortions in domestic costs and prices by evaluating domestic factors of production at their opportunity cost and evaluating output at international prices. If, for a product, the DRC ratio is positive but less than one, it may be classified as efficiently produced; the firm producing that product has a comparative advantage in manufacturing it domestically. The smaller the ratio, the higher the comparative advantage. On the other hand, if the DRC ratio is greater than one, it is better to import that product, and the firm producing it does not have a comparative advantage. Cases where DRC ratios are negative mean that the value added at international prices is negative and the firms producing that product are definitely suffering from severe comparative disadvantage even if they are making high financial rates of return on the basis of market costs and prices. Table 7 shows the results of DRC ratios that were calculated once on the basis of historical cost and an accounting rate of interest of 6 percent, and once on the basis of replacement

TABLE 7
Comparative Advantage of Public Sector Industries (1980-81)

Industry	*Aggregate Domestic Resource Cost (DRC)*	
	Historical Cost ARI = 6%	Replacement Cost ARI = 10%
Textiles		
Cotton Textiles	0.629	0.889
Other Textiles	0.994	0.281
Food		
Edible Oils	0.566	0.843
Processed Food	0.314	0.516
Alcohol, Beverage	0.395	0.562
Chemicals		
Paper	1.714	2.803
Basic Chemicals	1.838	3.457
Miscellaneous	−0.651	−1.156
Metals		
Basic Metals	−27.558	−45.146
Transport Equipment	−6.431	−8.467
Electric Machinery	0.591	0.800
China and Glass	−3.931	−5.431

Note: ARI stands for Accounting Rate of Interest.
Source: World Bank estimates.

cost and an accounting rate of interest of 10 percent. The results are consistent in both calculations. Egypt enjoys a clear comparative advantage in the textile and food industries, where all DRCs are less than unity. At the same time it suffers from a comparative disadvantage in chemicals and metals, where all DRCs (except electrical machinery) are either negative or greater than unity. The degree of comparative disadvantage is apparently greater in metals, where the incidence of negative value added is more frequent. This is perhaps because many metal industries are extremely energy-intensive. Since they use up energy at heavily subsidized prices, the evaluation of inputs and outputs at economic or world prices produces negative value added. In many of these industries, the foreign exchange used in importing inputs is greater than the foreign exchange generated by exporting output.

The ranking of firms according to DRC coefficients gives a broad indication of where comparative advantage resides. It should be pointed out, however, that the methodology is subject to important limitations.[9] In the first place, DRC is a static concept which measures comparative advantages at a given moment in time. It fails to capture changes over time which could substantially affect the relative position of different industries. Moreover, it would be wrong to generalize about a whole sector or subsector. Some firms are more efficient than others in the same economic activity. They may be classified as enjoying a comparative advantage even though the sector as a whole shows a comparative disadvantage coefficient. Despite these limitations, the concept underlying domestic cost ratios remains a useful guide to policy.

Investment allocations under both the 1982-86 plan and the 1987-91 plan do not seem to have been influenced by considerations of comparative advantage. In fact the pattern of investment under both plans differs from what one would expect on the basis of domestic cost ratios. Thus, the major share of investment in the industrial sector goes to chemicals, metals, and engineering industries.[10] By way of illustration, the current Five-Year Plan envisages a substantial increase in the output of passenger cars (117 percent), trucks (218 percent), buses (92 percent), cement (292 percent), and caustic soda (251 percent), during 1987-91. In contrast, the planned increase in food and textile industries, where the country enjoys a clear comparative advantage, is relatively modest: sugar (13 percent), edible oils (25 percent), cotton spinning (22 percent), cotton weaving (32 percent), and ready-made clothes (119 percent). This pattern of investment is hardly surprising, given the declared objectives of the plan. Aside from the replacement and completion of on-going projects, which account for over 50 percent of total public investments, the criteria for investments in new projects are primarily self-sufficiency, augmenting productive capacity, and reducing import dependence. There is nothing wrong with these objectives except that they are so broad as to justify practically any investment decision. At the same time, concepts such as efficiency pricing, opportunity cost, comparative advantage, and international competitiveness are conspicuous by their absence from plan documents.

The Public Sector and Income Distribution

It is often argued that efficiency is not the sole criterion by which the public sector should be judged. There are other important considerations. Prominent among these is the redistribution of income. The public sector, so the argument runs, is an important instrument for redistributing income in favor of the low income groups. It is able to offer a wide range of essential goods and services at prices that the poor can afford. Admittedly, these prices may not reflect the economic cost of goods and services. But considerations of equity should weigh as much as efficiency.

Before commenting on this argument, it should be made clear that the goal of a more equitable income distribution is not at issue. However, the present system of using pricing policies as a vehicle for income redistribution raises three questions:

1. The effectiveness of the present system in achieving the stated goals;
2. The cost involved in deviating from efficiency pricing for the attainment of social goals.
3. Whether there are alternative policies which are more effective in reducing inequality of income distribution.

The effectiveness of the present system is questionable at both the macro and micro levels. At the macro level, there is a close correlation between the present pricing policies and the magnitude of the deficit in the national budget. As mentioned earlier, many public enterprises have large financial deficits. These deficits have a great deal to do with the fact that prices are frequently set at levels which fail to reflect the costs of goods and services. The excess of cost over price is largely financed by a direct subsidy from the national budget. The impact of such subsidies is evidently to raise the level of public expenditure. This is not, however, the only burden on the national budget. In many cases, the subsidy is implicit and has the effect of reducing public revenues. Such is the case when the government supplies foreign exchange, energy, or other inputs at prices well below the free market costs. Whether the pricing system is expenditure raising or revenue reducing, it has the same impact on the national budget; it contributes toward the overall budget deficit. In fact, about one-third of the budget deficit is directly related to overall deficits of public enterprises.

Presently, the budget deficit in Egypt stands at the high rate of 15 percent of GDP. This is partly financed by borrowing from foreign and domestic sources, and partly by borrowing from the banking system, that is, by an expansion in money supply. It is estimated that domestic bank financing of the budget deficit runs at about 7 percent of GDP. Clearly, this is a highly inflationary form of deficit financing. To a large extent, it is responsible for a current rate of inflation in excess of 20 percent per annum. It is well recognized that inflation has a highly regressive impact on income distribution. Thus, the benefits that might accrue to the low or fixed income groups from subsidizing the price of a few goods and services could be more than offset through inflation caused by budget deficits attributed to the operations of public enterprises.

At the micro level, it is not clear that the present pricing policies have a positive effect on income distribution. Subsidized products are available to both rich and poor. In fact, they are more accessible to the rich than to the low income groups, and to the urban centers more than to the countryside. Under these circumstances, the presumed distributional impact of subsidized goods and services becomes highly questionable. There is another aspect to the present system which is relevant to income distribution. For every subsidized commodity there exist two markets: one is controlled and largely administered by the public sector; the other is free and run by private traders. The free market price is often much higher than the controlled price. Accordingly, the temptation to divert subsidized supplies illegally to the free market is overpowering. Some individuals have reportedly made fortunes out of the system. This is particularly the case in subsidized building materials and in certain basic commodities. Petty middlemen have also been abusing the system to make quick and easy profits. If account is taken of shortcomings at both the macro and micro levels, it is not clear how much benefit is left for the initial target group in whose favor the system was established in the first place.

Suppose, however, that the system is working fairly smoothly. The question arises as to whether the cost involved justifies the benefit. The deviation of subsidized prices from opportunity cost gives rise to a serious misallocation of resources. This means that the contribution of real resources—capital, labor, land and management—to national output is less than it would otherwise have been. The fact that the prices of the principal agricultural commodities are set at less than their economic level has resulted in a distortion in the allocation of resources. The effect of such a misallocation of resources is not only a significant loss of output but also a widening food gap and heavy dependence on food imports. The same can be said of energy pricing. The fact that energy is being consumed at less than its true scarcity value means: (a) loss of foreign exchange that could have been earned by exporting oil at international prices; (b) the establishment of industries which are economically unviable. The fact that capital is used at less than its scarcity value means a disincentive to save and the encouragement of highly capital-intensive industries in a country which is labor-abundant. Examples can be multiplied. The gradual elimination of subsidies would admittedly deprive the low income groups of the benefits of subsidized prices. But it would simultaneously increase national output by much more than the lost benefits. In the language of welfare economics, society can compensate the losers fully for their loss while leaving others better off than before.

It is in the best interest of all income groups to use the price system for what it is made for; namely, the allocation of scarce resources among alternative uses. Using the price system for income redistribution may represent the course of least resistance politically. But it is both ineffective and costly. To bring about a more equitable distribution, there is no substitute for direct taxation. At the same time, relative prices should reflect the relative scarcity of resources to ensure the highest attainable growth rates. It is within the framework of a vigorously growing economy that the issue of income redistribution can be most effectively addressed. However, the present system of subsidized prices can only be phased out gradually. As a practical way of compensating the low income beneficiaries, consideration might be given to either a direct increase in income or a system similar to that of food stamps.

Redefining the Scope of the Public and Private Sector

The preceding analysis points clearly to the conclusion that the public sector is over-extended. Today's economic philosophy and development strategy are radically different from those which previously determined the scope of the public sector. It has been shown that the present system is too costly. Egypt was able to afford the cost in the seventies when its external resources were growing rapidly. With the sharp decline in oil revenue and workers' remittances, the situation facing the country radically changed. This can be seen from a comparison between 1975-81 and 1981-1986. Table 8 reveals a marked slowdown in all indicators between the two periods. This is true of Gross Domestic Product, saving, investment, consumption, exports, and imports. It is disturbing indeed to note that during the period 1981-86, the volume of investment was virtually stagnant while gross national savings declined in absolute terms. At the same time, the last few years have witnessed a significant acceleration in the rate of inflation, serious deficits in the balance of payments, and a growing debt service burden. Such a situation is hardly sustainable.

TABLE 8
Principal Economic Indicators Average Annual Rates of Growth
(Percent in Real Terms)

	1975-1981	1981-1986
Gross Domestic Product	9.4	4.6
Agriculture	2.5	1.7
Industry & Petroleum	12.6	6.4
Services	11.2	5.1
Consumption	8.2	4.6
Gross Investment	7.6	0.1
Exports of GNFS	8.4	4.1
Imports of GNFS	5.8	1.1
Gross National Saving	46.2	–5.7

Note: GNFS stands for goods and non-factor services.
Source: World Bank, *Egypt: Review of the Finances of the Decentralized Public Sector,* Vol. I, p. 1.

Under the present conditions in Egypt, privatization does not mean the transfer of all or even most public enterprises to the private sector. This is neither politically feasible nor economically desirable. What is needed is a delineation of the scope of the public sector in order to bring it into line with the requirements of the present stage of development. According to the proposed strategy, the role of the public sector will continue to be important for development. In addition to the conventional functions of government in health, education, defense, social security and the like, the public sector should continue in the following areas:

1. Control over important natural resources. This is particularly the case with respect to the Suez Canal and petroleum. Public enterprises in both fields have been fairly successful, constituting an important source of public revenue.

2. Natural monopolies. These are activities where considerations of efficiency require the existence of a single enterprise. Railways, ports, tramways, telephones, water, sewerage, and most other public utilities fall in principle under this category. Privatization in such cases would substitute a private monopoly for a public one. There is no reason to assume that such a change would result in a net improvement from the viewpoint of efficiency or distribution of wealth.

3. A substantial divergence between private and social benefits. This is the case of external economies where the benefits to the private entrepreneur from a certain economic activity are substantially less than the benefits that accrue to society. In such cases the profit motive will not ensure an optimum level of investment. There are many enterprises which belong to this category, particularly in such fields as training, research, and development.

4. Areas where capital requirements and/or high technology go beyond the capability of domestic private enterprise. Some of the heavy and defense industries may be classified under this category.

Enterprises in the above four categories will constitute the core of the public sector, where government involvement is justified in terms of specific and identifiable needs. In contrast, there is no justification for the government to continue to be involved in such activities as grocery and department stores, bakeries, flour mills, printing, bookshops, newspaper and magazine publishing, advertising, hotels, travel agencies, contracting, and cattle raising, etc. By no stretch of the imagination could such activities be qualified as "strategic" or "commanding heights" in terms of current development policy. On the contrary, most public enterprises in these areas are run at a considerable financial loss, thus burdening the national budget. The government continues to be involved in these activities because they were nationalized during the sixties. Reference was made to the fact that the public sector in these areas is used to deliver goods and services at reduced prices. Evidently, however, prices are low not on account of efficiency but because of direct or indirect subsidization by the government. The shortcomings of such a policy have already been pointed out. However, should the government continue with its current subsidization policies, there is no reason why it could not do so through the private sector. Indeed, the private sector has been involved in the distribution of "rationed" goods at government-controlled prices since the inception of subsidization policies during the Second World War.

So far, the foreign trade sector has not been dealt with. Presently, it is mostly under the control of public enterprises. There are a number of state trading companies which, until recently, monopolized the export and import of the principal agricultural and industrial products. Their monopoly has been diluted by allowing private exporters and importers to enter certain fields which were not open before. However, the participation of the private sector is still quite limited. By and large, the foreign trade of Egypt continues to be controlled by public sector companies. In principle, the public sector should be gradually phased out of the export and import business. These are typically the kind of activities which are better handled by the private sector. The problem is, however, complicated by certain considerations. Some of the foreign trading companies, particularly on the export side, are sources of public revenue. This is the case with respect to state trading companies for the export of cotton and rice. Procurement prices are set at levels well below world market prices with the difference going to the coffers of the trading companies. On the import side, the opposite is true. The Public Authority of Supply Commodities, for instance, is heavily subsidized from the state budget by allocations of foreign exchange at extremely favorable rates to be able to offer consumers essentials such as wheat flour, cooking fats, and sugar at reduced prices. However, these considerations do not constitute insurmountable obstacles to privatization. The revenue-yielding companies can continue in the public sector pending adjustment of agricultural pricing policies. In fact, this is already taking place. As a consequence, the relative importance of the state trading companies in agricultural commodities as a source of public revenue has declined significantly. As for the importing state companies, it has been pointed out that there is no contradiction between privatization and the continuation of subsidization policies.

Problems of Transition

The case for privatizing those activities which do not belong to the "core" public sector would seem to be compelling. Privatization would certainly reduce the burden on the national budget, eliminate a major source of waste and inflation, and make a positive contribution to the balance of payments position. These benefits would be greatly enhanced if privatization is coupled with the implementation of adjustment policies aiming at the elimination of price and cost distortions as well as macroeconomic imbalances. At the same time, privatization need not be associated with a regressive income distribution. If it is well designed and if it helps reduce inflationary pressures, the overall impact on income distribution should be favorable.

While these are weighty benefits, the problems of privatization should not be underestimated. To nationalize is easy, but to privatize is fraught with difficulty. The nationalization of the Egyptian economy was effected within a very short span of time. During a period of only a few months in 1961 there was a thorough transformation from a private enterprise, market-oriented economy to central planning. To reverse this process poses a challenge of major proportions.

The public sector has a momentum of its own. It has created powerful vested interests whose income, status, and authority are perceived to be closely linked to the continuation of the status quo. Moreover, there is a web of relationships among the public sector, the national budget, the foreign exchange budget, the banking system, and the employment of university and school graduates. Each element of the system is related to others under conditions of precarious balance. Privatization may not be endorsed by policy makers, as it is seen to disturb this delicate equilibrium. The inertia of the present system is perhaps the most formidable obstacle to reform.

This does not mean that privatization is doomed. It simply underscores the crucial role that has to be played by the political leadership in explaining the reasons behind privatization, its objectives and benefits, and in allaying the fears of those who might be adversely affected. On several occasions the political leadership of Egypt emphasized that economic reform should proceed within a framework of social equity and stability. One cannot take issue with such objectives. However, there is a trade-off between short-term expediency and long-run viability. As one economic report observed:

> In the short run it may appear easier to preserve existing mechanisms and to postpone difficult decisions. Political constraints may seem to forbid bold and wide ranging reforms. But as time passes the problems will become more difficult to solve and the magnitude of the required changes will become even greater. What may appear to strengthen short-term stability could very well lead to major social and political difficulties in the longer run. This trade-off is at the center of Egypt's search for optimal economic policies.

Political commitment apart, the privatization program will have a better chance of success if it anticipates the obstacles and pitfalls and formulates effective solutions to overcome them.[11] The following elements are particularly important:

1. Privatization should be interpreted broadly so as not to be limited to divestiture in the sense of the sale of public enterprises to the private sector. While divestiture might be the most appropriate form of privatization, it should be supplemented by other mechanisms. One possible alternative is the privatization of management as distinct from the ownership of assets which may continue to be vested in the public sector. It may also be convenient to resort to partial privatization of public enterprises by converting them to joint stock companies which are only partly controlled by the private sector. When it proves difficult to apply any of these techniques, reform may be limited to the removal of regulations and restrictions which prevent the private sector from entry into certain fields or from competing on equal terms with the public sector.

2. The privatization program should recognize the great differences that exist among enterprises in the public sector. There is a need for the classification of enterprises for the purpose of privatization according to whether they are making profits or losses, the debt-equity ratio, the size of employment, the scale of operations, and so on. Classification of enterprises is important in three respects. It

helps in choosing the appropriate form of privatization whether through divestiture or otherwise. It specifies what action is needed in each case. Firms which are making losses or suffer from a heavy debt overhang, for instance, will perhaps require a major restructuring prior to privatization. Finally, the classification of enterprises is important in defining successive stages in the privatization program. In order to minimize the cost of, and opposition to, privatization, it may be necessary to start with those enterprises which have a relatively small labor force, limited assets, and a favorable debt-equity ratio.

3. Along with privatization, steps should be taken to revitalize the domestic capital market. One of the major constraints on privatization is limited private savings. Accordingly, there may not be enough private capital to acquire public enterprises which become candidates for privatization. This constraint takes on special importance, since privatization should not lead to the concentration of wealth in a few hands, nor should it result in the control of important enterprises by foreign capital. The experience of other countries, both developing and developed, shows that privatization is likely to be more successful if it increases popular participation in the ownership of national assets. In Britain, privatization is seen as a way to bring stock ownership to the grass roots.[12] Brazil is selling stock in its public enterprises as a way to democratize ownership while raising capital. Several techniques have been applied in many countries to ensure that the ownership of privatized firms is broadly based. In Egypt, the problem may be less acute in view of substantial savings by Egyptians abroad. This, however, does not obviate the need to formulate ground rules for acquisition of stock, to eliminate loopholes in existing laws and to tighten regulations on accounting, auditing, stock trading, and conflict of interest.

4. The privatization program will have to include provisions relating to workers and employees of enterprises subject to privatization. The main purpose is to ensure that the burden of reform does not fall upon the work force of these enterprises. To that end, the following techniques should be included in the program: participation of the work force in owning privatized enterprises on favorable terms, generous compensation for those whose service will be terminated and, finally, provisions for the reassignment and retraining of redundant labor.

5. The formulation and implementation of the privatization program should be the responsibility of a special entity to be established for

that purpose. Privatization is complex and requires expert information on the specific conditions of each unit in the public sector. Such specialized knowledge and skills can only be acquired and developed by a competent authority. Moreover, it is unrealistic to expect that the initiative for privatization will come from the managers of public enterprises.

The General Accounting Office may play an important role in preparing, initiating, and designing the privatization process. Since its establishment, it has acquired extensive knowledge of the conditions and operations of the public sector. It enjoys some of the autonomy and independence which is essential for the discharge of this responsibility. Another possible candidate is the Public Authority for Investment and Free Zones. In either case a special privatization department will have to be established within these organizations and their charter will have to be amended for them to perform that function.

Notes

1. Richard Hemming and Ali M. Mansour, *Privatization and Public Enterprises,* Occasional Paper 56 (Washington, DC: International Monetary Fund, 1988), p. 9.

2. John Waterbury, *The Egypt of Nasser and Sadat: The Political Economy of Two Regimes* (Princeton: Princeton University Press, 1983), p. 76.

3. Khalid Ikram, *Egypt: Economic Management in a Period of Transition,* A World Bank Country Economic Report (Washington, DC: World Bank, 1980), p. 26.

4. See also Sadiq Ahmed, *Public Finance in Egypt: Its Structure and Trends,* World Bank Staff Working Papers No. 639 (Washington, DC: World Bank, 1984); Sadiq Ahmed et al., *Macroeconomic Effects of Efficiency Pricing in the Public Sector,* World Bank Staff Working Papers, No. 726 (Washington, DC: World Bank, 1985); Mary M. Shirley, *Managing State-Owned Enterprises,* World Bank Staff Working Papers, No. 577 (Washington, DC: World Bank, 1983). In addition, there is valuable material in the World Bank's *World Development Report* (Washington, DC, 1983).

5. The methodology of calculating overall deficits and rates of return is explained in the World Bank's *Egypt: Review of the Finances of the Decentralized Public Sector,* Vol. II, Annexes A1 and A2.

6. It should be mentioned that the net fiscal burden in Table 2 is not comparable to overall deficits in Table 1 due to the fact that the former is only concerned with net transfers from the national budget excluding those parts of deficits financed from other sources.

7. It is interesting to note that the "Islamic" investment societies in Egypt distribute "dividends," which reportedly run at about 24 to 30 percent per annum.

8. World Bank, *Industrialization in Egypt: Performance and Policies* (Washington, DC, 1984).

9. Ann O. Krueger, "Evaluating Restrictionist Trade Regimes: Theory and Measurement," *Journal of Political Economy* (January 1972). See also Michael Bruno, "Domestic Resource

Cost and Effective Protection: Clarification and Synthesis," in the same issue of the *Journal of Political Economy*.

10. Egypt, Ministry of Planning, *Summary of the Second Five-Year Plan: 1987/88-1991/92* (Cairo, 1987), p. 30.

11. Elliot Berg and Mary M. Shirley, *Divestiture in Developing Countries,* World Bank Discussion Papers No. 11 (Washington, DC: World Bank, 1987); Steve H. Hanke, ed., *Privatization and Development* (San Francisco: Institute for Contemporary Studies, 1987).

12. See A.A. Walters, "Privatization: Some International Lessons," a paper presented at the Fifth Annual Convention of Private Argentine Banks, Buenos Aires, 1987. See also David Gills, "Privatization and Internationalization of Securities Markets," International Finance Corporation, 1987.

3 PRODUCTION, PUBLIC OWNERSHIP, AND PRIVATE OWNERSHIP

Fouad Sultan

Introduction

Recent Egyptian economic history has witnessed two distinct eras of national economic management. The first started in the early 1960s and was characterized by the massive nationalization of medium and large-scale private enterprises, as well as the imposition of rigid controls and regulations on all economic activities. This period was also characterized by an average rate of economic growth of about 6 percent per year resulting primarily from relatively intensive public investment spending financed by external borrowing, mainly from countries of the Eastern bloc. When this flow of funds dried up, the economic growth rate fell to almost zero and became negative in some years of the late 1960s, due to the low productive efficiency of many projects which had been envisaged for political and prestigious purposes rather than on the basis of rational economic considerations which took account of their potential added value to the national economy.

During this period and subsequently, the Egyptian economy had to confront a multitude of problems:

1. The impact of successive wars and the burden of excessive military outlays, as well as related expenditures for reconstruction. This was related to a continuous decline of domestic savings, and the subsequent inability of the level of investments to accommodate rising population growth.

2. The increase of inflationary pressures due to imported inflation and a continuous reliance on the banking system to finance the growing budget deficit.

3. The low growth of labor productivity and the shortage of managerial skills and leadership in the public economic sector.

4. A weak balance of payments structure reflecting the severe internal budget deficit.

The Egyptian authorities, responding to the above problems, ushered in a second stage of economic management with a policy of economic reform after the October War of 1973. The policy represented a shift away from socialism toward liberalization through the encouragement of private initiative and the improvement of relations with Western countries that possessed economic experience and know-how, as well as neighboring Arab countries which enjoyed large capital surpluses. Nevertheless, the relatively high annual economic growth rates (estimated at 9 percent) that were achieved during the first years of the open-door policy did not result from increased productive capacity and efficiency in the commodity sectors, which in fact grew at a slower rate than the overall growth rate. The high growth rates were primarily induced by coincidental developments, the most important of which were the recovery of the Sinai oil fields, higher oil export proceeds as a result of world price increases, active tourism, the reopening of the Suez Canal, and increases in remittances from Egyptians working abroad. The improvements in foreign exchange receipts stimulated import demand for both consumer goods and intermediary goods to activate the idle capacity in industry, which in turn augmented the rates of capital formation and assisted the realization of relatively higher rates of investment.

Production continued, however, to be characterized by low productive efficiency—both in quantity and quality. Consequently, Egypt's dependence on the external world to cover a large portion of increased consumption demand continued. This situation was facilitated by the continuation of fiscal and monetary policies (particularly in respect of the level of prices and exchange rates) which aimed to preserve a price structure based on social and political goals and did not reflect the economic costs of production or importation. It was not, therefore, conducive to the rationalization of the demand for imports or the stimulation of the growth of domestic output in the commodity sectors. The result was an increased external deficit in both the trade balance and the balance of payments on current account. The latter was partly offset—and sometimes even more than matched in the late 1970s—by capital inflows to Egypt either in the form of concessional financial flows based on political considerations, or capital flows attracted by economic investment opportunities.

A number of factors explain why there was a large boom in the trade and service sectors during this period, but not in the commodity-producing sector. They include:

1. The legal restrictions and obstacles imposed during the preceding period to restrict private sector activity in the field of commodity production.

2. The urgent and pressing need to satisfy the repressed demand for consumption that had accumulated over the preceding years of deprivation.

3. The natural response of such activities to market forces and profit motivation.

4. The then-prevailing discrimination vis-a-vis the private sector in favor of the public sector in areas of price control, input subsidies, energy prices, and exchange rates.

5. The limited capability of the newly evolving money market to fund the long-term needs of productive investments.

At the beginning of the open-door policy, had the government been aware of the nature of the new tools of national economic management required to move the economy gradually toward a market economy, it could have avoided a period of extended economic disorder and prevented an inconsistent monetary and fiscal policy.

In short, the declaration of the open-door policy was not in itself sufficient to realize a major improvement in efficiency and productivity, nor was it conducive to substantial capital inflows seeking viable investment opportunities. Such drastic changes in economic policy could not be effective unless accompanied by a comprehensive reform capitalizing on the then-prevailing positive elements in the economy.

Comprehensive reforms would have required:

1. The elimination of the dual price system through the gradual elimination of subsidies on a number of less essential goods, passing on their increased cost of production to consumers.

2. Constraints on public consumption to allow for a substantial reduction in the government's recourse to the domestic and foreign banking systems to finance the budget deficit.

3. An improvement in the tax collection system.

4. The elimination of all discrimination between public and private sectors in areas of taxes, custom duties, energy, the prices of inputs and outputs, exchange rates, the cost and availability of finance, and similar costs which seriously affect the competitive position of the production unit.

5. Investments in vocational training to improve the quality and quantity of skilled labor.

The principal need of the Egyptian economy is to maximize private initiatives in the field of production, and increase reliance on market forces to achieve equilibrium within the society and to direct resources toward their best use. A reliance on administrative decisions and directives is unwise, since even a relatively efficient central bureaucracy will always fall short of grasping the complexity of the economic environment of the production sector. This does not, however, mean neglecting planning, which is as beneficial to any national economy as it is to individuals. But the required planning, within the context of a market economy, should be concerned only with macroeconomic variables and achieving a balance between the growth of various sectors within the community. This may be achieved through financial incentives to encourage factors of production to move toward the sectors or areas where they are most needed, and also through a sound fiscal and monetary policy aimed at mobilizing domestic savings and directing them toward productive purposes. Thus, the private sector—which owns the largest portion of domestic savings—may bear a greater share of responsibility for achieving economic development, leaving public funds available to meet the requirements of investment in infrastructure.

Key Economic Problem

The main features of Egypt's present economic problems may be summarized as follows:

1. The actual deficit realized in the government budget over the past years has been larger than the budgeted deficit. This reflects the weakness of the available information base and/or the continuous optimism of the budget planner, a matter which annually contributes to the internal imbalance which has already grown out of proportion and prevents the achievement of the hypothetical equilibrium sought in the development plan.

2. The direct impact of a continued government budget deficit of that size will be to increase the domestic effective demand, in money terms, compared to the growth in real terms in productive capacity. This results in large increases in demand for imports of consumer goods. With the recent adoption of a managed float of the Egyptian pound, the continued government budget deficit at such rates will certainly be reflected in a continuous depreciation of the rate of exchange of the Egyptian pound in the free market, and thus will lead to further internal and external disequilibria. This will also encourage hedging operations aimed at preserving the real value of domestic savings by purchasing foreign currency, which will in turn fuel the demand for foreign currency and lead to further depreciation.

3. While the rate of increase of domestic liquidity recently has fallen to a level slightly exceeding the rate of growth of GDP, this should not be considered a healthy phenomenon. The drop has mainly been induced by the deflationary effect of the balance of payments deficit and by the reduction in the rate of increase of domestic credit available to the private sector as a result of the current credit policy. This has imposed an overall credit ceiling favoring the public sector and the government.

4. While the state budget is showing a large deficit in financing available for the required investment level, the economy is suffering from excess liquidity in the banking system which reaches double the liquidity level prevailing in similar economies. This puts pressure on consumption and consequently results in large increases in inflation rates.

5. Another factor is the lagging rate of growth of output in commodity-producing sectors compared to overall rates of economic growth. This is due to low productivity levels in the commodity sectors and to the attraction of higher returns on investment in the service sectors. In the meantime, population growth is continuing at an increasing rate, requiring the creation of about 400,000 new job opportunities per year.

6. The success of comprehensive planning depends on the efficiency and comprehensiveness of the information base. It is generally agreed that an appropriate information base is not currently available in Egypt. Moreover, even in the socialist countries which have applied comprehensive central planning, experience has shown the need for liberalization and for an at least partial return to a market-oriented policy, which depends primarily on the equilibration mechanism of the price system in rationing resources and signaling decisions.

A Possible Solution

The previous analysis has suggested that Egypt's problem is due to the large existing production gap, that is, the gap between production and consumption. This gap does not result from the lack of a solid production base—as is the case in many other developing countries— but is rather due to the low levels of production and productivity in relation to the installed capacities reflecting the accumulated invest- ments made by the public sector over the past years. Thus, increasing production in the case of Egypt does not require the time or the effort at the domestic and international levels which is otherwise needed to secure necessary financing and create the investment climate conducive to a new production base.

Whatever the degree of efficiency of the management of the public sector may be, the weakness of its productive capacity may be attributed mainly to the following:

1. The rigidity of management regulations and governmental procedures controlling the economy.

2. The poor financing arrangements and limited credit facilities, which are insufficient to finance the expansion and modernization of existing installations, or their working capital needs.

There is no way to optimize the use of this productive capacity other than through liberalization of the public business sector, and a gradual shift from public to private ownership.

Liberalization of the Public Business Sector

Public business entities should be placed under the jurisdiction of the "Companies Law," which clearly provides for the separation of ownership from management. Management performance should be assessed on the basis of the extent to which set targets and objectives are achieved, without interference in the daily administrative decisions necessary for running the firm. Supervision of management performance by the owners would then be exercised through the annual meetings of the "General Assembly" of the firm concerned, where accomplishments can be weighed against the targeted objectives. This requires a modification of the prevailing laws governing the public sector and the accountability of its management.

The public business sector should no longer have its annual investment requirements financed from appropriations of the state budget. Public business enterprises should become accustomed to going to the market to finance their needs for both working capital and expansion. They should both borrow funds, and rotate their equity holdings in those of their fully-owned subsidiaries which offer good investment prospects. In many cases, the access of public enterprises to the financial market must be preceded by a correction of their present financial structure.

Separating public sector investments from the state investment budget would by no means be destructive to governmental plans. What is called for is a revision of the underlying philosophy of the current Five Year Plan. Rather than being comprehensive, planning should offer guidelines to the business sector, both public and private. It should be based on sectoral studies of needs and of actual and potential bottlenecks so as to enable the business sector to identify economically viable projects in the light of real resources available for investment. The task of achieving equilibrium should be left to market forces, which tend to rationalize consumption and to direct resources toward their optimal value through the price system. Nevertheless, through financial incentives provided by monetary and fiscal policies, the plan could influence the pattern of investment allocation and attract investments toward sectors or specified geographical areas to be developed.

Once liberalized, the public business sector should take the lead in encouraging the private sector to step into the various fields of production. Only through the development of an active capital market could this policy be made viable. What is needed in practice is for the public business sector to play a leading role in providing the financial assets to stimulate trading in the capital market by rotating its equity holdings through public offerings of shares in the equity capital of its successful operating units. This would represent a major contribution to the mobilization of national savings currently attracted by unorganized fund-hunting companies. It would also augment the ability of the public sector authorities and enterprises to finance new investment initiatives which utilize their production experience and are in conformity with the indicators and objectives of the national development plan.

I would like to stress here that rotating holdings of equity in the public sector is not the same as selling or liquidating the public sector. On the contrary, it emphasizes the public sector's pioneering role in development by allowing it to enter new fields of production and launch investments in remote geographical areas. The degree of risk associated with investments in these new fields in remote areas is relatively large, and is usually beyond the ability of the private sector to sustain. It can only be approached initially with the backing and support of the state, until the time comes for reoffering the shares of the equity capital of such new projects to the private sector through the capital market. To ensure that the new system does not hinder investments in projects of national importance, it would be possible in addition to establish a special provision by which the Ministry of Planning or the National Investment Bank support the implementation of imperative investments which fail to arrange for their own financing due to their marginal viability.

The Gradual Shift to Private Ownership

I would like to emphasize once more that a shift to private ownership is not a goal in itself, but a powerful tool to link national savings to investments and to bridge the gap between national production and consumption through increasing efficiency and productivity. This will permit a gradual correction of internal and external imbalances. Ultimate success in attaining these objectives assumes of course that Egypt will adopt comprehensive economic reforms based on an increased reliance on the free interaction of market forces and on a price system reflecting the true scarcity of all economic factors, including foreign exchange and domestic credit.

The implementation of this reform, with the related austerity measures, should be phased over a span of time in order not to destroy the foundations of Egypt's economic development and political stability.

The necessary steps to be followed are:

1. To free the management of public companies from all restrictions. This may sometimes require changing the management itself and starting a series of negotiations between management and the government to determine the future relationship, if any, between company and the government. The extent to which the financial structure of the company needs to be corrected before offering it for sale has also to be determined. The right valuation of the offering price of the shares of these companies should be given special care and attention. This price has to be a realistic reflection of the future profitability of the company, so that the prospective shareholder does not experience a loss when the shares circulate in the secondary market. Overpricing of the early issues would abort the whole program prematurely.

This process may require several years to be completed, particularly in the case of losing enterprises, which will have to be reorganized and readjusted in order to become profitable before being offered for sale. In most cases, this readjustment will require a change of management. The new management, aware that its success in improving the company's performance is a basic condition for sale to the private sector and that otherwise the company will face the probability of liquidation and/or of a second change in management, will thus be highly motivated to speed up the process of restructuring and of the shift from public to private ownership.

2. In all these stages, the advice of specialized consulting firms in the field of management or finance is essential. Also essential is the

mobilization of the necessary financial support from the banking system and various other investment institutions through the application of appropriate monetary policy.

3. New shares should be issued with low par values to enable the average citizen to subscribe. In order to enlarge the subscription base, they should be sold at a discount to some low-income groups, with repayment by installments over several years allowed.

4. Assistance to workers within an enterprise to help them subscribe, and thus strengthen their commitment to the company, should also be considered.

5. The pace of privatization should initially be slow and consistent with the thin absorptive capacity of the market after long years of previous inactivity. The sale of a company would only take place after it first realizes a reasonable rate of profit, which would inspire confidence and ensure the success of this policy. I believe that naming the target enterprises would be a useful tool to enhance production and productivity, since it would be a challenge to the management of such enterprises.

6. When shares are offered for public subscription, it is essential to insure against malpractice. Lessons learned from the experience of other countries should be fully taken into account, including those relating to the participation of foreign capital while preserving the national interest and safeguarding against the excessive concentration of shared ownership in pressure groups.

In conclusion, the gradual shifting of ownership from the public to the private sector, through public subscription in the capital market, will secure the following economic benefits for the community:

1. The enhancement of productive efficiency through competition, deregulation, and the creation of a link between workers and the return on capital invested. This will help to close the gap between production and consumption and thus the gap in the external trade balance.

2. The achievement of an appropriate return on past public investments. This will alleviate the burden of subsidies and increase tax revenues, thus helping to achieve the required balance in the state budget.

3. The reduction in the size of internal debt, which will result in a corresponding reduction in the burden of debt servicing. This will be directly reflected in a decrease in the state budget deficit, and in a movement of domestic savings toward productive capital investment.

4. The inspiration of confidence in the prevailing economic system. This would stimulate external capital inflows to finance domestic

investments from Egyptian savings held abroad, and foreign capital flows. These flows will be particularly encouraged if shares of the equity capital of newly created joint stock companies are offered for subscription in Arab and other foreign capital markets. Appropriate restrictions may nevertheless be imposed and may differ from one project to the other, or from one industry to the other.

5. An improved internal balance both in the field of production and in the state budget will result in a corresponding improvement in the external balance. This will in turn lead eventually to a relative stability in inflation rates and in the exchange rate of the domestic currency, hopefully permitting the generation of an external surplus to meet the burden of external debt servicing.

6. The enlargement of the ownership base of capital through the capital market would in turn lead to the greater social and economic stability needed to effectively offset the social implications of the economic reform.

One example of the application of many of the above principles has been the recent policy of the Ministry of Tourism—particularly in the case of some public sector touristic units which suffered from deterioration in the quality of their services or rigidity in their management. Some of these units have been offered to the private sector for management, provided that it makes the investments needed to increase their efficiency. Others have been offered for sale so as to mobilize part of Egypt's domestic and foreign savings. At the same time, the experience and skill of employees in the public sector has continued to play a developmental and promotional role, particularly in the development of remote touristic areas. This has all been achieved without adding any burden to the public treasury—an important consideration in view of the scarcity of resources allocated to tourism in the last Five Year Plan.

The tourism industry is one of the few industries in which Egypt enjoys a comparative advantage. The Ministry of Tourism, when drafting and implementing its policies, relies mainly on market forces in all fields of promotion, marketing, investment, and the development of tourism awareness.

Liberalization has also been applied to air traffic, where restrictions have been removed, especially on charter traffic, which reserved at least 50 percent of the traffic to Egypt for the national airline company. The restrictions aimed only at protecting the national carrier without due consideration to the national economic interest. The result of such deregulation on tourism has been positive. At the same time the load factor on the national carrier went up and not down.

Egypt must press forward with a structural adjustment of its economy, draw upon its inherent strength, and make efforts to respond to the challenges of the present. These efforts should include preparing a competitive environment, maintaining an appropriate balance between savings and investments, reviewing the role of the public sector and consolidating the fiscal budget. Privatization can be one of the most effective tools for speeding up the achievement of such policy objectives. A careful government policy can minimize the social costs normally attached to the austerity measures required for the implementation of an economic stabilization program.

4 EGYPTIAN LABOR MIGRATION

Ann M. Lesch

In the past decade Egypt has come to depend on labor migration abroad, both as a source of revenue and as a safety valve. It has reduced internal pressure to generate employment and has enabled the population to maintain a higher standard of living than production at home would warrant. The downturn in oil revenue in the mid-1980s, however, has reduced the outflow of migrant labor and diminished the hard currency returning to Egypt. Many observers are concerned that this shift could have serious economic, social, and political implications for Egypt, particularly as the government and the economic system as a whole appear ill-prepared to cope with the returning migrants.

It must be remembered that the large-scale movement of labor is a recent phenomenon in Egypt. It dates back only to the early 1970s, when emigration restrictions were ended and job opportunities swelled in the oil-rich states of the Arabian peninsula. Labor migration has undermined the stereotype of the Egyptian peasant as a person wedded to his land and his village. More importantly, migration has altered social and economic relations in Egypt in ways which are just beginning to be comprehended. Most individual migrants would argue that work abroad has enabled them to increase their living standards in tangible ways. But not all could claim that they had augmented their earning capacity in the long run. Moreover, inflation has eroded their savings and this inflation has been caused, at least in part, by migration itself. The demand for consumer goods has risen faster than internal production, thereby pushing up prices, and the cost of certain kinds of agricultural and skilled labor has risen dramatically with so many workers abroad.

For the country as a whole, migration has brought in much-needed hard currency in the form of worker remittances. But government policies that allow the import of consumer goods and maintain multiple currency exchange rates have encouraged returnees to bring home foreign goods and channel their earnings through the currency black market. The long-term effects on development depend on how workers' savings are invested. Do they increase the productive capacity of the

90

economy or do they merely result in more imports of food and consumer goods?

In recent years, the government has expressed concern about a downturn in migration. Many oil-producing countries have completed their infrastructures, and so the demand for large numbers of construction workers has fallen. Moreover, the severe drop in the price of oil in early 1986 has forced the states to revamp their development programs, cutting back or cancelling many projects and even running serious budget deficits. Foreign workers are being affected significantly by those measures. The failure of Egyptians to find jobs abroad and the return of large numbers to Egypt, without adequate planning to reabsorb them into the economy, could have a ripple effect throughout the country. Their return could reduce the hard currency available to lubricate the economy, could harm the construction and trade sectors which rely on migrant earnings, and could depress wages as returnees compete for scarce jobs. Moreover, a large-scale return and the frustration of the aspiration of others to go abroad would impact the political and social forces within Egypt, increasing the dissatisfaction among residents with government policies and priorities.

Despite the pervasiveness and massive impact of labor migration, the Egyptian government lacks precise figures on the numbers of Egyptians abroad, the duration of their stay, and the amount of remittances transferred home. Figures obtained from the Ministry of Foreign Affairs and the Ministry of Migration indicate that as of 1985 3.5 million Egyptians lived in other Arab states of whom 1.4 million were in Saudi Arabia and 1.25 million in Iraq. (See Table 1) Those figures included families as well as workers, and accounted for approximately 7 percent of the total Egyptian population, which numbered 49 million in mid-1985. Those figures are only estimates, however, and must be treated with extreme caution.

There has been a remarkable increase in the number of Egyptians living abroad over the past fifteen years. In 1970, 100-200,000 were abroad (excluding permanent emigrants), but in only five years the figures swelled to 500,000. They reached a million in 1980 and peaked at 3.5 million in 1985.

There has also been a shift in the countries to which Egyptian labor has been attracted. A decade ago, one third went to Libya, and a fifth to Saudi Arabia. Now the Libyan share has dropped below 5 percent and Saudi Arabia accounts for 40 percent. Iraq, which imported 1 percent of the total in 1975, now absorbs at least one third. These shifts reflect the rapidly changing economic circumstances and political relations in the region.

Official Policy

The main factors that promote or inhibit migration have been Egyptian government policy toward migration, in the context of overall Egyptian economic and foreign policy, and the economic policies and conditions

TABLE 1
Egyptian Workers and Families in Key Arab Countries
(in thousands)

	1970[a]	1975[b]	1976[c]	1980[d]	1982[e]	1985[f]
S. Arabia	n.a.	95-120	100-140	150-250	800	1,400
Iraq	n.a.	7	32.5	223-342	1,250	1,250
Libya	60.8	200-230	250	250-340	300	100[g]
Kuwait	17.7	40-60	139	60-105	200	220
Jordan	n.a.	5.3	4.5	56-70	125	160
UAE	11	13-15	12.5	28-50	150	110
Qatar	0.6[h]	3-5	12.2	6-20	25	30.5
Oman	n.a.	4.6	5	5-6.3	11.5	8.7
Bahrain	n.a.	1-3	2-3	1.4-5	6	n.a.
N. Yemen	n.a.	2	n.a.	4	12	n.a.

a. International Labour Organization figures, cited in Nazli Choucri, *Migration in the Middle East*, TAP Report, 1, 1983, p. 3-2A.

b. Giuseppi Pennisi, *Development, Manpower and Migration in the Red Sea Region* (Hamburg: Deutsches Orient Institut, 1981), p. 25; Choucri, *Migration . . .* , 1, p. 3-5A.

c. J.S. Birks and C.A. Sinclair, "Egypt: A Frustrated Labor Exporter?," *The Middle East Journal*, Vol. 33, No. 3 (1979), p. 295; and Fatma Aly Khafagy, "The Socio-Economic Impact of the Spending of Remittances by Emigrant Egyptian Labour" (Doctoral Thesis, University College, London, 1984), p. 21.

d. Mahmoud Abdul-Fadil and Ibrahim Saad al-Din, *Intiqal al-Umala al-Arabiyya* (The Movement of Arab Labor) (Beirut: Center for Arab Unity Studies, 1983), p. 70; J.S. Birks, C. A. Sinclair, and J. Socknat, "The Demand for Egyptian Labor Abroad," in Alan Richards and Philip L. Martin, editors, *Migration, Mechanization, and Agricultural Labor Markets in Egypt* (Boulder, Colorado: Westview, 1983), p. 113; Pennisi, *Development, Manpower . . .* , p. 26.

e. *Al-Ahram*, September 1983, quoting Ministry of Migration figures; Khafagy, "The Socio-Economic Impact . . . ," p. 24; *al-Ahram al-Iqtisadi*, May 9, 1983.

f. Mimeographed sheet from the Ministry of Migration, based on figures from the Ministry of Foreign Affairs, received on January 15, 1986 (undated).

g. *Washington Post*, September 3, 1985; *The Middle East* (London), July 1985; *New York Times*, September 29, 1984.

h. Robert J. LaTowsky, "Egyptian Labour Abroad," *MERIP Reports*, May 1984, p. 12.

in the receiving countries. Egyptian government policy toward labor migration has undergone three stages, and has now entered a fourth.[1] At each stage, the interactions among factors have differed. Moreover, the policies and conditions in all the countries of the region are profoundly affected by shifts in the world economic system and the balance of international political forces.

Phase One: Before the mid-1960s, the Egyptian government maintained highly restrictive policies in relation to migration. Officials argued that all of Egypt's manpower was needed to promote economic and social development. The government was especially concerned about a possible brain-drain to the West, and so it required individuals who studied abroad to return to Egypt to work for a specified time. Moreover, it was extremely difficult to obtain an exit permit or even a passport, and permission to travel had to be obtained from one's superior at work as well as the security office.

The Egyptian government encouraged and organized one kind of labor movement to the Arab states, in the form of missions and the seconding of educated manpower. In those cases, either the Egyptian or the host government paid the salaries, living expenses, and travel costs for Egyptian teachers and administrators to work in another Arab country for a specific time period, after which they would return to their previous jobs. Thus, in the 1950s Egyptian lawyers, administrators, and teachers staffed the bureaucracies and school systems in Saudi Arabia and several Gulf states, where the indigenous population lacked the requisite educational qualifications.

Nevertheless, the numbers remained small. In 1967, for example, perhaps 80,000 Egyptians were abroad, including families, of whom half were teachers and 22 percent managerial and commercial personnel.[2]

Phase Two: Egyptian policy began to shift in the mid-1960s. Difficulties experienced in the nationalized industrial sector and a mounting foreign debt were exacerbated by the profound political and economic crisis that arose in the wake of the June 1967 military defeat by Israel. With soaring military expenses, deep political demoralization, and an economy at a standstill, the government was hard put to contain the pent-up social forces. Student and worker demonstrations in 1968 called for economic reforms, democratic practices, and an activist foreign policy.

The government tried to contain the pressure in part by drafting more educated youths into the military forces and in part by offering employment in the public sector to all university graduates, irrespective of the actual labor requirements. Moreover, it eased restrictions on emigration, both to syphon off surplus labor and to attract hard currency remittances.

The Ministerial Committee for Manpower recommended in October 1967 that the government institute a coherent migration policy and simplify bureaucratic procedures for emigration. The following year, the government began to allow emigrants to open foreign currency accounts in Egyptian banks with a 35 percent bonus over the official exchange rate, in the hope of winning back some of their earnings. In 1969, it set up a Migration Department within the Ministry of Foreign Affairs and a Committee on Emigration and Work Abroad, chaired by the Minister of Labor.

These signs of a more favorable attitude toward emigration led to a flood of applications, totalling 28,000 in 1969. This reflected the pent-up demand in the educated sector, but compelled the government to establish quotas for each profession.

Demand for Egyptian labor, however, remained limited in oil-producing states, with the exception of Libya. After the September 1969 coup d'etat, the oil sector was nationalized and ambitious development plans were sketched. Libya's ill-educated population of only two million could not provide the manpower for those projects. And so thousands of construction workers and agricultural laborers crossed the border from Egypt, joining the teachers and bureaucrats who were seconded there in growing numbers. In less than a year, the number of Egyptians in Libya leapt from a few thousand to nearly 61,000, and more than tripled again by 1975.

Phase Three: A rapid increase in migration did not start until 1974, following the October War and the accompanying rises in the price of oil. At that time, the countries of the Arabian peninsula embarked on large-scale development programs for which, like Libya, they lacked sufficient labor at all skill levels. Moreover, under Anwar Sadat, Egypt began to encourage foreign investment, private enterprise, and the import of foreign goods. Freeing the movement of labor was integral to this shift in ideology and policy. Moreover, the demobilization of thousands of soldiers in mid-1974—coupled with the high rate of growth of population—exacerbated the problem of absorbing new entrants into the labor force and made labor migration attractive as a safety valve.

The Constitution promulgated in 1971 had set the stage for these changes by specifying in Article 52 that all Egyptians have the right to emigrate. This was implemented in an eighteen-point government program that abolished the exit visa, replacing it by a travel permit obtainable at the individual's place of work; eased procedures for obtaining and renewing passports; and gave emigrants a 50 percent bonus over the official exchange rate, instead of the 35 percent approved in 1968. This increased their incentive to remit through the banking system instead of the currency black market. Further modifications over the next five years allowed dual nationality in certain cases, extended the validity of passports from two to seven years, enabled Egyptian social insurance to cover Egyptians working abroad on personal contracts as well as official secondments, and cancelled the requirement that migrants transfer a specified portion of their earnings home.

Decrees issued in 1981 eased the system for renewing leaves of absence and for reinstatement in a comparable government post, even after the person had resigned. Those measures culminated in the appointment of a Minister of State for Migration Affairs in December 1981 and the issue of comprehensive regulations on labor migration in August 1983. Those moves marked the shift to the fourth phase of consolidation and an increased effort to protect Egyptian workers against cutbacks and retrenchment in the oil-producing states.

Receiving Countries' Labor Policies

The large-scale development plans of the states of the Arabian peninsula, funded by the dramatically increased oil revenues of the 1970s, were the major determinants of the scale and composition of labor migration from Egypt and other countries.[3] Oil prices increased 70 percent during the October War, and nearly quadrupled by 1975. From 1974 to 1980, oil revenue throughout the Middle East doubled, reaching $100 billion.

Those increases on their own need not have led to massive labor migration, since oil production requires only a limited, highly-skilled work force. Rather, the kinds of projects in which those funds were invested determined the need for such labor. The second Saudi Five Year Plan (1975-80), for example, allocated half of government expenditure to infrastructural projects and another sizable component to educational expansion, since those sectors would lay the basis for long-term industrialization and reduce the country's dependence on oil, a non-renewable resource.[4] But the construction of highways, airports, schools, and industrial complexes was very labor-intensive.

Saudi citizens numbered only 5-6 million, of whom nearly half were rural. Only a quarter of Saudi adults were literate, and practically all the women were excluded from the labor force. In order to meet its goals, the government had to import increasing numbers of foreigners. In the mid-1970s, 1.5 million foreigners lived in the Saudi kingdom, constituting a quarter of the population but more than 40 percent of the labor force. Almost 15 percent of the foreigners came from Egypt. By 1980, the total rose to 2.1 million, 53 percent of the labor force.

Although 40 percent of Arab migrant labor was drawn to Saudi Arabia in the 1970s, nearly a million workers found jobs in other oil-rich states in the Persian Gulf and another 300-400,000 worked in Libya. By the 1980s, Iraq and Jordan also began to import foreign workers. In 1980, three fifths of the half-million foreigners working in Iraq came from Egypt. The war with Iran accelerated this trend, since a growing proportion of the Iraqi men were conscripted into the armed forces. Expatriate replacement workers soared to two million by 1985, three-quarters from Egypt alone, constituting a third of the labor force there. In Jordan, the migration of educated and skilled Jordanians to the Gulf caused a domestic labor shortage. In the mid-1970s only 5,000 Egyptians worked in Jordan, but a decade later 125,000 worked there, constituting 80 percent of the migrant labor force and a quarter of the total labor force.

The receiving countries obtain important economic benefits from labor migration. Moreover, migrant laborers can be controlled more easily than indigenous workers. They come on short-term contracts, can be replaced when their term ends, and have no political rights. Most workers are not allowed to bring their families. When families do accompany them, their children are often barred from schools and restricted in the use of government hospitals.

However, recipient countries also have been concerned about the impact of migration on their economies and societies. They fear that the cultural and national identities of their countries could be transformed if a large number—or even a majority—of the labor force remains foreign. They all have declared policies of indigenizing their work force through increased training and educational programs for nationals, and they seek high-technology industries that would require relatively few workers to operate.

Nearly all recipient countries have stringent conditions for immigration, in order to maintain control over the foreign labor force. Almost all require visas and work permits prior to the person's arrival in the country. They limit the presence of migrants' families to the upper-level educators and administrators. Moreover, most compel workers to leave as soon as their contracts expire, if they are unable to find a new employer. It is virtually impossible for expatriates to obtain citizenship.

Oil production and revenues peaked in most Arab countries in 1980-81. Subsequently, the price of oil dropped precipitously and there were severe production cutbacks. Saudi Arabia earned $115 billion in 1981, but only $47.1 billion in 1983. Kuwaiti oil income peaked in 1980 and dropped 51 percent by 1982, and Libyan revenue dropped by one third in the same two years.[5]

The governments subsequently cut back on their development programs, initially announcing that they would complete projects but would postpone new ones until the budgets could be balanced. Saudi Arabia reduced its budget expenditure by one third in 1983, and Kuwait ran a $1 billion deficit in 1982, which forced it to freeze public sector salaries and hiring and sharply retrench on infrastructural projects.

The impact on labor migration was not immediate, since foreigners remained essential to administration, services, and schools, and since many projects still in the pipeline had to be completed. It was estimated that even with the cutbacks Saudi Arabia still needed 3.3 million workers in 1985, of whom 2 million were foreign. Nevertheless, the Saudi government announced that it would remove 600,000 expatriates that year. Other small Gulf countries began to delay payments to foreign contractors and remove foreign labor. Qatar, for example, removed 7,000 workers in 1983-84 as projects ended and only skeleton crews remained. But an Egyptian official maintained that most of the remaining expatriates were essential to the country and that Asian labor was apt to be affected more severely than Arab in future reductions.[6]

Libya is the only Arab country that has forcibly deported large numbers of its foreign labor force, along the lines of Nigeria's expulsion of two million Ghanaians. In 1984 the government halved its development budget, banned most imports, and introduced austerity measures. Cutbacks necessitated the termination of contracts for many foreigners: half of the 180,000 Egyptians who worked in Libyan farms and factories in January 1984 had left by September.[7] Thousands more were expelled in the summer of 1985. They were allowed to take half of their earnings with them, but were denied their other benefits and were stripped of their electrical appliances and often even household goods at the border.

The labor situation has been significantly different in Iraq, which allows Arabs to enter without any visa or work permit. As restrictions have mounted in other countries, a considerable proportion of the migrant labor has been diverted to Iraq. Nevertheless, the migrant takes risks in travelling there, since he has no guarantee of a job and must bear the cost of transport himself. A former Egyptian labor attache in Baghdad commented that migrants must often take jobs below their skill level and for low wages, and that they are under psychological pressure to volunteer for the army.[8] Moreover, although Iraq does not have restrictions on entry it does have restrictions on exit. Since 1983, a migrant on secondment to the government can remit only half his salary, must cover the cost of his transport himself, and has reduced housing benefits. Restrictions are tighter in the private sector, where only a quarter of the salary can be remitted, and all expatriates must transfer their savings through the official bank.

Jordan also has a policy of unrestricted entry of Arab labor but, unlike Iraq, it does not restrict remittances. With the return of skilled Jordanians from the Gulf and a slowdown in construction that was funded by remittances, job opportunities for foreigners are starting to be reduced.

The overall picture in the oil-producing countries is one of considerable reduction in their labor forces as price falls necessitate sharp cutbacks in government spending and cause financial difficulties for private firms. Sending countries such as Egypt are hard pressed to adjust to the drop in remittances, the return home of many workers, and the failure of others to find jobs abroad.

The Economic Impact

The Egyptian economy has undergone major structural changes in the past decade, reflecting a reorientation in its governing political philosophy. Under Nasser, emphasis was placed on industrial pro-duction, limitations on imports, and the retention of indigenous manpower to serve its economic and educational institutions. Under Sadat, the open-door policy encouraged the import of foreign goods and technology, fostered private investment in commerce and services as well as production, and allowed large-scale labor emigration in order to alleviate unemployment and gain foreign exchange.

The 1970s were a boom period, at least on the surface.[9] Real economic growth was 9 percent a year, based on rising oil prices and increased oil production, tolls from the Suez Canal, substantial aid from the United States, growing tourism, and worker remittances. The swing toward the West and accords with Israel appeared to be paying off: Egypt regained control over the oil fields in Sinai in 1975, the Canal reopened the same year, and Western aid and tourists poured into the country. Remittances were a key component of this boom. In 1983, officially recorded remittances were nearly 9 percent of the Gross National Product and, at $3.3 billion, equalled the combined revenue from oil ($2.4 b) and the Canal ($974 m).

Nevertheless, disturbing trends were evident in the economy. Overall agricultural production was not only failing to keep pace with the 2.7 percent annual population growth but was even falling in some sectors, as a result of the low prices paid to farmers and the unrestricted import of foreign produce. The country became heavily dependent on foreign food, not only luxury items but essential wheat. As a result, the food import bill soared, totalling $3 billion annually in the mid-1980s and eating up nearly all officially-recorded worker remittances.

Imports also increased in other sectors, and inventories piled up in Egyptian factories as consumers purchased foreign products instead of locally produced goods. This shift was caused in part by returning workers, who increasingly sought electronic appliances and other consumer durables that either were not produced in Egypt or were thought to be of better quality abroad. Consequently, although Egypt had balance of payments surpluses in the late 1970s and early 1980s, its deficit grew in the 1980s as remittances declined and oil prices dropped. Moreover, tourist revenue was affected negatively by hijackings in the Mediterranean in 1985 and the security forces' mutiny in Cairo in February 1986.

Egypt also suffered from an inflation rate of nearly 30 percent. Inflation was partly attributable to labor migration, since workers returned with a purchasing power greater than local production, and thereby fueled price rises in the private sector. Moreover, migrants generally sought to purchase land for housing or agriculture.[10] Given the limited area available, land prices increased more than fivefold in a decade, without a comparable rise in the land's productivity. Finally, shortages in certain skills, such as construction, carpentry, plumbing, and electrical services, could be directly attributed to labor migration and led to higher wages without an increase in quality or productivity.

The currency black market also expanded, undermining government efforts to stabilize the Egyptian pound and to improve the balance of payments. This expansion is a direct result of government policies that make it difficult for businesses to obtain hard currency through legal banking channels. Worker remittances are soaked up by these businesses, which are thirsty for dollars.

The official figures for worker remittances represent the tip of the iceberg. One observer noted that, if three million persons work abroad and each remits $1000 a year, the total would be $3 billion, matching the government data. However, the observer argued, it is far more likely that each person was remitting $7,500, bringing the grand total up to $22 billion.[11] Even if that figure were excessive and each individual remitted, say, $3,000, the total would reach $10 billion a year.

In fact, an official in the Ministry of Migration stated in January 1986 that actual remittances totalled $10 billion: $2 billion through legal channels and $8 billion through illegal routes.[12] These "uncaptured" funds entered Egypt at the black market rate. However, the problem was not caused by the remittances themselves. Rather, the government's maintenance of multiple exchange rates and restrictions on business access to hard currency underlay the situation. Efforts since 1986 to unify the exchange rate and crack down on black market dealers have improved the situation marginally.

The actual composition of remittances cannot be known so long as the unrecorded sums cannot be detailed. One study estimates that, of the official remittances for 1979, 43 percent entered through the banking system or as bank notes whereas 57 percent entered as goods.[13] The bulk of the goods comprised consumer items and only one third could be clearly identified as intermediate or capital goods. This tallied with the general finding that 25-30 percent of the savings are used to import consumer goods.

Nevertheless, it is also evident that substantial sums are available for investment, either through imported intermediate and capital goods or through savings accumulated in the bank. In 1980-81, a quarter of gross investment in Egypt came from remittances, a sum which represented 81 percent of private sector investment.[14] Moreover, a sizable amount is invested in building new houses or repairing old accommodations, thereby improving the general living conditions and expanding employment in the construction sector. But, as noted earlier, this also has inflationary effects as it has artificially raised the prices of land and labor.

Researchers find that the ability to save from work abroad is the key motivation for migration.[15] The differential in wage with the prior job in Egypt is, of course, a crucial component. However, the rate of saving also depends on the cost of living in the recipient country and the policies of that country concerning the remittance of earnings. If a high proportion of the salary must be used to cover daily expenses while abroad, and if only a part of the savings can be remitted, then the incentive to migrate is significantly reduced. This has generally not been the case in the past, but is becoming an important concern as labor-importing countries cut back on fringe benefits such as travel and housing.

In any case, the savings "target" appears to be used to meet basic needs and purchase consumer durables that could not have been afforded previously. Since many of the migrants and their families were underfed and relatively poorly housed and clothed before, expenditure for a plot of land, house construction, debt repayment, and household items, upgrades the living conditions of such persons. Even the use of remittances for a marriage dowry or jewelry is viewed as a better investment than putting money in a bank.

Many migrants have utilized their savings to open a shop, purchase a van or truck, or improve their agricultural holding. These investments enable them to augment their earnings within Egypt after their return. But others appear to place their savings in the bank and then draw down their account to meet daily or special needs. In such cases, they find it difficult to sustain the higher level of consumption underwritten by remittances once their savings are gone, particularly if their only regular income comes from a meager salary from clerical or teaching posts in the government. Therefore, they usually seek another secondment or contract abroad. Migration becomes a kind of addiction that temporarily alleviates the situation but does not augment their earning capacity within Egypt.

Some argue that all of Egypt has become addicted to migration, and that the government thinks that it can export part of its economic crisis instead of resolving it internally.[16] This may be too harsh a judgment, but it does reflect a widespread view among Egyptian analysts that the costs of migration outweigh the benefits. Even if the individual migrant improves his living standard, they argue, Egypt as a whole pays an economic and social price. Their critique is based on the arguments that remittances have a minimal developmental impact, that they fuel inflation and sustain the currency black market, and that they deplete the country of its best minds and most skilled persons.

Moreover, some sociologists maintain that migration has damaged the family structure, since husbands are absent for extended periods. The result has been an increased sense of individualism and materialism at the expense of social goals and values, and has deepened public discontent with conditions in Egypt.[17] These concerns may prove exaggerated, but it does seem likely, as one Egyptian economist noted, that returning migrants "have been relatively well paid, well fed and well housed. They are unlikely to be impressed by unemployment, housing shortages and rising food prices" at home.[18]

The core argument of these Egyptian critics appears valid: that it would have been better to concentrate on increasing agricultural and industrial production inside Egypt, rather than relying on the windfall of remittances to ease the balance-of-payments problem and to postpone making difficult economic decisions. If development is defined as an increase in the country's productive capacity, then remittances do not automatically promote development. As a Jordanian economist argued, countries such as Egypt should create import-substituting and export-oriented industries. In this way, they would export goods and services rather than exporting human capital, and they would promote the long-term development of their country.[19]

Current Government Policies

As labor migration soared, the government increased its attention to the economic and social ramifications of migration. In December 1981 a Minister of State for Migration was appointed whose responsibilities included protecting the interests of Egyptians residing abroad and devising a comprehensive plan for Egyptian migration in accordance with the country's economic and social development goals.[20] The ministry was charged with finding ways to involve emigrants in programs inside Egypt by using their experience and encouraging them to invest in Egypt. It was expected to offer educational, economic, and tourist facilities to them and their children, and to involve them in conferences in Egypt and abroad on migration.

Ministry activities as well as the consolidated migration law of 1983 appeared to give primary attention to the problems facing permanent migrants in North America, Europe, and Australia.[21] However, the new law did exempt bank deposits by temporary migrants from taxation, treat their investment in Egyptian projects on the same favored basis as foreign investment, and confirm that migrants who resigned from public sector jobs but returned in two years could apply for reappointment and regain their previous job or an equivalent one. Even those who migrated for more than two years could be reappointed if they still qualified for the post.

Finally, unions and clubs have been promoted in receiving countries in order to enhance communication between the Egyptian consulates and the migrants and help the latter overcome any problems encountered while living abroad. A Union of Egyptians Abroad was set up in 1985, with its headquarters in Cairo and branches in receiving countries.[22] A conference of temporary migrants had already been held in Qatar in January 1984, which resolved to establish a branch of the pending Union of Egyptians Abroad and pressed for more facilities to transfer remittances and invest in Egypt. In 1986 branches opened in other Gulf states as well as New York.

The government has taken action in two key areas involving temporary migrants: first, the conditions encountered by workers in the receiving countries and, second, the remitting of savings in a manner that would benefit Egypt's economy.

Early attempts to protect Egyptian laborers were embodied in bilateral agreements with Libya and Qatar in 1971 and 1974, respectively. These specified the terms and conditions of employment and methods of resolving disputes. The Libyan government violated the protocol by its expulsion of laborers in August 1985, and so the Egyptian and Tunisian government have filed a joint suit against Libya to enforce international labor conventions relating to migrant labor.[23] The bilateral accord with Qatar went into abeyance when diplomatic relations were frozen after Egypt's peace treaty with Israel in 1979. But a delegation came from Qatar to Cairo in May 1983 to revise and renew the accord.[24] The Ministries of Labor and Foreign Affairs have also worked to draft agreements with Arab countries that will protect laborers against unscrupulous travel agencies and private contractors that either take the potential migrant's money and then disappear without providing the promised visa and job, or alter the terms of the contract to the disadvantage of the worker once he reaches the job site. Since 1982 the Ministry of Labor has tried to eliminate fraud by licensing travel agencies and has set up a special office to try to match potential migrants with interested Arab employers.

The main responsibility for protecting workers has fallen on the shoulders of labor attaches posted to Egyptian embassies. The attaches coordinate with the host government to ensure that contracts are enforced and that workers' interests are protected. Their impact remains limited. They can be effective when the worker has entered with a valid work permit and contract, which has been approved by the Egyptian Ministry of Labor and authorized by the host government. However, migrants who fail to register at the embassy upon their arrival and who have come with no contract or with one that has not been vested with the appropriate authorities usually cannot be protected by the labor attache.[25] This is particularly a problem for low-level, illiterate workers. Even migrants with valid contracts may fear to protest violations, out of concern that their employer might precipitously deport them before they can obtain legal redress. Officials hope that conferences held in Egypt and abroad on issues of labor migration, and the Union of Egyptians Abroad, will serve to make workers more aware of their rights and more willing to insist on attaining them. However, participants in such conferences tend to be educators and administrators rather than workers.

The second major concern has been obtaining remittances for investment in Egypt.[26] Monetary policy is the preserve of the Ministries of Finance and Economy, which have tried through government bonds, incentive rates in banks, "own exchange" imports, and crackdowns on black market activities, to increase the share of remittances entering through legal channels.[27] By the late 1980s, those efforts, coupled with the gradual unification of exchange rates, caused a higher proportion of remittances to enter Egypt through legal channels.

The Ministry of Migration has a more direct role in encouraging investment by migrants in specific developmental projects. As an outcome of the conferences on migration, an Egyptian Expatriate Company for Investment and Development was established, headed by Ahmed Mashhour, former director of the Suez Canal Company.[28] This company is setting up subsidiary enterprises for cooperative housing, international trade, and the promotion of industries. The Qatar branch of the Union of Egyptians Abroad has been studying the possibility of a large-scale poultry project in the Delta, and the Kuwaiti branch is developing 6000 acres in Sinai. The ministry has also arranged for a quarter of the housing plots in new towns to be set aside for migrants, and for tracts to be allocated for land reclamation by migrants. Bank Misr has formed an investment and development company, 51 percent of whose capital is to be reserved for migrants.

Yet, just as the migrants' unions appear to be dominated by high-level administrators and educators abroad, so too do their schemes appear to be addressed to the wealthier migrants, who have large sums available to invest and the know-how to deal with the governmental apparatus. The average worker, who has a small sum available and does not trust large-scale institutions, is not apt to be attracted to these schemes and, so far, has not been provided with any organized way in which to invest his savings.

Moreover, the return of workers has now become a serious issue. By 1988 an estimated 1.4 million Egyptians (plus families) were abroad, a drop of one million in less than three years.[29] With 2.8 million persons unemployed out of a domestic work force of 14.8 million, the economy was evidently finding it impossible to absorb new entrants into the labor force, much less returning migrants.

Nevertheless, official statements did not reflect a serious concern about the situation. In late 1985, the Minister of Labor claimed that returnees "would be easily absorbed at home" and the Minister of Planning commented: "Since we have severe labor shortages in several sectors, our problem is not their return *per se*. It is where they will go when they return. We're trying to build new communities in the desert because Cairo simply can't handle any more people."[30] Foreign Ministry officials also stated to this author that jobs await them in Egypt, in their former posts or in agriculture or industry.

Others, however, have expressed alarm and warned about the need to plan for the return of migrants so that the economy can absorb the shock. Staff at the Institute of National Planning are particularly vocal in demanding comprehensive planning, including retraining programs, analyses of the local wage structure, and new possible job outlets abroad, and the search for alternatives to remittances to finance Egyptian development.[31] The National Council for Social Development and Services, meeting in January 1986, finally asserted that short and long-term plans must be prepared to cope with the return of workers.[32]

Egyptian economists and sociologists had already expressed concern that no serious planning to reabsorb migrants was taking place. A leading economist outlined several basic requirements.[33] They included reaching agreements with the receiving countries for a planned and phased return of Egyptian labor according to specific quotas and guaranteeing that returnees receive their end-of-work payments, travel allowances, and compensation for the liquidation of their businesses. He also stressed that special business loans and retraining programs should be available to all levels of returnees, and that studies should be made on which countries in the Gulf or elsewhere could still use Egyptian labor. Finally, he urged that labor-intensive industries should be established in Egypt to absorb returnees as well as new entrants into the labor force.

Egypt is at present confronted by serious economic and political problems that its government is hard pressed to handle. Under Hosni Mubarak, it has moved haltingly to strengthen democratic institutions, restructure its diplomatic relations, and rationalize the open-door policy. Egypt's relations with its Arab neighbors have improved despite its ties with Israel. Government efforts to undo the excesses of the open-door policy by restricting imports and encouraging domestic production have met with mixed results. Hard-currency reserves are under greater strain, making the country more dependent on its aid relationship with the West.

In this context, the already-apparent reduction in remittances and return of a portion of the migrant workers are part of a complex of economic and political issues that the government must address. It is evident that the government has a limited capacity to cope with a downturn in revenue from remittances, on which it has relied. It has few ideas as to how to absorb the returning workers and to encourage productive investment before the remittances are consumed and disappear.

Migration has contributed to altering economic patterns and social attitudes in ways that have raised expectations for improved living standards. Migration may have served in part as a safety-valve for Egypt, but it has also generated its own pressures on the country. And the apparent failure to use the buoyant period underwritten by remittances in order to stabilize and propel forward internal production may haunt the country in the coming years.

Notes

1. This paper is based on the author's "Egyptian Labor Migration: Economic Trends and Government Policies," Universities Field Staff International (UFSI) *Report*, No. 38 (1985). For the background on labor migration, see Ali E. Hillal Dessouki, *Development of Egypt's Migration Policy, 1952-1978*, Technology Adaptation Program (TAP) (Cairo University/Massachusetts Institute of Technology, 1978). See also Nazih Ayubi, "The Egyptian Brain Drain," *International Journal of Middle East Studies* 15 (1983), p. 4; Saad Eddin Ibrahim, *The New Arab Social Order* (Boulder, Colorado: Westview, 1982); Fatma Aly Khafagy, "The Socio-Economic Impact of the Spending of Remittances by Emigrant Egyptian Labour (A Case Study of Two Villages)" (Doctoral Thesis, University College, London, 1984); Robert J. LaTowsky, "Egyptian Labor Abroad," *MERIP Reports*, Vol. 14, No. 4 (May 1984); and Naiem A. Sherbiny and Ismail Serageldin, "Expatriate Labor and Economic Growth: Saudi Demand for Egyptian Labor," in Malcolm H. Kerr and El Sayed Yasin, eds., *Rich and Poor States in the Middle East* (Boulder: Westview, 1982).

2. Dessouki, *Development of Egypt's Migration Policy, op. cit.*, p. 9.

3. The principal sources for the section on receiving countries are: *al-Ahram al-Iqtisadi* (Cairo), May 2, 1983; Judith Marie Barsalou, "Foreign Labor in Saudi Arabia" (Doctoral

Thesis, Columbia University, New York, 1985); J.S. Birks, I. Serageldin, C. A. Sinclair, and J. Socknat, "Who is Migrating Where?," in Alan Richards and Philip L. Martin, eds., *Migration, Mechanization and Agricultural Labor Markets in Egypt* (Boulder: Westview, 1983); Nazli Choucri, *Migration in the Middle East: Transformations, Policies, and Processes,* Vol. I, TAP Report, 1983; Nader Firgani, *al-Hijra ila al-Naft* (Migration to Oil) (Beirut: Center for Arab Unity Studies, 1983); Rostam M. Kavoussi, "Oil Exports and the Changing Occupational Structure in Saudi Arabia," *Arab Studies Quarterly,* Vol. 6, No. 4 (1984); Guiseppi Pennisi, *Development, Manpower and Migration in the Red Sea Region: The Case for Cooperation* (Hamburg: Deutsches Orient-Institut, 1981); and Naiem A. Sherbiny, "Expatriate Labor Flows to the Arab Oil Countries in the 1980s," *Middle East Journal,* Vol. 38, No. 4 (1984).

4. For information on Saudi Arabia, see Barsalou, "Foreign Labor . . . ," *op. cit.,* pp. 4, 68, 73, 105, 118; and Sherbiny and Serageldin, "Expatriate Labor . . . ," *op. cit.,* pp. 227, 234.

5. On production and plans, see Barsalou, "Foreign Labor . . . ," *op. cit.,* pp. 104, 114; and Sherbiny, "Expatriate Labor . . . ," *op. cit.,* p. 649.

6. Interview with Mahmoud Mahdi, formerly in the Egyptian Embassy in Qatar and currently Minister Plenipotentiary, Migration Office, Ministry of Foreign Affairs, January 16, 1986.

7. *New York Times,* September 29, 1984; *Washington Post,* September 3, 1985; *Egyptian Gazette* (Cairo), September 4, 1985; *The Middle East* (October 1985); *International Herald Tribune,* January 14, 1986.

8. *Al-Ahram al-Iqtisadi,* March 11, 1985; see also the issues of April 11 and May 9, 1983, May 21, 1984; and Mahmoud Abdul-Fadil and Ibrahim Saad al-Din, *Intiqal al-Umala al-Arabiyya* (The Movement of Arab Labor) (Beirut: Center for Arab Unity Studies, 1983), pp. 161-63.

9. On the Egyptian economy, see Osama Hamed, "Egypt's Open Door Economic Policy," *International Journal of Middle East Studies,* Vol. 13, No. 1 (1981); Mihssen Kadhim, "Labor Export and Economic Development in Egypt," *Journal of South Asian and Middle Eastern Studies,* Vol. 7, No. 4 (1984); N. Choucri and Supriya Lahiri, *Macroeconomic Impacts of Remittances in Egypt: An Exploratory Analysis,* TAP Report, 1983; and U.S. Embassy, *Economic Trends Report: Egypt,* Cairo, April and December 1985.

10. For details see the author's "Impact of Labor Migration on Urban and Rural Egypt," *UFSI Report,* No. 39 (1985).

11. Nazli Choucri in *al-Ahram al-Iqtisadi,* December 9, 1985; clarifications on the currency black market are provided by Frederic Shorter.

12. *Al-Ahram,* January 29, 1986; comments by Mahmoud Mahdi and his colleague Hussein al-Bahrawi, cited in footnote no. 6 of this paper, and comments by Muhammad Marzouk Hamid, Undersecretary in the Ministry for Migration, January 15, 1986.

13. Khafagy, "The Socio-Economic Impact . . . ," *op. cit.* pp. 87, 91, based on *al-Ahram al-Iqtisadi,* September 28, 1981, p. 20.

14. Galal A. Amin and Elizabeth Awny, "International Migration of Egyptian Labour: A Review of the State of the Art" (Manuscript Report, International Development Research Center, Ottawa and Cairo, 1985), p. 86.

15. The following paragraphs are based especially on the writings of an economist at Cairo University, Mahmoud Abdul-Fadil; see "The Economic Impact of International Migration with Special Reference to Worker's Remittances in Countries of the Middle East" (Proceedings of the International Population Conference, International Union for the Scientific Study of Population, Florence, Italy, June 1985) and the interview with him in *al-Ahram al-Iqtisadi,* May 16, 1983. See also Riad Tabarah, "Demo-Economic Consequences of International Migration," in the above-mentioned conference proceedings.

16. M. Abdul-Fadil in *al-Ahram al-Iqtisadi,* May 16, 1983, and the comment by Nader Firgani, January 12, 1986.

17. Interviews with Dr. Ramzi Zaki, expert at the Institute of National Planning; Abdul-Basit Abdul-Mu'ti, sociologist at Ain Shams University; and Saad al-Din Ibrahim, sociologist at the American University in Cairo, in *al-Ahram al-Iqtisadi,* April 25, 1983.

18. Unnamed economist quoted in *The Middle East,* August 1985, p. 21.

19. Ahmad K. Katanani, economist at Jordan University, "Economic Alternatives to Migration" (Paper, Conference on International Migration in the Arab World, UN Economic Commission for West Asia, Nicosia, Cyprus, May 1981), pp. 15-18.

20. Khafagy, "The Socio-Economic Impact..," *op. cit.* pp. 27-28, quoting *al-Ahram* newspaper, October 15 and November 22, 1981.

21. Law Number 111, 1983: memorandum and text in an Arabic pamphlet; text also reproduced in *al-Ahram al-Iqtisadi,* August 29, 1983.

22. See the text of the decree and statements by the President, Prime Minister and Minister of State for Migration, *al-Ahram al-Iqtisadi,* June 11, 1984; interview with Ambassador Mahmoud Abdul-Hadi, Director of the Migration Office, Ministry of Foreign Affairs, Cairo, January 14, 1986; and interview with William Nagib Safain, Minister of State for Migration, Cairo, January 15, 1986.

23. Comments by H. al-Bahrawi and M. Mahdi, see footnote no. 6.

24. *Al-Ahram al-Iqtisadi,* May 2 and 9, 1983.

25. Comment by M. Mahdi, see footnote no. 6 of this paper. The conferences include annual gatherings in Cairo since 1983, local meetings such as January 1984 in Qatar, and the first conference on Egyptian labor abroad organized by the Egyptian Federation of Trade Unions in December 1984.

26. Quoted by J.S. Birks and C.A. Sinclair, "Egypt: A Frustrated Labor Exporter?" *Middle East Journal,* Vol. 33, No. 3 (1979), p. 302.

27. See interviews with Gulf bankers in *al-Ahram al-Iqtisadi,* February 3 and June 11, 1984.

28. Interviews with Ambassador Abdul-Hadi and Minister Safain, cited in endnote 22. The minister described land allocated for industries by migrants in Sadat City in *Journal d'Egypte,* February 21, 1986.

29. *Middle East Times,* February 28, 1988, p. 7.

30. *New York Times,* October 6, 1985; see also *al-Ahram al-Iqtisadi,* May 9, 1983, and *The Middle East Reporter* (Beirut), September 17, 1985.

31. Interviews with Acting Director Abdul-Fattah Mungi and expert Abdul-Fattah Nassif, in *al-Ahram al-Iqtisadi,* May 16, 1983.

32. *The Egyptian Gazette,* January 12, 1986.

33. Mahmoud Abdul-Fadil, *al-Ahram al-Iqtisadi,* May 16, 1983, and Mahmoud Abdul-Fadil and Ibrahim Saad al-Din, *Intiqal al-Umala . . . , op. cit.,* pp. 262-66.

5 FIFTEEN YEARS OF US AID TO EGYPT: A CRITICAL REVIEW

Heba Handoussa

Introduction

The fifteen years from 1974 to the present encompass a period of radical transformation of the Egyptian economy from the socialist model toward a decentralized market system. Egypt's adoption of the open-door policy has been supported and encouraged by a generous flow of $1 billion per year in US economic assistance. This transformation also coincided with Egypt's ten-year boom (1975 to 1985) in foreign exchange income from petroleum, the Suez Canal, worker remittances and tourism, which raised annual current account receipts to an average of $13 billion in the mid-1980s, up from only $3 billion in the mid-1970s.

Paradoxically, the protracted economic stagnation of the late 1960s to early 1970s which had been largely responsible for this shift to a liberalized Western model of development has again afflicted Egypt's economy since 1985. After a period of unprecedented growth of Gross Domestic Product per capita from $334 in 1975 to $700 in 1985, the years from 1985-1988 witnessed virtually no increase in per capita income. Egypt's economy is once again suffering all the symptoms of structural imbalance and indebtedness as severe (if not more so) as those of the early 1970s. Indeed, Egypt's foreign debt (including military debt) has multiplied sevenfold, from $6 billion in 1974 to $44 billion in 1988 or 180 percent of GDP, one of the highest ratios in the world today.[1]

The initial enthusiasm for the new partnership between Egypt and the US, heralding an era of peace and prosperity, and the ensuing negative turn in the economy's performance is cause for great disappointment and concern. Both donor and recipient have understandably pointed a blaming finger at each other. While America claims that poor economic management is responsible for Egypt's chronic deficits in the budget and balance of payments, Egypt contends that the nature of the US aid package is responsible for the exponential growth in the country's foreign debt.

The purpose of this paper is to reappraise the strengths and weaknesses of the Egyptian-American aid relationship as it affects Egypt's long-term development and America's interests.

Aid Transactions: A Non-Zero Sum Game

A useful way to approach any aid relationship is to treat it as a transaction or as a mixed motive game rather than as a zero sum or purely cooperative game. Dependency on aid, like on trade, stems from the opportunity cost of foregoing the relationship to either partner.[2] The term "aid" is perhaps a misnomer, since the obligation to reciprocate is at the basis of the exchange. Unfortunately, a number of misleading concepts have crept into the vocabulary of the aid dialogue, including those of "unilateral transfer," "no strings attached," "absorptive capacity," and "fungibility." The first of these misconceptions implies that the recipient alone stands to gain from the aid flow. The second suggests that conditionality does not exist. The third concept presupposes a limit to the ability of the recipient to utilize large amounts of aid, and the fourth casts doubt on the value and usefulness of aid in kind.

A closer examination of the size and nature of US-Egypt aid transactions will dispel these distorted notions and convey a more objective assessment of the reciprocal nature of aid. This clearer perception is of benefit to both parties in the interest of a more productive relationship. Thus, the concept of "no strings attached" has contributed to the belief that a full $1 billion of highly concessionary US economic aid has been annually available to and utilized by Egypt with no indirect costs attached. In fact, indirect costs have been significant in the form of excessive US consultancy services imposed by the donor, procurement conditions stipulating use of often overpriced American goods and services, and, what is more important, donor selection of project priorities often at odds with Egypt's priorities. This has resulted in the emergence of an inflated US AID bureaucracy, often referred to as Egypt's "shadow cabinet," the presence of which contrasts sharply with Israel's relative autonomy in the allocation of its $1 billion of American aid in cash per year with no interference from a single US AID official in the country. It is, therefore, fair to conclude that in Egypt's case, the additional strings attached to US aid also assign a greater responsibility to the US for the success or failure of its aid program.

In addition, the size of aggregate aid disbursements has itself been far short of commitments because of the donor's rigid procedures whereby project funds are frozen according to implementation schedule per project. Thus, by the end of 1982, as much as $2.7 billion (or 86 percent) of the cumulative value of project aid was still "in the pipeline." The ratio improved significantly, but there remained in 1986 a sizable 33 percent of undisbursed project aid. This pipeline effect has often been blamed on Egypt's absorptive capacity when in fact the problem has been due to the lengthy implementation time typical of large-scale projects such as sewerage, electricity, waterworks, and other rehabilitation schemes.[3]

Absorptive capacity refers to problems arising from the recipient's inability to make use of available investment funds due to a lack of viable project opportunities, to infrastructural bottlenecks, or again, to a shortage of trained labor or management. For Egypt, the reverse has been true; ever since the 1960s in spite of an abundance of skilled labor and a long established industrial tradition, the shortage of capital resources has always been the major constraint on development. It is true that bureaucratic red tape has been responsible for delays in the implementation of some projects, but it cannot be held accountable for the countless viable projects that have been identified by both donor and recipient but are not implemented for lack of funds.

Similar to the accusation levelled at Egypt with regard to its perceived limited absorptive capacity is an accusation levelled at American food aid to Egypt. It has been argued that this aid was not fungible and that it discouraged Egyptians from producing cereals, and encouraged the consumption of more cereals than would have been the case without the PL 480 Food for Peace aid. It is fair to say that US food aid to Egypt is entirely fungible since it accounts for only a small proportion of total cereal imports, more than 70 percent of which are purchased on commercial terms. In fact, PL 480 has been fungible ever since the 1950s, when Egypt's population was less than half of today's and the country had reallocated a significant proportion of land from cotton to wheat since any further shift away from cotton would jeopardize the country's comparative advantage in exporting cotton and importing wheat. Although Egypt's per capita consumption of cereals may be the highest in the world, this is clearly the result of the government's domestic price and subsidy policy rather than a function of food aid being available to the country.

As for "unilateral transfers," this concept implies that aid benefits flow in one direction, from donor to recipient. The evidence shows, however, that in the case of the US-Egypt transaction, the benefits to the US are considerable if not always quantifiable. Thus, in the decade 1975 to 1985, the aggregate disbursements of US economic aid to Egypt of $8.7 billion have been accompanied by equally significant commercial and political gains to the US.[4] American investments in Egypt's petroleum sector have earned profits estimated at

Table 1
US Economic Aid to Egypt, 1975 to 1988
(in $US millions)

	1	2	3(1+2)	4	5	6(1+2+4)
	PROJ C	CIP C	ESF C	ESF D	PL 480 C	Total C
1975	85	150	235	25	111	346
1976	458	314	772	94	192	963
1977	245	437	682	167	193	875
1978	429	297	726	523	189	916
1979	472	334	814	367	230	1036
1980	510	334	844	605	299	1144
1981	506	300	806	737	298	1104
1982	412	350	762	597	292	1054
1983	447	301	748	868	258	1006
1984	450	402*	852	905	264	1116
1985	515	550*	1065	1272	236	1301
1986	553	515*	1068	n.a.	219	1287
1987	n.a.	n.a.	806	n.a.	171	977
1988	n.a.	n.a.	705	n.a.	171	876

* Cash transfers of $102 million, $350 million and $360 million are included for the three years 1984, 1985, and 1986, consecutively.

Note: PROJ = Project aid: C = Commitment: D = Disbursement
CIP = Commodity Import Program
ESF = Economic Support Fund (PROJ + CIP)
PL 480 = Public Law 480 (Title I and Title II)

Source: For the years 1975 to 1986, all figures on commitments are from the Ministry of Planning and International Cooperation, US Economic Cooperation Division, *Status Report on Use of US Loans and Grants to Egypt for the Period 1975 to End 1986* (Cairo, 1989). For the years 1987 and 1988, and column 4 (ESF disbursements), see the issues of *Egyptian Economic Trends,* a publication by the US Embassy in Cairo.

about 70 percent of the aggregate profits (after cost recovery) transferred by all foreign petroleum companies at $9.5 billion over the decade.[5] American banks which began operating in Egypt in the mid-1970s have also reaped substantial profits on their modest investments. Starting from a zero base in the early 1970s, the foreign currency accounts of Egyptian residents stood at $9.9 billion in 1985,[6] and the bulk of these deposits have been placed abroad by the joint venture and local branches of foreign banks (which are American). This has therefore deprived the Egyptian economy of these valuable sources of finance. Again, American exports to Egypt have long surpassed the $2 billion annual total of economic and military aid to Egypt. For example, roughly 40 percent of American sales of agricultural products to Egypt have, since the early 1980s, been made on strictly commercial terms, and US millers consider Egypt their largest foreign customer.[7] Egypt's exports to the US have met with protectionist barriers, with total exports to the US averaging $218 million as compared to total imports from the US at $2,305 million over the 1983 to 1987 period.[8]

On balance, therefore, it would seem fair to say that American aid to Egypt has reaped substantial American dividends in terms of investment and trade, and that both parties are better off in terms of economic transactions, without accounting for the additional benefits from their political and military cooperation.

The Political Dimension of the Aid Relationship

By the end of the 1963 to 1973 decade, Egypt was emerging from three wars which had exhausted its economy and drained its budget on military expenditure. The net flow of Soviet economic and military aid (available to Egypt since the 1950s) was decreasing as debt servicing started to claim a large portion of aid disbursements. Arab aid flows were generous but only sufficient to compensate for the loss of the Suez Canal revenues and of the Sinai oil fields since the 1967 war. Egypt's leadership was seeking radical solutions, both on the domestic and international front.

At this time the US was seeking to contain Soviet influence in the Middle East after a decade which had witnessed the shift of many states to socialism. The region was becoming increasingly powerful and independent as a result of its oil wealth. The oil embargo of 1973 was a dramatic example of how far Egypt's friends in the region, including Saudi Arabia and the Gulf states, were willing to wield the oil weapon and thus challenge Western interests.

Within the Arab world, Egypt's size, strategic location, and military strength made it an ideal ally for the US effort to expand the American military, diplomatic, and political presence in the area. For Egypt, renewed ties with the US were perceived as essential to breaking the Egyptian-Israeli stalemate and to bringing new injections of capital to Egypt's war-torn economy. This convergence of interests led to the open-door policy and to the resumption of diplomatic ties and economic aid from the US to Egypt in 1973-74. America's big foreign policy gain came with the signing of the Egypt-Israeli peace treaty in 1979.

Although the Camp David accords were ostensibly designed to bring peace to the troubled Middle East, America's reward to Egypt was to match its annual economic aid package of $1 billion with annual arms sales of another $1 billion, the cost of which almost neutralized the benefits of the economic aid flow. In the space of five years of peace, the cumulative military debt to the US was thus to reach the staggering figure of $4.55 billion (by the end of 1984) in comparison to the modest $2 billion of military debt that accrued to the Soviet Union over a twenty-year period during which Egypt had witnessed four major wars. The size of a US military aid package too large for the Egyptian economy to support, given the fact that counterpart domestic finance was required to complement the annual $1 billion, and the terms of the transaction were equally onerous. These stipulated that the principal would only start to be amortized after 30 years, while the "concessionary" rate of interest of 14 percent would be charged annually. The servicing of America's military aid to Egypt at $650 million per year in interest alone is thus almost as large as the average annual disbursement of US economic aid (ESF + PL 480) received by Egypt at $721 million over the decade 1975 to 1984 (see Table 1).

In retrospect, it seems that both donor and recipient had embarked on a military spending spree which Egypt could not afford, given its meager resources and the pressing developmental claims on the government budget. When in 1985, it became obvious that Egypt could no longer continue accumulating military debts at this unprecedented pace, the US shifted its military aid transfers to a grant basis, an arrangement which has continued to this day. The question arises as to why the US used and Egypt accepted such paralyzing commercial terms up until 1984. The fully concessionary flows of military aid since 1985 have meant a heavy drain on the government budget with regard to the size of the counterpart military expenditure in domestic currency. Budget figures on defense show that these expenses have in fact increased more than fivefold from an annual average of EP 265 million in the 1969 to 1974 period (which witnessed the 1973 war) to an average of EP 1.42 billion in the 1979 to 1984 period (post-Camp David peace), consuming 18 percent of total budget revenue.[9]

The issue is not the role which Egypt has willingly assumed as watchdog in this volatile part of the world, nor should a reduction in military capability be suggested. Rather, the issue is the cost of assuming this role, which weighs heavily on the Egyptian economy. It is sometimes forgotten that Egypt's purchase of weapons from the Eastern bloc back in 1955 came as a result not of ideological preference, but as a pragmatic response to the inflexible US conditions for arms sales, which required direct cash payments in US dollars in advance. Therefore Egypt had to give up its first choice of American weaponry; but, as a country in the throes of development, it had to be conservative in expenditures and could not ignore the attractive terms available from the Eastern bloc. These included long-term credit at 2.5 percent interest repayable in Egyptian exports.

At present, an essential complement to the grant basis of US military aid would be an arrangement for the US to support Egypt's effort to restructure its arms industry by providing the technology to produce and export a range of US weapons or their component parts. This would transform Egypt's defense sector from being a net burden to becoming a net generator of income, employment, skills, and foreign exchange for the economy.

Structural Imbalance and the Policy Dialogue

In addition to the glaring imbalance between economic and military aid which has hindered the development of the Egyptian economy, another serious maladjustment has gradually evolved since the mid-1970s. This is a major structural imbalance resulting from poor macroeconomic policies, which have upset the pattern of investment, consumption, and trade in favor of nonproductive economic activities and culminated in unmanageable deficits in Egypt's balance of payments and government budget.

Throughout the 1975 to 1985 decade of prosperity, many economists warned that this prosperity might be a short-lived phenomenon, and that policy makers should hedge against a drop in windfall incomes in case external conditions led to a return flow of Egyptian migrant workers, or a decline in petroleum revenues or foreign aid flows. The warnings went unheeded as Egypt basked in the luxury of its short-lived boom, and as Western creditors peddled the surplus petrodollars as though there was no tomorrow.

The decade-long boom was fed by worker remittances which grew from $366 million in 1975 to $3.93 billion in 1983-84, petroleum exports which grew from $381 million in 1976 to $4.96 billion in 1984-85 (of which Egypt's share was $2.89 billion in that year), and net official loans and grants from Arab and OECD countries which averaged $2.33 billion per year between 1975 and 1984-85. The reopening and expansion of the Suez Canal also contributed earnings which leveled off at $1 billion after 1983-84.[10]

Increased incomes accrued both to the government and to the household sectors, and both proceeded to raise their consumption and investment levels. Unfortunately, macroeconomic policies were not conducive to an optimal allocation of resources and a chronic deficit developed in the balance of payments and the government budget. Three major areas that were affected were investment, trade, and government expenditure.

The Pattern of Investment

Although a significantly high and unprecedented ratio of investment to GDP was sustained at 29.4 percent over the entire boom period, public and private investment was concentrated in the nontradeable sectors of the economy or in petroleum.

The bulk of private domestic investment was in the housing sector, whose prospects for long-term income generation, employment, or exports were nil. Foreign investment via the newly enacted investment encouragement law (Law 43 of 1974) was negligible and the only sectors which attracted direct capital flows were petroleum, banking, and tourism. By the end of 1977, the cumulative value of American investments in Egypt stood at $1.7 billion, 82 percent of which was in petroleum.[11] In fact, by 1984-85, the export performance of all Law 43 companies (domestic and foreign investments outside housing and petroleum) amounted to only $26 million, in contrast to their import bill of $609 million, and to the estimated value of their capital investment of $8.6 billion.

The government and public sector investments, reflected in the two Five-Year Plans of 1977-82 and 1982-87, allocated only 35-38 percent of investment resources to all of the productive sectors combined—agriculture, manufacturing, petroleum and mining. The lion's share of investments went to infrastructure and utilities, with transport and communications receiving 27-29 percent, public utilities 8-11 percent, and electricity 9-10 percent. Project aid (mostly American) was specifically earmarked for expenditure on these three infrastructural subsectors, as opposed to the commodity producing sectors which could have generated much-needed income, employment, and exports as well as provided sufficient returns for the servicing of the fast-accumulating foreign debt which reached $40 billion in 1987.

It has been argued that Egypt's infrastructure was in desperate need of rehabilitation and expansion and that American aid could not have financed all of Egypt's required investments. Yet, given the overall scarcity of available funds for development, whether foreign or domestic, both donor and recipient should have worked closely to design an optimal package of aid projects over time and sectors. It seems that too much US project aid was allocated to doubling the number of telephone lines ($247 million), increasing rural electrification (from 19 percent of households in 1975 to 79 percent in 1985),[12] or spending $764 million on the Cairo and Alexandria sewage systems. From Egypt's standpoint, these non-productive investments, although necessary, have had very high opportunity costs in foregoing industrial and agricultural expansion.

What is disconcerting about US aid policy is the radical volte-face vis-a-vis industry which took place after 1978. In the first four years of US economic cooperation, 40 percent ($504 million) of project aid was committed to the industrial sector. This share fell to less than 4 percent over the following decade. One possible explanation for this attitudinal shift was the marked anti-public sector bias of the Reagan administration.

However, during the mid-1980s, Egypt's public sector still accounted for about 40 percent of GDP and about 90 percent of installed capacity in the formal industrial sector.[13] Private manufacturing on the other hand was originating from a very small base and therefore had limited absorptive capacity. US policy was followed by other Western aid donors and international institutions such as the World Bank, which became increasingly prejudiced with regard to public sector efficiency, its monopolistic advantages, and the perceived threat posed to "the free play of market forces." Thus, after a number of highly successful loans to public enterprises in textiles, steel, fertilizer, cement, and other sectors, finance was withheld.

This indiscriminate condemnation of public enterprise has been a major contributor to unbalanced development, since ultimately neither public nor private enterprise was able to take up the challenge of self-sustaining growth. Moreover, since the enactment of Law 43, there has been a growing complementarity and healthy competition between the two sectors which could conceivably have evolved into the sought-after liberalized environment of a market economy with minimum dislocation to the social fabric. Egypt's government did not have sufficient resources to meet the minimum requirements for restructuring and rehabilitation of this vital public enterprise sector of economic activity.

One of the most destabilizing repercussions of ignoring the structure of Egypt's economy with state capitalism at its base, has been the loss of the employment-generating capacity of industry at large. Whereas the public sector was not given the opportunity to expand, the private sector could not and did not fill in the massive gap. The two Five Year Plans (1977 to 1986/87) forecast that 60 percent of the employment increase of 4 million people would be generated by the productive sectors of the economy, with industry taking the leading role in job creation. Instead, open unemployment increased from a rate of 7 percent in the 1976 census to 15 percent in the 1986 census. Equally striking is the fact that the productive sectors (both public and private), including manufacturing, have provided less than half of the targeted increase in employment. Although the detailed results of the 1986 census are not yet available, estimates show that employment growth declined to 0.2 percent in public sector manufacturing and 1.3 percent in private sector manufacturing starting in 1980.[14]

The Pattern of Trade

In their trade and exchange rate policies, Egypt's policy-makers began to implement IMF recommendations in 1974. These policies were strongly supported by the US as a means of promoting its own exports and enticing its multinationals into Egypt. Bilateral trade agreements were dismantled in favor of free trade and the government monopoly on imports and exports was abolished. The early removal of trade restrictions and exchange controls, along with the real appreciation of the Egyptian pound, led to an upsurge in imports, a thriving foreign currency black market, and a sharp decline in the competitiveness of Egyptian non-oil exports. Another serious problem that ensued was capital flight and the holding of foreign currency balances in local banks. The impact of the government's liberalized trade and exchange regime was therefore a current account deficit of $3.59 billion in 1984-85, up from $2.43 billion in 1975. This occurred in spite of the dramatic leap of 330 percent in current account receipts over the decade.

The export performance of Egypt's manufacturing sector has suffered as a result of the overvaluation of the country's currency prior to the 1980s, while the protectionist policies of Egypt's new trading partners in the West can be blamed for the poor results achieved by Egypt's export drive, which began after 1980. With the decline in windfall revenues from petroleum and related sources, the government offered manufacturers a number of export incentives including a market-determined exchange rate, full retention rights, and a simplified drawback scheme. However, the imposition of quotas on Egypt's chief manufactured products—cotton yarn and textiles, which account for 60 percent of total manufacturing exports—was to prove a major impediment to the growth of these exports to the US and EEC markets.

US protectionism should be singled out in particular, given that the US was now Egypt's major trading partner (accounting for one third of Egypt's import bill in 1984), with US exports to Egypt having increased significantly from $610 million in 1976 to $2.32 billion in 1985. In contrast, Egypt's exports of textiles to the US, which had started from a negligible base, were subjected to tight quota limitations in spite of prolonged negotiations. By 1987, the 6.5 percent quota increase meant that Egypt's textile exports to the US (yarn, fabrics, knitwear and clothing) had only reached $70 million in a market which imports textiles worth approximately $21 billion per annum.

Egypt was thus caught in the impossible situation whereby it accepted donor advice to promote its exports, to phase out import restrictions, and discontinue bilateral trade worth hundreds of millions of dollars, and yet was prevented from making the expected transition to the status of a semi-industrialized mixed-economy exporter. This transition had in fact been made smoothly by many other developing countries a decade or so earlier. Egypt's non-petroleum exports declined from $1.6 billion in 1974 to $1.3 billion in 1984-85, and the country's dependence on petroleum exports thereby continued. In spite of falling international prices, these exports still accounted for 48 percent of Egypt's total merchandise exports to the world and for 68 percent of total exports to the US in 1987.

Clearly, unless Egypt's new aid and trade partners, led by the US, give special treatment to the exports from Egypt's textile industry, the dominant source of comparative advantage, employment, and linkages in the economy, there can be no prospect for Egypt to redress the balance between its exports and imports, or close its savings gap, which had reached 15 percent of GDP by the mid-eighties.

Fiscal Policy

The government's attempt to sustain the living standards of the poorest segments of the population has led to an extensive system of explicit and implicit subsidies and a general price freeze on the output of public enterprises. These price controls have taken a heavy toll on enterprise profits and state dividends, with negative repercussions on the size of the budget deficit. However, even the threefold increase in the explicit subsidy bill over the decade 1975 to 1985 from EP 661 million to EP 2.28 billion seems modest in comparison to the growth in three other major items of government expenditure on current account. By 1985, the wage bill had multiplied sixfold to reach EP 3.2 billion, defense expenditure had multiplied fourfold to reach EP 2.39 billion, and interest payments multiplied fifteen times to reach EP 1.28 billion and continued to grow exponentially, paralleling the accumulation of domestic and foreign debt.

Explicit subsidies can be justified as a means of correcting the serious maldistribution of income resulting from the open-door policy, in a country where one third of the population live below the poverty line, and where no system of unemployment benefits exists. On the other hand, the outcome of the guaranteed employment scheme for graduates—introduced by Nasser in the 1960s—was the exponential growth of wages in government administration. It has been argued that these funds could have instead been productively used in employment-generating investments, had policy-makers taken advantage of the prevailing boom to reform higher education and employment policy. However, the state chose to continue absorbing into its bureaucracy over one hundred thousand graduates each year. The abnormal growth in defense expenditure was also symptomatic of the extravagant fiscal "laissez-aller" of that period. On the revenue side of the budget, no effort was made to improve tax administration.

The bulk of government income came from the rent-earning Suez Canal, petroleum, and from taxes on international trade. Thus, the budget balance was becoming increasingly precarious.

The end of the boom came with the 1985 crash in the petroleum market. Egypt's oil revenues dropped by 40 percent, while income from all of the other major sources stagnated. Hardest hit were budget revenues, forcing the government to significantly cut down planned investment expenditure and to trim its guaranteed employment scheme drastically. Even so, these measures left the budget deficit at the unmanageable level of 22 percent of GDP. Thus by 1986, the government was constrained to admit to its creditors that Egypt was unable to meet its debt obligations. The IMF stepped in, and structural adjustment and conditionality became the order of the day. Egypt's massive foreign debt of $40 billion was rescheduled and a program of economic reform negotiated.

The major components on the reform agenda were designed to reduce aggregate consumption and investment: adjusting the exchange rate, raising the rate of interest, reducing implicit subsidies on energy, raising the price of agricultural products and of public sector output, and rationalizing explicit subsidies. The government has moved on each front, but the steps taken have not gone far enough to satisfy the IMF. The commercial exchange rate was devalued by 63 percent in 1987, but the government has insisted on maintaining its official rate at only one third of the market rate. Electricity and fuel oil prices have been raised several times, but are still selling at a fraction of their world price equivalent. The same is true of agriculture and industry, where price liberalization is far from complete. Explicit subsidies on food and other basic commodities have been reduced in real terms by reducing the range and availability of subsidized products. Moreover, although the guaranteed employment scheme has not been officially abandoned, annual recruitment into the bureaucracy has been drastically curtailed.

The US has been a strong advocate of economic reform, although its emphasis has been on those measures (such as the increases in energy and in agricultural prices) which do not directly threaten social and political stability. There are two areas in particular which the US wishes to see treated with sensitivity. These are food subsidies and the level of private investment. The general buoyancy of the economy is considered important insofar as it affects business confidence and ensures the steady growth of the nascent private sector. The US therefore leans towards the expenditure-switching policies of the reform package, unlike the IMF, which also insists on a strong dose of expenditure-reducing measures.

The critical variable in the policy dialogue between Egypt and its aid donors is the pace of adjustment, and the trade-off is between the slow and cautious reform process adopted by Egypt as against a more risky (if speedier) recovery proposed by the IMF. Egypt's preferred option would require donor support both in principle and in additional injections of aid channelled to the appropriate sectors of the economy.

Conclusion

There is little doubt that on balance, both Egypt and the US have substantially gained from their mutual cooperation over the past fifteen years. For the US, the benefits have included foreign policy successes such as its increased regional influence following the American-brokered peace treaty between Egypt and Israel, the replacement of the Soviet presence in Egypt and the emergence of a viable alternative to the socialist economic model. The commercial gains for the US have included the phenomenal growth in exports to Egypt, which has turned the US into Egypt's major trading partner, as well as large profits from its investments in Egypt's petroleum and banking sectors.

For Egypt, the benefits have included an uninterrupted and substantial flow of aid on highly concessionary terms, alleviating the government import burden for food and other intermediates. The aid has largely financed the rehabilitation of basic utilities and social services, as well as refurbished the network of research institutions. Moreover, US support has been instrumental in democratizing and decentralizing the domestic political and economic environment, with major gains achieved in the development of a multi-party system, interest groups, a free press and a reinvigorated private sector.

However, the combination of poor economic management, and the disproportionately high emphasis of US aid on military expenditure, and infrastructural projects, as well as the anti-public sector bias of the aid policy have contributed to the misallocation of the country's scarce resources. This has diverted the economy from its self-sustaining course of development and accentuated the structural imbalance of the economy. Today, the government of Egypt faces an unprecedented crisis, not only in the management of its massive foreign debt but also in the finance of basic goods and services for over one third of the population who remain below the poverty line.

On the Egyptian side, the government has recognized its policy shortcomings and has implemented a major part of the reform package proposed by the aid donors and the IMF. The effect has been a sharp reduction in real incomes and growing unemployment, and projections indicate a further worsening of the situation for the foreseeable future. In other words, the magnitude of the problem is such that when structural adjustment is fully implemented, it will, at the very least, exacerbate the trend of falling living standards and at worst create serious social upheavals.

Egypt's principal aid donor—the US—could take a number of measures to cushion the strains of structural adjustment and support a reorientation toward long-term growth. The bulk of the project aid package should be redirected to favor the productive sectors, including agriculture and industry, without discrimination against the public sector. The military aid package should be restructured to support the development of an export-oriented defense industry. The trade relationship should be reviewed and Egyptian textile exports given preferential access to the now-protected US market. The US should also embark together with Egypt on a well-designed campaign to promote direct US investment in Egypt's productive sectors of the economy. Finally, the US should seriously consider forgiving most if not all of Egypt's $11.7 billion of outstanding debt to the US.[15]

Given the symbiotic nature of the aid relationship between the US and Egypt, it is to the advantage of both parties that the policy dialogue become more transparent, so that the legitimate interests of each are attended to in a spirit of pragmatic and effective cooperation.

References

1. World Bank, *Arab Republic of Egypt: Country Economic Memorandum,* Vol. II. Report No. 7447 (Washington, DC: World Bank, 1989).

2. David A. Baldwin, *Economic Statecraft* (New Jersey: Princeton University Press, 1985), p. 306.

3. Heba Handoussa, "Conflicting Objectives in the Egyptian-American Aid Relationship," in Earl L. Sullivan, ed., *Impact of Development Assistance on Egypt,* Cairo Papers in Social Science (Cairo: The American University in Cairo, September 1984).

4. Cumulative Economic Support Fund (ESF) disbursements equalled $6.2 billion (see American Embassy, Cairo, *Economic Trends Report: Egypt,* December 1985, p. 12) and cumulative PL 480 disbursements reached $2.6 billion (see Table 1).

5. Heba Handoussa, "The Impact of Foreign Assistance on Egypt's Economic Development: 1952-1986," a paper completed in July 1988 and presented to the Conference on

Aid, Capital Flows and Development in Talloires, France. The conference was jointly sponsored by the World Bank and the International Center for Economic Growth.

6. *Ibid.*

7. Adel A. Beshai, "Egypt and the Helping Hand," in Earl L. Sullivan, ed., *op. cit.*, p. 69.

8. American Embassy, Cairo, *Egyptian Economic Trends,* March 1989.

9. Heba Handoussa, "The Burden of Public Service Employment and Remuneration: A Case Study of Egypt," a monograph commissioned by the International Labor Office in Geneva in May 1988 and revised in September 1988, pp. 21-24.

10. Unless otherwise indicated, all of the statistics in this section can be found in Heba Handoussa, "The Impact of Foreign Assistance on Egypt's Economic Development: 1952-1986," *op. cit.*

11. American Embassy, Cairo, *Egyptian Economic Trends,* March 1989, p. 19.

12. Central Agency for Public Mobilization and Statistics, *Preliminary Results of the 1986 General Census of Population, Housing and Establishment* (Cairo, 1987), in Arabic.

13. Heba Handoussa, "Reform Policies for Egypt's Manufacturing Sector," paper presented to the Conference on Employment Strategy in Egypt. The conference was sponsored by the International Labor Organization, the Ministry of Manpower and Training, and the United Nations Development Program in Cairo in December 1988.

14. *Ibid.*, p. 9.

15. American Embassy, Cairo, *Egyptian Economic Trends,* March 1989, p. 21.

6 BUREAUCRACY AND FOREIGN AID IN EGYPT: THE PRIMACY OF POLITICS

Denis J. Sullivan

For all the attention paid to political economy in Egypt in the past decade, there is a notable gap in this literature on the fundamental question of whether Egypt has been developing. The research done on bureaucratic-authoritarianism, dependent development, and Sadat's *infitah* in Egypt discusses the economic growth and political changes in a period of two decades or more. Whether these changes translate into real economic and social development is something that surprisingly has yet to be determined.[1]

A notable exception to this gap is filled by Richard Adams who concludes that there is "growth without development" in Egypt's rural sector. He attributes this phenomenon to the government's determined policy of *control* of agriculture instead of *management* of it. It is a political technique used to maintain law and order and to extract a surplus out of agriculture, ostensibly for national development purposes. This is in fact a political technique designed to thwart opposition to the government as it caters to a potentially disruptive urban population. Politics takes priority over economic development. As will be demonstrated below, this priority is espoused by Egypt's foreign patrons as well.

To manage, on the other hand, is to seek to increase the flow of surplus out of agriculture by qualitatively changing the social and economic character of peasant production. Economic growth has occurred in Egypt's agricultural sector (as well as in industry and the service sector). But "development, in the sense of qualitative changes in the units of economic production, has not taken place in rural Egypt. As a consequence, rural poverty and inequality have been slowly increasing."[2] A general rise in rural wage rates in the 1980s notwithstanding, Korayem has pointed out that any improvement in rural incomes is due more to the inflow of remittances from family members working in the Gulf and other countries than it is to any specific program by the government to promote growth and development.[3]

Most observers of Egypt's rural economy agree overwhelmingly that Egypt has tremendous potential that is not being met. The principal reasons are government policies of control, manifested through such practices as price controls, ill-directed and/or insufficient subsidies, government quotas and procurement mandates placed on *fallahin* (farmers), and the improper management of marketing facilities, etc.[4] Government rationality is not in question; but it is the *type* of rationality that matters. The government maintains these policies more for *political* priorities than for *economic* development goals. The desire for regime maintenance and stability overrides economic objectives.

Aid for Development?

The United States and other governments generally share these priorities, as is reflected in their policies toward Egypt. Since 1975, Egypt has received over $14 billion[5] in economic assistance from the United States and a similar amount from other foreign donors. Yet Egypt has not demonstrated any profound ability to utilize this huge amount of economic assistance to promote its own economic development to a significant degree. Nor have foreign donors, especially the US, been able or willing to require Egypt to utilize these funds more effectively. This reflects the priority assigned to regime stability over economic efficiency.

TABLE 1
US Economic Assistance to Egypt, 1975-88

	1975-86	1987	1988
ESF*	10,467.20	815.0	815.0
of which:			
CIP**	3,610.50		
Cash Transfer	811.94		
Project Aid	4,944.76		
PL 480***	2,781.23	189.4	182.5
TOTAL	12,148.43	1,004.4	997.5

 * Economic Support Fund, a special category of aid designed for political support, its name notwithstanding.
 ** Commodity Import Program, designed to allow recipients "needed commodities from the US."
*** Food for Peace Program, Titles I and II, designed to allow recipients to import quantities of wheat and other products on lenient terms.

Source: USAID, Cairo Mission and Washington

In a period of vast influx of foreign aid, the Egyptian economy has grown, to be sure. Gross Domestic Product grew at an average of 8.4 percent in the period 1970-82 versus 4.3 percent in 1960-70.[6] That rate slowed, however, to roughly 5 percent between 1984 and 1987. Moreover, Egypt's inflation, trade and budget deficits, and foreign debt have also climbed dramatically. For instance, the amount of foreign exchange needed just to cover its debt obligations rose from 35.1 percent in 1984 to 45.8 percent in 1986. In short, the case of Egypt is not a major economic development success story, as are the cases of other semi-periphery states such as Brazil and South Korea, two "graduates" of American economic aid programs.

TABLE 2
Key Egyptian Economic Indicators
(US$ Million)

	1981	1982	1983	1984	1985	1986
GDP				20400	21300	22100
Trade Balance	-3920	-3715	-3823	-8400	-8200	-8100

Sources: USAID, IMF, OECD

The chief question here is why has Egypt not been able to take better advantage of the billions of dollars in economic aid it receives every year to promote its own growth and development with the ultimate objective of being able to lessen its dependence on such aid in future? There are obviously many reasons for Egypt's continuing dependence on foreign aid and continuing state of economic *crisis*,[7] including the vagaries of the international market place, internal economic structural imbalances, misguided government policies, and problems associated with foreign aid programs.

Without discounting the importance of any of these or other reasons, primary attention should nevertheless be directed toward a problem that is common to virtually all political and economic systems, whether in more developed or less developed countries, in socialist or capitalist economies. The problem is one of bureaucratic and political struggles inherent in the policy-making process. Bureaucracies and other political units compete for power to make or, at least, to influence policy. This competition is found not only *between* bureaucracies but also *within* them. Such competition is enough to cause numerous problems when it is engaged in by one government or political system. But when another government becomes involved, as in the case of a foreign donor, then the problems are not just doubled but increase exponentially. Not only does the government of Egypt (GOE) compete within and against itself, and between itself and the US, but the US is also competing within and against itself as its different bureaucracies have different goals for the aid program their government has established in Egypt.

Officials within Egypt's Ministry of Agriculture (MOA) are under great pressure not only from US Agency for International Development (AID) officials but also from Egyptian bureaucrats in other ministries and politicians in their government. AID is pushing the MOA to reform its policies in agriculture to allow a freer market system to determine cropping patterns, marketing and distribution of products, and overall prices, thus sending more appropriate signals to farmers and others as to which crops Egypt should be producing, selling domestically and even exporting. While many officials in the MOA are in considerable agreement with the AID argument and have been attempting to accomplish at least some of these goals, they are facing tremendous opposition from within the government, their own ministry, and other ministries, especially Irrigation, Industry, Supply, and Planning.

It is no small task to have to confront these pressures, from within the Egyptian bureaucracy and from American (principally AID) circles, especially in the face of continued uncertainty or lack of consensus within one's own ministry. There is so little agreement within Egypt on the appropriate economic and social path the country should be following—i.e., socialist, capitalist, Islamic or other[8]—that various voices dominate the policy debate within individual ministries and across the bureaucracy as a whole. These voices compete for President Mubarak's attention and in their quest for acceptance of their point of view, no consensus emerges. The result is that no serious action is taken to mend an economic system that has been in a state of crisis since 1984-85 and has since worsened. The decline in Egypt's principal foreign exchange earners—Suez Canal tolls, tourism, worker remittances, and oil[9]—only hastens the need for and lessens the ability to attain consensus on sound economic planning and policy reform. In the absence of this consensus, it falls to President Mubarak to outline the course of action his country will take to mend the shattered economy.

TABLE 3
Four Pillars of Egypt's Economy
(US$ Million)

	1981/82	1982/83	1983/84	1984/85	1985/86
Remittances	$3100	3750	3800	3550	3550
Oil	3329	2807	2957	2770	2100
Tourism	1000	1000	1050	1000	800
Suez Canal	909	957	974	897	900

Sources: Central Bank of Egypt, IMF, Ministry of Economy, US Embassy, and American Chamber of Commerce, Egypt

The main reason for this competition between Egyptian ministries supersedes ideology and comes down to individual and organizational self-interest. As various studies suggest, Egyptian organizations exhibit characteristics similar to bureaucracies in much of the world, regardless of geographic location or political circumstance. As Crozier explains, power—in various forms and wielded by numerous actors within a bureaucratic organization—is the universal phenomenon inherent in any hierarchical system. Bureaucracies, says Ayubi, concurring with established Marxist contentions, are essentially conservative and

> even if bureaucratic leaders desire change (and it is an important "if"), they are made so weak by the pattern of resistance of the different isolated strata within the bureaucracy, that they can use their power only in truly exceptional circumstances.

Yet, rather than tearing the organization apart, power is a necessary (since inevitable) part of the functioning of all bureaucracies, which maintain stability and a *minimum* of consensus through shared norms, especially the realization that each group's privileges depends to a large extent on the maintenance of other groups' privileges.[10] Beyond this minimum, consensus breaks down as bureaucrats compete against each other to increase their power, especially in a government facing changes due to proposed administrative reform, as in Egypt, or limited budgets, as in the US. Thus, regardless of the cultural-specific contention, most recently suggested by Springborg, that "competition has a negative connotation in Egyptian society as being against solidarity,"[11] such competition, even rivalry, is indeed alive and well in Egyptian bureaucracy and politics.

Egypt: The Bureaucratic State

The significance of bureaucracies in Egypt has long been apparent. Egyptian society as a whole is highly bureaucratized, with government agencies encroaching on virtually all aspects of life and death (and everything in between). It has been this way since Pharaonic times, say Weber and Ayubi, who separately explain how Egypt, throughout its 7000-year history, was and remains an example of "relatively clearly developed and quantitatively large bureaucracies" (Weber, 1947, p. 315), rendering it a "purely bureaucratic state" (Ayubi, 1980, p. 80). Education, religion, politics, agriculture, industry, banking, tourism, and much more are regulated and controlled by the state. Given the dominance of various bureaucracies in virtually all aspects of Egyptian economic, social, and political life, any hopes of changing any part of the system require working within (or possibly manipulating) the system. This is especially true of any attempts to promote economic development in Egypt, whether made by the Egyptian government, AID, the World Bank, General Motors, or any other donor or investor: development efforts inevitably come into contact with several agencies, each of which has some say in how those efforts are to be undertaken. Having said this, it is recognized that the government often works *outside* the system (i.e., its own system) when it needs things done[12] in a hurry (or at all), and AID officials express a similar desire to emulate the GOE in this respect.[13] In fact, working "outside the system" really means working outside the *normal* channels of operation, utilizing a more efficient—but nonetheless bureaucratic—agency or agencies over which an official or organization has power (meaning the ability of a "requesting agency" to obtain that which the "implementing" agency would not otherwise do on its own).[14]

In addition to the universal bureaucratic phenomenon of power, Egyptian organizations exhibit certain unique traits that render these bureaucracies more complex, less efficient, and less susceptible to reform than similar organizations elsewhere in the semi-periphery (e.g., states such as Brazil, Pakistan, South Korea, etc.). One of these traits is the ability for any college graduate to become an employee of the state, either as a civil servant or as part of a state industry. This guarantee of a job to college graduates was a promise made by Gamal Abdul-Nasser in his drive to change Egyptian society into a "technocracy,"[15] where technology, as the new ideology of the state, would require a highly educated body-politic, primarily relying on a technical elite to push Egypt along the path toward national (especially economic) development. The guarantee had the equally significant benefit of giving a job to those who would be educated and who might otherwise organize against the regime if job opportunities were lacking and economic conditions remained poor. This guarantee was retained by Sadat for similar reasons. Mubarak, in his first years as president, maintained the guarantee but soon realized its great cost to the government payroll, which was supporting nearly one-third of Egypt's labor force. Mubarak began to undertake the risky, but essential, task of backing away from this inherited promise. The waiting period between graduation from college and being hired by the government expanded from 1-2 years to 2-4 years. Then, word spread throughout government agencies that a college degree no longer guaranteed its holder a position in the public sector.[16] The promise was never really rescinded publicly, but by 1987, the public's realization of the long waiting period for a job and the bureaucrats' admissions of their intolerance for hiring just *anybody* greatly reduced the frequency of recruitment by this method. The bureaucracy continues to grow, but holding a degree no longer guarantees someone that he or she will be part of that growth.

Bureaucracy and Development

Bureaucrats remain key figures in Egypt's quest for economic growth and self-sustaining development. They have a great deal of power in planning and implementing development objectives. Their efficiency and effectiveness is crucial to the success of such planning. In short, they can promote or inhibit economic development, depending on the role they choose to play in this quest. For instance,

a bureaucracy may contribute to economic development in two major ways: (1) the provision of services and other aspects of the infrastructure needed for economic growth; and (2) direct participation in the economic field as an "entrepreneur," either out of ideological choice or as a result of other practical considerations.[17]

In other words, an efficient, activist-type bureaucracy may provide the necessary services and leadership to promote development. However, administrative bottlenecks are "among the main causes

behind the fact that economic plans too often fall short of expectations. . . . Administrative deficiencies could be as crippling to economic
growth as lack of capital."[18] Bureaucrats who work for their own
personal interests and advancement (economic, political, or other)
may also do much to inhibit governmental or ministerial plans for
development. When bureaucrats of different ministries begin to compete
against each other, or even when the tasks given to different ministries
result in unintended competition with other agencies, the struggle to
maintain or increase one's power in the organization often obscures
and transcends in importance the national struggle for economic
development.

Traditional bureaucracies entrusted with the responsibilities of
formulating, planning, executing, and monitoring Egypt's development
objectives have, to a large extent, failed in their tasks.[19] Other
organizations, most notably the Egyptian army and Islamic groups,
have recently taken on these tasks. The army is building roads,
developing cities (including providing basic infrastructure to support
these), growing crops to feed its own troops and even marketing and
distributing the surplus to the Egyptian public—for a profit. Islamic
groups have developed efficient social services, most notably schools
and hospitals, out of frustration over the government's inability to
recognize the needs of specific communities and to target these
communities with development projects in response to those needs.
Thus, the entrepreneurial role so necessary to promote growth and
development is not being taken up by the government or most of its
individual ministries. Moreover, development is further inhibited by
the competition of these ministries against one another, either in
their individual approaches to development or in their sheer struggle
to survive, to maintain their power, their position, their "status."

Bureaucracy in Egypt has become very defensive and non-activist
as the government struggles with economic crisis. Instead of being
able to work to promote development, the government is by necessity
more involved in crisis management, in averting financial collapse.
It has little energy and even fewer resources to work on such "luxuries"
as *development!* The government is, of course, devoting time and
money to its development priorities.[20] It is able to do so, to a large
extent, with the assistance of foreign donors, principally the United
States. The problem remains, however, that the Egyptian government is
often at odds with these donors—especially the US—over how to
promote development and where to invest the financial and human
resources to do so. The prior existing problem, again, is finding

agreement within its own bureaucracy (i.e., between its various bureaucracies) on what "*the* government position" on development is.

The Government of Egypt and Development

We will not speak of *the* Egyptian government's view of and approach to development, as we do not speak of *the* US government's view or approach. Rather, we must attempt to look at the numerous views and approaches of the various ministries and governmental bodies, especially the perceptions of development held by the political heads of these groups. Personalities remain important in Egypt, both in pushing for reform and in leading efforts to resist economic initiative or upset other ministers' attempts at economic reform.[21] Given the size of the Egyptian bureaucracy plus the diversity of opinion among its leaders, it is essential to differentiate between various agencies and their leaders as well as to highlight the consensus of opinion when and where that does exist.

In an attempt to suggest that there is indeed consensus of opinion on the overall approach to development, the government appears to speak with one voice, and in fact to use only one word: *gradualism,* which describes the pace at which it is willing to undertake economic and possibly political reform. Officials from various ministries— Planning and International Cooperation, Agriculture, Economics, Finance, Foreign Affairs, Industry, and Irrigation—all say Egypt agrees with donors on the need for economic reform as a prerequisite to development, but will undertake such reform only on its own timetable, taking into consideration its political and social environment, which they say AID, the IMF, the World Bank, and other donors ignore. Yet within this unity there is a diversity of opinion that often descends to open inter-ministerial rivalry on what economic reform entails and how it will be achieved. Such opinions obviously reflect each ministry's organizational responsibilities as well as individuals' interests.[22]

Egypt's Ministry of Agriculture, especially under the leadership of Yusuf Wali, has remained a major force in promoting economic development. The focus, obviously, is to increase productivity in the agriculture sector; but the hope is to use growth here to promote development throughout the economy. Many MOA officials recognize the need for economic reform, not only on the macroeconomic issues of exchange rates, energy prices, subsidies and interest rates, but more directly on the micro-level of agricultural production costs, government quotas and procurement mandates placed on the farmers.

Still, the MOA does not speak with one voice on these issues as many assistant secretaries and project directors worry how such reform will affect their own power bases and pocketbooks. One MOA official suggests that the MOA

> wants the free market; we want to help the producer *[fallahin];* we'd like to get rid of subsidies on inputs [fertilizers, seeds, credit], but it is hard to do. There is a network of interconnected interests so we'll do it in our own way, in our own time.[23]

This advocate of gradualism feels that it will take time to move Egypt to a free market. He agrees that "every Egyptian would like the private sector to take care of everything because it would have the flexibility to do it better." But he suggests that the "private sector is not ready, not mature enough yet. It may therefore hurt the consumer more than help him." To illustrate his resistance to quick change, especially as demanded by AID, he feels that succumbing to AID's pressure on Egypt to open its doors to imported frozen meat would hurt Egypt. He argues that opening wide Egypt's doors to imported frozen meat would force local meat prices down, making this sector less profitable and lessening the demand for animal fodder. He agrees that the result would be that Egypt would then use less of its scarce land resources to raise feed and could turn those resources over to food production for people. But the long-term problem is that Egyptians would also change their food habits, become accustomed to frozen meat, as they became accustomed to rice in upper Egypt,[24] and would soon have to pay even higher prices for this meat because it is currently being subsidized by European and American governments, subsidies he says are scheduled to end in 3 or 4 years. What this official failed to say is that his own *gamoosa* [waterbuffalo] herd, which is quite substantial and is sold off in the domestic market as fresh meat, would also become less profitable if Egypt relied more on imported beef, and he would lose a substantial part of his real livelihood.

A top official of Egypt's principal bank for development and agricultural credit is another staunch opponent of AID's demand that Egypt open its doors to beef imports. He also heads up a beef cooperative and obviously does not want the increased competition that would come from unlimited imports. This pattern of dual and related jobs is more the norm than the exception in the MOA. Various undersecretaries have large farms, are beef producers, or have stakes in the various fertilizer and seed companies in Egypt. Given the low and unchanging salaries for government employees, such outside economic endeavors are a must for the vast majority of these workers, including the high-level ones who can use their positions of authority in government to help private sector and foreign companies hoping to invest in Egypt's large and potentially profitable market.

An important question is whether these officials (a) use their position to contravene existing policy decisions made by their superiors or (b) actively work to prevent such decisions from being made. The first part of this question cannot be answered without a more extensive analysis of the policy implementation process; but knowledge of other bureaucracies' acts of both commission and omission suggest that such a move on the part of Egyptian officials in the MOA is certainly possible.[25] The second part of the question is answered very strongly in the affirmative. By their own admission, numerous civil servants in the MOA and elsewhere in the Egyptian bureaucracy actively lobby their superiors, as well as friends in other ministries, to avoid reform.

Lack of consensus within the MOA is thus due, in part, to outside economic interests that many officials have, interests that might be undercut if the MOA pursued certain reforms or policies. Such disagreements are also due to a great deal of intra-ministerial rivalry over "turf." These power struggles are often quite blatant and are evident in casual conversations with MOA officials and even more in meetings within the MOA and between MOA and AID officials.

The events of one such meeting underscore this continuing battle over turf. The meeting was scheduled to discuss a certain AID-funded, US Department of Agriculture-contracted project to improve data collection and analysis (DCA) in Egypt's agricultural sector. AID brought in a highly respected American consultant to discuss how this project should proceed now that the USDA was ending its participation as contractor. The agricultural economist's suggestion in his presentation at the meeting was to support the efforts of a certain undersecretary in the MOA "to establish a data base; to access it; to do micro-economic analyses on commodities, cost of their production, etc., in order to do accurate *forecasting* of Egypt's agricultural potential" and ultimately to utilize this data to make suggestions to the GOE on economic and policy reform in agriculture. The office best suited to handle the responsibilities of continuing this project,[26] suggested this consultant, is an MOA office headed by a young Egyptian with direct access to Minister Wali. The first question raised, after the presentation by the American agricultural specialist, was one which most AID and MOA officials were expecting. It came from another undersecretary in the MOA, one who heads up an agriculture research center in Egypt, which was created essentially with American aid. This undersecretary, who is much older than his young rival, asked "where is the link between my young colleague's office and my center?" What he was asking really was "will it be under my control since my center was set up to do what you now want this office to do: economic analysis!?" The question was a "hot potato" that was passed from the speaker to a high-level AID official to an advisor to Minister Wali to the younger undersecretary and to several others who wanted to "address" this significant question but not to answer it.

At one point, an official of Egypt's Agricultural Economics Research Institute, yet another bureaucratic structure designed to utilize the thousands of Egyptians trained as agriculture specialists and the parent bureaucracy to the elder undersecretary's research center, pointed out that "the rough draft [of the project paper] subordinated the center to the office," i.e., the older undersecretary was intended to answer to his younger rival. The latter, as well as the American consultant, scrambled to explain that the *final draft* "corrects this." The young protege of Minister Wali tried to clarify the situation by saying "the output of your center is research, which then becomes input to my office and the output of my office is policies." Yet even while trying to allay the fears of the other MOA officials who saw this young "upstart" as encroaching on their turf, threatening to chip away at their power bases, the undersecretary also let it be known that the matter had in fact already settled between Minister Wali, AID and his office:

> We have a system of research with *some* problems. Data is collected on an ad-hoc basis and the results of erroneous data are erroneous decisions. The existing system has gaps which reflect on policy decisions. My office is to fill in those gaps. To do so, we will call on the expertise of my colleague's research center, universities, outsiders, etc.

The entire discussion session continued along these lines. Even Minister Wali's advisor, who is also a professor of agriculture at an Egyptian university, asked that the final draft be amended to include the word "universities" after "USAID/MOA" as recipients of information collected from this project. After the meeting, one agriculture officer laughed in frustration over the futility of the meeting. "Do you believe it!? Not *one* question about a budget or financing or the ability to fulfill project goals. It was all a matter of turf!"

This line of discussion had been expected all along, before the meeting even took place. In fact, the young undersecretary even asked AID officials to send the invitations to the meeting to all the appropriate MOA officials because if *he* had done so, those being invited might not have come. He told his colleagues at AID that his MOA colleagues/rivals might be "offended," or would surely have realized that this data collection project was already under his control, not subject to discussion or bargaining. In effect, the meeting was a "trap" of sorts, and AID collaborated in it. It brought into one place several MOA officials, many of whom were vying for control of the project and thus for the money and prestige that these projects can bring both to the office and the person in charge of them. It was then made clear to all of the officials present who would be heading this project—which is, in fact, insignificant money-wise by AID standards in Egypt, being only a $5 million project. The elder undersecretary already directs two AID projects[27] worth several times more than that. But the younger protege of Wali recognized that the real significance of the project was the concern with economic and policy reform. While this is a politically risky area, it is an issue whose time has come which is thus likely to bring great benefits to those who are seen as being in the forefront of suggesting how that reform should take place. Also, given that Minister Wali faced enough resistance in the Cabinet to his policy reforms, he needed someone he could trust to head this initiative in his own ministry, which is still struggling to build a consensus on the issue of reform.

This example highlights not only the intraministerial rivalries and struggles for power, prestige, and project funding that are rampant in the MOA and doubtless throughout Egypt's sprawling bureaucracy. It also highlights another reason for the continuing growth of bureaucratic structures. Certain ministers or other government officials lack the political courage to take a clear stand (e.g., saying that one research center is subordinate to another) for fear of alienating certain bureaucrats (who probably have powerful patrons in the government). As a result, the government builds *parallel organizations,* entrusted with tasks similar to existing agencies but staffed by "insiders" who are given the necessary authority (including finances) to implement the tasks with which those existing agencies were already charged. The latter continue to attempt to achieve their goals but are without any real authority to accomplish anything. Thus, Egypt has numerous agricultural research agencies, but the one given the real power depends on domestic and international patronage. This pattern is repeated in other spheres as well. In foreign affairs, for instance, there are parallel bureaucracies in the Cabinet Ministry of Foreign Affairs, and the Ministry of State for Foreign Affairs. In population planning and defense we see the same pattern. Which bureaucracy dominates its shadow bureaucracy depends almost entirely on the personalities who head them.[28]

Interministerial Competition

Organizational and personal rivalries, based on related interests, are evident and endemic between bureaucracies, not just within them. And even if a particular minister decides on certain initiatives to change, reform, or otherwise improve the operation of his/her organization or the economic or social concerns for which he/she is entrusted, rival ministers—especially in Egypt, but in any country—may have something to say about any proposed changes. Even if the changes cover areas which otherwise appear to be wholly within one ministry's range of responsibilities (e.g., prices of crops), other ministries can find a reason to assert themselves and disrupt any plans for change. For instance, one would assume (as most AID officials new to Egypt did) that since the government was controlling prices, cropping patterns and marketing of many crops, such control would be the responsibility of MOA. However, this is not the case.

While the MOA has fought internally as well as with AID over which crops to "free up" and which ones to continue to control, the more intense and significant struggle is occurring between the MOA and those ministries which stake a greater claim to certain crops. In the list of agricultural policy reforms that MOA has undertaken, a consistent set of crops seems above complete manipulation—cotton, sugarcane, and rice—because other ministries fight to maintain control over these.

Nevertheless, Wali has been somewhat successful in reforming the agricultural sector. Some of the reforms that he was able to push through the Cabinet include:

1. In December 1986, procurement prices for rice, sesame, soybeans, wheat, lentils and sugarcane were *increased an average of 25 percent,* but not freed up completely.
2. In January 1987 delivery quotas for all crops were removed, except for cotton, sugarcane and 50 percent of rice. Mandated cropping quotas were terminated for corn, broad beans, and wheat, but not for cotton, sugarcane or rice. Cotton procurement prices were increased 20 percent, with increases to be passed through to final consumers. This still leaves local cotton prices at half the world market prices.[29] Procurement prices are administered prices set by the government and used by it to buy products from farmers. Delivery quotas are mandatory and fixed amounts of crops to be sold by the farmer to the government. Procurement prices are at least 25 percent lower than the open market price in the immediate post-harvest period.[30] Table 4 lists the delivery quotas for several crops *before* the reforms listed above went into effect. With the reforms, only cotton, sugarcane, and rice are to retain their delivery quotas.

TABLE 4
Delivery Quotas by the Government, 1985

	Output to be sold to government*	Average Yield	Proportion of output procured by government**
	Units per feddan		%
Cotton (metric qantars)	all output	6.8	100
Wheat (ardeb)	1–2.5	10.5	17
Rice (ton)	1–1.5	2.5	50
Sugarcane (ton)	all output	37.6	100
Onions (ton)	6–8	8.7	80
Lentils (ardeb)	1–2.5	3.5	50
Sesame (ardeb)	1–2.5	3.5	50
Groundnuts (ardeb)	2–8	10.9	46
Horsebeans (ardeb)	2–3.5	6.8	40

* The upper and lower limits of the range depend on the estimated productivity of the land.
** Estimated on the assumption that the average quantity delivered to the government falls at the midpoint of the range of procurement.

Source: Ministry of Agriculture as quoted in Simon Commander, *The State and Agricultural Development in Egypt Since 1973* (London: The Overseas Development Institute, 1987).

Thus, Wali has made some progress in moving the government away from the business of trying to dictate agricultural production toward putting much of those decisions in the hands of the actual producers, the *fallahin*. Nevertheless, resistance to his efforts remains strong within the Cabinet and other political circles, including the governors of key agricultural regions.[31] Certain crops are beyond reform at present because other ministries assert an interest in how these crops are priced and in the quantities available for "public" (read, state) consumption.

Cotton. Cotton is a major input to the clothing industry in Egypt and the Ministry of Industry does not want any increase in the price of this input, nor does it want the MOA to make decisions on the quantities of its production. Since cotton is Egypt's principal export, various other ministries have a stake in its production and price, including the ministries of Economy, Finance, Supply and Foreign Trade. In fact, this is the only crop that AID officials admit Egypt should control since it has a near monopoly on long-staple cotton trade in the world market. Yet, according to AID officials, the control should be in the opposite direction from what is occurring now, i.e., the GOE should raise the procurement price *above* the world market price, instead of keeping it at *half* that price, in order to give an incentive to more *fallahin* to produce more of it. Prices are low so that state companies run by the Ministry of Industry can make clothes inexpensively while turning a profit. The government as a whole also profits as its Ministry of Trade buys the crop at half its real price and sells it abroad at its market value. Once again, the farmer loses as the MOA can do little to help in the face of more powerful rivals in the government.

Rice. Rice production requires a great deal of water, an agricultural input that is provided free of charge to the *fallahin*. The Ministry of Irrigation thus has a greater say in the cropping pattern and price structure of this crop than does MOA. The former obviously does not want to relinquish any of its control over decision-making regarding the production and pricing of rice. Power granted to a bureaucracy cannot be take away—at least not without a struggle. This inter-bureaucratic squabbling over turf continues despite the fact that Egypt is on the brink of being a net importer of rice for the first time in its history.[32] Cooperation between these key bureaucracies is essential to turn the situation around. Otherwise, Egypt will lose a previously important foreign exchange earner and will even have to expend more of its already scarce hard currency to meet local consumption needs for rice. This scenario also interests and worries the ministries of Supply and Trade as well as Finance, Planning and Economy. Instead of allowing the MOA to take the lead in trying to reverse this trend through an innovative, if common-sensical, reform of rice cropping and pricing, these ministries propose alternative plans, ranging from even greater control to maintaining the status quo for fear that nothing can be done anyway to reverse the trend toward losing a once valuable export, especially in the face of unceasing population increases and soil erosion compounded by a declining water table. Cooperation seems unlikely as these ministries scramble to retain as much control and power as has been granted to them throughout the years.

Wheat. Domestic wheat production plus wheat imports are probably the most crucial commodities to bureaucrats in the Ministry of Supply, which is charged with providing substantial amounts of cheap food—primarily wheat, but also sugar, rice and beans—to all of Egypt, and especially to Cairo. Efforts by MOA to reform wheat production are resisted strongly by the Ministry of Supply for fear that such a change would diminish its ability to provide the supplies in the quantities and at the price the government feels is necessary to prevent social unrest. Not only does the Ministry of Supply resist such change in order not to relinquish any of its authority or power, but if the reform led to a shortage of supplies or an increase in prices, the result could be a repeat of the food riots of January 1977 and it would most likely be the Ministry of Supply that would pay the political price. Food aid is considered essential by most in the MOA as well. There are few in Egypt's bureaucracy (i.e., in its various ministries) who would say that food aid is a disincentive[33] to Egyptian farmers and thus should be stopped. The need for food—especially low-cost food—is just too great in the short-term for any responsible government official to look a gift-horse in the mouth, even if the long-term consequences are recognized, as indeed they are by some in the MOA.

Citrus. One crop that does not often come up in conversations between AID and the MOA in discussions about reforming agriculture is citrus. There are controls on the growing and marketing of this group of crops and there was even one instance when the MOA placed its name on a list of crops to be excluded from a complete "freeing up" of prices and production. In a one-on-one meeting between an AID official and a young undersecretary at MOA, the latter told the AID agricultural economist that his ministry did not want to include citrus in the policy reform conditions being discussed between the two agencies for the simple fact the "oranges are not dealt with by MOA. The Ministry of Trade deals with this crop because it is used as barter with the Soviet bloc."[34] At the same time, this aide to the Minister of Agriculture suggested that this was merely a negotiating chip his ministry would use in meetings between AID and MOA as well as within the Cabinet to decide on reforms. In negotiations between the Minister and (then) USAID Director Frank Kimball, "[The Minister] will say that political pressures force him to exclude cotton, rice and oranges from reform. Kimball won't like any exclusions and Wali will concede by giving up oranges and that'll be the compromise." The Minister of Agriculture would not budge on cotton or rice mainly because he did not have the authority to include them in reform, for reasons described above. And in his negotiations with his fellow Cabinet members, he would be able to say that he was forced to give up oranges in his discussions with Kimball but would suggest that by his efforts, cotton and rice were not compromised.

However, all did not go as the MOA aide had suggested. To be sure, Director Kimball protested to the Minister that no crops should be excluded from reform and the Minister did indeed say that cotton, rice, and citrus were beyond his control. Citrus remained on the list of crops to be excluded from reform, but the AID-MOA statement did express the hope that all these crops would be reformed but that this would require "action by several ministries."[35]

The Ministry of Planning is charged with overseeing all of these various bureaucratic interests, primarily in order to formulate and execute Egypt's five-year plans. The Ministry of Planning is one of the bureaucratic holdovers from the Nasserist era, a time of major state-dominance in the economy, indeed in all of Egyptian society. The nature of this organization is to plan, to oversee and to insure the performance of economic enterprises—in short, to control. It is thus not interested in allowing "the market" to determine supply or prices.

Dr. Kamal Ganzouri, the Minister of Planning, clearly sees his role not as being to oversee the Ministry's gradual obsolescence but to assure its success in managing Egypt's economic performance. Indeed, Ganzouri, who was also Minister of International Cooperation until 1987, is widely regarded as opposed to much reform of the policy structure. Yet he recognizes that Egypt's economy is in a shambles and that even he cannot do much to reverse this situation to any considerable degree. He thus acknowledges the need for some policy reform, but has been the main proponent of the "gradualism" approach to such reform. His commitment to a slow pace and piecemeal approach to reform has distinguished him from colleagues in the Cabinet who favor a more extensive and faster approach. Minister for Cabinet Affairs Atif Obaid is said to be the intellectual force behind those Egyptian politicians calling for more thorough economic reform. He claims as like-minded colleagues Yusif Wali, Salah Hamad of the Central Bank of Egypt, Fuad Sultan, Minister of Tourism, and Muhammad Abdul-Wahab, Ministry of Industry. USAID officials have been doing what they can to promote the political fortunes of these officials, especially at the expense of Ganzouri.

Much of the competition between Ganzouri and Wali is more than a clash of bureaucratic interests. In his seven years in office, Mubarak has yet to name a vice-president, i.e., someone designated by President Mubarak to be his successor. Wali is Secretary General of the ruling National Democratic Party and in 1987 was thought to be the main candidate for Vice-President. Ganzouri, as the head of planning in Egypt, wields enormous economic and political clout, and is said to be in competition for that same position, as are several others. Mubarak recognizes this rivalry and has tried to placate leading ministers by designating them as deputy prime ministers. Despite the various changes of prime ministers by Mubarak, the following individuals have been deputy prime ministers since 1985: Wali, Ganzouri, and Foreign Minister Ismat Abdul-Maguid.

The rivalries and struggles for power between numerous ministries keep the organizations from cooperating to improve the functioning of a bureaucratic structure which has an inordinate say in the running of Egypt's economic system.

Inside and outside the Egyptian government, many argue that the answers to Egypt's problems are to be found in the private sector along with a reform (an Egyptian *perestroika*?) of Egypt's bloated public sector. While there may be a good deal of truth to these suggestions, the state will continue to be an important actor in Egyptian economic decision making, as the state is in virtually every society. Turning to the private sector as a panacea would be to ignore the equally important task of improving the capabilities of the public sector.

If Egyptian bureaucrats were better managers, perhaps the economic system over which they have power would be performing better. If they relinquished some of their power to the private sector, perhaps the same could be said. But we cannot expect bureaucrats in any society, or any organization, to give up easily that which they struggle to maintain, i.e., their power. Given the primacy of politics in the bureaucracy and in the various aid programs in Egypt, one hope for economic development may be found in administrative reform. This would entail either a complete overhaul of a bureaucracy, which may require a political revolution, or improvement in the managerial capabilities of existing bureaucratic structures[36] (i.e., training bureaucrats or recruiting good managers).

There may also be hope in accepting the fact that political disputes exist between bureaucracies and exploiting that reality to deal with bureaucratic hold-ups which inhibit economic progress. Some ministries struggle to control certain crops (or other commodities) even if the effort is non-rational in an economic sense, because this control may be all the power they have. They may be willing to use that power to barter with another ministry to gain control over something they covet more. For instance, in a meeting between Egypt's Minister of Industry and an AID economist, the Minister said that if the MOA "let me sell fertilizer at world prices, I'd give them [control over] cotton."[37] When one of the young aides of the Minister of Agriculture heard this from AID officials, he said without hesitation, "We'll take it!" MOA officials did not know prior to this that the Ministry of Industry was even interested in such a deal. The competition between Egyptian ministries is obviously so stiff that there is little discussion between them. It thus, at times, requires an outsider to act as a go-between or a catalyst for change.

Whether "reformists" or "gradualists," whether in the MOA, Ministry of Planning, Ministry of Economy, or Ministry of Irrigation, the consistent answer to the question of how can Egypt better utilize foreign aid to promote development was: "good management." To the gradualists, this meant improving government control through increased efficiency to operate state-run industries and services better as well as to improve the government's overall planning apparatus, especially to improve the extraction of revenues from companies, farmers, and citizens. To the reformists, it meant allowing the private sector an increased (but not total) role in the economy, as well as recruiting into the bureaucracy a more diverse group of trained professionals, people who are not only good with ideas but who have the ability to implement those ideas. The head of the office in the Ministry of Agriculture dealing with USAID Affairs bemoans the poor quality of managers in his ministry. When asked about the Ministry's approach to development, he said:

> Maybe we need good management. We have thousands of people who hold M.A.s and Ph.D.s in agriculture in Egypt; but who has an M.A. or Ph.D. in agricultural *management*? Maybe two or three. How can we then prepare or choose who will *lead* us in agricultural development? All of our workers are sinking in papers. Where is the time to think, to develop projects? We suggest thousands of projects, but they are not well thought-out. Who will take the initiative to develop these? Where is the political *will* or even the *ability* to lead? *Mafish!*[38]

This person's concern, reiterated by many Egyptian bureaucrats, is that Egypt is devoid of effective leadership from the top of the political structure down through the bureaucracy. Another MOA undersecretary and former director of an AID-funded development project echoes his colleague's concern for better management in the ministry while asking that AID fulfill its stated intentions:

> AID brought a new idea into Egypt, which I hope it achieves, and that is to *develop* Egypt, instead of just helping to increase production. That [latter idea] was all the US Embassy thought was necessary. Now, AID realizes that it should help Egypt and all LDCs to stand on their own feet [to build institutional capacity]. Egypt must develop its own resources, but it needs effective leadership to do so. Otherwise, if Egypt just sits around and waits every year to get money from abroad, dependency will continue without development.[39]

This official's fear is that Egypt is doing just that, "sitting around," becoming ever-more dependent, especially on the US, yet not utilizing the enormous financial resources available to it year after year to promote its own development—i.e., its own institutions whereby trained Egyptians rely on their own resources to achieve economic progress. Yet there is a commitment to improving their record on development, if only the politics of the aid program and their own bureaucratic rivalries can be transcended. Perhaps Egypt could put the billions of dollars of aid to better use if that aid were targeted less at demonstration projects and capital investments and more at promoting the human resources of the country. A similar statement might be made about the government's own budget priorities, the typical "guns vs. butter" argument. As one MOA official put it, "Development means developing the *persons* first and the persons will develop the country."[40] This perception of development is the same as that of many development agencies throughout the world. The Ford Foundation seeks to help developing countries help themselves by relying on the talents and resources available in their own countries. The Italian government's aid agency is in Ethiopia to build institutional capacity. ANERA, the American Near East Refugee Association, is working with Palestinians to build institutions, and to develop economic and social infrastructure on the West Bank and Gaza Strip in the absence of government efforts to help them.[41]

Ministry of Irrigation officials also cry out for better-trained civil servants:

> We don't have enough staff to do the research necessary to improve water use and management here [in Egypt]. We didn't even have enough qualified engineers available to us until recently. But we still are in great need of more, better trained personnel. We have to send our workers to the US for training, to get Ph.D.s and M.Sc.s.[42]

The problem, of course, is that once these people are trained abroad, a good percentage of them stay abroad. There is also a considerable "internal brain-drain" in that many Egyptians are finding work in the Egyptian private sector or with foreign companies or agencies (e.g., roughly 100 Egyptians work in the AID offices) because the pay is substantially better than civil servants' salaries. Thus, while the need in Egypt is to pare down the overgrown and crushing government bureaucracy and public sector while allowing the private sector to thrive, the government needs at the same time to improve the salaries of its employees in order to attract the best (or at least better) qualified and trained workers. This reform of the bureaucratic structure would, however, require a major initiative on the part of numerous key figures in the Egyptian government, including President Mubarak and several current Cabinet members, especially Atif Obaid, Yusif Wali, and Kamal Ganzouri. Given the rivalries between ministers, this kind of innovation and initiative is unlikely.

The rivalries so obvious and often detrimental to development plans on the Egyptian side find their counterpart on the American side of this aid relationship. And given that the US government has committed itself to supporting Egypt economically, politically and militarily, a review of Egypt's efforts at promoting development necessitates a look at how American bureaucracies interact with one another, as well as with their Egyptian colleagues.

USAID and Development

Since its inception in 1961, AID has attempted to become a major voice for promoting development in the Third World. However, given that "the organization is always a subsystem of a more comprehensive social system," such as the US government, it necessarily accepts "the generalized values of the superordinate system."[43] In other words, AID's values are subordinate to the overtly political values of the US government and AID has thus been doing more to promote US interests in the Third World than to promote development there. Nevertheless, while its developmental efforts are generally overshadowed and often undercut by political machinations within donor and recipient governments, the ideas and determination to succeed in these efforts remain. And while AID officials' preferred goal to promote development has remained relatively constant over its 25-year history, its definition of development and thus the methods it uses to achieve it have changed due to a great deal of organizational and individual learning.

One significant change in AID's approach to development has come about in the last decade or so, beginning during the Carter presidency[44] but being strengthened and encouraged under the Reagan administration.[45] This change in approach to promoting development resulted from a great many AID officials becoming frustrated with what they believed to be the failures of many Third World states to utilize foreign aid efficiently. The AID officials blamed this failure especially on statist policies subsidizing urban consumers as well as protecting and supporting inefficient industries, placing the economic burden for this urban bias on the farmers and indeed the overall agriculture sector—generally, the largest sector in Third World economies and the one with the potential for being an engine of growth for the entire economy.

AID officials have also become increasingly frustrated[46] over their own government's tying their hands by compromising with Third World governments for reasons that are political but have had negative economic effects. From this frustration over numerous experiences with state-dominated and inefficient economies, AID officials and the organization as a whole adopted a "new orthodoxy," a new approach to promoting development. The original goals of promoting economic growth and satisfying basic human needs, while still desirable, have become upstaged by AID's new desire to promote private sector interests and efficient government management of the economy. The private sector is viewed by AID as the best—and maybe the last—hope for economic development; it is also a traditional favorite of many in Washington as the engine of political development and democratization.

AID officials in various mission offices around the world are the direct sources not only for gaining experience and learning the problems of trying to promote development in Third World countries, but also for making use of such experiences and putting new ideas to work. The frustration with specific host governments and their policies is expressed by AID officials in various parts of the world in different ways. For example, in Pakistan, AID officials' frustration with the government of Pakistan's urban-biased cum agriculture-restrictive policies has been expressed in a confrontationalist and outright hostile fashion, with AID officials outwardly provoking a run-in with the host government by publicly criticizing the policies.[47] This open hostility also occurred in Egypt,[48] but AID officials have now moved on to a new stage of frustration: one manifested more by resignation with the political reality within Egypt and between Egypt and the US than by provoking the government in the hope of pushing economic reform.

AID set up its mission office in Cairo in 1975 to pursue its traditional goals, but when the funding grew dramatically in the late 1970s as a reward to Sadat for signing the Camp David accords and the Egyptian-Israeli peace treaty, AID's role went "beyond issues of equity, basic human needs, and the poor majority [because] the concerns of the poor can only be met within the framework of economic growth."[49] Through its experiences in Egypt and much of the Third World, AID has opted for or been given increasing responsibilities in Egypt. From 1975 to 1989 and beyond, AID has been expected to fulfill the monumental task of assisting the government in: rebuilding a war-damaged economy; developing a modernized urban infrastructure (sewers, telephones, transportation, utilities, port facilities) supportive of economic growth; promoting the private sector in an economy which is highly state-controlled, -subsidized, and -planned; satisfying basic human needs in a society where the government has already done much to establish a far-reaching minimum; and promoting overall economic development, especially by encouraging a complete overhaul of the economy through drastic economic reforms of foreign exchange and interest rates, government procurement policies and monopolies, and massive subsidization of food and energy consumption. In other words, AID has undertaken a major plan of reworking an entire economy in a more perfect image. The task is monumental but AID has had the money to attempt it—more money than it has ever had to work with in any one country in so short a time. To spend such huge amounts with such a major goal of radical change of an economy inevitably led to AID's need to do more than merely monitor the distribution of funds between a contracting third party and the recipient government, which is the theoretical and legal requirement. It led also to AID's desire to have a major voice in the implementation end of the process—a voice which is technically to be supervisory, not dictating.

Despite the lackluster performance of their efforts in Egypt, AID officials are nevertheless convinced of the correctness of the approach they are taking in Egypt to promote development. The approach is: (1) the funding of various and diverse projects, from agricultural and industrial to population planning and health projects; (2) promoting the private sector at the expense of state enterprises; and (3) generally pushing for economic liberalization and the decline of state domination of economic concerns (e.g., subsidies, state industries, etc.). These officials are also quite sure of what is the wrong approach to development: cash transfers and PL 480 Title I food aid. They say that these two methods of transferring aid to Third World countries not only do not promote development, but in fact inhibit development as they make Third World governments ever more dependent on the US (or other donors). The governments thus become "welfare states," not working to reform their own systems to promote agricultural and industrial productivity and greater self-reliance. AID officials, especially in Egypt, are increasingly vocal in their opposition to these forms of aid funding in developing countries as they face more influential lobbies in favor of these forms: lobbies such as US Embassy officials in Egypt, a few members of Congress (who determine how aid will be spent in general terms), United States Department of Agriculture (which has been quite successful in keeping PL 480 food aid alive for the benefit of American farmers regardless of its impact on farmers in recipient nations), and White House officials, whose prime interest is in maintaining a stable, friendly government in Egypt.

Watching billions of dollars being spent in numerous and diverse economic and social fields but with no significant overall impact on development, AID officials in Egypt have become quite frustrated. The Egyptian government has proved unable to provide a better policy climate, which could take more advantage of the economic aid provided Egypt. Certain elements of the American government have also often undermined AID's efforts, usually by siding with the government of Egypt in rejecting AID demands for reform and in lobbying Congress to turn the aid program into a cash transfer, as is done with Israel, instead of the current system, a largely project-funded program. This frustration at seeing their efforts achieve little led AID officials to reevaluate their role in helping Egypt and to redefine their goals in a much broader context.

While each administrative unit or office in USAID-Egypt has its own specific goals for their projects (such as agriculture, industry, health, local development and energy) the officers in the program and director's offices rely on more general, broad-based goals. Essentially, these goals are: economic reform; privatization; and institutionalization. Economic reform is the goal that has been given much attention lately, especially in view of the recent (1986-87) IMF talks with the Egyptian government and the crisis situation of the Egyptian economy. This goal, however, has long been on the agenda of AID-Egypt, as its officials have been trying to talk the government of Egypt into a thorough economic reform package for years. For a variety of reasons, they have not been successful. A chief reason for this is that Egypt is of such strategic importance to US interests in the Middle East that government officials have been able to convince Congress and the White House that drastic changes would lead to political instability in Egypt, as everyone learned in January 1977 when Sadat attempted to end various food and other subsidies at the insistence of the IMF. This led to the January 1977 food riots and several days of uncertainty regarding Sadat's stability. It also led eventually to the return of these subsidies.

The White House and American Embassy in Egypt have often backed the Egyptian government's position, overriding their own AID mission office in Egypt. They have adopted the view that political stability is primary and Egypt should not be pushed too far too fast. The White House (under Presidents Carter and Reagan) has sent the same message to the IMF time and again so that the IMF has continuously found itself backing down on its demands for economic reform.[50] Even the most recent standby agreement between Egypt and the IMF had the latter making what in its view was a major concession, one which gave the government of Egypt 18 months to unify its foreign exchange rates—i.e., its various "official rates" (numbering about four) with the "free [black] market rate"—instead of doing it overnight, as the IMF virtually always insists. The IMF's compromise or fall-back position would have been for Egypt to take six months to unify the rates.[51] The 18-month figure was Egypt's idea and many people in AID (in Washington and in Egypt) predicted that Egypt would once again win out over the IMF, with the White House supporting Egypt.[52] Their predictions came true.

> The US pressured the IMF into softening its conditions [on the Egyptian government]. One IMF director resigned in protest, complaining of undue interference by the US. On May 15, 1987, the IMF accepted most of Egypt's reform program.[53]

It is thus obvious that Egypt has sufficient political clout in Washington to fend off those who seek to press it too hard on economic reasons alone. We see this clout manifested in the increasing competition between the AID mission office and the US Embassy in Cairo, as these two entities of the same US State Department pursue often conflicting goals, AID focusing on what is economically rational and the US embassy seeing what is politically possible and supposedly best for continued Egyptian stability.[54]

Aside from these inevitable, and probably insurmountable, rivalries, several problems remain in the way AID attempts to work in Egypt. Egyptian bureaucratic processes, about which many AID officials constantly complain, have come to roost in the AID offices in Cairo. As many Egyptians and some Americans have told me many times, "AID has done a good job of copying the Egyptians." This applies to project feasibility studies, approval and oversight, backstopping and evaluation (at various stages of a project's life), extension (when goals are not reached within a projected time horizon), and ultimately project wrap-up (*in sha allah* [God willing], as most AID officials say, using a phrase which often implies that something is to be done in the distant future, if at all). In addition to the extensive procedures necessary to implement each project, there is a considerable expense for the procedures, outside the cost of the project. For instance, an AID feasibility study on whether to construct a highway overpass in Cairo to relieve very little of the ever-increasing traffic cost $1 million. The study was ordered by ex-director McPherson. Even when his replacement, Frank Kimball, came to Cairo in November 1985 saying that AID would not be involved in any such projects, the study could not be stopped, even though it had not been completed. In 1987, Kimball's replacement wanted to see such a project for Cairo as it would be the type of monument project many Egyptians and some Americans are calling for to demonstrate the benefits of American aid to "the masses." The problem is, according to an AID official in the Program Office in Cairo, that the old feasibility study is now outdated and a new, more expensive one (i.e., costing over one million dollars) would be necessary.

Mid-project and final evaluation reports are also expensive formalities with questionable utility. Each evaluation costs about $100,000 or more to bring in American consultant teams who travel to project sites around Egypt, interviewing AID officials and American contractors but very few Egyptians involved in the projects. (Most of their reports have a disclaimer saying that time limitations and language barrier prevented them from contacting many Egyptians.) One AID official in the Program Office in Cairo said that these evaluations are:

> often such a waste of money. Usually, the recommendations are not even followed by AID and very often these are given in a vacuum—they are not realistic given the *political* situation in Egypt, about which most of these American consultants know nothing. Also, the recommendations can be contradictory. For example, in the urban health delivery project, the evaluation says the project is not good because of certain problems in the region which can't be overcome. Yet, it is suggested later in the report that this project be replicated elsewhere! In other words, this report—as others—goes through a process, a necessary "back-patting" of AID telling AID what a good job it is doing.[55]

This back-patting is also probably a good way of endearing these consultants to AID, in the hope of gaining further invitations to evaluate AID's efforts on other projects.

AID officials in Egypt do not escape the well-known and endemic problem of virtually all State Department personnel who are rotated out of their country assignments every two or four years. (Some do come back to Egypt after several years of absence, but these are few in number.) Because of this short time-frame, most AID officials lack sufficient knowledge about Egyptian society, politics, language, and culture.[56] While they quite quickly develop an in-depth *knowledge* about economics, they never fully develop a thorough *understanding* of Egyptian economics, which can only come with an appreciation for and knowledge of politics and society. AID personnel also work in a vacuum, focusing on economics and development issues and hoping to ignore the political nature of their program. Even Egyptian "direct-hires" working as AID officials find it difficult to come to terms with the politics of the program. One such official in the Agriculture Office in Cairo said:

> We're technicians; I'm an entomologist. We don't have great experience with politics. We're here to help Egypt develop; we're not here to promote US interests over Egyptian ones. Others [i.e., the US embassy, USDA] do that. We need a few political scientists here to deal with the overtly political nature of the aid program and let us technicians work in productive, helpful fields: basic human needs, education, health.[57]

US embassies do have such specialists, of course, but the experience that AID officials in Cairo have had with the US Embassy there suggests that these separate and competitive bureaucracies do not share their own expertise and experts with each other. Indeed, I often felt that I was relaying messages between the two groups while I was conducting my interviews with them. In one incident, the Science Attache under Ambassador Frank Wisner needed my assistance in acquiring AID's 1986 Status Report on its program in Egypt. Until I mentioned the report, he did not even know that one existed and was almost totally unaware of the types of science and technology projects that AID was funding in Egypt.

It would be possible to cite many more such examples of how the two entities do not mix, either professionally or socially. This aloofness from one another is detrimental to both of their individual and combined efforts. This designed separateness is probably unavoidable given the rivalry, lack of interest, and indeed lack of respect between the two organizations. Yet those interested in improving the aid program in Egypt should be aware of this situation, in order to develop some type of working relationship, if not a *rapprochement,* between these reluctant partners in America's aid program in Egypt. If this is not achieved, the rivalry could easily deal a staggering blow to this program, which has had its share of successes, but which is so large, so omnipresent, and less than significant in many respects, that its critics find numerous examples of failure, of inequities, and of what appears to be Egyptian subservience to and dependence on the US.

Such competition, whether between AID and the US Embassy in Cairo, or between AID and USDA, or AID and Congress, as well as the competition between American agencies (in general) and their Egyptian counterparts, is an impediment to the development process. AID and Egyptian government officials work to overcome such rivalry and competition, but it is often at cross-purposes. Frustration with the magnitude of the problems has led to a sense of resignation, if not withdrawal. Much needs to be done to improve the Egyptian-American aid relationship, especially if the political relationship is to last, since it is the aid relationship that is the foundation of the political relationship. Sadat was instrumental in establishing the economic foundation and Mubarak has done much to build upon it in political terms. But if the cracks that are indeed evident in the foundation are not sealed, the edifice will be severely weakened, if not doomed.

Conclusion

Bureaucratic-authoritarian regimes have had some success in promoting growth and economic development. In studies on Taiwan, South Korea, Brazil, and other such states, various observers have pointed out the competence, effectiveness, and strength of the governments of these states—especially in dealing with MNCs—and their ability to promote their own growth and economic development.[58] From these examples, we see how strong, stable, effective governments— i.e., ones that are fairly well developed politically although undemo- cratic—facilitate economic development. This is not to suggest, however, that authoritarianism is necessary for economic growth. Kaufman argues that states run by non-authoritarian elites are as able to develop economically as are states run by authoritarian elites; in fact, the latter are not always successful in their efforts because some bureaucratic authoritarian elites come to power with no economic strategy at all.[59] Ajami, Richards, Waterbury, and Aulas each discuss how Nasser and the Free Officers came to power in 1952 with no economic blueprint on how to effectively promote growth and development.[60] Things seem not to have changed much from 1952, as Egypt remains yet another good example of an authoritarian elite that has failed to push its economy anywhere near a stage of self- sustaining growth. While the state elite is stable and strong, it is far from effective. The results of this study suggest that there is an association between ineffective management in political organizations and continuing economic stagnation.

Egyptian government officials are not taking the lead in promoting development. Instead, the army, Islamic groupings, and some private businesses are taking the lead, acting as the necessary entrepreneurs in promoting economic and social development by working outside the inefficient government and bureaucratic structures supposedly entrusted with the goal of promoting development. Ayubi explains that bureaucracies are not innovators, even if they are given that role by government:

> If a bureaucracy of some "guardianship" orientation is still growing in size and influence under the pretext of promoting economic development, how can one expect such a bureaucracy to give up its powers and privileges?[61]

He reminds us that bureaucracies are "essentially conservative," resisting changes both from within and from without, able to discourage "the emergence of innovative individuals and even more to retard the adoption of whatever innovation [does] appear."[62]

This characterization certainly applies in Egypt. Regardless of their stated positions on the question of the need to reform Egypt's economic system, the bureaucrats and politicians in charge of the system are essentially conservative, i.e., resistant to change for fear of losing control, which is the source of their power. Even those considered "reformists" add their voices to those advocating "gradualism." The difference between the two groups is that reformists want change only gradually so that they can adapt to the changing situation as it occurs and are able to use the changes to maintain whatever power they can, even in the face of reform. But by using the right language—reform privatization, open-door, free market— they are essentially pandering to, and thus supported by, powerful foreign interests (e.g., the US, the IMF, multinationals). Gradualists want even less reform than the reformists but feel it necessary to use the language of reform, with the qualifier that it is to be gradual, to placate these same foreign donors and investors while continuing to use their positions of power to resist any change at all.

While this struggle over reform goes on at the upper levels of the Egyptian government, that is, within the Cabinet, the fundamental nature of bureaucracies seems to be assisting those who seek to avoid reform. Ayubi points out that administrative reform is unlikely, given the bureaucratic ability to resist it, short of revolution. And if "changes introduced are so fundamental and radical that they are more of a 'revolution' than 'reform,' then they can no longer be described as 'administrative' "[63] and are in fact political. This characterization may apply to the Gorbachev "revolution" in the Soviet Union. It is, however, too early to speculate on how successful Gorbachev will be in his attempt at political and economic restructuring.

Such sweeping political change could occur if Egypt's economic crisis situation continues unabated. Crozier argues that a crisis environment gives impetus to reform:

> Crisis is a distinctive and necessary element of the bureaucratic system. It provides the only means of making the necessary adjustments, and it therefore plays a role in enabling the organization to develop and, indirectly, for centralization and impersonality to grow. . . . During crises, individual initiative prevails and people eventually come to depend on some strategic individual's arbitrary whim. Forgotten, strained dependence relationships reappear. Personal authority at times supersedes the rules. [Such] exceptions continually create a new demand for authoritarian reformer figures in the midst of the bureaucratic routine.[64]

In other words, a crisis situation might allow certain powerful individuals to reform a bureaucracy that is, with far too few exceptions, overstaffed, under-trained, inefficient, and directionless. This pre-supposes that change will come from within the existing bureaucratic and political structure. Yet this is hardly inevitable, especially in Egypt, where the latter structure continues to be challenged from without, most recently by a variety of Islamic groups. And if such reform, pushed by leaders responding to crisis, does not come from within, it is nonetheless necessary—and the only other source for change is from outside the system.

Notes

1. See especially Gouda Abdel-Khalek, "Looking Outside, or Turning Northwest? On the Meaning and External Dimension of Egypt's Infitah, 1971-80," *Social Problems,* Vol. 28, No. 4 (April 1981), pp. 394-409 and Gouda Abdel-Khalek and Robert Tignor (eds.), *The Political Economy of Income Distribution in Egypt* (New York: Holmes and Meier, 1982) for discussions of *infitah* and economic dependency; John Waterbury, *The Egypt of Nasser*

and Sadat: The Political Economy of Two Regimes (Princeton: Princeton University Press, 1983), for an excellent political-economic analysis of Egypt using bureaucratic-authoritarian and dependent development frameworks; and Marvin G. Weinbaum, *Egypt and the Politics of US Economic Aid* (Boulder: Westview Press, 1986), for a thorough review of the politics of the US-Egypt aid relationship.

2. Richard H. Adams, "Growth Without Development in Rural Egypt: A Local-Level Study of Institutional and Social Change," Ph.D. dissertation, University of California-Berkeley, 1981, p. 2.

3. Interview with Karima Korayem, November 9, 1986.

4. See especially Alan Richards, *Egypt's Agricultural Development, 1800-1980: Technical and Social Change* (Boulder: Westview Press, 1982); and Ahmad H. Ibrahim, "Impact of Agriculture Policies on Income Distribution," in Gouda Abdel-Khalek and Robert Tignor (eds.), *The Political Economy of Income Distribution in Egypt* (New York: Holmes and Meier, 1982).

5. This is an amount obligated by Congress but not fully spent. Roughly $12 billion of it has been spent. Military aid to Egypt in this period has also been around $12 billion.

6. *World Development Report, 1984* (New York: Oxford University Press, 1984).

7. President Hosni Mubarak began using this term, *azma* (crisis), in 1984 in his public addresses. The US Embassy in Cairo also uses the label in its pronouncements concerning Egypt's economic situation.

8. See especially Samir Radwan, *"Ishtirakiya 'am Rasmaliya?"* [Socialism or Capitalism?], *al-Ahram al-Iqtisadi,* October 11, 1984 for an assessment of the state of the debate within Egypt and for an outline of the arguments in this debate.

9. See Paul Jabber, "Egypt's Crisis, America's Dilemma," *Foreign Affairs,* Vol. 64, No. 5 (Summer 1986), pp. 960-80.

10. See especially Nazih N.M. Ayubi, *Bureaucracy in Contemporary Egypt* (New York: Oxford University Press, 1980), pp. 51, 167; Michel Crozier, *The Bureaucratic Phenomenon* (Chicago: University of Chicago Press, 1964).

11. Springborg refers us to Andrea Rugh, *Family in Contemporary Egypt* (Syracuse: Syracuse University Press, 1984), in support of his observation regarding competition. Springborg's comments come from a lecture which he delivered entitled "The Politics of Agricultural Development in Egypt," at the American Research Center in Cairo, November 4, 1986.

12. Interview with the head of a private voluntary organization (PVO) in al-Minia, Egypt, October 28, 1986.

13. Interview with USAID official, Cairo, December 3, 1986.

14. See Robert Dahl, "The Concept of Power," *Behavioral Science,* II (July 1957), pp. 201-15.

15. Ayubi, *op. cit.,* preface. Ayubi calls Egypt a "bureaucratic polity which, in reviving some old traditions, adopted technology as ideology and replaced politics by organization. . . . This programme [relied] heavily on the bureaucracy, headed first by a militocracy but then increasingly by a growing technocracy."

16. Interview, MOA official, August 1987.

17. Ayubi, *op. cit.,* p. 43.

18. *Ibid.,* p. 38.

19. Notable exceptions to this norm include the consistently effective and efficient Suez Canal Authority as well as the High Dam Authority.

20. In Egypt's Second Five Year Plan, 1987/88-1991/92, investment is projected at EP 45.5 billion, up from EP 39 billion in the 1982-87 plan. Priorities are new lands reclamation, desert community development, scientific research and technology development, and projects that use existing, underutilized capacity, most of which are in the public sector.

21. There are numerous works on the importance of political will in promoting political and economic development. Even when these works deal exclusively or predominantly with political development, I assert that these arguments apply equally to notions of economic development.

22. These interests might be to use one's office to gain economic power, either by working a second job in which this official can help his or her private employer by providing information available to him/her from his/her government position or by corruption, such as selling government licenses to a company hoping to import restricted merchandise.

23. Interview with MOA undersecretary, February 22, 1987.

24. A similar argument is often heard about food aid to Nigeria and other countries, whereby large amounts of cheap food led to a major change in consumption patterns, making residents dependent on foreign sources for basic essential commodities.

25. The well-known problems that Mikhail Gorbachev and Deng Xiao Ping are having with low-level bureaucrats opposed to their reforms in the Soviet Union and China are the most recent examples of active resistance to reform. President Kennedy's assumption that missiles he had ordered removed from Turkey were removed and his later realization that his simple order got mislaid or ignored in the chain of command is perhaps an example of how bureaucrats can neglect an order, even if not actively resisting it.

26. Officials at MOA and AID (and even some at USDA) felt that USDA contractors for the DCA project, funded by AID from 1980-87 at a cost of $5 million, failed to fulfill the project goal of collecting and analyzing data on Egyptian agriculture.

27. He was already in charge of two AID-funded development projects that put over $40 million at his ministry's disposal.

28. For instance, George Simmons, in research on Egypt's population planning efforts, identified several agencies entrusted with halting and reversing the spiraling birth rate in Egypt. The agency given the most authority (and of course the biggest budget) under Sadat was headed by Jihan Sadat's personal gynecologist.

29. Sources: *al-Ahram,* USAID-Egypt, and USAID-Washington.

30. Simon Commander, *The State and Agricultural Development in Egypt Since 1973* (London: The Overseas Development Institute, 1987), p. 182.

31. The heads of six or seven agricultural governorates voiced their concerns, indeed their opposition, to Minister Wali's proposed reforms for various agricultural products. These governors feared that the proposed price increases would lead to increased competition between their governorates and while there certainly would be improved efficiency in production, this would likely result in decreased prices for these crops in the long run with fewer returns coming back to individual governorates. These governors say they are already suffering enough since the national government is facing ever-increasing budget and trade deficits and is thus withholding investments and funding for basic services from the governorates. The contents of this meeting were relayed to me by an aide to Minister Wali, February 5, 1987.

32. *Middle East Economic Weekly,* November 2, 1984.

33. The claim of disincentive is made vigorously by USAID officials in Cairo and Washington. The agency has been trying, for several years, to put an end to PL 480 Title I food aid to Egypt, and to much of the developing world, on the grounds that it stifles wheat production in recipient countries and perpetuates these countries' dependence on foreign sources.

34. USAID-MOA meeting, Cairo, February 5, 1987.

35. "Policy Reform Element," February 12, 1987, p. 2 (USAID-MOA joint statement).

36. Many observers believe that training sessions for Egyptian bureaucrats are one of the most effective ways of improving the performance of otherwise inefficient employees.

37. These comments were related to me by someone present at the meeting.

38. Interview with MOA official, Cairo, November 4, 1986.

39. Interview with official of MOA's USAID Affairs Office, November 9, 1986.

40. Interview with official of MOA's USAID Affairs Office, January 29, 1987.

41. The above perceptions of development were gleaned from a variety of sources, including discussions with the Ford Foundation's coordinator of projects in the Middle East; and newsletters from development agencies, including ANERA and World Development Forum.

42. Interview with Ministry of Irrigation official, Cairo, November 19, 1986.

43. Parsons (1978), pp. 98-99.

44. US Ambassador to Egypt Frank Wisner puts the approximate date of this ideological evolution at 1978.

45. Robert Springborg, *op. cit.*, claims this new orthodoxy came in with the "Reagan Revolution" and the President's ability to clean out the bureaucracy and replace it with like-minded conservatives. Most State Department and USAID officials I spoke with disagree with this view. They say that Reagan could not have accomplished such a thorough cleaning out of AID and that the new orthodoxy is much more an evolutionary development, resulting from 25 years of AID dealing with Third World governments.

46. This frustration was related to me by the overwhelming majority of AID officials whom I interviewed in Cairo and Washington. The same sentiment, using remarkably similar phrasing, has been expressed to Scott Gates during his research on AID in Pakistan.

47. See Scott G. Gates, "Micro Incentives and Macro Constraints of Development Assistance Conditionality," Ph.D. Dissertation, Department of Political Science, University of Michigan, (forthcoming).

48. Former Director of USAID-Egypt, Michael P. Stone, and former US Ambassador in Cairo, Nicholas Veliotes, were both often open and vociferous critics of their host government. There was little disappointment on the part of most GOE officials at the departure of both US officials from Cairo.

49. US House of Representatives, "US Mission and Office Operations: Egypt," Hearing before a Subcommittee of the Committee on Government Operations, 96th Congress, 2nd session, February 11, 1980.

50. Interview with AID official on TDY [temporary duty] in Cairo, October 15, 1986. See also Hamied Ansari, *Egypt: The Stalled Society* (Albany: SUNY Press, 1986), chapter 8.

51. Ali Lutfi, *al-Ahram al-Iqtisadi* (March 1987).

52. Interviews with AID officials in Washington and Cairo, September 1986 and January 1987.

53. Dirk Vandewalle, "Egypt and its Western Creditors," *Middle East Review,* Vol. 20, No. 3 (Spring 1988), p. 29.

54. This was the situation up until 1988. By that time, USAID officials were saying that any previous dispute or competition with the Embassy was over: "State has now moved to our [USAID] position of being resistant to giving money before we see any reform measures. State and AID are now at one voice on the policy dialogue process." (Interview with USAID official, August 24, 1988.) Apparently, an internal State Department memo was circulated in 1988 criticizing State for its leniency on Egypt and for "asking" the IMF to be lenient in the past as well.

55. Interview with AID official in Program Office, Cairo, December 4, 1987.

56. See Marvin G. Weinbaum, *Egypt and the Politics of US Economic Aid* (Boulder: Westview Press, 1986), p. 105.

57. Interview with Agriculture Officer, Cairo, February 5, 1987.

58. See Richard E. Barrett and Martin K. Whyte, "Dependency Theory and Taiwan: Analysis of a Deviant Case," *American Journal of Sociology,* Vol. 87, No. 5 (1982), pp. 1064-89; John Boli-Bennett, "Global Integration and the Universal Increase of State Dominance, 1910-70," in Albert Bergesen (ed.), *Studies of the Modern World System* (New York: Academic Press, 1980); and Peter Evans, *Dependent Development: The Alliance of Multinational, State and Local Capital in Brazil* (Princeton: Princeton University Press, 1979).

59. See Robert Kaufman, "Industrial Change and Authoritarian Rule in Latin America," in David Collier (ed.), *The New Authoritarianism in Latin America* (Princeton: Princeton University Press, 1979). Also see Jyotirinda das Gupta, "A Season of Caesars: Emergency Regimes and Development Politics in Asia," *Asian Survey,* 18 (1978), pp. 315-49, who points out that emergency regimes in Asia are not necessary for economic development given that their achievements do not justify their existence.

60. Fouad Ajami, *The Arab Predicament: Arab Political Thought and Practice Since 1967* (Cambridge: Cambridge University Press, 1981); Richards, *op. cit.*; Waterbury (1983), *op. cit.;* and Marie-Christine Aulas, "State and Ideology in Republican Egypt," in F. Halliday and H. Alavi (eds.), *State and Ideology in the Middle East and Pakistan* (New York: Monthly Review Press, 1988).

61. Ayubi, *op. cit.*, p. 46.

62. *Ibid.*, p. 51.

63. Ayubi, *op. cit.*, p. 54.

64. Crozier, *op. cit.*, pp. 196-97.

7   EGYPTIAN DEBT: FORGIVE—OR FORGET?

Delwin A. Roy

Introduction

Egypt remains an economic enigma for the development professional. For the past several decades, the national economy has alternately improved (often significantly) and deteriorated, but seldom appears destined for sustained growth or complete collapse. Reform remains the major topic of concern, but it becomes less clear with each passing year that the Egyptian government is able to do more than nominally rectify the basic problems which beset the economy. Progress has been made, but of an insufficient magnitude to keep pace with the demand and expectations of a burgeoning population.

Foreign indebtedness now heads the long list of economic issues that have traditionally plagued Egypt. It looms as possibly *the* problem of the 1990s, raising serious questions about the country's future financial integrity. In the past twelve years, Egyptian debt has increased tenfold to its present level of approximately $53 billion—about $42 billion in public and private sector debt and $11.4 billion in military debt. In total indebtedness, Egypt now ranks seventh in the developing world. In terms of government-to-government debt, it ranks number one.[1] (See Table 1.)

TABLE 1
The Structure of Egyptian Debt:
Total Foreign Debt, 1988
(US$ Billions)

Public Sector		$36.7
Private Sector		$ 5.3
Military Debt		$11.0
US	($5.9)	
USSR	($3.0)	
Other	($2.5)	$53.4
TOTAL	11.4	

Source: Author, based on interviews with US Embassy, Cairo; Egyptian Central Bank officials; and World Bank, May-June, 1988.

At the present time, Egypt must provide total debt servicing in excess of $5 billion annually (see Table 2), something that it is increasingly unable to do. The most that Egypt has ever been able to pay against its principal and interest obligation is $3 billion and there has been little sympathy by non-US debt holders such as the People's Republic of China, France, West Germany and Spain, for the idea of forgoing principal payments due them. On the Egyptian military debt to the United States alone, almost $1.4 billion in interest due has had to be amortized into the guaranteed debt outstanding. Not only has Egypt failed to meet its interest obligations, but it has had to increase its long-term debt burden. The result is that debt rescheduling will remain a more or less permanent fixture of economic policy well into the early part of the next century.

TABLE 2
The Structure of Egyptian Debt:
Projected Public and Private Debt Service 1987-1994*
(US$ Millions)

Public Debt Creditors

Year	Official	Private	Private**	Total
1987	1,648.9	1,690.8	258.4	3,598.1
1988	1,324.7	1,584.5	228.3	3,137.5
1989	1,304.1	1,528.0	199.5	3,031.6
1990	1,316.0	1,352.7	177.9	2,846.6
1991	1,314.9	287.6	143.1	1,745.6
1992	1,266.7	234.6	125.2	1,626.5
1993	1,213.5	190.0	103.0	1,506.5
1994	1,190.7	159.9	0.0	1,350.6

* Public and private sector debt service (interest and principal) excluding military and any new debt creation for which additional service requirements might prevail.
** Non-guaranteed debt service.

Source: World Bank

It is possible that a major turnaround in oil prices, coupled with substantive and immediate reforms, *could* lead to a more positive growth scenario in the latter part of the 1990s. A price rise for oil is predicted but nevertheless uncertain, although possibly less so given a sustainable truce in the Iran-Iraq War. Also, if Iraq's vast and expensive plans for reconstruction are even partially realized, the demand for Egyptian labor and professional skills could increase dramatically, leading to a substantive improvement in the level of repatriated earnings and conceivably to improved exports in the form of construction materials and services. However, all of this remains highly speculative and the time necessary for such "windfalls" to be realized, much less exert any positive effect on the debt situation, is not in Egypt's favor. The predilection of Egypt to await for events outside its direct control to allow it to come to grips with its economic problems serves to reduce any real motivation to undertake serious reform. Substantive reform thus does not appear in the offing.

At least one observer refers to the rapid growth in debt as the "Latinization" of the economy, referring to the growing similarity between debt-ridden Latin American economies such as Mexico, Brazil, and Argentina, and the Egyptian case. In the view of some observers, maintaining even a semblance of integrity in the national economy over the next decade-and-a-half will be a "tall order."

The main focus of this chapter is the structure of Egyptian debt and its possible long-term political implications—especially that component of it ($7.6 billion in nonmilitary and $5.9 billion in military aid) that has been provided by the United States. In 1974, President Sadat looked to links with the US as an economic panacea, and notwithstanding the financial dependency question, a means by which the national sovereignty and national unity of Egypt could be preserved. In 1988, that dependency is painfully clear. Renegotiating its terms and mitigating its more inimical political effects will in all probability dominate the US-Egyptian political dialogue for the next ten years.

The Dimensions and General Structure of the Egyptian Debt

Egypt borrows heavily to finance capital needs, military equipment and to a lesser extent, current consumption. It is estimated, however, that annual direct subsidies to consumers cost $3 billion. The latest officially reported figure for debt was $28.6 billion in 1986, the bulk of which—$23.7 billion—was public guaranteed long-term debt.[2] At that time, a reasonable estimate of the amount of military debt was $9 billion.

One analyst (Choucri) places the June 1987 total debt, including the military debt, at $40 billion, representing a ratio of foreign debt to GDP of 53.5 percent and foreign debt to export revenues of 300 percent.[3] By way of contrast, total non-military debt was $18 billion in 1980, about $3.6 billion of which was short-term. Hence, virtually all of the $13 billion increase in debt between 1980 and 1987 was long-term in character.

The author, based on information gathered in mid-1988, places total debt in 1988 at $53.9 billion inclusive of military and private sector non-guaranteed debt. The US portion of the government-to-government debt is in excess of $13 billion or about 27 percent of debt outstanding. (See Tables 3 and 4.)

Commanding over one third of total export reserves to service this debt, the government has been increasingly hard pressed to meet its obligations. Since 1985, there has been a serious decline in major foreign exchange earning activities: worker remittances, oil, tourism and canal revenues. The result is that Egypt must continuously reschedule its debt repayment, resorting on occasion to amortizing interest payments due in the form of long-term debt.

TABLE 3
The Structure of Egyptian Debt:
National Origin, 1986*
(EP Billions)

Country	Amount	%
USA	5.3	24.9
Other Western Industrial (Europe, Japan and Canada)	6.4	30.0
Arab and Islamic	2.5	11.7
Arab Financial Assistance Agencies	1.9	8.9
International Financial Assistance Agencies (IDA, World Bank, IMF)	2.0	9.4
Eastern Bloc and China	0.7	3.3
Other	2.5	11.8
Total: (EP)	21.3	100.0
(US$)**	30.3	

* Public sector and foreign-held excluding the military and private sectors.
** Converted at EP 0.70 = US $1

Source: World Bank

TABLE 4
The Structure of Egyptian Debt:
US Military Assistance, 1974-1985
(US$ Millions)

Year	FMS Credits* Guaranteed	Forgiven	Amort.** Int.	IMET Grant	Total
1974	0.0	0.0	0.0	0.0	0.0
1975	0.0	0.0	0.0	0.0	0.0
1976	0.0	0.0	0.0	0.0	0.0
1977	0.0	0.0	0.0	0.0	0.0
1978***	0.0	0.0	0.0	0.2	0.2
1979	1.500.0	0.0	0.0	0.4	1,500.4
1980	0.0	0.0	0.0	1.0	1.0
1981	550.0	0.0	0.0	0.8	550.8
1982	700.0	200.0	0.0	2.0	902.0
1983	900.0	425.0	0.0	2.0	1,327.0
1984	900.0	465.0	0.0	2.0	1,367.0
1985	0.0	1,175.0	0.0	2.0	1,177.0
1986/87	0.0	n/a	650.0	n/a	650.0
1987/88	0.0	n/a	650.0	n/a	650.0
Total	4,550.0	2,265.0	1,350.0	10.4	8,125.4

* Foreign military sales.

** Amortized interest represents interest due on guaranteed debt. As Egypt has not had the foreign exchange to meet interest payments, the amount due is capitalized as additional guaranteed debt.

*** Camp David accords signed in late 1978; Khomeini Revolution in Iran begins.

Source: US Dept. of State; Office of Management and Budget.

The inability of the domestic economy, as presently constituted, to generate sufficient revenues to meet current and upcoming debt servicing requirements is worrisome in its own right. But even more serious is the longer term question of whether debt-financed capital will have gone to capital-producing projects that can be made profitable. Egypt has in effect mortgaged its future, but tended to absorb the borrowed capital in an economic structure that remains seriously distorted.

Egypt is not dissimilar in this respect to a number of other developing countries. What is disconcerting is that all the trends point to a worsening in the debt situation, leading to the conclusion that there is not much "light at the end of the tunnel." Despite the $20 billion in US aid that has been pumped into the Egyptian economy since 1975, few reforms have been enacted for the substantial increase in debt incurred. Egypt continues to use external aid and debt to maintain the status quo, or at best, nibble away at the edges of core structural problems in the economy. On that basis, future increases are to be expected in the size of the debt outstanding, while there is simultaneously likely to be a diminished ability to meet debt servicing requirements. This presupposes, of course, that major creditors, especially the United States, will have no other recourse but to pump up the Egyptian economy in view of its continued geopolitical significance in a much troubled Middle East.

Debt and the US-Egyptian Economic Relationship

As the United States is the largest single Egyptian benefactor—providing over one quarter of total debt, roughly one half of the military debt, and considerable bilateral aid—the tenor of the economic relationship between these two countries is important. As Egypt is unable to service its present debt load, it requires IMF support through standby agreements, both as a means of accessing scarce foreign exchange and as a precondition for debt rescheduling consideration by the Paris Club. The Paris Club might reschedule without a standby agreement but this has never been done for any other country. Whatever proves to be the case, the United States plays the crucial role in getting the IMF and the Paris Club to go along with Egyptian requests.[4]

The present rate of interest on the Egyptian debt held by the US is, on average, in excess of 12 percent. Recently, when Egypt has had to reschedule or, in effect, amortize interest payments on the military portion that it could not meet, the rate of interest applied has been 8 percent. Debt held by other countries earns equally high rates of interest, although for obvious reasons, the rate of interest on non-US military debt is not generally available to the public. The rate of interest on World Bank loans is, on average, 9 percent or more. In the past four years, Egypt has simply balked at the World Bank rate and therefore no new lending has taken place.

At what rate of interest could Egypt conceivably handle its debt loan without continuous and massive rescheduling? Egypt has pressed the US for something on the order of 7 percent and therefore it might reasonably be assumed that, at that rate, Egypt believes that it could manage. However, it must be borne in mind that the continuing failure of Egypt to deal with the fundamental factors that cause debt-dependency would mean that relief through interest-rate reductions on present debt would at best be temporary. With world interest rates on the rise, there will be little sympathy for a concessionary stance by Egypt's debt holders.

The "debt relief" question, at least between Egypt and the United States, takes an even more interesting turn when one considers that the *casus belli* of relations over the debt question has in recent times seemed to hinge on a single issue: the forgiveness of military debt owed to the US. In fact, alternatives being considered, almost all of which fall short of outright forgiveness of the debt, appear to offer only marginal relief *even if* a compromise is struck.

As can be seen in Table 4, much of the Egyptian military debt owed the US was incurred in the period 1982-1985, a period of high interest rates. Loans issued during that period were tied to Treasury Note rates, with the result that Egypt agreed to pay interest on the $4.6 billion in Foreign Military Sales (FMS) at an average rate of 11.8 percent.[5] The subsequent precipitous decline of interest rates after 1985 put considerable pressure on Egyptian authorities to renegotiate the debt to the US.

TABLE 5
The Structure of Egyptian Debt:
US Economic Assistance Debt Repayment, FY 1980-FY 1989*
(US$ Millions)

Year	PL 480 (Title I)	US AID ESF Loans	EximBank	Total
1980	282.5	24.8	0.0	307.3
1981	303.4	33.2	0.0	336.6
1982	249.2	40.8	0.0	290.0
1983	71.8	46.9	104.0	222.6
1984	55.9	48.4	103.2	217.5
1985	55.1	50.7	130.5	236.3
1986	54.4	53.3	169.4	267.1
1987	55.6	30.8	204.8	391.2
1988	59.0	89.0	209.1	257.1
1989	70.3	101.9	n/a	172.2

* The statistics are for combined interest and principal repayments. The statistics for FY 1980 to FY 1986 are actual, while those for FY 1987 to FY 1989 are estimated.

Source: US Office of Management and Budget

The military debt question has assumed a disproportionate importance, given the overall debt situation. The Egyptian government
has placed considerable emphasis on getting relief from the American
portion of the debt (as noted, non-US Western country suppliers
have been unwilling to reschedule principal or interest payments as
due). However, as one negotiator puts it, "from just about everyone's
point of view, the FMS debt is really a political, *not* [emphasis
added] an economic issue."

There is some sentiment in the US Congress for the provision of
relief to Egypt, albeit there is less direct apparent concern for the
Egyptian situation than for Israel.[6] In early 1988, Congress mandated a
debt refinancing plan that calls for the issuing of 90 percent US-
government-backed guarantees on Egyptian military debt. In effect,
this would permit the commercialization of the debt at a lower
interest rate, providing some relief to Egypt.

However, those charged with researching the feasibility of this
form of refinancing found little favorable sentiment among private
banks for commercializing the military debt on less than a 100
percent basis. There is a degree of congressional premeditation
involved in the exercise. The Egyptian military debt relief issue has,
in effect, become a "stalking horse." The main interest of those in
Congress who are advocating relief for Egypt is to provide military
debt relief for Israel. Egypt is an additional concern, but undoubtedly of
less importance. The goal had always been for 100 percent guarantees.
Congressional sponsors of this proposal assumed that there is at
present more public sympathy for Egyptian than Israeli debt problems.
The 100 percent guarantee position is more likely to be achieved on
behalf of Egypt. If agreed upon by Congress as a whole, then according
to the concept of parity of treatment, the refinancing scheme would
be applied to Israel as well.

Aside from the political machinations involved in dealing with the
US portion of the military debt, there is very little to be achieved in
the economic sense through this refinancing scheme. If the 100
percent guarantee formula is passed, then at best the debt could be
commercially refinanced at a rate of interest of about .75-1 percent
higher than the US Treasury rate. Given the interest rates prevailing
at the time this remedy surfaced in Congress, the average interest
rate on the debt of 11.8 percent might be reduced to 9 percent, or
about 2-3 percent savings.

In the exercise of influence on the IMF and the Paris Club, and in the congressionally-mandated military debt refinancing scheme noted above, there is no serious effort to deal with the principal causes of Egypt's debt problem.

The Consequences of Egyptian Debt

Several observations can be made regarding the present and prospective debt situation in Egypt:

1. Since 1973, the debt problem of Egypt has become perceptibly worse, although the national economy has made significant improvements.

2. The uses of the capital for which Egypt is indebted do not appear to have eased the major constraint on economic growth, but rather to have shored up a structurally defective economy. A degree of reform has ensued that is of insufficient magnitude to reduce the causes underlying future debt.

3. Egypt cannot now or in the foreseeable future service its present debt level without considerable and continuous rescheduling. It cannot be assumed that the present pace of incurring additional debt, or the reasons for that new debt, will abate significantly in the future.

4. In the most positive development scenario, even assuming a strong economic reform package, debt would still be a major impediment to future growth. Obviously, without a strong policy package, the situation would be even worse and a creditworthy Egypt might not emerge until after the year 2000.

5. Even given an optimistic growth scenario, which would include an optimistic oil price situation *and* the continuous rescheduling of debt, no positive impact on the economy would be felt before the mid-1990s.

6. Watered-down reforms, such as those advocated in the last IMF Standby Agreement, are in no one's interest: they weaken the IMF as a credible institution and provide no incentive whatsoever for the undertaking of serious reform.

One is drawn to the conclusion that for the next ten years or so, the prospects for putting the Egyptian economy on a growth footing are at best discouraging. Yet the alternative of allowing the situation to languish uncorrected is not attractive. Egypt's economic problems will only compound under the twin pressures of continuing population growth and economic distortion, waste and inefficiency. This is clearly not in the interest of the United States or of the cause of political moderation in the Middle East. The fundamental question posed in the early 1970s thus remains: is there any possibility for serious reform of the Egyptian economy?

Egyptian Debt and Egyptian Reform: Where Next?

History shows that, in the absence of serious reforms, lenders will lend anyway, but this cannot be construed as being in the long-term interest of Egypt. It weakens any reform-minded constituency and exacts future economic consequences of an unknown but certainly potentially serious character. An economy that does not generate adequate resources for current consumption and needed growth capital cannot be expected to do it miraculously in the future. Obtaining credit is at best only a temporary and short-term tactic that resolves little.

The Egyptian View

For the Mubarak government, as for that of Sadat, the overriding concern about any bold economic reform policy remains the potential for political instability that might follow. The Sadat government could not, in 1973, articulate and implement any policy that would have had as its objective a major reordering of the economic system. The economic management ability of the bureaucracy had proved inadequate to generate the Nasserist version of the ideal economy in which social justice would prevail, and the bureaucracy was no better able to deliver the new Sadat version, economic liberalization.

Sadat was thus forced to interpret and implement his liberalization policy in a manner consistent with his analysis of the forces in Egyptian society that might produce instability. Fundamental reform, arguably more affordable after 1978 given Egypt's good fortune in oil and remittance earnings, was instead eschewed in favor of increased consumption through the freeing up of imports. Mubarak inherited the cumulative negative effects of the past: the distorted sense of social justice of Nasser, best characterized by the sardonic phrase "equal poverty for all," and the "consumption binge in favor of quieting domestic waters" of Sadat.

Even more telling than the lame economic policy legacy left to Mubarak are three silent features of the debate in Egypt on whether or not to change economic policy. Each feature poses a significant obstacle to any Egyptian leader vigorously pursuing a program of economic reform. Taken collectively, the three features constitute a formidable barrier.

First, there is the strong belief within Egyptian leadership circles (from Nasser to Mubarak) that, bad as the system may be, Egypt has enjoyed unprecedented internal political stability since the Revolution. What other country in the Middle East has achieved so enviable a record? And in part, it is the distorted economy that has contributed to this domestic peace.

The second feature of the debate is more pertinent. It is extremely doubtful that Egypt possesses the requisite professional capability to effectively manage its way out of its present economic state. There are very few Egyptian economists left who can muster sufficient knowledge of the current structure of the Egyptian economy to undo in timely and expeditious fashion the damage done.

Finally, there is a pervasive attitude evident in the Mubarak government that further impedes any reform sentiment: the US financial assistance package is, after all, seen as only a just payment to Egypt for having taken the very difficult step of establishing peace with Israel. To attach *any* further conditions to the use or continuance of the aid package is thus seen as representing a degree of thanklessness on the part of the United States.

In sum, then, Egypt does not appear to have the political will in its leadership, the management capability among its bureaucrats or technocrats, or even the inclination that would be needed to pursue serious economic reform. Most importantly, many intellectuals and professionals *believe* that tinkering with the system could well bring very serious consequences. Previous food riots and general civil disorders occasioned by attempts to change policies have occurred often enough to cause one to pause.

The American Response: An Attitude Problem

After spending almost $20 billion in Egypt since 1975, there is little to which the United States can point in terms of major, or indeed minor, economic reform. While it would be unfair to state that there is a total lack of interest in inducing reform, the combined weight of a fickle and unpredictable Congress and a technical assistance program that is considered "political" in its primary intent, have made the application of consistent pressure for reform virtually impossible. When applied to foreign aid, the term "political" has become analogous to "short-term" and antithetical to the concept of "sustainable economic development." In short, the US aid and lending program is more oriented toward shoring-up a bad situation than enabling a fundamental change in that bad situation.

On occasion, either in frustration or in an attempt to let Egypt know that it is serious, the US has withheld an installment of aid, most recently in March 1989. The intention was to provoke signs of an Egyptian willingness to "bite the policy reform bullet." But in the first instance of such punitive action, 1985, the US proved unable to stay the course. In any event, such actions, conducted on an *ad hoc* basis, are unlikely to be viewed as serious by Egypt.

In addition to the many criticisms that should be leveled against the US aid program to Egypt, the one particularly sticky point between Egypt and the US has been the latter's unwillingness to provide any support to the public sector. Although the sector is highly inefficient, it makes little sense for the US to totally ignore a sector that, after 12 years of economic liberalization, still accounts for 90 percent of capital investment in industry and 75 percent of total industrial production. The domestic political clout of the Egyptian public sector has not been seriously diminished, even with so-called economic liberalization. The US may be able to continue to avoid supporting that sector, but the price may prove to be its own interest, however ephemeral, in eliciting economic reforms.

Concluding Observations

The attitude of both Egypt and the United States can potentially harm both their national interests *and* interests held in common. In Egypt, the official attitude is best summed up by the statement of one senior representative: "Sure you [Egypt] have these debts but you can't pay them, so why worry?" The US has for some time, as noted, considered major economic policy issues in Egypt as falling within the realm of the "political," not the economic. Whatever current initiatives may be under way to alleviate the Egyptian debt crisis, or to bring about economic reform, appear to this author to be short-term political responses serving a variety of special political interests but doing little else.

The issue is not so much a matter of who is at fault—either lender or borrower—as of Egypt's future economic and political stability. Debt forgiveness and rescheduling in and of themselves, in the absence of a joint US-Egyptian strategy starting to resolve the causes of economic problems, do little to alter or relieve the factors that led to debt creation in the first instance.

In the interest of breaking this impasse in the US-Egyptian dialogue on the future course of economic relations, new options must be considered. Before turning to the specific recommendations of this author, two important factors must be taken into account. These factors constitute "preconditions" to any successful bid to get the Egyptian reform movement off dead center:

1. The Egyptian economy will continue to labor under its present burden of the mistakes of the past until there is a region-wide solution to the Arab-Israeli conflict, including the resolution of the Palestinian question. Any sympathy for reform is necessarily weakened in the absence of significant progress on this front.

2. Not only must there be a fundamental reconsideration of the present Egyptian economic system, there also needs to be a major attitude change on the part of Egypt and the United States. Continuous short-term, "crisis-like" dealings with each other have sapped the search for innovative and creative solutions on the terms of a partnership built on trust and mutual understanding. The cynicism evident in the present relationship is palpable; any real prospect for a significant departure is thus dependent on a commitment by both parties to "take a fresh look" at their respective postures.

Within that context, the following general recommendations may be relevant to the present impasse:

1. The United States should offer a moratorium on Egyptian debt interest and principal repayment for two years in exchange for evidence of a commitment to undertake fundamental economic reforms to be initiated on or before the expiration of the moratorium. Further, the US would consider further debt relief measures *after* the two years had elapsed, subject to solid evidence of the subsequent implementation of the reform plan.

2. In the interim period of the two years between reform plan formulation and implementation, the US would commit itself to maintaining the present aid and assistance level, with a further commitment to enter into good-faith negotiations as to the form and uses of the aid package. This would include a commitment to review the present prohibition on providing substantive aid and assistance to the public sector. *After* the two-year period, future US aid and assistance packages would be directly keyed to the realization of specific reform measures to be implemented.

3. The US and Egypt must find suitable institutional means by which jointly to devise both a reform plan and an implementation

schedule. How this is accomplished is critical: the Egyptian public would not long endure any institutional arrangement in which it appeared that the US was dictating reform measures to Egypt. Without such cooperation, however, there is little hope that either Egypt or the US would have sufficient "equity" in the reform plan upon which to base the trust and understanding so critically needed in the implementation phase.

4. Simultaneously with the declaration of the moratorium, the United States and Egypt should jointly devise and implement an institution-building technical assistance package, the primary purpose of which would be to enhance directly Egypt's capability to manage, monitor and revise the reform plan to be implemented after 1992. This package should be devised on a separate and autonomous basis from the US Agency for International Development and should be separately funded, i.e., costs involved should not be included within the general aid and assistance levels to be maintained until 1992.

5. Egypt should commit itself to set up new quasi-governmental planning and economic management bodies that may, realistically, have to be built upon at least some elements of the present institutions. However, the devising of a reform plan and the subsequent implementation of its detailed measures cannot be wholly dependent upon the present bureaucratic organization and capability.

6. The question of continuing military aid and its terms must be placed completely outside the context of any continuing US aid and assistance package linked to the implementation of a reform package. Further, the US should commit itself to good-faith negotiations on the repayment of military debt incurred in the past, *including* a commitment to consider debt forgiveness in exchange for evidence of solid progress on the reform front. Any military debt relief schedule devised for the post-1992 implementation phase should be tied, serially and progressively, to mutually agreed reform success indicators.

7. The United States should enter into a commitment *in principle* to Egypt to stay the reform course, in partnership, up to the year 2000. After 1992, there should be established performance benchmarks to which conditions would be attached for any subsequent disbursements of financial support, debt relief or any other appropriate incentive measures. These benchmarks, to be negotiated and mutually agreed upon, should be incorporated into a "loose" or "rolling" economic plan which will form the basic framework within which to fit specific measures to be adopted in the reform plan and subsequently implemented.

By committing to the longer term, and taking the aid and assistance question out of the "on again, off again" approach of Congress, there is at least the *prospect* of exacting meaningful reforms. Simply soldiering on with the past approach, only to find that in the year 2000 another $20 billion, or more, is expended for solid reform purposes makes no sense whatsoever. Anwar Sadat could have had his "Marshall Plan" and then some *if* the US had made a $20 billion, or a $40 billion, commitment in 1975. The United States is simply piecemealing its potential clout "to death" and no good purpose.

Even under the terms set forth above, can Egypt pull off reform? In the final analysis, any reform of the Egyptian economy is essentially a matter for Egyptians to resolve. In part, stripping Egyptian administrations of the ability to procrastinate on the matter or to blame everyone else (always with a degree of truth inherent in the exercise), is in part what initiating meaningful reform is about. It is time to put in front of Egypt a reform assistance package which it must either accept or reject. Anything short of this will only provide an incentive to persist in the present course.

The recommendations set forth are meant only to stimulate a reconsideration of the tenets of the present US-Egyptian economic relationship. It presumes that both Egypt and the United States stand to benefit, individually and in combination, from a serious review of the present logic of that relationship. The United States has, since 1975, granted aid and issued loans that now total many billions, for which precious little has been done in the way of constructive structural change in the economy. Economic brinkmanship, occasioned by Egypt's geopolitical significance, has to date brought little improvement to the ability of Egypt to sustain itself in the longer term. If that does not change, then the continuing client-state status of Egypt will be more than obvious to a population long indisposed to overt foreign influence in domestic economic and political affairs.

Notes

1. US Embassy, Cairo, economic staff discussion, May, 1988.
2. International Bank for Reconstruction and Development, *World Debt Tables* (March, 1988), p. 114.
3. Nazli Choucri, *Dimensions of National Security*, Egypt, March, 1988 (unpublished monograph),pp. 6-9b.
4. There is a strong opinion expressed among some elements of the international donor

community that US pressure led to a very "watered-down" Standby Agreement concluded in the summer of 1987. As one official puts it, given Egypt's need to reschedule $5 billion in debt servicing due on June 30, 1988, "the only alternative is a still weaker [than the 1987] IMF Agreement. Official creditors may force the IMF into this situation. However, if you abuse the IMF's own guidelines, then you weaken the institution overall."

5. Discussion with officials of the US Department of the Treasury, March 1988.

6. The economic safety net provided to Israel through legislation enacted by the US Congress is indeed prodigious and includes a trade agreement establishing a generalized schedule of preferences (GSP) which allows 2,700 manufactured items to enter the US without duties; providing an annual $3 billion aid package in the form of grants which are exempted from repayment; and the extension of a variety of special privileges, some of them unprecedented in American foreign relations. With respect to the latter we have: an unmonitored, lump-sum payment of economic aid at the *start* of the fiscal year, enabling Israel to earn some $40 million in interest annually; the waiving of the requirement that most of the money received for military aid be spent in the US, allowing Israel instead to bolster its own defense industry; deleting from defense contracts with Israel a number of administrative and research and development costs which allow Israel, for example, to save about $90 million on the replacement of 60 F-16 fighter bombers; and, of particular interest here, a recent military debt scheme.

This new scheme, passed just prior to the adjournment of the 1988 Congress, allows Israel to finance any military debts to the US in excess of 10 percent of that debt. This takes the form of a refinancing by allowing the debtor nation to make a special offer on Wall Street with a US government guarantee. While this agreement appears to be consistent with the ultimate intent of the plan mandated by the US Congress in early 1988 (and referenced here), it is only Israel thus far that has been permitted to refinance portions of its $5.6 billion military debt owed to the US under this new legislation. This does not suggest that the US will deny Egypt the same privilege; it is to say that thus far, it has not agreed to any Egyptian request to refinance its military debt under the terms of this new legislation.

8 ECONOMIC EVOLUTION SINCE 1800

Charles Issawi

The economic difficulties which Egypt is facing today can be traced, to a large extent, to the pattern of its evolution in the last two hundred years. I shall examine this under four headings: Egypt's relatively unfavorable position in 1800; its lop-sided growth in the nineteenth century; its accumulating difficulties in 1922-52; and lastly and briefly, its achievements and failures since the 1952 Revolution.

The Situation in 1800

Partly because of such external shocks as the Black Death and the diversion of the trade routes, partly because of the nature of Mamluk government, and partly because of the cultural stagnation affecting the whole Middle East, Egypt's economic and social condition around 1800 was profoundly unsatisfactory. This is brought out by comparison not only with Western Europe but with such regions as Russia, Japan, China, the Balkans, and Latin America.

Egypt's agriculture compared very favorably—in terms of yield per acre and, unless my sums are wrong, also per man—with those of most other parts of the world. Its transport system was also adequate, thanks to the magnificent Nile and its branches and canals; I say this although aware that there were no man-made ports, no roads, no carts and only a couple of carriages in the whole country. Technology had shown no improvement since ancient times. The level of the crafts may have actually declined. The tax system was oppressive and inefficient. And there was no remote equivalent of the commercial and financial institutions and devices that had developed in Europe and were also to be found in Russia, Japan and parts of Latin America— banks, insurance, double-entry book-keeping, stock or produce exchanges, and so on.

In the cultural field the gap was still wider. Egypt's literacy rate must have been below 5 percent—after all, at the end of the ninteeth century, it was only 7 percent. Its ancient university, al-Azhar, showed no signs of life that I can discern, though I should immediately add that some scholars whom I respect disagree with me. The official curriculum did not include the philosophical or scientific works of the great Muslim thinkers, not even al-Ghazzali's. Printing had not been introduced. When Muhammad Ali started his reforms, he could not find a single Egyptian who knew a European language and, as far as I am aware, no one had a clue regarding Western science. This may be contrasted not only with Europe but also with the other regions which I mentioned. In Japan, by 1850 overall male literacy was about 40 percent, and in the cities 75-80 percent. In the 1780s some 3,000 books were being published each year, editions of 10,000 or so were not uncommon (in Europe the usual run was 500-1,000), books were cheap, both free and commercial lending libraries were active, and many books aimed at diffusing improved industrial, commercial and agricultural methods.[1] In eighteenth- and early nineteenth-century China "perhaps 30 to 45 percent of males" had "some ability to read and write"[2] and printing had been practiced on a large scale since the seventh century.

In Spanish America, by 1820, there were over 20 universities, including a College of Mines, which between them had conferred 150,000 degrees. In addition, many students went to Europe, and the Latin Americans participated very fully in the Enlightenment and were familiar with, and often critical of, the work of the major European scientists and philosophers. Printing presses had been introduced from the beginning of the Spanish conquest.[3]

In Russia, though the economy was distinctly more developed, the level of literacy was probably not much higher than in Egypt. But, even more than in Latin America, there was a fairly large and very active intellectual elite—operating from universities, technical schools and various academies and societies. Three indicators may be noted: in 1820 the Imperial Library in St. Petersburg, with 300,000 volumes, was the fourth largest in Europe; in the late eighteenth century, Nikolai Novikov, an incisive social critic, ran a publishing house which put out 900 titles; and in 1787-92, an Economic Encyclopedia was published, followed by a Russian translation of Adam Smith's *Wealth of Nations,* only twenty-six years after the English edition. No wonder that soon after Russia experienced both an industrial upsurge and an amazing cultural florescence.

A similar phenomenon may be observed in the Balkans, especially Greece. Already in the eighteenth century students were being sent to Europe, books in the various vernaculars were printed in Europe and sent to the Balkans, and many schools were opened. Shelley, who in addition to being a marvellous poet was an acute though, I am afraid, partisan political observer, states, "The University of Chios contained, before the breaking out of the [Greek] revolution, eight hundred students and among them several Germans and Americans."[4] Following independence, and helped by the more egalitarian social structure which gave peasants enough land to lead a decent life, education spread rapidly in the Balkans and enabled them to make rapid progress.[5]

One can sum up the situation by saying that, unlike the above-mentioned regions, Egypt had neither a strong and enlightened government that promoted development nor an educated and active bourgeoisie. For thirty years or more, the first deficiency was remedied by the titanic energy of Muhammad Ali, who shifted Egypt's agriculture from basic to perennial irrigation growing cotton, developed transport by building the port of Alexandria and opening the Mahmudiya canal and, starting from scratch, set up an impressive industrial structure. At the same time he revolutionized education by sending students to Europe and opening numerous technical schools.

Lop-Sided Development, 1850-1914

The breakdown of Muhammad Ali's system—under foreign pressure but also because of his failing energy—shifted Egypt to another path, indicated by its comparative advantages in agriculture and transport. It became an export-oriented economy, sending out cotton and other agricultural goods and importing practically everything else. Helped by the shortage caused by the American Civil War, cotton exports shot up; between 1848-52 and 1908-12 they increased nearly twenty times in volume and almost as much in value and in purchasing power. This was achieved by a vast expansion in irrigation, crowned by the opening of the Aswan Dam in 1902, at that time the largest in the world. It required the laying down of a vast network of railways—and it may be pointed out that Egypt got a railway before Sweden, Central Poland, or the Balkans and long before Japan. It led to the enlargement of the port of Alexandria and the building of new ports at Suez and Port Said. Foreign banks were founded, and they and the foreign-owned cotton export firms financed the movement of the cotton crop and the return flow of imports. Alexandria was recreated, the population rising from 10,000 or 15,000 in 1800 to nearly 450,000 in 1917, and vast new quarters, provided with modern amenities, were built in Cairo and elsewhere. By 1913, Egypt presented many aspects of a developed country. Its per capita income, about $50.00, was higher than that of Japan, twice as high as that of India, and almost one-quarter that of France.[6] Per capita foreign trade (exports plus imports), at $24.30, was higher than in Spain, twice as high as in Japan, Greece, and Bulgaria, and two and a half times as high as in Russia. Its railway network per inhabited square kilometer or per capita was one of the highest in the world.[7] And there are clear indications of an improvement in the level of living of the masses.[8]

However, this development was lop-sided or asymmetrical.[9] On the purely economic side it had two grave defects. First, the large increase in output, income and exports had been dissipated in consumption or remitted abroad. The savings rate remained very low; for 1903-13, it is put at about 3.5 percent by Bent Hansen. To make matters worse, a huge foreign debt—about $1 billion—had been accumulated, making Egypt one of the most highly indebted countries per capita. Secondly, hardly any manufacturing industry had been developed. For this there were many reasons: the small size of the market, the scarcity of raw materials and power, the lack of skilled labor, the shortage of capital, etc. But the political factors were also very important. First, the Egyptian government's hands were tied by the Anglo-Turkish Commercial Convention of 1838, which prevented the lifting of import duties above first 5 and then 8 percent, or the imposition of a differentiated tariff. And secondly, Egypt's British rulers had no great wish—to say the least—to promote its industrialization.[10]

These two economic deficiencies were accompanied by an equally grave social one—the failure to develop Egypt's human resources. The most striking index of this, in addition to poor health conditions, is the extremely low literacy rate—in 1907, only 7 percent overall. This is far below the contemporary figures for the countries used for comparison—whether Greece's 39 percent or Japan's nearly 100 percent. Here too, the British have received most of the blame and there is no doubt that their zeal for education was less than overwhelming. But I cannot help believing that Egyptian society itself bears the greater responsibility, and that much more could have been done if the necessary will had been present. After all, it does not cost much to teach people to read and write, but it does take hard work.

Egypt was able to achieve quite rapid economic growth with a minimum amount of social development because it acquired the skills required to run a modern economy by importing its bourgeoisie en bloc. At the top of the social pyramid—along with the large

Egyptian landowners—stood the European capitalists—French, British, Italian, etc. Europeans ran the banks, insurance companies, cotton export firms, mines and factories, railways and public utilities. They also staffed the higher ranks of the professions: physicians, engineers, lawyers (in the mixed courts) and so forth. Below them came other foreigners and members of minority groups—Greeks, Armenians, Jews and Syrian Christians, who performed two main functions. The salaried group provided technical and administrative skills: as journalists, engineers, lawyers, doctors, employees in banks and other businesses, accountants, skilled workers, etc. The entrepreneurial group formed a link between the large capitalists, concentrated in Alexandria or Cairo, and the farmers and urban masses. They lent money to growers, bought their crops and moved them to Alexandria for shipment abroad, and in return supplied them with imported manufactured goods. This bourgeoisie of foreigners and members of minorities was surely essential for Egypt's development; without it, the machine could not have run. But its presence had two harmful effects. First, it inhibited the growth of an indigenous bourgeoisie, without which no durable development can take place. Secondly, it imprinted in the Egyptian mind the notion that capitalism was something alien, carried out by, and for the exclusive benefit of, foreigners. This idea was to bear bitter fruit in the 1950s and 1960s.

Accumulating Difficulties, 1922-1952

In this period Egypt began to face increasing difficulties. The development path it had been following for nearly a hundred years had led to a dead end. First of all, the reserves of arable land were running out and expansion of cultivation could be achieved only by increasingly costly irrigation works. In 1912, the cultivated area had been 5.3 million feddans; by 1952 the figure had risen by only 10 percent to 5.8 million. However, various dams had made it possible to convert some acreage from basin irrigation, growing only one crop a year, to perennial irrigation, growing three crops in two years, and the cropped area had risen by 21 percent. Secondly, the price of Egyptian cotton—along with other agricultural prices—fell sharply in world markets in the late 1920s and 1930s, Egypt's terms of trade deteriorated, and the purchasing power of its exports shrank. Thirdly, the growth of the population began to accelerate. From about 3.8 million around 1800, population increased a little over three times to 12.8 million in 1917. But between 1917 and 1960 it more than doubled, and since then has almost doubled again, standing at over 50 million. At present rates of growth, the population should double again in under 30 years. The combined effect of all these factors have been a shrinkage in the amount of cultivable land per head, a decline in per capita GNP and the conversion of Egypt—traditionally a grain exporter— into an ever greater importer.

Until the 1930s, Egypt's successive governments, preoccupied with the struggle for complete independence, showed little awareness of these problems. Measures were taken to intensify agriculture, by using improved seeds and more fertilizers and by expanding irrigation and drainage. This helped to raise cotton and grain yields, but also increased the costs of production. In 1930, the commercial treaties that restricted Egypt's tariff autonomy lapsed, and in 1936 the capitulations that restricted its fiscal autonomy were abolished. The government seized this opportunity to embark on an industrialization program, based on tariff protection and aiming at import substitution. The tax system was also reformed, income taxes being imposed for the first time. This program achieved a fair measure of success and created an industrial nucleus that served Egypt well during the Second World War. Like the First World War, the Second World War caused a great shortage of industrial goods, owing to the cutting off of sources of supply and the increased demand created by the Allied troops stationed in Egypt. However, this time, Egypt had an industrial structure that could seize the opportunity; output rose by over one-half and industrial profits expanded greatly. Much of these profits were reinvested after the war. Helped by further protection, output continued to expand. By 1952 industrial production was about 2.5 times the prewar level.[11]

Another important aspect of this period was the growth of an indigenous bourgeoisie, brought about by three factors. First, the expansion of certain sectors created opportunities which were seized by Egyptian entrepreneurs, e.g., in industry and navigation. Secondly, the expansion of education meant that many more trained Egyptians were available for employment in the urban sectors. Thirdly, the government used what pressure it could to promote "Egyptianization," i.e., the increased hiring of Egyptians in various foreign firms and, wherever possible, the replacement of foreigners by Egyptians. Lastly tens of thousands of foreigners, seeing the end of their privileges in Egypt and apprehensive about the future, left the country.

However, all these measures—intensification, industrialization, and "Egyptianization"—as well as a slight improvement in the tax structure and an increase in education and other social services—

could not offset the effects of a sluggish agriculture and rapid population growth. During the war per capita incomes, and the level of living, had declined sharply and the postwar advance had, by 1952, at best just restored the prewar level, and may actually have not quite reached it.[12] A sense of economic failure was certainly one—though by no means the main—factor behind the 1952 Revolution.

Egypt After 1952

In agriculture, in the period since the 1952 Revolution, three important measures may be noted. The successive land reforms have transformed Egypt's agrarian structure, which in the past had been marked by great inequality. Over 1 million feddans of land, or one-sixth of the cultivated area, was transferred from large landowners to small farmers, and one-tenth of the rural population benefited from this measure; a larger number benefited from the reduction in rents. Most observers agree that the reform did not disrupt production and may indeed have enhanced it. Some maintain that it has not really solved any major problems, having merely replaced a large landowning class by a middling one—but in our very imperfect world, this must surely count as an achievement.

Other important measures in agriculture include the building of the High Dam, extension of cooperatives, further intensification and a shift to more valuable crops. The Dam has come in for a lot of criticism—much of it, I cannot help feeling, arising from the fact that it was built by the Russians. It has certainly provided flood control, additional supplies of water, and vast amounts of electricity, admittedly at an ecological cost. Equally obviously, the vast reclamation of marginal lands envisioned in the plans has not come about,[13] but one can hardly blame the Dam for this. A shift to fruits and vegetables, for which Egypt is ideally suited and which I have been advocating for nearly 50 years, has also taken place.[14] Unfortunately, very little of the increase in production has been exported, going instead to meet the growing needs of the urban population. Intensification has continued but the results have been limited: in 1973-84, agricultural output grew by only 2.5 percent a year, or slightly below the population growth and well below the increase in demand. As a result, the per capita index of food production fell from 100 in 1974-76 to 91 in 1982-84. Concurrently, imports of cereals rose from 3.9 million tons in 1974 to 8.6 million in 1984.[15]

Industrialization has been pursued with much energy since the Revolution. It will be remembered that in 1945-52 private enterprise had produced a rate of growth of over 10 percent in industrial output, but following the revolution this fell sharply. The state therefore stepped in, at first to supplement and then to take over the private sector. Much was undoubtedly achieved; the output of existing industries expanded and new ones were created. Following the 1965 economic crisis, caused by overextension, sectoral imbalance, inadequate savings, shortage of foreign exchange, the war in Yemen, and the increasingly obvious inefficiency of the public sector, the growth rate of industrial output fell sharply, to 3.8 percent a year in 1965-73; however, following Sadat's new policies, this rose again to the very impressive figure of 10.3 in 1973-84.[16] Moreover, there were signs that some industries were becoming competitive and penetrating world markets: in 1965, 46 percent of manufactured exports went to the Soviet Union and East Europe and only 20 percent to industrial market economies; by 1983, the Soviet share had dropped to 40 and the Western had risen to 38. But when all this has been said it remains true that the public sector, which accounts for the bulk of Egyptian industry, is in the main a horror story, in terms of overstaffing, imbalances, low efficiency of investment, and low productivity per worker. I shall not repeat the usual examples but just point out the automobile industry: in the late 1970s the Nasr factory produced one car per man per year, whereas an identical Fiat factory in Spain produced over 8. It is worth adding that the present British figure is 17 and the Japanese figures range from 30 to 50.[17] John Waterbury, on whom I have freely drawn in this section, has an excellent analytic account of the development, and shortcomings, of the public sector.[18] Some years ago I stated that: "It is difficult to imagine a more cumbersome and inefficient instrument of industrial management than Middle Eastern bureaucracy," a judgment that was quoted approvingly by a reviewer in a Czech journal, who presumably was thinking of his own bureaucrats. I see no reason to revise this estimate, but am fully aware that in Egypt, as elsewhere in the Middle East and most of the world, including the United States, bureaucracy is there not only to stay but to grow.

Another of Nasser's objectives was to raise the investment rate, in order to promote overall growth. Indeed, this was surely one of the reasons for the massive industrializations of the 1950s and 1960s. At first some success was achieved and the gross domestic savings rate rose from 12 percent of GDP to 14 in 1975. But after that it dropped sharply, to a low of 4 in 1975, rising again to 12 by 1984. This was far below the investment rate and in 1984 Egypt's resource balance—i.e., the extent to which it drew on foreign resources to cover its consumption and investment—was no less than 13 percent of its GDP, a figure exceeded only by some very poor countries.[19] The reasons are only too clear. On the one hand, private consumption has grown quite rapidly. The government has not been willing to squeeze the population hard enough to extract greater savings from them—and who shall blame it? On the other, government consumption has shot up at a very high rate. This in turn has been due to the very high military expenditure, caused mainly by the conflicts with Israel—which at one time was absorbing the enormous figure of over 20 percent of GNP—and to the growth of bureaucracy, where numbers have multiplied several fold. In these circumstances there were only two possible outcomes: the elimination of investment, which would have spelled stagnation, or seeking foreign grants and loans. As a result, by 1984, Egypt's gross external liabilities amounted to over $23 billion and its debt service absorbed 34 percent of the value of its exports of goods and services.[20]

One last word about the development of Egypt's human resources. As noted earlier, at independence Egypt had achieved little in the fields of health and education. Since then, and more particularly since the revolution, very much more has been done. Three figures are indicative. Life expectancy at birth has risen from about 31 years in the 1930s and 47 in 1965 to 60 years in 1984; this reflects the massive reductions in the general death rate, and more particularly in infant mortality. Literacy has risen from 18 percent in 1937 and 38 in 1957 to close to 50 percent today; this reflects the great expansion of schools, which today provide for practically all children of school age. And, at the level of higher education, there is the great and impressive increase in the number of qualified Egyptian scientists, physicians, agronomists, statisticians, economists, and others. I need hardly add that this includes many women. To one who, like me, can vividly remember conditions prevailing 60 years ago, the change that has taken place is most gratifying.

However, there is no reason for complacency—far from it. For the sad fact remains that in the scale of social development Egypt stands low—lower indeed than in the scale of economic development. The best indicator of this is the Physical Quality of Life Index, compiled around 1980 and based essentially on birth rates, death rates, literacy and education. Egypt scored 52—the highest being Iceland with 98 and the lowest Guinea Bissau with 14. This is low compared to the poorer Asian countries, whose per capita incomes were not too different from those of Egypt: Sri Lanka 81, Thailand 75, Philippines 72, and China 71, though it is higher than India's 43.[21]

Today, technology has become the most important single factor of production and the future of nations is becoming increasingly dependent on how well they can absorb technology, including very advanced branches like computers and biotechnology.[22] Already South Korea, Taiwan, Hong Kong and Singapore, and others, have shown how countries with an educated, adaptive labor force can break into fields which were thought reserved for highly developed ones. In this coming race, Egypt cannot afford to remain behind and its performance will depend on how well it succeeds in developing its human resources.

Notes

1. Charles Issawi, "Why Japan," in Ibrahim Ibrahim (ed.), *Arab Resources* (Washington, D.C.: Center for Contemporary Arab Studies, 1983), pp. 283-300.

2. Evelyn Sakakida Rawski, *Education and Popular Literacy in Ching China* (Ann Arbor, Michigan, 1979), p.23.

3. For details and references see Issawi, "The Middle East," op. cit.

4. Preface to *Hellas*.

5. See John Lampe and Marvin Jackson, *Balkan Economic History, 1550-1950* (Bloomington, Indiana, 1982).

6. For figures, sources and qualifications see Charles Issawi, "Asymmetrical Development and Transport in Egypt," in William R. Polk and Richard L. Chambers, eds., *Beginning of Modernization in the Middle East* (Chicago, 1968), pp. 399-400.

7. See tables in *ibid.*, pp. 384, 394.

8. See Charles Issawi, *An Economic History of the Middle East and North Africa* (New York, 1982), pp. 104-105.

9. On this see Charles Issawi, "Egypt Since 1800: A Study in Lop-Sided Development," *Journal of Economic History* 2, no. 1 (March 1961).

10. See Charles Issawi, "British Policy and Egyptian Industrialization: A Case Study" (forthcoming).

11. See indices in Charles Issawi, *Egypt in Revolution* (London, 1963), pp. 113, 173.

12. *Ibid.*, pp. 111-13.

13. John Waterbury, *The Egypt of Nasser and Sadat* (Princeton, 1983), pp. 64-65, 297-300.

14. *Ibid.*, 290.

15. World Bank, *World Development Report,* 1986 (New York) Appendix Tables.

16. World Bank, *loc. cit.*

17. Waterbury, *op. cit.*, p. 105, citing Ali al-Graitli.

18. *Ibid.*, chapters 4-6.

19. World Bank, *loc. cit.*

20. *Ibid.*

21. Roger Hansen and V. Kallab, *U.S. Foreign Policy and The Third World* (New York, 1982), pp. 153-61.

22. W. Michael Blumenthal, "The World Economy and Technological Change," *Foreign Affairs* 66, no. 3 (1988).

PART 2: EGYPT'S POLITICAL SYSTEM

9 THE FORMATION OF THE CONTEMPORARY EGYPTIAN STATE FROM NASSER AND SADAT TO MUBARAK

Raymond A. Hinnebusch

This essay examines the formation of the contemporary Egyptian state as the outcome of the state-building project of the Nasser era and the attempt of Nasser's successor, Sadat, to accommodate the state to a threatening and unmanageable environment. Mubarak's Egypt inherits this double legacy. The formation of the Egyptian state has proceeded amidst fundamental international and domestic challenges. A credible response to them has required the forging of legitimate authority—a consensus between the leader and the rest of the elite on the objectives and limits of power, and the acceptance of state authority among the wider public.[1] It also demanded the creation of political structures able to control an increasingly mobilized political arena. This analysis examines the changing role of leadership and political structure under the three regimes in their search to cope with the constraints of the environment.

The Heritage of Nasser: The Legitimacy and Structural Foundations of the State

Nasser's major contribution to the formation of the state was to forge its dominant structures and to endow it with a nationalist-populist legitimacy. This went hand in hand with challenges to those forces which had dominated Egypt—Western imperialism and the largely agrarian bourgeoisie—for no autonomous state could be forged until their power over the country was broken. Thus, Nasserist state building took a radical nationalist-populist direction.

The key to state building under Nasser was charismatic leadership. Nasser's regime began as a military coup, not a charismatic movement. It rose, however, out of a "time of troubles," and Nasser, in a series of successful foreign policy victories over "imperialist" powers which made Egypt the acknowledged center of the Arab world, soon emerged as a charismatic leader, embraced by Egyptians as a national hero with unmatched personal legitimacy. It was this which consolidated and legitimized the regime, allowing it to transcend its purely military origins. Nasser was raised above the rest of his colleagues—turning them, in effect, into his "staff." The Nasser regime launched modernization and populist reform from above, chiefly through a rationalized bureaucracy. Nasser sought first to accommodate, then to replace, the private sector as the main motor of the economy in favor of state planning, entrepreneurship and investment. At the same time, he eschewed a full assault on the bourgeoisie and sought to win its cooperation with the state. The most enduring results of Nasserist public policy were land reform, the formation of a large public sector, import-substitute industrialization, and a series of "populist" policies which established certain economic "rights"—from reasonably priced food to education and employment—as part of the "social contract" between the regime and public. Through charisma and nationalism, a huge bureaucratic state incorporating a large segment of salaried middle class, and through populist redistribution, Nasser cut the previously dominant classes down to size, raised up and won the support of middle- and lower-class elements, and created a broad cross-class support coalition. By balancing the various elements in this coalition and mobilizing his mass support against recalcitrant elites, Nasser created a stronger, more autonomous state. In harnessing charisma, ideology and coercion in its challenge to the old order and the formation of a new one, the Nasser regime corresponds closely to charismatic authority; but the reliance on bureaucratic instruments rather than a mass movement made the regime a charismatic-bureaucratic hybrid.

The roots of Egypt's post-populist change must be sought in the Nasser regime itself, since some of its very strengths turned out to be vulnerabilities and because it stimulated the forces which generated pressures for change. Personalized charismatic rule, while an asset in imposing radical reform, retarded the development of political institutions in which charismatic legitimacy, to persist, must be infused. Perhaps because of the relative ease with which his popular support and the compliant bureaucracy at his command enabled Nasser to consolidate power and smash opposition, he never felt the need for a strong party system. After his regime defeated the old upper classes, it was exposed to embourgeoisement by its failure to create an ideological party which could replenish the elite from a popularly-recruited cadre and by the use of the army, bureaucracy, and a weak party/parliament, which chiefly coopted the local notability, as the main channels of recruitment. Moreover, in the absence of a strong party, Nasser lacked an instrument for institutionalizing mass activism on behalf of "Nasserism," a political motor to drive the statist economy, and a means to contain the patrimonial tendencies of the authoritarian-bureaucratic state. In part because of this, the regime soon showed signs of patrimonialization: growing corruption and clientalism, riddling the state apparatus, generated a "bureaucratic feudalism" at the expense of rationalization. The failure to institutionalize Nasserism meant that it would not survive its first and only leadership succession.

The very policies on which Nasser built his authority had certain built-in contradictions. While etatist and populist policies curbed and alienated the private bourgeoisie, the regime nevertheless tried to co-opt it into a subordinate role in the state development drive, and in certain ways actually stimulated a state-dependent bourgeoisie. Recruitment practices brought the bourgeoisie into the heart of the state economic sector, but it was deprived of the real political power which might have accommodated it to etatism. The bourgeoisie could not long rest content with statist control, Nasserist leveling, and political subordination. Despite the discontent of the bourgeoisie, Nasser actually sought to spare it excessive burdens, while also attempting to meet the needs of his mass constituency for a better life; this, however, constrained the regime's capacity to mobilize resources, making it vulnerable to a resource crisis which soon put the etatist model in jeopardy and opened the door to capitalist restoration. There was thus a contradiction between the ideological superstructure and the socio-economic base of the regime which ultimately would be bridged, once the charismatic leader passed, by a bourgeois recapture of state power.

Nasser's charisma was built on nationalism, which entangled him in costly conflicts in the Arab world. No authentic nationalist leadership could avoid challenging imperialist control of the region, but it was the intervention of external forces this challenge ultimately brought on—Israel's 1967 strike with American connivance at Egypt—which threw Nasserism into a fatal crisis. The 1967 war brought on economic stagnation and a foreign policy stalemate which badly shook the legitimacy of the regime and mass faith, not so much in Nasser, but certainly in his policies. Without the disillusionment and ideological vacuum engendered by the defeat, Sadat's radical reversal of Nasserism would hardly be conceivable. The defeat exacerbated all the vulnera-bilities of the regime, strengthened bourgeois forces opposed to it, and threw it into permanent crisis. All that was required to set in train a major policy transformation was a new ruler prepared to lead it. Sadat was that man.

Charismatic authority, though less constrained by institutions or customs, is more conditional than other forms of authority, specifically on the exceptional performance of the leader, and is hence vulnerable to over-extension. Egypt could not sustain the simultaneous drive for economic modernization, military and political power, and a mass welfare state, which Nasser promised and Egyptians expected. Nasser erected a strong new state in Egypt, but in challenging the dominant classes internally and the American-Israeli *combinazione* externally, without forging his populist coalition into a strong organized political force, he left the state vulnerable to a policy transformation after his death. Nasserism nevertheless left an enduring twin legacy of legitimacy and coercion. It created the structural foundations of the authoritarian state, the instruments which have made rule possible in spite of protracted economic and foreign policy crises; indeed, the instruments Nasser built to carry out his policies would serve Sadat equally well in their undoing. But Nasser also established new standards of nationalist independence and populist obligation which legitimized his authoritarian state. Herein lies the dilemma of Nasser's successors: to the extent they use the instruments of power he built to reverse the policies that legitimized them, they risk a mass alienation that is threatening to the long-term durability of this power.

Egypt under Sadat: The Transformation of Public Policy

Sadat's major contribution to the development of the Egyptian state was to accommodate its policies to the dominant forces in its domestic and global environment. Sadat's transformation of Egyptian policy was propelled by the interaction between his drive to consolidate his power and Egypt's struggle to extricate itself from the post-1967 economic stagnation and Israeli occupation. There was mounting pressure on the regime to find a solution to the occupation, but the Israeli-American *combinazione* seemed unbeatable and the Soviet Union to offer no way out. This, and the class interests of the elite, ruled out a left-wing solution. A major segment of the elite was convinced, partly by its class interest in a change, that Nasserism had reached a dead end, and that only accommodation with the US and economic liberalization could relieve the crisis. Sadat came to power favorable to such a reversal of Nasserism and the requirements for consolidating his power pulled him in the same direction. Though the presidency gave him a command post no rival could match, Sadat, lacking the stature to pursue Nasser's centrist balancing act between elite and mass, needed a solid support base underpinning his legal authority; since his rivals were on the left and his potential support on the right, a rightward course which would win over the powerful bourgeoisie made the most sense. Sadat found his initial support in the "state bourgeoisie." With a foot in high state office and assets in private society, this group was not only the most strategic social force, but the one most prepared to accept his leadership; its support was crucial to Sadat's consolidation of his power. By contrast his rivals, led by Ali Sabri, though they spoke in the name of Nasserism, lacked a strong party with which to mobilize mass counter-forces. The purges of the official left and the new waves of recruitment from bourgeois private society engineered by Sadat after the succession struggle further consolidated the bourgeois social composition of the ruling elite. Thus, the cleavage between a radical political elite and the dominant classes characteristic of the Nasser era was bridged and the stage set for a conservatization of ideology and policy.

Sadat began with a series of foreign policy decisions which pushed Egypt increasingly rightward and into dependency on the United States. The decision to seek American diplomatic help sparked the fall of the Ali Sabri faction, the main obstacle to major change. This and the expulsion of the Soviet advisors won Sadat bourgeois support and, in alienating the Soviets, narrowed alternatives to a westward turn. The conservative Arab forces on which Egypt was becoming economically dependent also pushed Sadat to the right. This all helped shape the strategy of limited war in 1973 which led Sadat to put all his eggs in the American basket in the "first disengagement." The latter led to a second disengagement, and then to the trip to Jerusalem, Camp David and the separate peace. As he was ever more deeply committed to an American solution, Sadat's alternatives were so narrowed and his prestige so staked on a "successful" outcome that he had to accept what he was offered despite the price: a separate peace at the expense of Egypt's leadership of the Arab world, an end to nationalist non-alignment, and an opening of Egypt to American and Israeli influence. *Infitah* accompanied this diplomatic realignment. It responded to internal economic decline, the wishes of the bourgeoisie and external opportunities such as the petrodollar boom, but also to the need to stimulate and reinforce American interest in Egypt, to make her a suitable client. Once begun, internal and external interests combined to extend and entrench *infitah*; it and the "peace process"

were each deemed necessary to the success of the other. As Egypt
became economically dependent, the mounting foreign pressures on
decision-makers and the proliferation of local interests with a stake
in the process reinforced Sadat's course.

The outcome of Sadat's innovations was mixed. Egypt was
disentangled from the costly Arab-Israeli conflict, but lost its central
role in the Arab world and was pulled into unnatural alliances with
the US against other Arab states. *Infitah*, Western aid and the
accompanying oil boom and labor export sparked an influx of revenues
and imports, fueling an investment and consumption takeoff, and the
formation of a larger, stronger bourgeoisie, but at the cost of growing
debt, dependency and inequality. All these factors had profound
political consequences: the breakup of the populist coalition and the
decline of the nationalist legitimacy which had supported the regime
under Nasser; and a consequent dependence of the regime on a
bourgeoisie which expected a share of power, in return for support.
Sadat had to begin an adaptation of the state to the new conditions
his policies had created.

The Post-Populist State: The Adaptation of the
Nasserist Regime under Sadat and Mubarak

The adaptation of the Nasserist state to its post-populist environment
had to satisfy the desire of the regime's bourgeois constituency for
power sharing and cope with the narrowed social base and eroding
mass legitimacy of the state. Under Sadat, adaptation took the form
of a departure from charismatic authority toward both limited
retraditionalization and limited liberalization. Under Mubarak, limited
liberalization has been consolidated. Two key dimensions of state
adaptation, the changing bases of presidential authority and the
pluralization of the party system, capture the essence of post-Nasserist
political change.

Presidency and Elite: From Charismatic Leadership
to Presidential Monarchy

The presidency is the command post through which the bureaucratic
state governs Egypt. It is the linchpin of the political elite. Its powers
are decisive for the outcome of intra-elite power struggles and

regime stability. This office has, however, evolved through the changing relationship of the chief executive and the rest of the elite —his "staff."

Nasser founded the authoritarian presidency, endowing it not only with tremendous constitutional powers—over the cabinet, parliament, and courts, etc.—but also with his own charismatic legitimacy. Nasser made the presidency a highly activist, interventionist office, using its powers to establish his autonomy of the elite and in pursuit of a revolution from above which ran roughshod over the interests of the dominant classes. Nasser had to contend with a certain intra-elite rivalry; but in the end he eliminated all rivals, securely establishing his unchallenged presidential authority.

The legitimized powers of the office were crucial to Egypt's post-populist transformation. The legal authority of the presidency was decisive in the victory of Sadat, a man of otherwise modest political stature, in the succession crisis over rivals entrenched in their bureaucratic fiefdoms; it was his legal prerogative which allowed Sadat to strike first at the Sabri group and deterred a similar attempt on their part, which rallied the support of the army around Sadat and gave him command of the only reliable coercive force in the struggle for power, the presidential guard. This was a measure of the extent to which legal authority retained the upper hand over patrimonial tendencies in the regime. Moreover, the powers of the presidency were indispensable to Sadat's subsequent success in redirecting Egypt. Without its authority, Sadat could never have turned back the political ambitions of certain senior generals and fostered a professionalism in military ranks that accepted legal authority. In addition, at every watershed in his rightward course, Sadat had to defeat opposition to the reversal of Nasserism from both elites and segments of the mass public. To be sure, the intra-elite support Sadat enjoyed as a champion of bourgeois interests and the neutralization of Nasserite forces by the legitimacy won in the October War and by the failures of Nasserism, gave Sadat a free hand during the crucial period of redirection (1974-76). His shrewd patrimonial manipulations also helped him divide and keep on top of the elite. But the political structure—an authoritarian state headed by a dominant presidency—was crucial to Sadat's enterprise. As long as policy conflicts remained confined to elite circles, the presidency was the dominant force and the authoritarian state, lacking traditions or institutions of mass participation, largely kept them so confined. Inside the elite, the office provided

Sadat the indispensable levers of power to stay on top. The routinization of Nasser's legitimacy in the presidency made it the most institution-alized part of the political system, against which all other elite institutions—party, press, even the military—proved impotent, and from which Sadat was able to purge all elite opposition and construct a deferent new team.

With the passing of the charismatic leader, either retraditionalized personal rule or legal rational authority is likely to emerge. Where charismatic authority is, at best, routinized in the position held by the leader, it is likely, when he passes, to turn into patrimonial authority. Sadat, in fact, presided over the emergence of a "Presidential Monarchy" at the apex of the state. His use of traditional techniques of rule—patriarchalism, clientalism, corruption, the formation of a kind of royal family at the center, the traditional legitimation he resurrected, and the essentially conservative objectives of his policies—all amounted to a traditionalization of authority. Moreover, Sadat played a patrimonial game of divide and rule in seeking to impose his controversial policies on recalcitrant segments of the elite. But simultaneously, as part of the deal with his elite and bourgeois supporters, Sadat had also to move in legal-rational directions, curbing the arbitrary power of the state and the presidency. While Nasser had stood above and balanced off the elites, and frequently used his popular support to curb them, Sadat's support rested on a new kind of tacit "social contract" with them. Sadat would retain a free hand in foreign policy, and the ultimate powers of the authoritarian presidency would not be overtly challenged. But the control of the state over society and the political arena would be relaxed and the interventionist role of the presidency under Nasser curbed. While Sadat retained the last word, he refrained from intervening in many domestic policy matters, allowing the bourgeoisie growing scope to advance its interests. The courts took on a new life and a limited pluralization of the political arena allowed the emergence of more effective interest-group activity. Parliament acquired much greater authority and became a major arena for the articulation of bourgeois interests. But this limited political liberalization took place in an unequal way favoring the regime's bourgeois constituency. While a multitude of bourgeois interests turned the newly opened channels of the state into vehicles of political influence, the regime sought the demobilization of the masses, containing any challenge to bourgeois hegemony. Thus a hybrid form of authority emerged, mixing traditional and legal-rational dimensions: a presidential monarchy presiding over a power-sharing alliance between the state and its bourgeois constituency. Although Sadat's patrimonial excesses and the occasionally arbitrary imposition of his major policies retarded the consolidation of this power-sharing experiment, it would be institutionalized under his successor.

Under Mubarak, the authoritarian presidency remains the centerpiece of the state. The smooth transfer of power from Sadat, free of intra-elite conflict, and Mubarak's 1987 reelection manifested the institutionalization of unchallenged legal legitimacy in the office. But Mubarak has used his power in the least activist way of Egypt's three presidents. While Nasser and Sadat sought to reshape Egypt and its place in the world, Mubarak's aim is stability. His values and personality are leaving a new imprint on the office: more cautious, lacking a strong ideological viewpoint and with a self-effacing style, he displays a pragmatism and predictability which made him a man appropriate to a time of rising constraints on state power. His personal integrity and genuine commitment to limited democratization also make him the most widely acceptable leader in a regime enjoying little popular trust. Patrimonialization has also receded before an increased rationalism in elite style; gone is much of the personalism, traditionalism and "royal entourage" of Sadat's rule. Foreign policy, now the province of professional diplomats, is no longer the victim of presidential impulse. Recent prime ministers have been colorless technocrats who typically made their careers in economic or financial management. Pragmatism and technocracy are the order of the day, and legitimacy is sought in legality and rationality, not patriarchalism or personality. The scope of presidential power seems clearly to have narrowed further, but, being less threatening, this power is also less in dispute than under Nasser and Sadat.

The advance of constitutional legality and political liberalization begun under Sadat has accelerated under Mubarak. Having no "mission" comparable to Sadat, he can afford to be more tolerant of opposition, and since his legitimacy rests squarely on legality, he has a greater interest in respecting it. Freedom of political expression, particularly of the press, has widened, and criticism of the government is much more unrestrained than under Sadat. The independence of the courts and their role in expanding constitutional rights and procedures has deepened: e.g., their overturning of a ban on the Wafd party, of the 1984 election law, and of a Sadat decree issued in the absence of parliament. The 1987 trial of police officers for torturing

Islamic activists, a product of press pressure, is a milestone in the protection of individual rights against the state. Political freedoms are still unequally enjoyed: dissent within regime institutions is tolerated, but when it crosses the line into mass action—such as Islamic street demonstrations for implementation of *shari'a* law, and anti-Israeli protests—it is regularly repressed. Generally speaking, the curbing of presidential power under Mubarak, the end to a presidential mission which must be imposed against elite opinion, and the widened access through parliament and cabinet for a multitude of elite factions and bourgeois interest groups, has consolidated the experiment in elite power sharing.

An increase in the power and politicization of the military elite under Mubarak seemed, however, to pose a certain patrimonial challenge to presidential and legal authority. Mubarak was less careful than Sadat to play the patrimonial game of periodic rotation of military chieftains or to balance them with rival officers or strong civilian politicians. As a result, Defense Minister Abdul-Halim Abu Ghazala, an ambitious politicized officer, appeared to establish unprecedented power and acknowledged status as the number two man in the regime. A pro-American rightist, he positioned himself as a champion of military privileges and arms spending, and widened the role of the army in the economy, making it a font of patronage and subcontracting to the private sector. But Abu Ghazala lacked the crucial control over appointments to turn the army into a personal fiefdom, and his right-wing image was a political liability; hence Mubarak had no difficulty removing him from the Defense Ministry in 1989. The professionalization of the officer corps, a tradition of respect for legal legitimacy, and the reluctance of an army utterly lacking in national vision to assume responsibility for Egypt's problems, all make it unlikely that any top general could carry the officer corps in an overt challenge to Mubarak. Mubarak has evidently tried to lessen his dependency on the military and "Sadatists" in the elite by backing technocratic elements in the bureaucracy and encouraging the political opposition. But the Right's ability to block a presidential appointment of the Nasserist Muhammad Hassanein Heikal to a top media post suggests that its power is formidable.

Egypt under Mubarak is inching its way toward a more rational-legal form of authority, but the persisting authoritarian powers of a presidency no longer infused with charisma and the continued potential for military politicians to build semi-autonomous fiefdoms, gives a continuing patrimonial quality to the state.

Managing the Political Arena: Pluralization and the
Formation of a "Dominant Party System"

A state may control the political arena through coercion, legitimacy, or the use of political institutions to incorporate political participation. A second major evolution in the post-populist Egyptian state has been the development of a new formula of political control.

Nasser used charisma and coercion to impose a nationalist-populist ideological consensus on Egypt's political arena and incorporate a broad support coalition in a single—albeit weak—party, the Arab Socialist Union (ASU). His charismatic legitimacy allowed him to balance rival social forces—notably to use popular support to curb the bourgeoisie—rather than accommodate their participatory propensities, and to repress those—the Wafd, the Ikhwan—which refused incorporation into his authoritarian-populist coalition.

Sadat pioneered the adaptation of the state to a more pluralized political arena. Lacking similar popular legitimacy and seeking to root his rule in the support of the bourgeoisie, he had to address its desires for political liberalization. Moreover, his "rightward" policy course shattered the Nasserist consensus and precipitated the emergence of leftist opposition, which Sadat sought to balance by allowing the mainstream Islamic movement and the liberal Wafd to re-enter the political arena. As Egypt's political arena was thus pluralized, Sadat attempted to incorporate it by a controlled political liberalization. The single party system was dismantled and loyal opposition parties allowed to form and compete in parliamentary elections. Islamic activists, Nasserists and the Left were even allowed "in" under controlled conditions, though they were vulnerable to exclusion when they pushed their case too far. Ultimately, when they refused to play by his rules, Sadat suspended the experiment. Toward the more passive masses, Sadat's strategy was to replace charismatic with traditional personal legitimacy, projecting himself as a pious and patriarchal leader, and after 1973 as a successful war hero; but as he pursued Westernization and accommodation with Israel, this gradually failed, leaving a legitimacy vacuum.

Mubarak inherited a regime lacking a credible legitimating ideology or leading personality capable of attaching mass loyalties to the state, and a faltering experiment in political liberalization. Indicative of the regime's ideological bankruptcy were its attempts to depict itself as both Nasserist and Islamic, all the while following Sadatist policies. In the absence of mass legitimacy, the Mubarak regime further developed the combination of limited repression and limited liberalization pioneered by Sadat.

Repression continues to play a role and the security apparatus, more massive than ever, has been relatively effective in containing the two main episodes of violent challenge to the regime—localized Islamic uprisings at Sadat's death and the 1986 police rebellion. Although the police rebellion had no political program and was mainly sparked by worsening treatment of the lower ranks, it could be a sign that politicization is making the use of conscripts from the poorest sectors of society to contain radical opposition to a bourgeois regime ever more risky.

But Mubarak's rule rests on more than coercion. Indeed, his first presidential initiative was to restore the limited liberalization of the party system begun by Sadat. This was both a sign that a reversal of the adaptation of the state to a pluralizing environment was too politically costly, and that the regime was confident that it could control the process. Given the solidity of the Egyptian state, resting on a huge bureaucracy and a history of mass deference, the risks of this adaptation were probably less than the dangers of alternative courses—widened repression or full-scale liberalization. The outcome is a dominant party system with a large government party straddling the center and an array of smaller opposition parties or forces on its right and left.

The ruling National Democratic Party (NDP) stands for the dominant alliance of senior bureaucrats, army officers, businessmen, and the rural notability behind a corresponding ideology: a massive state in an open economy. Although cooptation from the bureaucracy and academia remain the main channels of elite recruitment, party credentials and service have become a factor in this cooptation and the party represents a ladder of recruitment for the private sector bourgeoisie. The party does not make high policy, which remains a government prerogative, but its parliamentary caucus has assumed considerable authority over lesser matters: it is the source of a constant stream of initiatives and responses to government meant to defend or promote the interest of its largely bourgeois constituency. Thus, it incorporates major segments of the most strategic social forces into the ruling coalition; it concedes no accountability to them, but provides enough privileged access to keep them satisfied. The NDP lacks a strong extra-governmental organization, but by way of the clientage networks of the pro-government notability it brings a portion of the village and urban masses into the regime camp, denying the opposition access to them. The party also nominally incorporates large numbers of government employees, and has managed to place its partisans in the top posts of most of the professional and labor syndicates. It lacks an interest in mass mobilization; if anything its function is to enforce demobilization. But as an organizational bond between the regime and the local sub-elites which represent its core support and its linkage to wider social forces, it performs a basic function in protecting the government's societal base.

The formerly monolithic Egyptian political arena has given birth to a rich array of opposition parties. The National Progressive Unionist Party (NPUP) on the left brings together intellectuals and working class activists behind an ideology of nationalist populism. On the liberal right, the New Wafd stands for a coalition of liberal professionals and landlords committed to more thorough economic and political liberalization. And the Islamic movement led by *'ulama*, merchants and lower middle-class student activists commanding a following in the traditional *baladi* quarters is a true cross-class coalition; appropriately, it affirms an indigenous way against the Western penetration which favors the high bourgeoisie. It also combines populist policies with the defense of private property. Under Mubarak, the Wafd and the Islamic movement have emerged as the main opposition forces, the leftist NPUP has declined, and an Islamic "alliance" has joined the small center-left Labor and rightist Liberal parties under Ikhwan leadership and the slogan "Islam is the solution." This marks not only the growing influence of Islam and the decline of the secular left, but the rise of a new Islamic-secular cleavage cutting across class-based ones and putting the regime, the NPUP and the Wafd on the same side. The cross-cutting of cleavages tends to mute political conflict to the advantage of the regime.

Under the current limited liberalization, the opposition parties cannot hope to take power through electoral support. The NDP has dominated parliamentary elections under Mubarak by the same effective methods used under Sadat: fraud, police containment of opposition access to the public, and patronage. Indeed, Mubarak's electoral law, which gives the votes of any party failing to get 8 percent of the total to the dominant party, in excluding smaller parties from parliament, makes elections less liberal than in 1976. As long as the Interior Ministry runs elections they will not be seen by the public as providing real choices and, except in some urban constituencies, will remain rivalries between local notables. Mubarak has, however, been more tolerant of a greater opposition presence in parliament. In 1984, a

Wafd-Ikhwan alliance captured 58 seats and in 1987, the Wafd got 35 and the Islamic Alliance 60. The government remains unchallengeable in parliament, but its majority has declined and the opposition's greater roots in society may give it a voice out of proportion to its size. On the other hand, the exclusion of the NPUP from parliament, principally through the election law, marginalizes Egypt's only unambiguously populist voice, the one force free of wealthy patrons or powerful economic interests and with an alternative non-capitalist economic program. Parliament thus remains almost exclusively a preserve of the bourgeoisie.

Nevertheless, the opposition parties have a real function as "parties of pressure" within the dominant party system. They articulate the interests and values of sectors of the population ignored by the dominant party. They help frame the terms of public debate by raising issues which would otherwise remain off the public agenda. They may even sway government, for if they threaten to capture enough support, it may alter its policies to take the wind out of their sails. The Liberal party helped advance economic liberalization under Sadat, while the leftist National Progressives were a brake on the reversal of populist policies like food subsidies. The Islamic movement has won Islamization concessions from the secular regime, while the New Wafd has helped make partial political liberalization irreversible. A party of pressure may also act as an interest group advocating particular interests in elite circles or promoting the fortunes of aspirant politicians hoping for cooptation. Mubarak's more consensual style of rule and regular consultation with opposition leaders may marginally advance their ability to influence government policy.

The primary consequence of the system in the short run is the stabilization of the regime. The divisions in the opposition allow the regime to play them off against each other. The opposition parties have channeled much political activity which might otherwise take a covert, even violent anti-regime direction into more tame, manageable forms. Opposition elites, in playing the game, incorporate their followings into the system. One sign of the regime's success is the growing incorporation of the three most independent political formations under Sadat, the Wafd, Ikhwan and NPUP, into the system under Mubarak. For opposition activists, the rewards are either personal advancement—the chance of cooptation—or ideological—the chance to espouse ideas, reshape public opinion, and occasionally even influence policy. Even if the regime is the big winner, participation is thus meaningful for them, affects outcomes, and in the long run may lead to the institutionalization of greater power sharing. A tacit understanding now exists between government and opposition: the latter knows that if it goes too far in challenging the regime it invites repression, while the former knows that if it is too unresponsive or tightens controls too much, it risks anti-system mobilization.

In the longer run, the party experiment is deepening the pluralization of the political arena. That the political pluralization begun under Sadat was real is clear from the persistence of all the parties then founded. They have proved to be more than personalistic or official factions, and either revive some political tradition or are rooted in a major societal or issue cleavage: e.g., class or secular-Islamic divisions. The rough correspondence between the ideologies of the parties and their social bases indicates a modern "blocking out" of the political arena along lines of ideological and social differentiation, moving Egyptian politics beyond a mere competition of patrons and shillas without social roots. It is true that this pluralization has only begun to seep down to the level of the mass public, much of which remains politically apathetic or attached to traditional clientage networks. But mass indifference has, in part, been bought by the regime's eschewing of a frontal assault on food subsidies, the surest catalyst of class conflict and political mobilization. The dominant party system probably represents an adaptation to the current level of pluralization sufficient to stabilize the regime at least until mass politicization spreads further downward. Overall, despite its still limited character, Mubarak can be credited with institutionalizing the experiment in political liberalization, thus stabilizing a post-populist regime.

The Limits of Incorporation: The Rise of Political Islam

The social base of the state under Sadat and Mubarak is undoubtedly narrower than under Nasser. In some ways it is more solid, resting on the hard core support of the most strategic social force, the bourgeoisie, which has a major stake in its survival. Elements of the opposition are at least partially incorporated through the party/interest group structure created under limited liberalization. But the regime lacks the legitimacy to incorporate the broad mass public, and the limits of its incorporative capacity leave the door open to the rise of a counter-elite in the form of the Islamic movement.

The development of the Islamic movement is the most significant change in the political arena. It is a change with the potential to transform the system. Sadat originally unleashed the movement against his leftist opponents, but as Westernization and the *infitah* advanced, it became a vehicle of opposition, sometimes violent, to his regime. Though Sadat attempted to curb it, under Mubarak it has taken on new dimensions. The more violent messianic groups, such as al-Jihad, are the targets of continual repression and containment, apparently only partly successful. But the mainstream, now possessed of greater cohesion, organization, and mobilizational capability, has rapidly taken advantage of the legitimate channels of activity opened by the regime. The Jama'at al-Islamiyya recovered their control of the student unions which Sadat tried to break, although the secular opposition has recently made inroads into their dominance. The Jama'at have tried to impose a puritanical, sometimes anti-Coptic, Islamic regime on the campuses and in the towns of upper Egypt, where local government has sometimes bowed to their demands. A major contest between such Islamic groups and the regime is being waged over control of some 40,000 mosques, potential centers of Islamic mobilization; the influence of Islamic groups in *baladi* neighborhoods such as 'Ain Shams seems to be growing. The mainstream Ikhwan and its conservative cousins have also been incorporated into parliament, infiltrated the parties, judiciary and press and generally put secular forces on the defensive. Several victories indicative of their influence are the reversal of Sadat's law of personal status which gave women some modest rights, and a constitutional amendment making the *shari'a* the sole basis of legislation, the potential ground for ruling a whole corpus of secular law unconstitutional. Filling the vacuum left by the withering of state populism, the Islamic movement has also constructed an alternative social infrastructure—mosques, clinics and cooperatives—to bring the masses under Islamic leadership.

The movement is backed by the power of Islamic banking and investment houses, an enigmatic development which may be filling the gap left by the decline of the state. Claiming to represent an alternative economic way, they initially seemed better positioned than government or foreign banks to mobilize the savings of ordinary people. Yet while the Islamic movement grew in opposition to Westernization and *infitah*, these institutions have been linked to entrepreneurs enriched in the oil states and make huge profits on the same international connections and through many of the same speculative financial, black market and tertiary enterprises that the *infitah* has encouraged. Scandals have, moreover, shaken confidence in them, and the government has moved to curb their autonomy. It is thus unclear whether their effect will be to incorporate ordinary Egyptians into a more indigenous, broader-based capitalism accommodated to the *infitah* regime, to provide the economic basis for an alternative socio-political order, or to prove a mere flash in the pan. The regime's mix of hostility and wary tolerance towards them suggests that it is not sure itself.

The Islamic movement is emerging as a powerful cross-class political alliance, a potential counter-establishment. But, as its economic and political power grows, there are signs that its anti-regime populism is being overshadowed by an embourgeoisement of its leadership and a conservation of its ideology: a preaching of class deference, respect for elders, female submission, and the right to a fair profit. If this is the dominant trend, the outcome is less likely to be Islamic revolution than a gradual Islamization of the regime and embourgeoisement of Islam.

The Paralysis of Policy under Mubarak: The Cumulative Constraints of the Nasser and Sadat Eras

Public policy in the Mubarak era has largely been one of continuity, in which Sadat's initiatives have crystallized. The legacies of the Sadat era—a "consumption *infitah,*" massive dependency on the United States and the reliance of the regime on the bourgeoisie— have imposed sharp constraints, locking Egypt into the course Sadat set. Mubarak also inherited constraints from the Nasser period which were difficult to reconcile with the Sadat heritage. So hemmed in, the regime seeks merely incremental changes and has continued to avoid the hard choices between the legacies of Nasser and Sadat. While the regime may not be immediately threatened with revolution, it does not have the capacity to vigorously attack Egypt's accumulating problems.

The major domestic legacy inherited by Mubarak was the hybrid resulting from the opening of Nasser's state-dominated economy to the international capitalist market. On the one hand, the interests created under Nasser have proven durable. The public sector is still the main engine of investment (75 percent of the total), of the mobilization of public revenues and the production of "popular" consumption goods, and cannot be dismantled, at least until a dynamic private alternative has matured. Egypt's huge army has not been demobilized. Indeed, Sadat had to buy its acquiescence in his course by replacing Soviet with American arms. The bureaucracy, employing a large portion of the middle class, is a formidable constituency and instrument of control. Populist "rights" acquired under Nasser have grown into a tacit social contract by which the government provides subsidized food to the masses in return for their tolerance of growing inequality.

Sadat's *infitah* has yet to produce a dynamic capitalist alternative to statism. It did stimulate a growth and consumption boom which lasted into the early eighties. But it remained too dependent on "rent" and transfers vulnerable to external changes such as aid and loans from the West, oil earnings, remittances of workers in the Gulf and Suez Canal fees. Too little of these revenues was invested in agriculture and industry, and too much went into services, was exported or was dissipated on import-driven consumption. Meanwhile, high population growth continued, food production per capita fell, and Egypt had to import over half its food, much from the US. On top of this, despite the peace, Egypt bought large quantities of expensive American arms with high-interest loans. Sadat's legacy seemed no more able to support sustained productive growth than Nasser's populism.

Mubarak sought to reform the economy. He called for a productive instead of a consumption *infitah*, with fewer luxury imports. He also called for foreign investment in less tertiary fields and with better terms, such as the use of more locally-made components. His policy sought to rationalize the state sector, i.e., reduce subsidies, raise agricultural prices, and reform public sector management. But as long as external revenues poured in and the *infitah* boom continued, the political costs of reforms appeared prohibitive and little was actually accomplished.

By the mid-eighties, however, a major economic crisis enveloped Egypt, heightening the urgency of reform. *Infitah* spending had led to a burgeoning debt of nearly $40 billion, for which repayment started to come due. Simultaneously, a fall in oil prices produced a precipitous drop in Egypt's revenues of almost 50 percent. The result was an acute balance of payments deficit, shortages of foreign currency, and an inability to service the debt which brought growth to a halt. The International Monetary Fund (IMF) and Egypt's creditors pushed for austerity and cuts in government spending to curb budget deficits. The bills for Sadat's extravagant policies finally came due, and the hole into which they put Egypt gave the government few viable options.

The regime is boxed in by conflicting domestic constraints which block both a radical reform of *infitah* and the reorientation of policy needed to cut consumption and mobilize resources. *Infitah* has created a larger and richer bourgeoisie which is unprepared to give up opportunities for commercial and speculative enrichment or to trim its new life of consumption. Any reversal of the course which so favors this class would cost the regime its strongest social support. Since the embourgeoised senior officer corps has acquired a stake in *infitah* business, it could also prove very dangerous. The ability of the regime to raise domestic revenues to cope with the financial imbalance is similarly constrained because those who can afford to pay represent its own support base. The NDP parliamentary caucus thus turned back a proposal of its own government to tax lucrative urban real estate interests. The threat of capital flight in an *infitah* economy must give pause to any government wishing to impose such burdens. On the other hand, as the 1977 uprising showed, the regime cannot radically break with populist policies, such as food subsidies, without grave political risk. Indeed, an economic crisis on top of *infitah* would only increase the regime's vulnerability and hence the political necessity of the subsidies. The supersession of a period of rising living standards by one of hard times and dashed expectations is a classic breeding ground for revolutionary ferment. The contrast of conspicuous new wealth amidst mass poverty generates a profound moral malaise. The debt has already become a political issue, reflected in a slogan voiced during the police rebellion: "*We're* asked to pay the debt while *they* live in palaces and villas." The government began a gradual covert shaving of subsidies—e.g., replacing the one piaster loaf with a supposedly better quality one—and continued the neglect of public services for the poor. But, unable to do much more, it has concentrated on negotiations with creditors for a rescheduling of debts, a lowering of interest rates, and new loans to support the balance of payments—merely postponing the day of reckoning. If this predicament results in economic stagnation while population growth continues unabated, future prospects are grim.

The second legacy Mubarak inherited was the contradiction between the standards of nationalist legitimacy established under Nasser, on the one hand, and Sadat's unnatural foreign policy alignments on the other: the US and Israeli connections and isolation from the Arab world. Mubarak has only partially extracted Egypt from this contradiction. The regime's extreme dependence on the US continues: for arms, cheap food to maintain social peace, and—especially as oil-linked earnings plummeted—for $2 billion yearly in loans and grants to keep the government budget and the economy afloat. The price of this dependency is sharp constraints on policy-makers. It has kept relations with Israel intact despite the total lack of progress toward a comprehensive peace or Palestinian rights. Mubarak's passivity in the face of Israel's Lebanon invasion, made possible only by the neutralization of Israel's southern front, would have been unthinkable under Nasser. Dependency has also dictated a close political-military alignment with the US, manifested in joint military exercises and US facilities at the expense of Egypt's traditional non-alignment. To be sure, Mubarak's rejection of pressures for joint action against Libya marked a step back from the role of conservative American surrogate. But joint military planning is still aimed at radical nationalist forces in the Arab world—not Israel, Egypt's historic enemy. Of course, Mubarak has some leverage over the US. Washington has invested so much in Egypt and gained so much from Sadat's policies—defusing the threat of an Arab-Israeli war, and rolling back Soviet and radical influence in the Arab world—that it cannot afford to alienate the regime or let it go under. Although the US has tried to use its leverage to advance economic liberalization, US aid also cushions the regime against hard choices.

The Israeli-American connection has generated a profound crisis of nationalist legitimacy which deprives the regime of the support needed to really confront Egypt's problems. Israel is widely seen as having "betrayed" the peace by its rejection of Palestinian rights, its attempt for some time to keep the Sinai enclave of Taba, and its acts of violence against Lebanon, Tunis and Iraq. The making of Suleiman Khater, a policeman who killed Israeli tourists, into a folk hero indicates the deep-seated antipathy toward Israel. The US connection is also now a political liability. Economic dependency is resented, and Westernization and the pro-Israeli peace fostered by the US are a focus of Islamic grievances. The forcing down by the US of the Egyptian airliner after the "Achille Lauro incident" was viewed as a national insult and set off the first nationalist street demonstrations in years. This kind of sentiment has not yet become a mass political movement able to force a policy change, despite demands by opposition leaders and isolated attacks on Israeli and American officials by disgruntled "Nasserist" officers. But few governments anywhere can be saddled with a foreign policy with so many unpopular features.

Mubarak's reintegration of Egypt into the Arab world without prejudice to its Israeli links was, however, a major coup which reversed part of the price of Sadat's policies. The first break in Egypt's isolation, Arafat's 1983 flight to Cairo from Syrian pressures, enabled Egypt to assume patronage of the PLO. The Arab oil states' need for support against Iran consolidated Egypt's restoration to favor. Mubarak's astute diplomacy, taking advantage of divisions among his rivals, enabled him to demonstrate Egypt's indispensability to the Arab world. In 1989, Egypt's readmission to the Arab League crowned his efforts. Egypt views its current role as that of a mediator between Israel and the Arabs, trying to advance the peace process and a role for the PLO in it. But this "process" has so far proved illusory, in good part because Egypt's absence from the Arab war coalition relieves Israel of pressures to negotiate. The opening to the Arab world is pursued above all as a key to internal legitimacy.

Conclusion

The evolution of the Egyptian state since 1952 is a story of both persistence and change. Continuity is manifest in the durability of the structures built by Nasser. The authoritarian presidency remains the command post of the state. Nasserist policies—from Arab nationalism to the food subsidies and the public sector—created durable interests and standards of legitimacy. Under Sadat, Egypt entered a "post-populist" phase accommodating public policy to the dominant forces in the regime's environment. Charisma, social reform and leadership of the Arab world gave way to their opposites. Sadat also adapted the state to the new conditions generated by his policies, altering the goals and style of presidential power and liberalizing the political structure. The survival of most of Sadat's work under Mubarak suggests that, more successfully than Nasser, he had partially institutionalized it—in a sturdy political structure, an alliance with the dominant social forces and a web of constraints against significant change. Under Mubarak, the interventionist efforts of the state to manipulate and reshape its environment are in rapid retreat before rising societal forces or powerful external constraints. But Mubarak also consolidated the adaptation of the political system inherited from his predecessors to this intractable environment. Though it has been at the price of concession of its initial ideology, the post-1952 state has shown a remarkable capacity to survive in spite of intense pressures and constraints.

Yet Sadat's innovations, in stimulating rising autonomous forces while narrowing regime options, contain seeds of change that are bound to transform the system over the long run. While the massive bureaucratic state is sure to long dominate, *infitah* should continue to expand, giving rise in time to countervailing power, the social basis for further political liberalization. But the widening inequality and social mobilization precipitated by capitalist development are also likely to produce growing class conflicts. These, especially in a regime with precarious legitimacy, will raise threats of instability or revolution which may only be containable by maintenance of the authoritarian regime. If rising economic constraints force the abandonment of the residues of populism, such a regime may have an ever more conservative and mass-repressive face. If an accommodation between the regime and political Islam matures, this could bring on conservatization without mass repression; but if it does not, a crumbling of the secular state under pressures from the street and defections within, could still produce a new Islamic order. In the meantime, the regime will continue its current course, trying to stay on top of events by avoiding radical turns to left or right and mixing doses of limited liberalization, limited repression and limited Islamization.

Note

1. Much of the conceptual analysis in this study is based on Max Weber's study of political authority. See in particular *The Theory of Social and Economic Organization* (New York: The Free Press, 1964), pp. 324-424.

10 INTEREST GROUPS AND POLITICS IN MUBARAK'S EGYPT

Robert Bianchi

The presidency of Hosni Mubarak has been marked by a gradual revival of statecraft in dealing with civil society that is a welcome departure from his predecessor's penchant for brinkmanship and repression. Instead of deploring the growing diversity and vitality of Egypt's associational life, Mubarak has tolerated a more heterogeneous group universe that can be manipulated by the regime's supporters and opponents alike.

Anwar Sadat tended to view wide disparities in the structure and influence of organized interests as a threat to his monopoly of power; his solution was to impose a more centralized and uniform version of corporatism that would strengthen and enrich his associational allies, who could then more effectively stifle and crush dissent among their constituents. Mubarak, however, has carefully avoided all efforts to refashion group life into a coherent system of representation, rejecting proposals for a more cohesive corporatism as well as demands for an unfettered pluralism. Instead, he has opted for a loose and incoherent group network that allows a degree of maneuver for weak opponents.

The persistent heterogeneity of organized interests has had mixed consequences for state autonomy. On one hand, groups possessing very different resources have been able to carve out important niches in the state bureaucracy and the economy while broadening their alliances through the parties and the press. This has made it more necessary for the authoritarian elite to engage in bargaining and compromise, including some embarrassing reversals and retreats over economic policy. Indeed, in view of the multiplication of centers of power in Egyptian society, it is doubtful that it makes sense any longer to use phrases such as "Mubarak's Egypt," which imply that social organization is little more than the patrimony of an all-powerful ruler.

On the other hand, the continued fragmentation of associational life places formidable barriers in the path of regime critics who might wish to recreate the sort of powerful counter-coalition that rose against Sadat. By tolerating criticism and recognizing the limits of his own power, Mubarak has been able to tame many of his loyal opponents while isolating and hunting down his most dangerous enemies. The bitter experience of Sadat's drive toward autocracy seems to have made Egypt's rulers more willing to accept de Tocqueville's optimistic conclusion that "Freedom of association in political matters is not so dangerous to public tranquility as is supposed, and . . . possibly, after having agitated society for some time, it may strengthen the state in the end."

At first glance, Egypt's associational life appears deceptively simple and uniform because of the clear predominance of corporatist legal and organizational patterns in virtually every interest sector. However, looking beyond the formal facade of common structures, it becomes clear that Egypt's authoritarian regime is based on an unusually flexible and incoherent variety of corporatism that promotes great diversity in groups' power relations and that tolerates opposition from many dissident group leaders. The ubiquity and malleability of corporatist arrangements have provided an important measure of stability and adaptiveness to Egypt's authoritarian rulers, allowing them to implement and survive recurrent changes in their social bases of support, their economic policies, and their international alliances.

The persistent diversity of Egyptian interest groups reflects wide variations in the process of corporatization from sector to sector. In each area of associational life corporatization has occurred at different times, in different ways, and for different reasons. Broadly speaking, it is possible to identify four key phases in the historical evolution of public policy toward modern associations, each of which has been marked by the state's promotion of a different blend of pluralist and corporatist structures in various socio-economic sectors.

The era of British occupation (1882-1922) encouraged the persistence of traditional corporatism and the emergence of modern pluralism. Many vestiges of the pre-modern guild system survived until the end of the First World War and were perpetuated in the lawyers' syndicate, the first modern professional association to be established along corporatist lines. During the first two decades of the twentieth century brief periods of liberal colonial rule permitted the appearance of Egypt's first political parties which, in turn, greatly aided the formation of new voluntary groups among workers, farmers and merchants, and in both Muslim and Christian religious communities.

From the establishment of the constitutional monarchy until the outbreak of the Second World War (1922-1939) associational life was dominated by what might be termed "palace pluralism." A multitude of weak, divided and dependent groups struggled to represent the lower classes in the cities and the countryside, but remained easily manipulated by pro-palace politicians. Meanwhile, Egypt's dominant landholding and business interests became the only social groups capable of building strong representative associations which then frequently allied with the king to replace popularly elected Wafdist governments with aristocratic dictatorships.

The years from the Second World War until the beginning of Egypt's "socialist transformation" (1940-1960) marked the emergence of modern corporatism. As the monarchist state expanded its regulatory role by managing the wartime economy and promoting import substitution, and as the Free Officers consolidated their revolutionary regime, interest representation in one sector after another was gradually restructured from pluralist lines to corporatist lines. Within just two decades corporatism was extended to the chambers of commerce (1940), the chambers of industry (1947 and 1958), the agricultural cooperatives (1944 and 1952), the labor movement (1952 and 1959) and eventually all of the liberal professions.

Since the early 1960s a crisis-ridden, "populist authoritarian" regime has tried to buttress itself with a series of pseudo-reforms in which piecemeal concessions to corporatist occupation groups have been coupled with continued restrictions on overt partisan competition. Despite its authoritarian character, the regime has (both intentionally and unwittingly) strengthened the organizational resources and political influence of a wide variety of interest groups. Egypt's rulers continue to encourage great diversity in associations' internal structures, their responsiveness to members' demands, their ability to penetrate decision-making processes in the state bureaucracy and the legislature, their alliances with political parties, and their ability to undertake entre-preneurial activities in Egypt's mixed economy.

This periodic mixing and remixing of pluralist and corporatist elements has resulted in three types of sectoral organization, each of which is the product of a distinctive historical pattern of associational evolution. First, there are the "corporatist sectors" in which corporatism always has been the predominant and generally the exclusive mode of representation. These include virtually all of the professional syndicates. Second, there are the "corporatized sectors" in which originally pluralist organizations were transformed into or supplanted by corporatist organizations. The primary examples of this pattern are the labor movement and the agricultural cooperatives. Third, there are the "hybrid sectors" in which both pluralist and corporatist structures continue to coexist and compete for predominance. These include the private business community, where some important new voluntary groups are beginning to emerge, as well as religious associations, which remain the last major preserve of pluralism in Egyptian society.

Important variations in group activity and influence are observable not only between these three categories, but within them as well. Historically, the professional syndicates have been some of the least autonomous groups in the nation because of their semi-official status, their often small and highly specialized memberships, and their constant vulnerability to reprisals from government employers and licensing bodies. Nevertheless, some of the syndicates have become highly politicized, even taking on party-like functions when more overt partisan activity has been prohibited or severely constricted. Professional syndicates have adopted a number of different roles, ranging from sources of political opposition to agents of cooptation and social control.

The Lawyers' Syndicate has often operated as the preserve of opposition leaders seeking a safe house for illegal party activity and trying to mobilize aggrieved constituencies against the government's economic and foreign policies. The Journalists' and Commercial Employees' Syndicates have been open to a wider range of partisan forces, representing both the opposition and the government. They have been key arenas (and at times open battlefields) in which policy debates and electoral competition provide public tests of strength for the regime as well as its numerous rivals.

Still other groups such as the Engineers' Syndicate have become targets of concerted campaigns of colonization by the ruling party, intent on transforming a recurrent source of embarrassment into a reliable base of support and a showcase of economic collaboration between a generous state and a privileged associational client. The Engineers' Syndicate has become a prototype for restructuring corporatist professional groups into profitable business enterprises that are financed with public funds and managed by the private sector cronies of the National Democratic Party.

Labor unions and agricultural cooperatives both sprang from voluntarist social movements that originated before the First World War; both fell under greater state regulation during the Great Depression and the Second World War and both were thoroughly transformed by Nasser's corporatizing reforms. Despite many similarities in historical evolution, however, corporatization had strikingly different consequences in these two sectors—whereas the political power and economic resources of organized labor were substantially increased, those of cooperative agriculture were not.

Corporatization consolidated and strengthened the traditionally feeble and fragmented organizations of the Egyptian working class. Nasser bequeathed a highly centralized union movement that gathered the bulk of urban wage earners under the leadership of a single, nationwide confederation. Moreover, he dramatically enhanced the economic power of workers through far-reaching redistributive reforms, including codetermination and profit-sharing in the nationalized and state-run enterprises that still form the backbone of large-scale industry. Sadat enacted several reforms designed to bolster the union confederation, to insulate its leaders from rank and file pressures, and to coopt them more effectively as junior members of the authoritarian elite and privileged partners in the new capitalist economic order.

By the time of Sadat's assassination in 1981, the Egyptian Confederation of Labor had become the largest, wealthiest, and most influential association in Egyptian society. The Mubarak regime has tacitly recognized the labor confederation as a veto group whose prior consent is indispensable to the success of any major initiative in the public sector of the economy. Mubarak has, in effect, agreed to a partial surrender of state autonomy on many issues in exchange for the cooperation of labor leaders in implementing painful and highly unpopular economic reforms.

In contrast, the corporatization of agricultural cooperatives never provided the peasantry with enduring and effective instruments to defend their revolutionary gains or to further penetrate the policy-making process. Only at the very end of Nasser's life did the cooperative movement acquire a national confederation. It was never able to operate as a strong coordinating center and it could not develop stable alliances with party organizations and government agencies. Even during the heyday of Egypt's "socialist transformation" the village cooperatives remained susceptible to infiltration and subversion by local elites who opposed their redistributive and regulatory goals.

Later, when Sadat suspected that the cooperative movement would be used against him by pro-Wafd politicians, he faced little difficulty in abolishing the national confederation, smearing its leaders with charges of corruption, and shifting its resources to a new network of "village banks" controlled by local allies of the government party. Politically fragmented and financially enfeebled, the cooperative movement was powerless to prevent Sadat's reversion to openly inegalitarian, neocapitalist policies that eventually undid much of the revolution in the countryside.

Businessmen's associations and religious groups are unusually heterogeneous sectors marked by hotly contested rivalries between state-sponsored organizations created from above and private, voluntary organizations created from below. In both of these sectors new groups have proliferated spontaneously as a result of widespread dissatisfaction with the contrived nature of older corporatist structures. Nevertheless, these two recent examples of pluralist resurgence carry divergent (and perhaps contradictory) implications for the political system as a whole.

The emergence of more autonomous private capitalists may provide the ruling elite with an important new coalition partner whose support can be particularly welcome as the traditional populist and socialist slogans of the Egyptian revolution lose what little remains of their credibility. However, the chain reaction of organization and counter-organization in both Muslim and Christian communities is both sharpening sectarian conflicts and generating the most serious pressures for the reform or overthrow of the authoritarian regime.

Under the Sadat and Mubarak governments private businessmen have been able to fashion more reciprocal power relations between their traditional corporatist associations (the Chambers of Commerce and the Chambers of Industry) and the major economic ministries. Organizations that had operated primarily as state agents of economic regulation gradually became more effective channels of interest representation, especially as the National Democratic Party paved the way for its partisans in the business world to play a greater role in both the legislative and bureaucratic arenas.

Leaders of particular factions within the private sector have converted some of the new, white-collar professional syndicates into aggressive vehicles of special interests such as contractors, importers, and bankers. Several elections of the Commercial Employees' Syndicate, for example, have become platforms for former ministers trying to launch political comebacks after falling out of favor because of their overly zealous (and sometimes corrupt) defense of private and foreign business interests.

Some of the most powerful elements of Egypt's burgeoning private sector have chosen to bypass these older corporatist structures instead of trying to reform them from within. They have preferred to establish their own voluntary groups as more autonomous instruments for shaping, and occasionally for subverting, the government's economic policies. The Egyptian Businessmen's Association encompasses executives from about two hundred of the nation's most prominent private firms, including those most closely allied with foreign investors. An equally important, though illegal and underground, businessmen's network emerged among the black market currency smugglers whose organization stretched from Egypt's provincial towns and villages to overseas banks in Europe and the Gulf. Whether acting independently or in concert with the more traditional business associations, these two groups have played a decisive role in defeating and ultimately removing economic nationalists in the Mubarak government who have sought to restore a modicum of state control over foreign trade and the supply of money.

Among religious groups, associational heterogeneity is not only more pronounced, it is far more volatile as well. Whereas the coexistence of corporatist and pluralist groups has diversified and strengthened the representation of business interests, state sponsorship of religious associations has promoted a backlash of counterorganization by a variety of militant groups claiming to be more independent and more authentic defenders of Islam. Consequently, organized Muslims are divided into at least five different types of rival groups, spanning the spectrum from semi-official corporatist structures to clandestine revolutionary societies.

After a century of bureaucratizing and secularizing "reforms" the religious complex of al-Azhar has become an indispensable part of the state apparatus, supervising Islamic education and publishing, managing pious foundations and government-owned mosques, and upholding the traditional position of the *'ulama* as the most authoritative interpreters of Sunni Islam. Increasingly intimate connections with the state have provided the Azhari *shuyukh* with greater power and resources, but they also have eroded their credibility among the masses, who tend to view them as privileged and corrupted extensions of the authoritarian regime rather than as a correcting or countervailing force.

Especially after the outpouring of religious sentiment following the 1967 war, Egypt's rulers realized that the "over-cooptation" of the *'ulama* had weakened the state's ability to control mass religious activity. In search of more populist expressions of organized Islam, Nasser and Sadat turned to the leaders of the Sufi mystical orders. Large government subsidies encouraged a partial revival of the Sufi orders and induced their *shuyukh* to accept sweeping corporatist reforms that placed traditionally independent and competitive organizations under the control of a mixed commission in which government appointees and Azharis wield decisive influence.

Voluntary charitable associations and private mosques comprise a third category of religious groups that exist in a precarious twilight between corporatism and pluralism, struggling to preserve a measure of autonomy and coping with constant pressures to accept tighter government regulation as the price of greater government financial support. Periodic campaigns of nationalization have brought many private schools, clinics, orphanages, and places of worship under state ownership. However, the construction of new private mosques continually has surpassed the state's ability to maintain them and al-Azhar's ability to provide them with certified preachers. Thus private mosques remain the largest and most vigorous enclave of voluntarism in a society where independent local initiative quickly tends to become regulated or appropriated by the government.

The most independent religious groups are the extralegal Islamic associations *(al-Jama'at al-Islamiyya)*. Most of these groups are patterned after the older *Ikhwan al-Muslimin*—they refuse to register with the government as official voluntary associations, they do not request state subsidization or recognition, and they call on Muslims to bypass the *'ulama* in developing independent interpretations of the Qur'an and Sunna. Whereas the Ikhwan have sought greater integration into the existing regime by building new alliances in the party system, the younger members of the *jama'at* have focused on controlling more and more aspects of daily life on university campuses and on building a self-sufficient "Sunni counterculture" that eventually can rely on its own economic enterprises. The older and newer types of *jama'at* are united in demanding adoption of the *shari'a* as the law of the land, but the younger groups are not willing to wait for state action, preferring a more spontaneous "codification" through example, peer pressure, and occasionally intimidation.

Finally, a small and radical fringe of the *jama'at* is composed of illegal, secret societies of revolutionaries, including those who have mounted armed attacks against Copts and pro-government *'ulama* as well as those who assassinated Anwar Sadat. Although the state and the Azharis have portrayed these groups as aberrant cults equipped and sustained by foreign funds, it is clear that they are genuine expressions of widespread social discontent and deepening communal conflicts that have been generated by the government's own political and economic policies. The unusually high attraction of these groups to unemployed university graduates and to middle-class students from the provincial towns of Upper Egypt suggests that religious extremism is strongest precisely where the government has tried to exploit sectarian tensions for partisan gain and where its economic policies have deepened regional and class inequalities.

On the whole, this broad and diversified network of associations reflects the range of interests and views in Egyptian society more accurately than the handful of artificial and state-licensed political parties. Egypt's authoritarian rulers have carefully manipulated *both* group and party systems to insure that they would be instruments of repression as well as agents of representation, mechanisms for fragmenting public opinion as well as aggregating it, and means of excluding potential "troublemakers" from effective participation while including others who are more supportive of the regime. Nevertheless, Egyptian governments have tended to view the generally corporatist interest groups as more malleable and controllable than the pluralist parties, which they regard with far greater suspicion.

Accordingly, the state often has shown greater tolerance and flexibility toward the expression of dissent by association leaders than by leaders of the opposition parties. For example, although Sadat was unwilling to allow the Wafd to reemerge as an independent party organization, he did not prevent Wafdists from becoming a key force in the Lawyers' Syndicate. Mubarak has reluctantly permitted the establishment of the New Wafd party, but has rejected similar appeals from the Nasserists and the Ikhwan who have been forced to operate as influential minorities within the facade of existing parties and associations.

Both Sadat and Mubarak have preferred experiments in political liberalization that envisage greater bargaining with group leaders over more risky and unpredictable ventures in unfettered party competition. When Sadat became disenchanted with his original project to create a more open multi-party system he tried to induce interest group leaders to accept functional representation as an alternative strategy of reform. At the same time that he froze the creation of new parties and corrupted the electoral process he established a new "upper house" of the legislature, the *Majlis al-Shura,* in which one half of the membership was to be appointed from a wide cross-section of occupational associations.

Similarly, while Mubarak complains with increasing frequency that the "irresponsible" behavior of the opposition parties is jeopardizing his supposed plan for a transition to democracy, his government is becoming more open to and more divided by the pleading of special interests, particularly business and labor. Thus, after several years of trial and error with various projects of reform it is clear that the authoritarian elite is much more attracted to the prospect of actively fashioning a "corporatist democracy" than to standing back and observing the emergence of a "pluralist democracy."

The current structure of associational life lends itself to conservative experiments in power sharing in several ways. Most of the large occupational groups already have longstanding and mutually beneficial relationships with the major regulatory and welfare ministries. Although group contacts with target agencies often are mediated by the ruling party, the thrust of group activity is channeled toward isolated, dyadic relations with the state bureaucracy. Stable alliances between groups and political parties are rare; direct, intersectoral bargaining between groups representing different occupational and class interests is even more uncommon.

Hence, the government presides over a series of compartmentalized and easily alterable exchanges with group leaders who can be played off against one another. Privileges and concessions granted to one sector or faction need not spill over to others; indeed, the original beneficiaries often are unable to consolidate their gains and may find them reduced or revoked at a later time.

For nearly three decades, these arrangements allowed Nasser and Sadat to substitute one set of discriminatory social and economic policies for another, tilting toward different classes and sectors at different times while making only modest changes in political institutions. Under Mubarak these techniques have been stretched to their limits. Egypt's increasingly desperate economic situation precludes not only the promise of an expanding pie that can be shared by all, but even more modest expectations that the lot of particular groups can be improved substantially by threatening the already precarious positions of others. What the regime has to offer is no longer the prospect of larger shares of a small or shrinking surplus, but a virtually inevitable austerity that can be made palatable only if its effects appear to be apportioned more or less evenly across all sectors.

Egyptian notions of social justice no longer demand discrimination in favor of certain classes in order to correct the supposed historical abuses of others. Instead, for the first time since the revolution, there is serious discussion of "social symmetry" as the equitable and consensual distribution of hardship. Nasserists once were fond of the grim slogan, "justice is equality in the face of dictatorship"; Mubarak and his supporters appear to be moving toward a more "liberal" reformulation—"Democracy is participation in the negotiation of austerity."

The Egyptian state still retains the initiative vis-a-vis differentially organized sectors whose major preoccupations are the defense and expansion of their turfs rather than the subjugation or elimination of their rivals. The government's decisional autonomy is more limited than ever by the demands of foreign creditors and aid donors, by internal cleavages arising from the competing claims of its own ministries, and by interest groups that have become firmly embedded in the bureaucracy, the ruling party, and the economy.

Nevertheless, Mubarak is by no means a prisoner of foreign capital or of rigid domestic coalitions. He is neither the policeman of a newly hegemonic bourgeoisie nor the immobilized victim of a society on the brink of class warfare. Instead, he is gradually becoming the reluctant arbiter of fragmented but well entrenched groups who have their backs to the wall, knowing that they all will have to give up something voluntarily or risk an upheaval that could forcibly strip them of a great deal more.

What does the Mubarak regime have to offer Egypt's most influential groups in return for their cooperation in weathering unavoidable hard times and averting a possible revolution? When Sadat's assassination brought him to power Mubarak pledged that he would redeem all three of his predecessor's historic promises to the Egyptian people—the promises of comprehensive peace, economic development, and democracy. Now it is clear that no Egyptian government will be able to attain the goals of peace and prosperity in the foreseeable future. Both of these objectives are intimately tied to Egypt's relations with the United States and Israel. With the gradual deterioration of those relations, two of the unkept promises of the Sadat era are at the mercy of foreigners.

The only promise that remains is the one that depends solely on Egyptian initiative—the promise of democracy. Probably the only way that Mubarak can expect to elicit consent and support for painful and unpopular economic policies is to devolve greater responsibility for making and implementing those policies to the organized interests that have the most at stake. Naturally, Mubarak and his military-technocratic advisors do not relish the prospect of sharing power, but this could be the only card they have left to play. The diversity of political organization and the volatility of public opinion in Egypt today make repression far more costly and risky than expanding the modest experiments with "corporatist democracy" that were initiated by Sadat.

There is one area in particular where the regime could strengthen itself by broadening the political role of existing associations—through liberalizing reforms designed to increase interest groups' interactions with political parties and with one another. In Sadat's original scheme the principal intersection of the group and party systems was supposed to be the *Majlis al-Shura,* the Consultative Assembly that combines deputies appointed from various occupational categories and deputies elected from party slates. In practice, however, the *Majlis al-Shura* has become an even greater government preserve than the "lower house" of parliament, the People's Assembly.

Appointed representatives are chosen directly by the president, not by the professional associations themselves. Opposition parties have boycotted elections of the remaining deputies because of a winner-take-all voting system that virtually insures sweeping government victories. Thus, instead of blending functional representation with territorial representation, the *Majlis al-Shura* has undermined both. Reform of the Consultative Assembly would not only provide group and party leaders with a greater stake in the system, it also might help to reduce the cynical (but currently very accurate) perception that Egypt's electoral and legislative processes cannot escape corruption by the state.

11 THE ISLAMIC MOVEMENT IN EGYPT: SOCIAL AND POLITICAL IMPLICATIONS

Moustapha K. El-Sayed

Religion and politics have been closely integrated throughout Egypt's history. In ancient Egypt the Pharaohs were considered to be half-gods, while the clergy constituted a powerful segment of the ruling elite. The local identity of each province of ancient Egypt was marked by a specific cult prevailing in it.[1] The advent of Islam did not change that situation, for although the rulers of the country could not claim a divine character any longer, the *'ulama* always acted as intermediaries between ordinary Egyptians and their foreign rulers and were sometimes able to check the excesses of the latter.[2] In such respects, Egypt differed little from other traditional societies.

When Muhammad 'Ali and his followers established modern government institutions in Egypt, it seemed for a time that the link between religion and politics had been practically severed. Under the rule of his dynasty, the power of the *'ulama* was curtailed, despite the fact that they had brought him to the supreme post of authority in the country, with the Ottoman sultan having to acquiesce to their choice.[3] However, the new Egyptian bourgeoisie which gradually came into being after the early decades of the nineteenth century never turned its back on religion. Its most outstanding members were either Azharites who came into contact with Western civilization, or were disciples of reformist religious leaders. The 'Urabis, the founders of the 'Umma Party, were greatly inspired by the ideals articulated by Jamal al-Din Afghani and later on by Sheikh Muhammad 'Abdu. Both Mustafa Kamil and Muhammad Farid, founders of the National Party in the early years of the twentieth century, often declared their attachment to the Ottoman caliphate.[4] Moreover, the Wafd Party, which included Muslims and Copts alike within its leadership, was challenged as a champion of the cause of independence after the Muslim Brotherhood was established in 1928, less than a decade after the foundation of the Wafd Party. The Muslim Brotherhood was particularly effective after the Second World War. Finally, the army officers who overthrew the monarchy in July 1952 shared many ideas of the Muslim Brotherhood and knew Sheikh Hassan al-Banna, its first Supreme Guide, quite closely.[5]

It is true that the Society was outlawed two years after the military takeover of 1952. Some of its leaders were executed and thousands of its members thrown into jail. However, a rudimentary secret organization continued to exist, since those members who were not arrested strove to offer assistance to families of the jailed *ikhwan*. Meanwhile, those who managed to leave the country maintained a network of solidarity and mutual support.[6]

To describe the overt activities of the Islamic groups in Egypt since the mid-seventies as an Islamic resurgence, awakening or revival would suggest, therefore, that a break with the very recent as well as ancient past had occurred, when there was really no break. For religion in general and Islam in particular has always been present in the Egyptian polity, as a basis of legitimacy for all regimes or as an ideal of social order advocated by specific actors either within a single mass party or through private voluntary associations.

This paper argues that an Islamic social movement has been a constant feature of politics in independent Egypt. It has experienced ups and downs caused by the social, economic, and political conditions of the country which might push it to the fore at a certain moment or eclipse it at another, but it has never been eliminated altogether. The major focus of the paper will be the analysis of the social and political implications of the recent upsurge in the activities of that movement.

The Islamic Movement: Definition

Social movements are described in the *International Encyclopedia of Social Sciences* as incorporating "a wide variety of attempts to bring about a change in certain social institutions or to create an entirely new order."[7] In this sense, social movements are distinguished both from protest movements, which have more limited objectives, and mobs, masses, and crowds, who constitute only temporary gatherings of individuals. The social movement, although much broader than a political organization, may consist of organized groups without one overall formal organization. The relationships between the various organized groups constituting a movement are not always free of tension. However, what gives the movement its unitary character is the adherence of all its members to a set of beliefs which justifies the aims of the movement. Such beliefs are embodied in abstract principles concerning the nature of man and his destiny, as well as a critique of existing political, social and cultural institutions, and an image of an alternative social order.[8] The study of a social movement usually involves an examination of ideals held by its members, its structure, social background, strategy, tactics and functions in the broader social context in which it operates.[9]

Viewed in this way, the Islamic movement in Egypt can include all those citizens who are dissatisfied with the basic institutions of Egyptian society and who aspire to replace them by alternative institutions more in line with the teachings of Islam embodied in verses of the Quran or the traditions of the prophet. The alternative order could lead, in their view, to a revival of some of the institutions and practices which characterized an earlier Islamic golden age.

Those who believe in such ideas in Egypt are not necessarily members of organized groups. They could be sympathizers who read the movements' publications, attend its meetings, and support it in different ways. In fact, the success of any social movement depends very much on its capacity to influence public opinion so as to advance its goals through the impact it produces on the non-organized masses.

The Islamic movement in Egypt is active in many spheres. It is made up of a nucleus of organized groups which operate directly in politics, such as the Society of Muslim Brothers, the Jihad organization,[10] *Jama'at al-Salafiyyin,* the Islamic Liberation Party, *Jama'at al-Tabligh,* and the group that has been accused of plotting to assassinate two former ministers of the interior and the editor of an Egyptian weekly, referred to in the press as "survivors from hell" —al-Najun min al-Nar.[11] Other organized groups within the movement confine their activities to the cultural arena, disseminating what they believe to be a correct understanding of Islam through public lectures and various publications. This second category includes a large number of associations, the most important of which is the Young Muslims Society. A third component of the movement focuses on social work, offering a host of educational, health, and charitable services, often making mosques the center of their activities. Finally, a powerful component of the movement is embodied in the so-called Islamic investment companies, some of which were founded by members of the Muslim Brothers, e.g., the Sharif Company. Others claim to operate in the same way as the Sharif on correct Islamic banking principles. The most important of these are the Rayyan, al-Huda Misr, al-Sa'ad and Badr companies. Such companies are thought to control about 8 billion pounds and $12 billion of deposits, made up primarily of a large number of small savings, which originated mostly in Arab Gulf countries as remittances of Egyptian workers there.[12] Besides all these organized groups, the movement includes probably hundreds of thousands, if not millions of Egyptians who sympathize with the call for a social order more in line with an Islamic ideal, although the exact contours of such an ideal are difficult to define.

Thus, it is possible to discern within the movement two wings or orientations. One, made up of several organized groups, focuses mainly on political action. It is usually identified as political Islam. The other usually operates within economic, social and cultural institutions. This division of labor does not preclude a common understanding of a broader goal or cooperation and mutual support among all components of the movement.

The political wing of the Islamic movement in Egypt has been the object of several studies in the last seven years, particularly since the assassination of President Sadat on October 6, 1981. Such studies have suggested that members of these organizations pursue different, and at times opposed strategies. Some authors have discerned two basic strategies. One is described as moderate, seeking to persuade the majority of the Egyptian people to espouse the Islamic cause. This strategy is usually identified with the Muslim Brotherhood. A second strategy tends toward the use of armed struggle in the hope of overthrowing the existing order and establishing the Islamic City in its place. This strategy is believed to be typical of the *Jama'at al-Islamiyya*, made up of young people, who are mostly students. The most famous of these were al-Takfir wal-Hijra, i.e., the Repentance and Holy Flight Group, led by Shukri Mustafa, and the Jihad organization.[13] In an analysis focusing in detail on the political trends in the movement, Dr. Saad Eddin Ibrahim has distinquished four major orientations among their members.

1. An orientation which shuns political action and is accommodating towards the Mubarak regime.
2. A modern, gradualist, and constitutionalist approach characterizing most of the Muslim Brotherhood.
3. A radical trend inclined to use armed methods against the regime.
4. A fourth trend willing to use force against society itself, judging it to be only Muslim in name, but following heathen ways in practice.[14]

The first of these trends is not of much interest to this study, except to the extent to which it sanctions the broader goals of the Islamic movement and renders moral support to it. This study will instead focus on the last three approaches or strategies, bearing in mind that the three cooperate with each other in certain situations. The groups identified with each specific approach are capable of renouncing it at a certain moment or combining it with another approach.

The major leaders of the Muslim Brotherhood have advocated their strategy of gradualism on several occasions and in different fora. The writings of prominent figures in the society such as the Supreme Guide, Muhammad Hamid Abu al-Nasr, or other historical figures such as Mustafa Mashhur, Salah Shadi or Dr. Yusuf al-Qaradawy abound with arguments demonstrating the reasons for pursuing such a strategy. Mr. Salah Shadi, for example, wrote in *al-Sha'ab,* the official newspaper of the Islamic Alliance, that the goals of the Muslim Brotherhood were of two sorts:

1. An immediate goal of contributing to all that is good for the whole society through as much social service as possible.
2. A distant goal, i.e., the reform advocated by the Muslim Brotherhood and for which it is preparing itself. It is a complete and comprehensive reform (*islah*) carried out jointly by all forces of the nation and results in changing all existing conditions.

   Until such a goal is achieved the Muslim Brotherhood offers its advice to all Egyptian governments, wishes them all success and wishes that Allah will mend this corrupt situation through it.[15]

Such a strategy assumes that the majority of Egyptians, including many of their political activists and even members of the government, are good Muslims who might not know the correct Islamic behavior in certain areas. They should therefore be made to realize what the teachings of Islam require in all spheres of life.

Such a view of Egyptian society is the opposite of what has been advocated by Dr. Omar Abdul-Rahman, the leading intellectual figure of the Jihad organization, who was among those arrested and tried following the assassination of the late President Anwar Sadat. In his testimony before the state Security Court which tried him, he said:

We do not deny the existence of hundreds of millions of Muslims on this globe. We have no doubts about this. . . . But the presence of the Islamic *'umma* is another matter. For such an *'umma*—nation—to exist, certain distinctive features must be fulfilled . . . the first of which is the rule by the Islamic *shari'a*. If, there is no rule by God's *shari'a,* it follows directly that there can be no Islamic nation. As for that strange claim that the Islamic nation is there despite the fact that it is governed contrary to the Islamic *shari'a,* and that its existence is not interrupted unless it renounces its faith completely, it is a false claim that does not stand to any reason and cannot be accepted by religion . . .[16]

According to this view, Egyptian society and its rulers would hardly qualify as a truly Muslim society. But whom should be fought first, the society or the government?

Advocates of the different Islamic trends are to be found among all classes in Egypt. Founders of so-called Islamic investment companies are among the wealthiest people in the country. Mr. 'Uthman Ahmad 'Uthman, founder of the country's leading contracting company, boasted in his autobiography of his old association with the Muslim Brotherhood.[17] Many old members of the society run lucrative businesses.[18] However, studies of the social background of the militants, such as those carried out by Saad Eddin Ibrahim and Hamid Ansari, suggest that they came mostly from middle class backgrounds, with the leaders coming from the rural elite.[19] Ansari, moreover, has pointed out that almost two thirds of the militants came from upper Egypt, particularly Minya and Assiut provinces as well as Giza. Those who resided in Cairo lived in the northern and eastern districts which attract migrants from lower Egypt.[20] He does not point out, however, that some of the provinces of Upper Egypt, as well as Cairo districts which have higher "shares" of the militants, are areas which have a relatively large Coptic population.

The Islamic movement in Egypt operates through a large number of organizations using a variety of methods, including political parties, professional associations and many publishing houses. Mosques have become centers of religious, educational, health and social services rendered by the movement. Their services are at high quality and low cost, and attract numerous Egyptians, including middle class families and even the left wing.

The Three Strategies in Action

The evolution of the Islamic movement in the 1980s, particularly since the inauguration by President Mubarak of a gradual period of political liberalization, must give its supporters many causes for satisfaction and for guarded optimism about the future prospects of the movement. It is true that the movement is not in the government, and its principal demand for the application of the Islamic *shari'a* is not going to be fulfilled in the near future. However, the Muslim Brotherhood, using its moderate and gradualist strategy, has achieved many successes. Its leaders make no secret of their pride in what has been accomplished.[21] The Brotherhood's presence in the People's Assembly jumped from 8 members after the election of 1984, which the Brotherhood contested on the slate of the Wafd Party, to 38 after the legislative elections of 1987, in which the Brotherhood was the senior partner in an alliance with two smaller parties, the Socialist Labor Party and the Socialist Liberal Party. It is estimated that the Brotherhood polled 9 percent of the vote, receiving more than half a million votes, despite the heavy-handed methods of the Ministry of Interior, which supervised the election. The Alliance, led effectively by the Muslim Brotherhood, emerged as the largest opposition bloc of about 60 deputies, with the Wafd coming in second place.[22] Moreover, the lists of candidates of the Islamic movement won the majority of seats in the elections of the executive councils of major professional associations in the country, such as the Councils of Administration in Clubs of University Professors in Cairo, Alexandria, and Assiut. No election was held at the Club of Professors of 'Ain Shams University for no valid reason. Most student union councils in major universities were also won by Islamic militants for the fourth successive year. The leaders of such unions in Cairo, 'Ain Shams and Alexandria were declared members of the *Jama'at al-Islamiyya*. Moreover, the overwhelming majority of members of the Councils of both the Medical Association and the Engineers Syndicate belong to the Muslim Brotherhood.[23] On the other hand, the Brotherhood has been less successful among lawyers and journalists, though it enjoys a strong presence in the leading organs of both the Bar Association and the Journalists Syndicate.

The electoral success of the Muslim Brotherhood in these strongholds of the Egyptian intelligentsia has many causes in addition to the generally favorable disposition in the country toward any one who carries the Islamic banner. The followers of the Brotherhood have demonstrated an impressive capacity for organization in the face of their fractionalized and scattered adversaries. They have also devised better electoral tactics focusing on sectors of the community who were neglected by their opponents. In university elections they fared well in larger faculties such as those of Medicine, Science, and Engineering, where they mobilized masses of university assistants and junior professors. In contrast, they invested little effort in the smaller faculties, where their opponents obtained worthless majorities which did not affect the overall advantages enjoyed by the lists of the Islamic movement.

A statement published in one of the movement's magazines, allegedly made by a student who voted for an Islamic list, seems to illustrate the superior mobilizational skills of the Islamic militants.

> I voted for the Islamists because they are not like others who promise and do not deliver. The Islamists first print university books and notes, and they offer loans to those who cannot afford to buy them. They proposed a bus service for girl students to provide them with decent transport, which spares them humiliating experiences in crowded public transport. They take student problems to the university administration. They express student views on major events in the country . . . they organize entertainment as well as study trips which cost very little, and they encourage sports. Besides, they print series of Islamic books at a low price to disseminate Islamic thought and culture. Finally, they organize public lectures and debates to explain major Islamic issues. . . . Isn't all that enough to make us vote for Islamic student unions?[24]

Such a statement seems to reflect too much enthusiasm for Islamic student unions to be typical of ordinary students. However, it does represent a prevailing attitude among large numbers of students who gave their votes to the Islamist lists. It also indicates the variety of activities undertaken by Islamic groups among university students.

Two important observations should be made concerning the significance of such victories. They were initially obtained against the background of a very low turn-out rate at the universities, due to the heavy-handed methods of university administrations who disqualified a large number of candidates of different political trends simply because they were not known supporters of the National Democratic

Party.[25] Besides, the major electoral victories of Islamic groups were achieved mostly in natural sciences and technical faculties, particularly among students of medicine, science, and engineering. In professional syndicates, the strongholds of the Islamic movement are the Medical Association and the Engineering Syndicate. It is true that such strongholds include the sections of the Egyptian intelligentsia who are most knowledgeable about the scientific and technological advances of the West. Nevertheless, they are also those which lack a sophisticated knowledge of the social and political realities of Egypt and the world.

Islamic proponents of the alternative strategy of armed resistance have very little cause for satisfaction. Although the assassination of Sadat opened the way for a more liberal atmosphere in the country in which the Islamic movement could propagate its message and get more organized, the goal of an Islamic order does not seem to have been brought any closer. Moreover, armed confrontations between the Islamic militants and security forces ended in defeat for the former without advancing their cause very much. The last acts of armed resistance attributed to the followers of a strategy of violence included three assassination attempts on the lives of two former ministers of interior, al-Nabawi Abu Isma'il and Hassan Abu Basha, and the editor-in-chief of *al-Mussawwar* weekly. The three attempts failed, with Mr. Hassan Abu Basha suffering serious injuries from which he largely recovered after months of intensive treatment in West Germany.[26] These attempts were largely acts of revenge and intimidation, an expression of despair rather than a well-elaborated strategy for the takeover of the government by force in order to establish the City of God on earth.

The third strategy, which fights manifestations of societal deviation from what its adherents consider to be Islamic teachings in the area of personal behavior, did not fare any better. Some video clubs were attacked in Shubra, a district inhabited by many Copts in the north of Cairo, presumably because some of the videotapes carried obscene movies. A year later, in Assiut large crowds of Islamic militants used force in order to stop a party organized by other students. The program of the party featured music and a play in which no women would appear. The attacking students, however, considered the party a violation of Islamic teachings. Similar incidents have also been reported from Upper Egypt.[27]

The publicity given to such events was not to the advantage of the Salafiyya Group, which was allegedly behind some such outbursts.

Not a single journalist tried to defend the actions of the group, although some found much to criticize in the conduct of the security forces who intervened to stop clashes between the attackers and organizers as well as the public. Some religious authorities published articles in newspapers affirming that nothing in Islamic teachings proscribes music or decent songs. More importantly, the Salafiyya attitude toward such events did not seem to be shared by Islamic militants in the other Egyptian universities of Cairo, Alexandria, or Lower Egypt. Overall, the strategy of persuasion, constitutionalism, and gradualism promised to enhance the influence and prestige of the Islamic movement, while the strategies based on the use of force against the government or society carried with them the prospect of more damage to the whole movement and no good to those who take the initiative in the use of force.

Social and Political Implications

The diverse activities of the Islamic movement are bound to have an impact on the process of social change in the country. The movement reaches ordinary citizens through a complex network, including one party weekly newspaper (*al-Sha'ab*) and three monthly magazines (*Liwa' al-Islam, al-'Itisam,* and *al-Mukhtar al-Islami*). Various publishing houses disseminate the world view of the movement, the most important of which are Dar al-Shuruq, Dar al-Zahra, Dar al-'Itisam and many other institutions. Leaders of the movement address public opinion occasionally through the televised debates in the People's Council, and through public meetings hosted by various professional associations in which the movement enjoys a dominant or at least an effective presence. The Islamic groups in the universities have made thousands of students dependent on their services. Hundreds of mosques have become centers of educational and social services under the banner of the movement. Finally, hundreds of thousands of families in Egypt depend for their livelihood on the incomes they receive from savings deposited with the Islamic investment companies. All such activities affect personal behavior, political participation and the culture of the population. They could also have some bearing on political stability in the country, and thus the evolution of the Egyptian political system.

In the area of personal behavior, for example, it should be noted that Islamic groups, particularly in Upper Egypt, have posed as moral censors of activities of their student colleagues, and in some cases of their professors. They have attempted to disrupt gatherings which they thought were contrary to their own interpretation of good Islamic conduct.[28] The publications of the movement abound with articles on the proper Islamic dress, particularly for women, and on the corruptive impact of foreign tourism to the country.[29] Although there are signs of resistance to this self-assigned role of the Islamic movement in the press as well as among students, the movement does not seem to be discouraged by this hostile, though muted reaction and will definitely continue to assume the role of moral censorship in the future.

This role has been enhanced by the other activities of the movement. Islamic investment companies have recently tended to diversify their activities, establishing light industries, running large animal-breeding farms, building houses, offering durable consumer goods on credit, and financing health and educational services. Thus, as the multiple and long arms of the movement reach all areas of the country and make their presence felt in all spheres of social action, hundreds of thousands of Egyptian families have become dependent on the Islamic companies for their livelihood and their welfare. The movement is already replacing the state in such areas, by rendering services which the state was expected to provide, and in some cases doing so much better and at a lower cost. The movement and especially the Islamic investment companies can exert pressure on the government.[30] However, those families who depend on the movement for their livelihood will become more amenable to accepting the movement's ideal of an alternative Islamic social and political order.

The decision of the movement in 1984 to contest, first the legislative elections and later on the elections in professional associations, has led to an expansion of political participation by the public. It is difficult to measure this impact precisely since voting returns in Egypt are not very reliable. The election results of 1987 were not declared at the constituency level by the Ministry of Interior and have been the object of a judicial dispute in which the judiciary has so far sided with the opposition political parties against the government. Voting turnout rates in major urban centers remain very low, in some cases being no greater than 18 or 20 percent of the electorate, according to President Hosni Mubarak. However, there are indications that the low level of 1987 was even higher than that of 1984. According to official results, the turnout rate was 44 percent in the country as a whole in 1984 and rose to about 50 percent in 1987. The author, observing voting in several constituencies, came to the conclusion that it rose from less than 10 percent in provincial towns in 1984 to about 30 percent three years later.[31] The presence of a silent majority in Egypt is duly acknowledged by observers and political parties. Whereas each political party can claim that the silent majority includes some of its supporters, the Islamic movement has been the only political force in the country capable of getting that silent majority to act. Political parties confined their efforts in this respect to appeals to citizens in December of every year to go to register as voters before the annual deadline December 31. The Islamic movement made a stronger appeal on the walls of many buildings in Cairo during the same period: there were posters carrying the slogans of the Islamic movement calling on citizens to register as voters and equating voting with the performance of *shahada*-testimony—which is an important religious duty.[32]

Newspaper accounts have also pointed to a higher rate of participation in elections of professional associations contested by the Islamic movement. Although the situation has varied from one professional association to another, the leading organs in such associations had usually been won by government candidates—with the exception of lawyers and journalists' syndicates, student unions and some university professors' clubs. The movement had to count, therefore, on massive mobilization of its supporters in all these associations. The level of electoral participation rose considerably, and candidates of the movement registered landslide victories.[33]

This development, in turn, has placed associations in the middle of the political process. Thus, the Egyptian Medical Association, under a Council in which almost four fifths of the members belong to the movement, has emerged as an important political actor, organizing public debates on issues including religion versus secularism, the state of emergency, and solidarity with the Palestinian people. All these public debates were attended by leaders of the Muslim Brotherhood. The Council has also undertaken a campaign of fundraising in favor of the Palestinian *intifada* in the occupied territories.[34]

Rival lists of candidates commonly enter the elections of other professional associations. For example, an Alliance List contested the election of the President and members of the Agricultural Engineers Syndicate, though it was defeated in this case by a list supported by the government. On the other hand, the Islamic list won massively in elections of both the provincial and national councils of the Engineers Syndicate. Besides, a list supported by both the Left and the Islamic movement won the Pharmacists' Syndicate, in which the Islamic movement previously had little presence.[35] For the first time three rival lists contested the election in the Social Workers Syndicate. One promoted the slogans of the Islamic movement, the second was described as leftist, and the third was supported by the government.[36] The same pattern also characterized the election campaign in the Egyptian Medical Association which took place on April 8, 1988.[37] Thus, the electoral successes of the Islamic movement in some professional associations led to a tremendous change of scene in all the others. Professional associations in Egypt are moving toward the central stage of the political process, becoming new arenas for debating the major political issues and for seeking support by contenders for power.

The impact of the movement on Egypt's political culture is already manifest in the disposition of other political parties to incorporate Islamic thinking on a number of issues. Thus almost all political parties in Egypt now accept—at least verbally—that the Islamic *shari'a* should be considered a principal source of legislation,[38] and a provision to that effect has been introduced in the Permanent Constitution of Egypt.[39] While most view acceptance of such a demand as the end of the story, for the Islamic movement, it is only the first step towards the full application of the *shari'a*. The language of political discourse abounds with references to verses of the Quran and the traditions of the prophet as well as quotations from the writings of Muslim jurists and philosophers. All political parties, all newspapers, and early all mass media devote much of their message to religious issues. Some political parties, such as the National Democratic Party and the Socialist Liberal Party, publish special papers devoted entirely to religious themes.[40]

The attachment to an Islamic ideal is reflected in attitudes towards other countries. Solidarity with all Muslim peoples has become a basic principle in the platforms of most parties. No Egyptian party, for example, condoned Soviet intervention in Afghanistan. The Islamic movement attaches the first priority to consolidating relations with Muslim countries in general, particularly those ruled by Islamic regimes, i.e., Pakistan and even Sudan during the last years of Numeiri. Other parties, particularly the National Democratic Party, the Wafd or al-Tajammu', might view the Islamic circle as only one among many within which Egypt should seek close relations. The Islamic movement has joined other Egyptian political parties in their support for the Palestinian cause.[41] However, a spokesman for the movement underlined the mounting importance of Islamic groups within the Palestinian resistance and even attributed the upsurge of Palestinian struggle in the occupied territories since last December to the leadership of the Islamic groups.[42] Spokesmen for the Islamic movement in the universities, professional associations and the press have often linked the causes of the Palestinian and Afghan peoples.

As for relations with the two superpowers, the electoral platform of the Islamic Alliance called for a policy of non-alignment vis-a-vis both East and West as a necessary condition for the Islamic renaissance. It also rejected any special relationship with the United States in the economic and military fields.[43] The newspaper *Liwa' al-Islam* quoted at length a study denouncing the activities of American research centers in Egypt, warning of the dangers they posed to the national security of the country.[44] On the other hand, although communism, atheism and "crusaderism" are considered the joint enemies of the Islamic movement, a writer in the monthly magazine *al-'Itisam* called for establishing and consolidating links with the Muslims of the Soviet Union since they are likely to become an influential group in Soviet politics in the future, as a result of their increasing demographic weight.[45]

Future Prospects

The leaders of the Islamic movement, reflecting on the accomplishments of the movement during the sixty years of existence of the Muslim Brotherhood, can find many causes for satisfaction at its recent progress.[46] Will they be capable of moving to a position where they can leave their mark decisively on the country's basic institutions of government, economy, education, and culture? Will they be capable of eventually taking over government?

The answer to such questions can only be speculative. For the movement to succeed, the conditions which led to its expansion in recent years would have to continue. It would also need to be capable of overcoming the weaknesses admitted by its own leaders. Finally, it needs some help from its opponents, including the governing National Democratic Party and other opposition parties, perhaps in the form of their inertia in countering its advance or even by allying with it.

Part of the success of the Islamic movement has been due to the weak credibility attached to the non-Islamic alternative models of development, which have failed to resolve the basic problems of the country or to provide the Egyptian middle class with the decent living its members demand after many years in educational institutions.[47] The next few years have been rightly described by Egyptian leaders as a period of sacrifice as Egypt will have to repay much of its debt while continuing to develop its economy. Thus, the Egyptian middle classes can expect little relief from the policy of belt-tightening to which they have been already condemned for several years. On the other hand, the appeal of the Liberal and Socialist alternatives does not seem to be growing over time. The Wafd and the Tajammu' parties which stand for these two alternatives have shown a weak electoral performance. The first polled only 10 percent of the vote in the last election, losing about 5 percentage points in three years, and the second could not reach the 8 percent minimum needed to send deputies to the People's Council.[48]

The movement has several weaknesses, of which its spokesmen are fully aware. Dr. Yusuf al-Qaradawy, for one, has enumerated many of these, including the absence of self-criticism within the movement, its factionalism, the predominance of emotion over reason, and a haste which might lead the movement to confront its enemies before it consolidates its organization. He has advised members of the movement to study Islam as well as the realities of their country, to narrow the gulf separating them from other citizens, particularly intellectuals, and to be involved in social services. He recommended patient work for a period of twenty years until the foundations of a truly Islamic society have been laid. This would allow the elimination of all manifestations of extremism, which cause more damage than good to the movement. Much also depends on the reactions of the opposition political parties, the silent majority and the government of the National Democratic Party. There is no rival to the Muslim Brotherhood in terms of capacity for mobilization of support and organizational skill. However, the Islamic movement has not succeeded in bridging the gulf separating it from many sectors of the Egyptian society who remain unconvinced that the movement offers a viable program to solve the country's economic, social and political problems. Public debates in the country are not dominated by the call to apply the Islamic *shari'a*. The question of the country's economic difficulties and frequent violation of political and civic rights figure prominently on the agenda of all Egyptian political forces. Moreover, opponents of the Islamic movement have become more assertive in their rejection of its ideas, often formulating their arguments with references to verses of the Quran and traditions of the Prophet. Faced by this kind of opposition, spokesmen for the movement have slandered their opponents as disguised atheists and enemies of Islam, sometimes even calling on al-Azhar to censor their books. An example of this kind of reaction was the debate between Fahmy Noweidi, the Islamist writer, and Mohammad Said Ashmawi, a former head of a state security tribunal and author of a book on political Islam. The debate raged over the pages of the Egyptian daily *al-Ahram* in February and March 1988.

The movement may thus prove unable to attract the silent majority to its side or to persuade other political forces to join its march. Its reaction to such a situation may depend on the outcome of debates taking place within its ranks. Will proponents of armed struggle gain the upper hand or can the policy of gradualism and constitutionalism persist in the face of difficulties? There are no easy answers to such questions. It is probable, however, that the fate of the "moderate" trend within the movement, as well as political stability in the country, depend on a measurable improvement in the conditions of the Egyptian masses, in the situation of the new poor of the middle classes, and in the establishment of a truly democratic political order.

Notes

1. Elman R. Services, *Origins of the State and Civilization: The Process of Cultural Evolution* (New York: W.W. Norton & Company, Inc., 1975), pp. 225-36.

2. Dr. Sa'id Isma'il 'Ali, *Dar al-Azhar fi al-Siyasa al-Misriyya* [Al-Azhar's Role in Egyptian Politics] (Cairo: Dar al-Hilal, 1986).

3. P.J. Vatikiotis, *The Modern History of Egypt* (London: Weidenfeld and Nicolson, 1969), pp. 49-163.

4. *Ibid.*, pp. 176-237.

5. *Ibid.*, pp. 315-411.

6. Personal recollections of the author, whose father was a member of the Muslim Brotherhood.

7. Rudolf Heberle, "Social Movements," in *International Encyclopedia of Social Sciences*, 1972, pp. 438-39.

8. Ibid., pp. 439-44.

9. Ibid., p. 445.

10. Dr. Yusuf al-Qaradawy, *Ayna al-Khalal*? [What is wrong?] (Cairo: Dar al-Sahwa li al-Nashr, 1985), p. 41.

11. Sayyed Zaki, "wa Bada'at Muhakamat al-Najun min al-Nar" [The Trial of the Survivors from Hell Has Started], *Al Mussawwar* (Cairo), No. 3313, April 8, 1988, pp. 16-17.

12. Ahmed Ghoneim, "Sharikat Tawzif al-Amwal, Qunbula Mawquta fi al-Iqtisad" [Investment Companies, a Time Bomb in the Economy], *al-Ahram al-Iqtisadi* (Cairo), No. 995, February 8, 1988, p. 21.

13. Michael C. Hudson, "Islam and Political Development," in John L. Esposito (ed.), *Islam and Development: Religion and Socio-Political Change* (Syracuse: Syracuse University Press, 1980), pp. 10-11.

14. Saad Eddin Ibrahim, "Egypt's Islamic Activism in the 1980s," *Third World Quarterly,* Vol. 10, No. 2, 1988. Was available to the author in mimeographed form, pp. 17-42.

15. Salah Shadi, "al-Mujtama'at al-Rashida . . . Kayfa Taq'um" [Rightful Societies . . . How Do They Come into Being?], *al-Sha'ab* (Cairo), No. 428, February 2, 1988, p. 5.

16. Dr. Omar Abdul Rahman, "Kalimat Haqq" [A Word of Truth], Dr. Omar Abdul Rahman's address to the court in the Jihad case, Dar al-'Itisam, Cairo, no date, p. 112.

17. 'Uthman Ahmad 'Uthman, *Safahat min Tajrubati* [Pages from My Experience] (Cairo: al-Maktab al-Misri al-Hadith, 1981), pp. 351-84.

18. *Ibid.,* p. 374.

19. Saad Eddin Ibrahim, "Anatomy of Egypt's Militant Islamic Groups," *International Journal of Middle East Studies,* Vol. 12, 1980; Hamid Ansari, "The Islamic Militants in Egyptian Politics," *International Journal of Middle East Studies,* No. 16, 1984, pp. 123-49.

20. Ansari, ibid., 131-41.

21. See for example, Dr. Mohammed Yenya, "Harakat al-Ikhwan al-Muslimin fi 'Amiha al-'Ishrin" [The Movement of Islamic Brothers in its Sixtieth Year], *al Liwa' al-Islami,* No. 12, March 19, 1988, pp. 20-22.

22. Moustapha El-Sayed, "Analysis of Election Results," in Ali Hilal Dessouki (ed.), *The Election of the People's Council, 1987* (Cairo: Al-Ahram Center for Political and Strategic Studies), forthcoming. See also *al-Ahram,* June 1, 1984, p. 17; April 1, 1987, p. 1.

23. *al-Sha'ab,* No. 423, December 23, 1987, p. 1.

24. Amer Shammakh, "Na'am li al-Ittihad al-Tullabiyya al-Islamiyya" [Yes to the Islamic Student Union], *al-Liwa' al-Islami,* No. 9, December 22, 1987, p. 54.

25. Ibid., pp. 52-54.

26. See *al-Mussawwar,* April 8, 1988, *op. cit.*

27. Abdel Moneim al-Geddawi, "Man Yutfi'i al-Nar fi Bayrut?" [Who Would Put out the Fire in Beirut], *al-Mussawwar,* ibid., pp. 14-16.

28. Mustapha Bakri, "Jiniralat al-Din wa Mahakim al-Taftish fi al-Minya" [Generals of Religion and Inquisition Tribunals in al-Minya), *al-Mussawwar,* No. 3285, September 25, 1987.

29. See particularly pages addressed to the Muslim Sisters in *Liwa' al-Islam,* and the report on intervention by the Islamic Alliance deputies in reply to the statement of the Prime Minister, *al-Sha'ab,* No. 426, January 19, 1988, p. 3.

30. Ahmed Ghoneim, *op. cit.,* for a critical appraisal; Salah Abdul Maqsoud, "Sharikat Tawzif al-Amwal, wa al-Dawr al-Mawtub" [Investment Companies and Their Role], *Liwa' al-Islam,* No. 8, November 23, 1988 for a sympathetic view.

31. Moustapha Kamel El-Sayed, "Analysis of Election Results," *op. cit.*

32. *al-Sha'ab,* No. 422, December 22, 1987, p. 7 for a photo of that poster.

33. See the report by Muhammad Abdel Kuddous on elections in the Engineers Syndicate in *al-Sha'ab,* No. 419, December 1, 1987, p. 2.

34. Such activities were reported in *al-Sha'ab.* See for example, No. 424, Jan. 5, 1988, p. 4; No. 435, March 22, 1988, p. 2; and No. 436, April 5, 1988, p. 2.

35. Muhammad Abdel Kuddous, *op. cit.*

36. *al-Ahram al-Iqtisadi,* No. 1003, April 4, 1988, p. 65.

37. Ga'afar Mahmoud, "Man Yafuzu al-Yawm bi Mansib Naqib al-Atibba'?" [Who Wins the Post of President of the Medical Association Today?], *al-Akhbar,* April 8, 1988.

38. Moustapha Kamel El-Sayed, "Political Parties after the Revolution" in *al-Mash al-Ijtima'iyy, The Second Survey,* published by the Center for Sociological and Criminological Research, Cairo, 1984, General Report, Ch. 4, p. 279.

39. Article 2 of the Permanent Constitution, *al-Muhamat,* Egyptian Bar Association, Cairo, supplement to issue no. 586, 60th year, June 1980, p. 2. The article was amended to that effect on April 30, 1980.

40. The first publishes *al-Liwa' al-Islami* and the second publishes *al-Nur.*

41. Hala Seoudi, "Foreign Policy Issues in Electoral Platforms of Egyptian Political Parties," in Ali Dessouki, *op. cit.,* forthcoming.

42. *al-'Itisam,* No. 10, February, 1988, p. 15, characterizes the resistance movement in the occupied territories in *al-Ahram,* January 1988, p. 7.

43. *al-Sha'ab,* No. 425, January 12, 1988, p. 5.

44. Lutfi Abdel Lateef, "Akhtar min Thalathin Markaz Abhath Amriki fi al-Qahira" [More than 30 American Research Centers in Cairo] *Liwa' al-Islam,* No. 9, December 22, 1987, pp. 16-20.

45. General Dr. Kamal Abdul Hamid, "Madha Ya'ani al-Insihab al-Sufiyati Min Afghanistan" [Meaning of the Soviet Withdrawal from Afghanistan], *al-'Itisam,* No. 11-12, March-April 1988, pp. 12-13.

46. Muhammad Yehya, "Harakat al-Ikhwan al-Muslimin fi 'Amiha al-'Ishrin" (The Movement of the Islamic Brotherhood in its Sixtieth Year), *Liwa' al-Islam,* No. 12, March 19, 1988, pp. 12-13.

47. Lawrence B. Bruce, "Muslim Fundamentalist Movements: Reflections toward a New Approach," in Stowasser, *op. cit.,* pp. 15-36, for a survey of such explanations.

48. Mustapha Kamel El-Sayed, "Analysis . . . ," *op.cit.*

12 LAW AND COURTS IN EGYPT: RECENT ISSUES AND EVENTS CONCERNING ISLAMIC LAW

Enid Hill

The Context

The introduction into Egypt of modern courts and codes dates back more than 100 years. Although there have been alterations in the jurisdictions and structures of the courts since that time, and judicial institutions added and basic codes revised, this heritage is essentially unbroken. Complete judicial independence was undercut in 1969 but was restored in 1984. Both lawyers and judges have professional associations. Legal publishing also began in the nineteenth century. Today two official journals publish laws and ministerial decrees and regulations; decisions of each of the high courts[1] are published in separate series; a journal is published by the Egyptian Bar Association and others by the judges' associations and by the law faculty of Cairo University and others. There are five law faculties in Cairo and Alexandria and others in many of the provincial universities, several of which also issue journals. Extensive education in the *shari'a* is given only at al-Azhar, but the modern law faculties include courses on the *shari'a* in each year's curriculum.

Institutional Development

Although there were precursors,[2] the modern legal system of Egypt dates from 1876 with the establishment of the Mixed Courts which were given jurisdiction over all controversies that had a "foreign interest." Since this was interpreted broadly and foreign interests came to have a substantial control over the economy of Egypt, the Mixed Courts had a formative influence on the development of the legal culture. A system of National Courts was inaugurated in 1883. From 1936 the Mixed Courts began to be phased out and in 1949 were abolished altogether. Egypt henceforth had one unified system of National Courts with civil and criminal jurisdictions. *Shari'a* Courts for personal status matters were retained until 1956, when they were abolished and their jurisdictions also incorporated into the National Courts.

Specialized criminal courts were set up around the turn of the century. In 1931 a separate Court of Cassation was established, and in 1946 adjudication was added to the functions of the Judiciary Advisory Council and this body metamorphosed into the administrative court system known as the *Majlis al-Dawla*. A High Administrative Court was added in 1949. In 1969, a "High Court" was established to handle conflicts of jurisdictions and judgments (and nominally constitutional issues). In 1979 it was succeeded by the present High Constitutional Court. Prior to the establishment of a specialized constitutional court, pleas of unconstitutionality were decided by the regular courts.

The civil and criminal codes were revised during the 1930s and 1940s in anticipation of the merging of the two court systems, the former coming into effect in 1949 and the latter in 1950. The commercial code has not until today been submitted to an overall revision, although many amendments have kept it current with commercial change. Nor has there been a comprehensive codification of the personal status law. Comprehensive laws governing inheritance (testate and intestate succession), applicable to all Egyptians, appeared in 1943 and 1946, but revisions of the marriage and divorce law date back to 1929 and 1931 and were without substantive amendment until 1979.

Judicial independence was established with the Mixed Courts. The initiative for these courts came from Isma'il's prime minister, Nubar Pasha. Whereas the British, during the long years of occupation, manipulated the Ministry of Justice, they were never able to encroach on the independence of these courts. The National Courts assumed the mantle of judicial independence, and shortly after its establishment the *Majlis al-Dawla* appropriated to itself and the judiciary in general the power to rule on the constitutionality of legislation.[3]

Changes in the 1960s and 1970s

Although Nasser left the judicial system intact, there were several major confrontations with the judiciary in the course of that era. In 1954 the *Majlis al-Dawla* was attacked and its Chief Justice (al-Sanhuri) retired from public life. In 1955, another attack against the *Majlis al-Dawla* came to bring it more closely within executive supervision, but this effort was thwarted. The final onslaught came in 1969, with the so-called "Massacre of the Judges," when a substantial number of judges were in effect fired[4] and a new body to supervise judicial appointments, controlled by the Ministry of Justice, was established.[5] These changes were reversed in 1984, when both the regular judiciary and the *Majlis al-Dawla* had control over their appointments and internal organization restored to them.

Leaving the judiciary intact did not mean that the judiciary was, however, unaffected during those years. In certain matters the established judiciary was simply bypassed. Decrees intended to bring about basic socioeconomic change were declared to be outside the capacity of the judiciary to void because they were "political." Special revolutionary courts were set up for special purposes; there was also experimentation with "popular courts." These extrajudicial arrangements disappeared with the passing of revolutionary government. Another means of exercising executive influence on the judiciary, however, is still with us. A comprehensive Emergency Law was legislated in 1958 (with several subsequent additions) and a State of Emergency has been almost continuously in force ever since.[6] Under the Emergency Law, various statutory procedural protections are not applicable,[7] various acts (otherwise allowed) are designated as crimes,[8] and certain crimes specified in the Penal Code are subject to harsher penalties.

Concomitant with the 1958 Emergency Law, State Security Courts were established to prosecute "political" crimes. While other exceptional courts experimented with in the 1950s and 1960s have disappeared, the State Security Courts remain and a new exceptional court was created by Sadat in 1980: the "Court of Values."[9] Another exceptional jurisdiction utilized by Sadat and still very much used is the "socialist prosecutor."[10] Appointed by the president of the republic and directly responsible to him, this office serves as the executive's arm for investigations and for the preparation of accusations independent of the judicial apparatus.[11]

It is the continuation of the State of Emergency, the "political" laws and the exceptional jurisdictions (and most especially the socialist prosecutor) that are the issues about which most agitation has come in recent years from the judiciary and the legal profession as well as the opposition parties. Calls for legislating the *shari'a* are certainly made, as will be detailed below—such calls are an endemic feature of Egyptian political life—but with rare exceptions, active proponents of scrapping the existing legal structure and legislating the *shari'a* as the law of the land do not come from the leadership of the legal and judicial professions.

Islamic Law in the Present Legal System

In the latter part of the 1870s, when the establishment of national courts and modern codes was under consideration, codifications of the *shari'a* were prepared by Muhammad Qadri Pasha for the civil law[12] and for personal status.[13] However, the decision was made not to go this route in Egypt, but to use a civil code patterned on the one already in force in the Mixed Courts.[14]

However, the modern civil law of Egypt, from its inception in the codes of both 1876 and 1883, contained legal rules drawn from the *shari'a* governing transactions and obligations, and especially regarding property rights. When the new Civil Code was prepared in the 1940s, special care was taken (a) to include these and other provisions from the *shari'a* that were consistent with the socioeconomy and the legal culture of Egypt at that time, and (b) to insure that the new code would be in harmony with the *shari'a* in spirit and not contradict its general principles.[15]

The issues of interest and insurance were not dealt with head on but retained in the new (1948) code. Both are considered by strict *shari'a* advocates to contradict Islamic law; "interest" is interpreted as "usury" (*riba*) and insurance is considered a "speculative contract" —both forbidden by the *shari'a*.[16]

Opposition to the proposed revised code appeared when it was debated in the parliament during 1948. The objections were, however, rebutted and the opposition did not prevail. One of the opponents of the revised code, Hasan al-Hudaybi (then a senior judge on the Court of Cassation, later head of the Muslim Brotherhood) is on record as saying that any revision of the Civil Code should be based on the Quran.[17]

During the 1930s and 1940s, the Muslim Brotherhood had consistently advocated "the Quran is our Constitution," and urged a return to the *shari'a* in various specifics such as abolition of statutory and contractual interest and speculative contracts. Some members also advocated a return to the *hadd* punishments (e.g., amputation for theft and flogging for adultery), as well as stricter morality laws and the prohibition of consumption of alcohol.[18] The revised Penal Code did not include any of these features.

Substantive revisions of the Personal Status law in the 1920s were based on the *shari'a,* but utilized the more extensive provisions of the Malaki law, instead of Egypt's official Hanafi rite. Using Malaki law allowed amplification of the grounds on which a woman could petition the courts for a divorce. Other reforms were then enacted as administrative regulations, allowable under the *shari'a.* Child marriages, for example, were discouraged by denying judicial recognition to them and thereby withholding state protection to claims resulting from them. The same device was used for the intricate regulations governing guardianship. When inheritance laws were legislated in the 1940s it was on the basis of Hanafi law, with additions to compensate for lacuna. In the absence of specific legislation, the courts apply *shari'a* rules and principles in personal status matters.

Neither *talaq* (the man's unilateral right to pronounce divorce) nor polygamy were touched by the 1920s reform legislation, except that the "triple divorce"[19] was outlawed. Christians are allowed to apply their own rules regarding marriage and divorce, administered by church elders, provided that they are of the same Christian sect. Otherwise, they come under state law, which is essentially Muslim law.

Although the Muslim Brotherhood was vocal in the 1930s and 1940s and the issues were discussed and written about in the media, the issues of the 1950s and 1960s concerned national independence, Arab unity, and socialism rather than calls for Islamic law. Calls for *shari'a* legislation reemerged in the 1970s.

Islamic Legal Issues in the 1970s

The back of the Muslim Brotherhood was broken during Nasser's rule, mainly as a result of its being decreed illegal (1953) and the incarceration of large numbers of them in the 1950s and again in the mid-1960s. With Sadat, a different atmosphere developed. Most if not all were released. Political opposition to Sadat was, until his fatal end, seen as coming from elsewhere.

Beginning in 1972 private bills began to appear in the *Majlis al-Sha'ab* (parliament) asking for enforcement of the *shari'a* in general and in various specifics.[20] These calls went largely unremarked and (with the exception noted below) such bills never went beyond being referred to a parliamentary committee.

After several attempts and a number of revisions a law was finally enacted in 1976 prohibiting the consumption of alcohol in public places, but excepting tourist establishments and making no distinction between Egyptians and foreigners. It has had minimal effect but is still on the books. Another law came some years later prohibited the serving of alcohol to Muslims during Ramadan. This law is enforced, and a hotel or bar that violates it can be closed for some weeks and/or fined.

The existence of extremist tendencies in some of the Islamic groups that were rumored to have been formed hit public consciousness first in 1974 when members of such a group were caught scaling the walls of the military technical academy in Heliopolis.[21] There was a trial with prison sentences given. It remains unclear just what these lads (for they were all young) hoped to accomplish. Some two years later another group kidnapped and murdered a former minister of *awqaf,* Shaikh Dhahabi. These incidents were enough to establish the uncontrovertible existence in Egypt of an extremist tendency in Muslim fundamentalism.

Around the same time the "Islamic tendency" began to become prominent among the students in the universities. It is fairly generally believed that the government had a major role in fostering these groups in the universities—to counter the leftist opposition that was becoming more and more vocal. But whether the government did or did not do anything actively to promote their development, it did nothing until 1979 when it curtailed some of the student unions' prerogatives. For the past several years the students of the Muslim associations have continued to be heavy winners in the student elections.[22] From time to time there are incidents on the campuses.[23] The existence of organized Islamic groups within the army was demonstrated by Sadat's assassination in 1981.

The days of the once monolithic Muslim Brotherhood have, however, passed. It is now but one among many Islamic groups, even though it is still the most prominent. Until 1981 it was known mainly through its monthly magazine, *al-Da'wa.*[24] In both 1984 and 1987 elections for the *Majlis al-Sha'ab,* it entered candidates by joining with one of the regularly constituted parties.[25] Each time a number of its members were elected. The line today is conciliatory, advocating legislation of the *shari'a* but through the procedures established for law-making.

The regime has of course cracked down hard—and continues to do so—on *extremist* Muslim fundamentalism. It should be realized, however, that Muslim piety is part of state ideology. Whereas the minister of the interior may launch campaigns to round up "extremists" and "terrorists," the ruling politicians are not about to disavow the Muslim heritage of Egypt.

The basis of presidential and regime legitimacy shifted with Sadat away from revolutionary charisma to a legally-defined basis of rule. For all his pronouncements that he had established a "rule of law," however, Sadat appears at times not to have really understood or accepted that his legitimacy rested on a different base than that of his predecessor. Certainly the symbols of religious piety he consistently used to define himself and his regime seemed intended to ingratiate him with the believing masses and win him acceptance as paternalistic leader. Both president and politicians appeared ready to make certain concessions to those pressing for *shari'a* reforms in law and quite anxious to give the state a heightened religious profile.

At the same time, strong pressures continue to come from those intent on pushing the new, open economic order (*infitah*). This has meant continuing the development of the society according to modernization definitions of economic development, which in turn has added grist to the mill of those who condemn wordly, secular pleasures and the impious, immoral behavior they are seen as encouraging. Such were some of the contradictions that beset the regime in the 1970s.

The Constitutional Issues

In September 1971, Sadat promulgated a permanent Constitution. Some language in Article 2 of this Constitution appears to make the *shari'a* "a" basis of legislation.[26] This innovation went largely unremarked at the time. In 1976, however, we find a case decided by the High Court[27] which contested the constitutionality of a provision in the regulations governing personal status litigation. This court said in passing that conformity with the *shari'a* was a test of constitutionality and that this applied to past as well as future legislation.[28] Then, in 1978, the rector of al-Azhar University raised a plea of unconstitionality against a lower court verdict requiring al-Azhar to pay a debt plus the accumulated interest at the rate of 4 percent, the rate specified in Article 226 of the Civil Code for civil debts.

This case, finally decided in 1985, settled the issue of retroactivity, at least for the time being, but at the same time threw the onus on the legislature to align laws with the provision of Article 2 of the Constitution. Before the latter case came to decision, however, two things happened. The High Court became the High Constitutional Court, divesting itself of political controls, and a constitutional amendment submitted to referendum in 1980 made the *shari'a* "the" (rather than "a") basis of all legislation.

Following the 1980 amendment to the Constitution (and doubtless the greater confidence the legal profession had in the Constitutional Court once it had become an independent judicial organ in 1979), a rash of pleas appeared claiming unconstitutionality on the basis of legislation being in conflict with the *shari'a* (that is, with amended Article 2). What happens procedurally is that when a plea of unconstitutionality is raised in a lower or appellate court, the judge may, at his discretion, stop the hearings and send the case to the Constitutional Court for determination of the constitutional issue before continuing to hear the case.

Inevitably there were cases challenging the interest provision in the Civil Code as being contrary to the *shari'a*[29]; but cases were also brought challenging the constitutionality of the 1979 amendment to the Personal Status law[30] and the penal law.[31] And there were cases during this period where judges, while following the legal rules then in force, urged the legislature to amend the law in accordance with the *shari'a*.[32]

A Court of Cassation decision in 1982 precluded the 1985 decision of the Constitutional Court. In this case the plaintiff challenged the admissibility of evidence given by the victim of a crime. The court, while agreeing that the *shari'a* forbids the testimony of a victim, denied the plea and ruled that principles of the *shari'a* cannot be applied until they have been formulated as precise legal rules by the legislator, saying:

> The provision of Article 2 of the constitution to the effect that the principles of the *shari'a* are the principal source of legislation has no legal force in and of itself, but is only an instruction to the legislator to take the *shari'a* as a principal source of the laws it enacts; . . . the application of the *shari'a* requires that [the legislator] should determine which exactly of the manifold conflicting views of the founders of the law schools . . . must be used as a basis for [particular] judgments.[33]

In the 1985 decision of the al-Azhar case the Constitutional Court ruled similarly, but went further. "If all past legislation which contradicts *shari'a* principles were to be scrapped," said the court, this would "clearly lead to contradictions and confusion in the judicial process in a manner which would threaten stability." Moreover,

> had the legislator of the Constitution wanted to incorporate the principles of the *shari'a* into the Constitution specifically, or had he intended that these principles be enforced by the courts without the need to formulate them as specific legislative texts according to the set procedures of the Constitution—he did not lack the authority so to provide, clearly and explicitly.[34]

The court thus rejected the plea of unconstitutionality of the article of the Civil Code at issue, Article 226, which provided that interest be charged on unpaid debts, and held that

> only the legal enactments issued after the coming into effect of the obligation to conform to Islamic Law are affected; . . . legal enactments which antedated the amendment are not affected by the obligation to conform because they were in existence before that limitation became due for implementation.[35]

Restricting the applicability of the constitutional amendment to future legislation "does not exempt the legislator from responsibility for the past laws," continued the court, especially those "in contradiction to the principles of the *shari'a*." It is, however, the *legislator's* responsibility, said the court, "to take the initiative in shifting out any infringement of [*shari'a*] principles from the texts of these laws."[36]

Even after this case, during 1986 a judge in a lower court in the governate of Daqhaliyya refused to require a defendant, a local government employee, to pay an interest of EP 48 on money improperly taken, the amount not returned to the government amounting to EP 90. This judge expressed his consternation as follows:

> The court feels too embarrassed in front of God—be He praised and exalted—to give judgment for the plaintiffs (the governor of Daqhaliyya and the minister of health) or even to consider their claim, for it is in fact a claim of usury (*riba*) which in all its forms, is forbidden in the *shari'a*.[37]

The judge, of course, did not have to call on the *shari'a* to deny the government's claim. The fact that he did so intensified his rebuke to the government plaintiffs and indicates, I believe, something of the basis of the "Islamic law" movement as criticism of behavior that the regime tolerates in its officials.

There was another challenge of constitutionality pursuant to the injunction of Article 2 that legislation be based on the *shari'a*. Decided on 4 May 1985, it concerned the 1979 amendment to the Personal Status Law. Great controversy had surrounded this law, known as "Jihan's Law," as it was generally believed to have been enacted on the initiative of the wife of the president. It had appeared suddenly in August of 1979 as a presidential decree (pursuant to decree powers delegated to the president by the parliament).

The amendments had actually been much milder than proposals that had come out of the Ministry of Social Affairs earlier in the decade.[38] Neither the right to marry four wives nor the man's right of *talaq* were essentially touched. The features of the law occasioning most controversy were those requiring that a divorced wife be allowed to continue living in the home of the marriage if she had minor children, and making a husband's taking of a second wife automatic grounds for divorce within one year, if the first wife chose to petition the court.[39]

The court *did* find this law unconstitutional, but not on substantive grounds. The court based its ruling of unconstitutionality on the way the law had been enacted. It was not, said the court, a matter of sufficient urgency that justified the use of the president's decree powers. Thus this case has wider significance than its refusal to make a substantive pronouncement on the personal status issue for it set, in unequivocal terms, limitations to the use of the presidential "emergency" power.

A revised law was passed some six weeks later in substantially the same form, except that it allowed a "suitable" home (rather than the home of the marriage), and required that a first wife who petitioned for a divorce would henceforth be required to demonstrate to a court that she was harmed by her husband's marriage to another.[40] Other features of the law remained essentially the same.[41]

Inasmuch as the court—in what is presently the ruling case (of 1985)—has put the onus on "the legislator" to bring legislation in conflict with the *shari'a* into conformity, we now turn to the activities of "the legislator," which includes both the *Majlis al-Sha'ab* and executive organs.

Parliamentary and Executive Responses

In 1975 the minister of justice had appointed a committee chaired by the chief justice of the Court of Cassation to prepare legislation in accordance with the *shari'a*. This committee prepared eight proposals in specific areas of penal law.[42]

Taking its lead from this apparent government support for preparing Islamic legislation, al-Azhar also formed a committee and directed it to prepare proposals for amending existing laws in "accordance with the *shari'a*." They also began with the penal law and in 1977 presented a proposal to the prime minister and the *Majlis al-Sha'ab*. The al-Azhar committee then turned its attention to the matters of interest and insurance in the civil law.[43]

However, in 1978 a resolution was passed in the *Majlis al-Sha'ab* to form a special committee to study proposals for applying the rules of the *shari'a* and for their codification. The committee was instructed to consult the University of al-Azhar, other faculties of law and the judiciary. The al-Azhar committee shelved its independent activities in this regard when its advice was sought by the parliamentary committee and in January 1981 informed the *Majlis al-Sha'ab* that it approved the drafts submitted to it. Six draft codes were presented to the *Majlis al-Sha'ab* on 1 July 1982, and were referred to the Legislative and Constitutional Committee. There they have languished ever since.[44]

The regime obviously came to have second thoughts as to the advisability of substituting "Islamic Codes" for the existing laws (or others in the government became aware of the potential seriousness of what was afoot). The assassination of President Sadat in September 1981 surely gave the politicians cause to ponder the policy of submitting to pressures exerted by the energetic proponents of Islamic law, but there is another aspect. It appears to me, that just as with the Islamic organizations in the university, there had seemed no harm—at first—in acquiescing to pious demands that Islamic ideals be propagated. Indeed the regime accrued a certain amount of support from such quarters. But suddenly one day there they were, six "Islamic codes" ready to be passed into law!

Since relegating these codes to committee in 1982, the regime has made sure that such an eventuality did not occur. Such a far-reaching revision of the legal system obviously would have extensive consequences. One attorney said to me at the time that if the codes were enacted he would simply have to stop practicing law.

The court, in 1985, when advising the legislature that it was up to it and not the judiciary to conform preexisting law with the *shari'a,* completely ignored that there existed "draft Islamic codes." Rather, it cautioned that

> the change from the legal system presently existing in Egypt, . . . to a completely Islamic legal system will require patience and proceeding with the utmost care as regards practical considerations; . . . and if the legal system is to be changed in its entirety, a suitable period of time is needed . . .[45]

Also contained in the court's opinion was language from a report prepared at the time when what became the amendment to Article 2 of the Constitution was being discussed. This report stated that the amendment was not intended to mean

> the change from the present legal system of Egypt which goes back more than one hundred years and its replacement by a complete system of Islamic law.[46]

Having opened Pandora's box, however, it was not quite so easy to close it again. Pressures for the Islamic codes to be discussed in the *Majlis al-Sha'ab* continued. On the same day that the Constitutional Court handed down its two decisions of 4 May 1985 referred to above, there was a parliamentary debate scheduled on the issue of legislating Islamic law. The session was carefully managed.

First, the Committee on Religious and Social Affairs submitted a report which interpreted the constitutional amendment as meaning

> that the present laws should be reviewed in stages, in a scientific manner, and those features revised that contradict the principles of the *shari'a,* a matter on which all parties and political orientations agree.

But, the report continued, "what is not in contradiction with the principles of the *shari'a* should be left alone." Moreover,

> the rules of the present civil code were enacted after lengthy study and reflection. . . . The majority of them have their origin in the rules of the *shari'a,* except in a few rare instances, as is confirmed in the explanatory memorandum [of the code]. . . . [Therefore] there is no need to revise the rules of the present civil law; it is enough to amend the texts that conflict with the *shari'a.*[47]

A number of deputies were recognized to speak. Some advocated the application of Islamic legislation, others supported the sentiments expressed in the report. All, however, attested their support in general terms for the *shari'a*.

Debate was closed and a government position paper on the subject was read. It contained six points which are quoted below, inasmuch as they exemplify the way in which the government has now chosen to view the issue.

Egypt's legal system is one of stable laws which have their basis in the *shari'a,* the Civil Code being a good example.

The judiciary in Egypt is firmly established with its system embedded in the Constitution and the laws which agree with the principles of the *shari'a*; it would be no small matter to rebuild such a system and much of value in the past efforts would be destroyed in the process. Therefore, it is preferable to work on developing what already exists, according to the *shari'a*.

The principles of the Islamic religion call for a society of equality, justice, sufficiency, tolerance and other qualities of which we can be justly proud in front of the whole world; and our work is to assure such a society.

There is a consensus on the principles of the *shari'a* concerning civil transactions; only in some details is there controversy, and the controversial issues must be studied carefully.

Egypt has never been isolated from the world and interacts with what happens today throughout the world; we must find ways to surmount the present burdens of our international commodity transactions (amounting to more than fifty percent of GNP), so that we may benefit from them.

All sects of Egyptian society accept drawing our legislation from the *shari'a* and the application of *shari'a* principles in response to concerns of utility, necessity, and the avoidance of harm.[48]

The session voted acceptance of the government's position paper, and when the matter of the draft Islamic codes was raised the Speaker of the House explained that there were no draft laws or proposals for draft laws before the present session of the Assembly, any such matters before a previous session having died with the ending of that session.[49]

Voices continue to be raised, however, calling for the enactment of Islamic law. In November 1987 the *Majlis al-Sha'ab* established a new committee "to review and oversee all bills being discussed by the *Majlis al-Sha'ab* to make sure that they do not conflict with either the *shari'a* or the Constitution." It was to be composed of the deputy chairman of the *Majlis al-Sha'ab,* the heads of parliamentary groups, and legal experts, and had as its mandate not only the review of all new bills but also "to review all laws issued in Egypt since 1882, in order to eliminate any redundant or contradictory laws and laws which do not conform to the *shari'a.*"[50] In a speech during the previous month President Mubarak had recommended that there be a "stock-taking and review of all legislation and laws, in light of their present complexity and contradiction." The laws in Egypt are said to number about 8,000 together with some 10,000 "peripheral" decrees. Review and revision of all of these will not in all likelihood be completed any time soon.

One minister of state[51] has interpreted this "stock-taking" to include (but not be limited to) the expunging of

> laws which are in violation with the *shari'a,* because the basic tendency among us is commitment to the application of the *shari'a.* This does not mean the elimination of all the laws that exist now in order to apply the *shari'a* in one fell swoop, but we will try as far as possible to clean up the current laws.[52]

The present proliferation of laws in Egypt is, if anything, symptomatic of deeper problems. "Islam"—said the campaign slogan of the Alliance in the last elections—"is the solution." But the problems of Egypt presently are manifold and the call for legislating the *shari'a* is, in light of the larger problems, something of a side issue. The issues which are at the center of the political arena concern the viability of the economy and the democratization of the polity. There are, however, aspects of both that touch on the "Islamic law" issue.

The Islamic Investment Companies

In terms of the economy, the problem as the government has defined it and as it affects the law can be summarized as how to promote free enterprise and the private sector and still retain control over the financial resources of Egypt.

This covers a wide territory. One singularly recalcitrant problem from the beginning of the *infitah* has been control over foreign currency and the associated issue of regulating imports. Almost yearly there have been revisions in the currency control regulations and concomitant efforts to make private sector importation possible without draining the state's scarce supply of foreign currency.[53] It is in this context that the problem which the Islamic investment companies present to the government should be understood.

All of a sudden these enterprises appeared as gigantic monoliths operating virtually outside the control of the banking laws. They promise large returns for investors (well over 20 percent) and thus are attractive to workers abroad and the general population at home. They deal in both foreign and Egyptian currency. Not only do they represent yet another means whereby workers' remittances remain outside the state's financial institutions, but they seem to have succeeded (where the government has never been wholly successful) in inducing ordinary people to commit their savings which, in composite, can be used as investment capital.

The government is in something of a "catch-22" situation. Because these institutions operate outside of the laws governing financial institutions, for all practical purposes, there are no legal protections for the depositors. Should these companies go under, the government would have to confront myriad citizens with grievances demanding redress. Nevertheless, there is fear that if controls are legislated the vast amounts of foreign currency these companies reportedly have abroad (estimated in the billions) will be forever lost to Egypt. Moreover, should new controls cause these companies to "fold their tents and quietly steal away," the Egyptian populace will also blame the government. There were indications of the scope of possible repercussions when at least one of these companies lost heavily speculating in the European gold market.

There is yet another aspect of the problem facing those who endeavor to manage the Egyptian economy. With the amount of capital these companies are able to generate, they can corner the market on particular items. Prices can be driven up and great profits made, causing distortions in the economy. (Scrap iron has been mentioned as one of their interests.) Although the government is anxious to promote investment in productive enterprises, those in charge of the economy are filled with even greater apprehension with the potential of these companies for buying up property and businesses and thus exerting control over key sectors of the economy. In addition, these companies are also creating jobs—the insufficiency of which is another current problem.

In an interview in November 1987, the director of al-Rayyan, one of the most prominent of the Islamic investment companies, spoke of "three main directions" in the management of their funds: production projects,[54] "fast-return" commercial projects,[55] and an amount set aside to provide for liquidity for "the needs of our clients."

An indication of the sensitive nature of the problem was contained in two articles which appeared in the opposition Hizb al-'Amal party paper, *al-Sha'ab,* in July 1987. Written as editorials these articles intimated that hostility to these companies derived from a desire on the part of greedy politicians to deny to ordinary people the opportunity— otherwise only open to the rich, the powerful, and the *infitah* profiteers—to earn high returns on their savings. In several well-publicized corruption cases in recent years the collusion of some of the state-regulated banks with racketeers and with government officials and their friends was quite evident and disclosures during the course of these trials not such as to inspire either faith in, or liking for, such institutions.[56]

The Islamic investment companies have nothing to do with "Islamic banking" as such[57] except insofar as their claim to Islamic legality is that they do not pay interest (*riba*). They are not incorporated as joint stock companies, nor do they issue stock or have boards of directors in the legal sense of these terms. Rather, the depositors are considered investors who are "sleeping partners," in a *mudaraba* partnership. The companies ostensibly guarantee a specified minimum profit to their depositors ("investors") who are told that they may be given more. This "sleeping partner" arrangement is, incidentally, the formula advocated generally by those who seek to eliminate the anti-Islamic "interest" of the civil law and, in a variation, also the solution proposed (by some) to the presumed Islamic prohibition against insurance.

Nonetheless, a draft law has now been introduced into parliament designed to require such companies to turn themselves into joint stock companies subject to regulation by the Ministry of Economy and the Stock Market Authority. They will have a year to comply from the date of the passing of the law and penalties are prescribed for evasion.[58]

The director of al-Rayyan has gone on record as saying that he welcomes the government's efforts "to regulate the conditions of all investment companies" as this "shows concern about the welfare of citizens . . . and we thank it for its praiseworthy stand."[59]

Party Politics, the Election Law,
and the Islamic Tendency

The dominant rhetoric from the regime and the ruling National Democratic Party (NDP) is that democratization of Egyptian politics continues to proceed apace and that a commitment to "real democracy" came only with the Mubarak presidency. Nevertheless, present laws governing elections to the national legislature as well as local bodies virtually guarantee that the ruling party will maintain a substantial majority.

The efforts of the ruling party to retain power have taken on another significance since the Muslim Brotherhood joined with the legally constituted opposition parties for the purpose of entering candidates in the *Majlis al-Sha'ab* elections. It won seats in both 1984 and 1987 and presently has some 40 deputies.[60] There has been a court case that has dragged on since the 1970s contesting the government's refusal to allow the Brotherhood party status, until now without success.[61]

The multi-party system as presently constituted in Egypt is only some 12 years old. It was in 1976 that a tentative concession to "multi-party" politics began. The parties which stood for election to the *Majlis al-Sha'ab* in that year were presented as "tendencies" (*manabir*—literally "pulpits") of the one-party Arab Socialist Union. Soon all pretense was dropped (in fact, if not immediately in law) that the ASU was any longer relevant to political life in Egypt. A Parties Law was enacted in 1977 (with amendments in 1979) to regulate party activity. Its major feature was a prescription of requirements for the formation henceforth of new parties, including the prohibition of parties organized on a religious basis. A governmental committee was established to rule on each petition for party status. Cases in the courts (and there are presently several) from groups seeking party status arise as appeals from this committee.[62]

Whereas the election of 1976 is generally considered to have involved minimal manipulation, that of 1979 was notoriously interfered with—openly and extensively. In both of these elections the opposition parties obtained a minimal number of seats to become a parliamentary opposition whose size was slightly increased by members elected as "independents."

In preparing for the 1984 elections the government chose to pass a new election law. This law prescribed a complicated system of proportional representation, required candidates to stand for election under party lists, and abolished the possibility of running as an "independent." To be eligible for any seats a party had to pull 8 percent of the national vote. The new law also included the provision of 30 seats earmarked for women.

Although the opposition parties (some five by that time, to be joined by election time by a sixth) vocally objected to the new election rules—since it was clear that the cards were stacked against them—they nonetheless chose to play the game. And although the law was clearly designed to give the ruling party the advantage, instances of fraud and manipulation were reported. Two persons were killed. Only one opposition party—the Wafd, including allied members of the Muslim Brotherhood—won any seats.[63]

Shortly thereafter a court case was begun, claiming the unconstitutionality of the Election Law. As this case approached decision in winter 1986-87 it became known that an advisory report to the court advocated holding the law unconstitutional. The *Majlis al-Sha'ab* responded immediately by passing a new Election Law. The issue of constitutionality involved the failure of the 1983 law to allow candidates to stand as independents. The 1987 law summarily changed the thirty seats reserved for women to being "independent" seats. Features concerning proportional representation, party lists, and the required national vote of 8 percent for parties to qualify for seats were retained. The enlargement of election districts was also retained from the 1983 law which required independent candidates to pull substantial votes far beyond what had been for some, under the system used in 1976 and 1979, sinecures of local *izbas* and villages.

The issue of the legality of the existing *Majlis al-Sha'ab,* of course, still remained. It assumed heightened importance inasmuch as this body would, pursuant to the Constitution, nominate the president for reelection in October 1987. The president called a plebiscite on dissolving the *Majlis* and a new election was scheduled for April 1987. (Shortly thereafter, in May, the Constitutional Court handed down its decision confirming that the 1983 election law had been unconstitutional.)

Again the opposition parties made a weak showing, but better than before. Both Wafd and Alliance won seats, some 90-odd altogether (out of a total parliament of 450 deputies), representing an increase over 1984. Some members of the Alliance exhibit the Islamic tendency, although they are not affiliated with the Muslim Brotherhood. There are also, nominally, those of the Islamic tendency among the independents.[64] The Islamic tendency, although small, certainly has a presence in the present parliament, but then it has consistently had advocates there in the preceding parliaments. Both *Hizb al-'Amal* and *Hizb al-Ahrar* have developed a marked Islamic coloration—especially since the Muslim Brothers joined with them.

There are several court cases presently contesting the counting of the votes[65] and another case has been raised challenging the constitutionality of the new Election Law. There have been indications that the government and relevant committees in the *Majlis* are considering revising the Election Law yet again, to allow more independent candidates, and to be ready for use in local elections.[66]

There are compelling legal arguments for challenges in the courts. A lower court has already decided for the plaintiffs in at least one of the vote-counting cases. At the same time the Judges Club[67] has now gone on record as dissociating itself from the Committee prescribed under the Election Law, formed of members of the Judiciary and of the Ministry of Interior, that oversees the election.

Presently there is movement on various levels—in which the judiciary, lawyers, and opposition parties are all active—to force more acceptable legal formulas and practices in the electoral process in Egypt. However, the great unknown in the equation is: Will freeing the election process of its legal shackles (and finding a means to exercise proper, impartial supervision to reduce tampering and intimidation) open the doors to a greatly increased representation of the "Islamic tendency" in parliament?

There is another, related, political cum legal issue. Pressures have also been mounting from various directions[68] to do away with the "exceptional" jurisdictions (especially the socialist prosecutor) and the State of Emergency. However, it is procedures under the emergency laws used by the minister of interior and the investigations of the socialist prosecutor's office that are the regime's principal means for controlling potential terrorism and violence deemed to come from some groups of "Islamic fundamentalists." Thus, the classic dilemma of liberalism presents itself: Is it justifiable—or to what extent—for a (liberal) democratic regime to use undemocratic means in the interest of preventing those who seek the establishment of an illiberal regime from doing so? In Egypt there is a variant of this issue.

The present legal structure contains several non-liberal provisions in the emergency and other "political" laws while the gap between rich and poor is widening and a substantial number of Egypt's citizens suffer severe economic disadvantage. On the other hand, those who call for a regime founded on Islamic principles hark back to the first Islamic state, Medina, the political order established by the prophet, a political order embodying ideals that only the most extreme secular modernists consider not to have included superior standards of justice. Proponents of *shari'a* legislation obviously do not believe this will produce an illiberal regime. The Guide of the Muslim Brothers has recently said the following:

> The general atmosphere is not [now] conducive to the establishment of an Islamic state . . .

> The most important thing is to work for the implementation of the *shari'a,* and to try to persuade the authorities to abolish the freedom-restricting laws such as the Law of Shame[69] and the Emergency Law. Implementation of the *shari'a* is the basis. . . .

> We carry out our activities in the *Majlis al-Sha'ab,* which is the legitimate place for that . . . [as] the *Majlis al-Sha'ab* [is] the official institution that combines all views and trends. . . .

> The Muslim Brothers have their own exclusive principles and so do the parties, but we are all agreed on the implementation of the *shari'a* and the promotion of various freedoms such as freedom of speech and freedom of assembly. We proceed on that path in full, solid cohesion with the parties with which we are allied. . . .

> As Muslims, the officials are not really against implementation of the *shari'a*; it is just that there are pressures here and there to delay its implementation. In the end, however, only what is right prevails; everything else disappears. . . . Islam maintains that the difference between right and wrong is quite clear, that everyone must obey the rules of Islam and God's law. . . .[70]

Notes

1. The Court of Cassation (*Mahkamat al-Naqd*), the High Constitutional Court, and the High Administrative Court.

2. Notably Muhammad 'Ali's *Majlis al-Ahkam* and "merchants' courts." The major study of this period is Ahmad Fathi Zaghloul, *al-Muhamah* (Cairo, 1900).

3. In Case No. 65 of Judicial Year No. 1, decided on Feb. 10, 1948.

4. The "massacre" included 129 judges and 58 auxiliary appointments. See Mumtaz

Nassar, *Ma'arakat al-'Adala fi Misr* (The Battle for Justice in Egypt)(Cairo 1974), discussed in Enid Hill, "The Judiciary in Egypt," paper prepared for SSRC Conference on Contracting States and Expanding Societies in the Middle East, Aix-en-Provence, March 25-27, 1988.

5. The High Council for Judicial Organizations.

6. Most recently it was lifted in May 1980 but reimposed in October 1981 after the assassination.

7. Notably the provision for incarceration for up to six months without a court hearing. An addition to the Emergency Law in the late 1970s allows arrest for political crimes on "suspicion."

8. Such as the "gathering" of five or more persons or the public distribution of political (subversive) literature, etc.

9. Subsuming some of the functions of the Sequestration Court, it has been used primarily to impose judicial penalties on persons prosecuted under the illegal gains legislation. It was in this court that a number of political personalities such as Rashad Osman and Ismat al-Sadat and family were brought to trial for crimes connected with accusations of "unjust enrichment." It was also here that the black marketeers were tried in fall 1985.

10. *Al-muda'i al-ishtiraki*—another retreading of a previous creation. Although this office in its present form was established by Sadat in 1971 (incidentally with the beginnings of desequestration), its status and powers were not fully spelled out in law until 1980.

11. It was from the socialist prosecutor's office that the list of 1,536 names on the arrest order in September 1981 emanated.

12. Published as *Murshid al-Hayran*. Codification of *shari'a* rules for civil law had been the route followed for legal reform by the Ottomans with the *Majalla,* which was promulgated in the Empire from 1876.

13. To be found in manuscript form in the Egyptian National Library (*Dar al-Kutub*), according to Farhat Ziadeh, *Lawyers, the Rules of Law and Liberalism in Modern Egypt* (Stanford: Hoover University Press, 1968).

14. The government at that time seems to have hoped and expected an early demise of the Mixed Courts with the National Courts assuming jurisdiction over all civil controversies. Thus, it was deemed advisable—to hasten this eventuality—to have a code acceptable to foreigners. This is Ziadeh's interpretation of why Qadri Pasha's codes were not adopted.

15. Elaborated in Enid Hill, *al-Sanhuri and Islamic Law* (Cairo Papers in Social Science) (Cairo, 1987), Chs. 6, 7 and 8.

16. Muhammad Abduh had issued a *fatwa* which interpreted the *shari'a* as allowing interest on savings accounts. From time to time other religious scholars have argued that the *shari'a* does permit banks to pay moderate interest.

17. Ziadeh, p. 143; discussed in Hill (1987), pp. 66-68.

18. I am indebted to a manuscript by Rudolph Peters, "Divine Law or Man-made Law? Egyptian Politics and the Application of the *Shari'a,*" publication forthcoming in *Arab Law Quarterly,* August 1988, for these details. Sources he cites are Richard Mitchell, *The Society of the Muslim Brothers* (London, 1969) and Jan Brugman, *De betekenis van het Mohammedaanse recht in het hedendaagse Egypte* (Leiden, 1960).

19. A pronouncement of *talaq* is revocable the first two times to insure that hasty action can be reconsidered. A practice had, however, grown up of making a *talaq* divorce final by pronouncing divorce three times at once to produce an irrevocable divorce.

20. According to Peters, *op. cit.,* these private bills included the following: A proposal of amputation for thefts, (1972); proposals to make employment of male hairdressers in women's coiffeurs illegal, and to prohibit production, consumption, and sale of alcohol, (1973); proposals to prohibit interest (*riba*), while allowing "investment loans," under a *mudaraba* partnership, to amend articles in the Penal Code to accord with the *shari'a,* (1976); and proposals to collect *zakat* (the Islamic tax), to make it a criminal offense to break the fast in public during Ramadan, "to protect women and society against temptation and perversion" especially as regards mixing of the sexes in public places like buses and the universities, and to prescribe female attire, and to prohibit certain professions for

women (e.g., air hostess, private secretary), and "sensual" advertising (1977).

21. This became known as the *"faniyya 'askariyya"* incident.

22. In the November 1987 student union elections members of Islamic groups won large majorities in Cairo University and in the universities of 'Ain Shams and Assiut (90 percent of the committees in various colleges). And "for the first time in the history of student elections the Islamic groups won in al-Azhar University with 70 percent" (*al-Wafd,* November 27, 1987), although the students complained of "continuing harassment of Islamic group members and politically and ideologically active students." *al-Sha'ab,* November 25, 1987.

23. Examples include the intimidation of other students, book burning, and a confrontation with the university administration two years ago when a veiled medical student was denied entry to a final examination. The fashion of veiling among female students ebbs and flows as does that of beards among male students.

24. In 1981 *al-Da'wa* was required to cease publication. Today there is a proliferation of popular Islamic books, journals, and newspapers, including publications of the government. Some journalists who are members of the Muslim Brotherhood now publish from time to time in both opposition party newspapers (notably, but not limited to, *al-Sha'ab*) and in the mainstream journals and newspapers.

25. In 1984, it joined with the Wafd, and in 1987 with the Socialist Workers Party and the Liberal Party to form "The Alliance" (*al-Tahalluf*).

26. While this was the first time that such language had appeared in an Egyptian Constitution, Article 1 of the revised Civil Code of 1948 had directed the judge to the *shari'a* as one source for guidance in the absence of applicable statutory provisions or custom (*'urf*).

27. The High Court was the predecessor to the High Constitutional Court but at that time a "political" court, as its appointments, while from members of the judiciary, were controlled by the Ministry of Justice and thus ultimately the president.

28. This case concerned the provision in the *Shari'a* Court's Ordinance (the law governing personal status litigation) which prescribed imprisonment for debt of a husband who, although financially able, failed to pay his wife's maintenance. The Court found this provision to be in agreement with the *shari'a* and included in its decision its opinion that Article 2 had retroactive effect. I am grateful to Rudolph Peters for calling attention to this case, discussed in Peters, *op. cit.,* note 32.

29. Some six such cases are cited in Peters, *op. cit.,* between 1980 and 1986.

30. Alleged restrictions in the 1979 law on the man's right of *talaq* and of polygamous marriage were at issue.

31. One such case concerned a bus accident involving 13 dead and 38 injured, which the judge sent to the Constitutional Court to determine the constitutionality of Articles 238 and 244 of the Penal Code (prescribing punishment for accidental homicide—ten years maximum imprisonment) and Article 220 of the Code of Criminal Procedure (concerning the award of civil damages for a crime). The court argued that these rules were incompatible with the *shari'a* which subscribes to a philosophy of justice making the punishment fit the crime, none of which applies in accidental crimes. While the Islamic *diyya* (indemnity for physical injury) requires civil compensation it takes account of differences in crimes and the persons involved.

32. In a case of Beni Suef the judge endorsed "the new draft penal code prescribing *hadd* ["defined"] punishments for theft," which he "yearned to apply" because "it is an example of laws which protect values, national unity, social peace and personal status." But he sentenced the accused thief before his court to three years imprisonment with hard labor. *Al-Ahram,* January 10, 1981.

33. Quoted from Peters, *op. cit.,* (citing *al-Ahram,* April 7, 1982).

34. High Constitutional Court Decision in Case No. 20 (May 4, 1985) in *al-Jarida al-Rasmiyya* 20 (May 16, 1985), p. 999. An English translation of this case appears in

Arab Law Quarterly, 1(1), pp. 100-107. This case is more fully discussed in Hill (1987), pp. 123ff and in Peters, *op. cit.*

35. *al-Jarida,* p. 997.

36. *Ibid.,* pp. 999-1000.

37. *al-Jumhuriya* (Cairo), February 5, 1986. The case involved a clerk in the office of the Health Administration in Mit Ghamr who took 480 EP for more than 15 days without permission. When it was given back it was EP 90 short. The court passed sentence that he repay the remaining EP 90 but refused the government's claim of interest.

38. There had been proposals in 1972, 1974 and 1977, each containing less ambitious changes than the one before. The 1974 proposal elicited a protest march from al-Azhar *'ulama* and students, whereupon Sadat promised that no action on the proposal was presently contemplated. Accounts of these proposals are contained in *al-Ahram,* February 16 and March 15, 1972, March 25 and April 1, 1974, and May 6, 1977. None of them was acted upon. Ironically, the 1979 law was an extremely watered down version of preceding proposals.

39. The law also gave statutory force to the abolition of the *bayt al-ta'a* (literally, "house of obedience"), which allowed a husband to enlist the help of the police in having his wife—who had left him—returned. The 1979 law set forth procedures whereby the husband must petition and the wife was given the opportunity to state her case. *Bayt al-ta'a* had in practice been discontinued somewhere in the early to mid-1970s. It is presumed that this followed a police directive as no one has been able to come up with the documentation.

Other features of the law included raising the ages for the mother to retain custody of children after divorce, requirement of State notification to a wife that she was divorced, and the *muta'* payments. The latter (literally "enjoyment") were lump sum payments to a wife upon divorce, the amounts depending on the husband's income and the length of the marriage.

40. This was basically a reversion to the 1929 law where "harm" was specified as one ground (among others) for divorce. In practice marriage to another woman by a husband was used by the first wife as the basis for claiming "harm." The difference is that she had to convince a judge that the second marriage of her husband had harmed her. It was not automatic. See Enid Hill, *Mahkama! Studies in the Egyptian Legal System* (London, 1979), chapter 3.

41. Aspects of reaction, especially among women, to the court decision are discussed in *The Middle East* (June 1985), pp. 17-20, to which this author contributed. Features of the new law are discussed in *Cairo Today* (1986), including a partial translation.

42. Texts of these proposals and discussion appear in the issues of *al-Muhamah* (Bar Association Journal) in 1980 and 1982 as follows: 60(1-2), pp. 212-27; 60(3-4), pp. 164-80; 60(5-6), pp. 166-92; 60(9-10), pp. 108-46; 62:(1-2), pp. 166-75. Discussed at some length in Peters *op. cit.*

43. I am indebted to Peters, *op. cit.* for these details.

44. A fuller discussion can be found in Peters, *op. cit.* Information concerning the legislative history of these draft codes is to be found in *Madbatat Majlis al-Sha'ab* (Transcript of Daily Proceedings of the Legislature), 70th Session, July 1, 1982, and 74th Session, May 4, 1985. These draft codes were printed as appendices to the *Madbata* of July 1, 1982 under imprint of the *Majlis al-Sha'ab.* See Hill 1987, pp. 124-25. Articles discussing their content appeared in *al-Ahram* on July 12, 1982, November 11, 1982, November 14, 1982 and December 6, 1982.

45. *al-Jarida al-Rasmiyya* 20 (May 16, 1985), p. 998.

46. Discussed in Hill (1987), pp. 125-28.

47. *Madbatat Majlis al-Sha'ab,* 74th Session, May 4, 1985, p. 14. See also Hill (1987), p. 129.

48. *Ibid.,* p. 35.

49. *Ibid.*

50. *al-Tadamun* (London), November 21, 1987.

51. Dr. Ahmad Salama, minister of state for *Majlis al-Sha'ab* and *Majlis al-Shura* Affairs, in an interview with *Akhir Sa'a* (Cairo), Oct. 21, 1987.

52. *Ibid.* The main problem is here identified as the proliferation of laws and decrees and the need for "an overall view and the necessity for issuance of flexible, not rigid, legislation."

53. Discussed in Enid Hill, Khaled Fahmy, and Ziyad Baha al-Din, "Legislating *al-Fitah* (1971-1987)," paper presented to the Annual Conference of the British Society for Middle East Studies, July 12-15, 1987.

54. The director spoke of seventeen companies "established in record time" which include factories producing tiles (automated with modern equipment from Germany and Italy), hollow cement blocks, industrial cleaners, fiberglass for bathtubs, automobile spare parts and tanks, a large agricultural-industrial enterprise, and projects to produce seeds and processed meats. Planned projects include a group of language schools ("al-Rayyan for Languages") beginning with primary school, embroidered clothing, "al-Rayyan Farm" with 5,000 head of cattle, a factory for processing dairy products, and an integrated housing project. Their exports include processed meat products, cleaners, fiberglass and natural juices "to the Arab countries, especially Saudi Arabia." *October* (Cairo), November 15, 1987.

55. These include restaurants, automobile service stations, jewelry, lumber and hardware businesses. Also mentioned were "some investments overseas, such as farms and restaurants in Saudi Arabia, and pill and drug companies in America." *Ibid.*

56. From its beginning, in the fall of 1980, the *Mahkamat al-Qim* or "Court of Values" had cases of corruption brought to it under illegal gains legislation whereby judgments of judicial sequestration were passed. The most famous: Rashad Uthman (1981), Ismat al-Sadat and family (1982-83), Tawfiq Abd al-Hayy (1982-83), Sami Ali Hasan and other "money merchants" (1985). All involved certain of the banks in one way or another. These cases are discussed in Gamal Zahran, "al-Dur al-Siyasi li al-Qada fi 'Amaliyyat San' al-Qarar" (The political role of the judiciary in decree-making), paper given at Annual Conference on Political Studies in Egypt, Center for Political Studies and Research, Cairo University, November 1987.

57. The Islamic banks are subject to the banking laws.

58. *al-Sha'ab* (Cairo), January 12, 1988. There are 36 articles in 8 sections reported as being in this draft law, comprising: (1) the legal form of companies; (2) the financial structure of joint stock companies having variable capital; (3) the total amount of variable capital; (4) the model and change of legal form; (5) stopping the activity of companies and their liquidation; (6) supervision and balance sheets; (7) special provisions for existing companies, and (8) penalties. In Article 1 it is stated that there is to be no "public subscription" for companies not organized as joint stock companies. The Stock Market Authority and the Ministry of the Economy, as well as the board of directors of each company, are given supervisory control over various of their activities. There is a requirement of depositing funds in the Central Bank, and "the companies will not be permitted to keep any former deposits or certificates in any bank or financial organization abroad."

59. *October,* November 15, 1987. He added: "We have been active for four years in the area of investing funds. We obey all the regulations and laws that protect the funds of clients."

60. *al-Sharq al-Awsat* (London), January 11, 1988.

61. Recently it was reported that a new twist has appeared in their case. Their lawyers are claiming that they were never legally abolished, as the government has been unable to produce in court the decree which outlawed them in 1953, the implication being that it was never put into writing and signed (that is, never promulgated and therefore not a valid decree). *The Middle East Times* (Cairo), November 15-21, 1987.

62. See Hill (1988), pp. 1ff.

63. About 65 seats were won. Estimates are that 15-20 of these deputies belong to the Brotherhood.

64. Few of the "independent" seats were won by true independents in the 1987 election. Both government and opposition parties ran candidates on independent ballots. Usually the government candidate won. A notable upset for the government, however, was the Helwan district, which elected a shaikh.

65. The issues are complex and are not relevant here, but are discussed in Hill (1988).

66. Discussed further in *ibid*.

67. This is the professional association of judges, which has had no small measure of influence as an instrument of pressure at times in the past, when it has chosen to use it.

68. These include all the opposition parties, which consistently publish diatribes in their newspapers; the Judges Club, which held a special Congress in 1986, where opposition was couched in suitable judicially-responsible language; and the executive council of the Bar Association, which is controlled by civil libertarians.

69. This was one of Sadat's "political" laws passed in 1980, which also established the (exceptional) Court of Values.

70. Hamid Abu al-Nasr, Guide of the Muslim Brotherhood, interview in *al-Sharq al-Awsat* (London), January 11, 1988.

13 SOCIETY, POLITICS AND SECTARIAN STRIFE

Amira Sonbol

Sectarian strife sometimes results from religious causes of long historical standing. It can also be the result of more recent developments, ranging from demographic changes to a lack of political participation in a state where power is controlled by one religious group. Typically, such non-participation is accompanied by social and economic inequalities which exacerbate the problem and act as a catalyst that can lead to sectarian violence.

The case of Egypt is illustrative. There are long-standing grievances between Muslims and Copts, who have been kept separate for centuries by a political and legal system that based individual identification on religious affiliation. The growth in population of the country and the fears of each group that its rights would be undermined or swamped by the other, have only increased the tension. This tension has, in turn, been escalated by the movement of population and urbanization, accompanied by demographic transformations through which the spatial distribution of Copts throughout Egypt has changed. Previously Copt-heavy areas, e.g., the towns of Upper Egypt (Assiut, Luxor, Qina), and quarters of cities, e.g., Shubra, are now inhabited by larger percentages of Muslims. The population pressure, a yearly increase of nearly 1.5 million, or one person born every 21 seconds, has only helped to extend the problem.[1]

Even though Egypt today has an "open" multi-party electoral system, in which, at least theoretically, any Egyptian is allowed to run for elections, it has not provided for true representation for either the Coptic or Muslim communities. This situation is exacerbated by Coptic anger over the 1980 inclusion in the Constitution of an article making the *shari'a* the main source for legislation.[2] However sincere the belief may be that the *shari'a* would guarantee Coptic rights, by the very inclusion of this clause the Egyptian Constitution sanctioned what amounted to religious preferment and belied the claim that Egypt was a true democracy. It also reinforced the separation of communities along religious lines, giving new life to the traditional basis of identity according to religious affiliation, thereby undermining the secular fundamentals that bind a nation-state together.

This is a study of Egyptian society, religious revivalism, and sectarian strife. Taking the above-mentioned points as a basis, it considers the phenomena of religious revivalism and sectarian strife to be part of an ongoing class conflict, paralleled by a struggle between Church and State, in which the legitimacy of the government is questioned and its ability to rule is therefore undermined. Because the state represents a dominant elite which has kept tight control over real political participation, and assures its continuation in power by force, arbitrary manipulation of the law, and legitimization by an official religious hierarchy, it has managed to alienate a majority of its population who cannot identify with its policies or benefit from its rule.

Revivalism, both Muslim and Coptic, is a reflection of the wish to be involved in the process of decision-making. Being unable to participate in a modern political structure such as a nation-state, Egyptians have turned to traditional forms of self-identity. By recreating what they believe to be "true Islam," the institution of a just society, or the call for an independent state for Copts, revivalists are expressing a wish to have some form of control over decision-making in their personal lives, as well as to have their wishes heard by pressuring for changes in the laws of the state and its political institutions.

The government of Egypt, faced with the continuing appearance of radical elements that threaten the stability of the state, has helped reinforce the religious phenomenon for its own ends. There are strong practical reasons for this approach. The ruling elite has found it expedient to use the *'ulama* as a means to combat the radical Islamic groups as well as to act as justifiers of their rule. Whether it is the Sadat regime using the religious groups to combat socialist influence or the Mubarak government using the *'ulama* of the Azhar to combat the radical elements, the result has been the same: religious and social matters have been turned over to the keeping of a religious leadership that the government considers to be safe for the stability of the state. This has meant the introduction of that group's conception of what form the state should take, which is invariably a dogmatic one, based on the authority of their class, by which the *shari'a* becomes not a law given by God, but a law interpreted by this very class, influenced by its own social and economic background. What had once been considered civil liberties and right of choice, are now seen as anti-Islamic actions.[3]

The increased activities of Islamic revivalist groups, and the role played by the Muslim clergy in shaping society, have pushed the Copts to further emphasize their self-identity in religious terms.

There is a definite correlation between increased Islamization and sectarian strife. The closer the movement towards establishing Islamic law as a common law for all the people, the more intransigent and radical are the actions of the Church.

Foreign pressures have also had a significant role to play in the political activism of the Coptic community in Egypt. First, the specter of sectarian strife and the fate of minorities in other Islamic countries, particularly Lebanon and Sudan, have contributed directly to fear and anxiety amongst Copts. Second, the Coptic population of Egypt, one of the largest minorities in any Islamic country, has close connections with large immigrant communities in the US, Canada, and Australia. The latter have provided financial and political support, and have used their leverage and lobbying with the governments of their new countries to exert pressure on Egypt. Because of the importance of relations between the US and Egypt since Camp David, the Coptic lobbying activity in the US Congress has strengthened the Church's resolve to take matters into its own hands, and to wage a real, if hidden, conflict between it and the State, a struggle which the latter cannot ignore and has to handle with great care.

Religion and Class

We can divide Egyptian society into two major groups:

First, an upper-class elite whose position is based largely but not exclusively on wealth; this elite is best defined as those who hold the reins of power in their hands, who have an actual say in the process of decision-making, and who, by virtue of wealth or prestige, control their own role and fortune within the community. Included here would be the upper echelons of the government hierarchy and of the army officer corps; intellectuals, including high-level journalists, writers, and the top-level teaching staff of universities; the leadership of the six government approved parties; a particular group of high level urban professionals, including doctors, lawyers, engineers, and artists; and wealthy merchants involved in export-import and large-scale retail activity, land owners and bankers, all of whom benefitted from *infitah* policies.

The second group would consist of the rest of the population, notwithstanding the differences in class, wealth, education, or religion. Here we would include the middle echelons of the various departments and institutions of the government, as well as the public sector; the lower ranking officers with slow potential for promotion; the lower staff of academic institutions, including school-teachers and the *ma'ahid*; shopowners and other members of the petty bourgeoisie; and university students facing difficult or bleak futures. These can be considered a middle-class in economic terms, a group hardest hit by inflation, and the lack of fulfillment of rising expectations. Urban labor, privately employed or otherwise, as well as most shopkeepers, can be added to this group of disillusioned, even though culturally and educationally they form a different class. While this second group, which we can call the *raqaya,* has traditionally formed a base of support for nationalist governments, it happens to be a politically sophisticated and dissatisfied group, that is now divided between those who believe in a nation-state with a democratic structure, and those who have turned towards religion for self-identification and political activism.

The peasantry, the newly urbanized, the unemployed, and the various other groups that form a subclass, enforce the stand of the second group and the role of religion in society. Having yet to break out of traditional mores, and being left out of the political process, it is only normal that they belong to the group that is emphasizing the very principles most familiar to them.

There is undoubtedly a strong correlation between class and religious revivalism. In the first group, we see that the problems faced by the members of the two religions are common, as are the answers, ideologies, and outlooks across sectarian lines. Thus, while the elite is involved in the world of business, high-finance, party-politics, and foreign affairs, the people's main concerns include widespread poverty, extreme overcrowdedness, a daily struggle for mere survival, and day-to-day friction on a personal basis that can easily lead to violence. One of the dilemmas that faces Egypt is that the ruling elite may understand the problems facing the second group, but has tried to present solutions that proved unsuccessful because they reflected elite interests rather than those of the country as a whole. The perception of the elite amongst the general populace is that of an oligarchy, well-connected through marriage and political alliances, who use power to extract wealth. Such a picture also characterized both the Arab Socialist Union (formed in 1961), and the *shillal* that marked the rule of President Sadat.[4] Today, there may be a wish to move away from such elitism, but the shape of the political system and the role played by the National Democratic Party seem to emphasize its continuation.

Demographic and Security Issues

However much the government builds or the economy grows, the results seem to be eaten up by the growth of the population, which is expected to reach 70 million by the beginning of the twenty-first century.[5] The problem of overcrowding has had its repercussions on every aspect of life in Egypt, including sectarian strife. The growth of the Coptic population meant a need for larger numbers of churches to serve the spiritual needs of the community. Egyptian laws regarding religious minorities allowed for only limited building of churches. Copts were given the right by President Nasser to add twenty-five churches a year, and the number was increased by Sadat to fifty, but this proved to be insufficient.[6] To face the shortage in churches, the Coptic community, which has been experiencing a revivalist movement under the leadership of Pope Shenouda, resorted to building churches in secret and without the permission of the government. Because land is at a premium in the towns and cities of Egypt, and people are living too closely together, such actions brought on clashes between Copts and the Muslim community, which was undergoing its own process of revivalism. The most important episode of sectarian conflict in Egypt, that of the Dar al-Ahmar, reflected this. A dispute over ownership of a piece of land in an area of high population density, which was "illegally" turned into a church, brought about a clash between members of the two communities.

The frustrations of everyday life are worsened by a sense of insecurity and fear for the future, particularly among the young. Of Egypt's current population of 53 million, 40 percent are under 15 years of age. Social mobility has become very difficult, and the movement downward on the social ladder is a fearful reality experienced by members of the middle classes. There is widespread unemployment, and there is a sense that only those with the right connections can get the right job. Every year about 350,000 new graduates enter the job market, 120,000 with university degrees, and 230,000 from specialized agricultural, industrial, trade, and teachers' schools. In 1987 the government employed 220,000 of them, even though it needed only 60,000 new employees; this has in turn meant the over-staffing of the government bureaucracy, at a time when priority is being given to bureaucratic rationalization.[7]

The government has come up with some interesting solutions to the problem of the estimated four to five million unemployed Egyptians. Suggestions have been put forward that emphasize traditional structures, one of which is to give financial assistance to the unemployed to help them in opening small industries or craft-shops.[8] The president himself is encouraging crafts, "family industries," and small industries as a solution for unemployment and for making a living for the poorer families. Another old idea being revived is that of allotting parcels of government agricultural land at nominal fees to university graduates to cultivate, thereby providing them with a living.[9]

The big discussion going on among the elite today is the role of the government as a developer undertaking massive capital projects, such as readying land for cultivation, and then turning it over to private investors. The fact that the practice of the public sector doing business with the private sector has been exposed as an excellent way by which the heads of these projects have extracted wealth (the latest celebrated case is that of the governor of Giza) does not seem to have made much difference.[10]

Meanwhile, government control over events is diminishing. It is no secret that Egyptians today have a sense of insecurity about the government's ability to protect life and property. Companies have appeared, owned interestingly enough by formerly high-ranking policemen, which provide expensive security services to businesses. Among the less fortunate who can afford no such service, anarchy reigns. Thugs often take advantage of the situation and the government's inability to provide adequate protection. Since large numbers of the police have been turned into a political police force which concentrates on hunting down and fighting anti-government radical Islamic groups there is a deficiency in the number of police required to maintain law and order. In this vacuum, gangs have become the arbiters of law in a number of areas, where they use violence to extort money from the poorer members of the community.

Two examples can illustrate this lack of security. The first involved one man with an eighty-member gang who took over a major intercity taxi-stop in Cairo, and allowed only taxis owned by him, as well as the taxis that paid a set fee, to take passengers.[11] The second involved a group of young men who had taken over the mosque of Adam in 'Ain Shams and ruled over the people inhabiting that quarter of Cairo. They set up a whipping post which they used to flog those who did not follow their commands. This continued for some time and it was only when they had killed a policeman and were identified as members of a *Jihad* cell that the police moved in and took action against them. A shootout took place in which three of the leaders were killed and about two hundred persons imprisoned.

Since security is lacking, so too is respect for the government.[12] The makeup of those involved in the mosque of Adam takeover should act as a warning bell for the future. Many were still high-school students, others were unemployed, still others gave their profession as *hirafiyyin,* such as electricians or carpenters. They were also very well armed, with guns and homemade bombs. The group was different from the previous *Jihad* cells, whose members were mostly university graduates; it is rooted in the coming generation of the most volatile and dispossessed members of society.

Religion and Politics

The electoral system in Egypt is supposedly democratic, and President Mubarak may be sincere in his wish to institute full democracy. However, the process has been too slow and too cautious and has meant that there is small potential for people other than the elite and their supporters to win seats in either the *Majlis al-Sha'ab* (National Assembly) or the *Majlis al-Shura* (Consultative Assembly). Religious parties have not been legalized, which has meant that the Copts cannot have a party of their own. Islamic groups have either had to enter their candidates as independents or form short-lived alliances with other parties, as in the *Ikhwan's* alliances with the Wafd in 1984 and with the al-Ahrar for the April 1987 elections.

Other parties have only lately appeared to be viable alternatives, and proof of their effectiveness as an opposition able to produce actual change is yet to be tested. The president, inheriting a political system and a presidential party from his predecessor, has continued to align himself with the National Democratic Party, whose leadership is composed of the main body of Sadat supporters who are not willing to allow for participation by outsiders, nor for an opening of the political system that could cause them a loss of power. The whole political structure appears to the outsiders to be merely a system of legitimization of government stands and decisions. The discussions that go on in the *Majlis al-Sha'ab* are lively and give the semblance of democracy, yet internal and external policy matters, and all major decisions, continue to be the full prerogative of the government. The *Majlis* has yet to oppose a president on any of these issues.[13]

The inequalities of the system are perhaps reflected best with regard to the Coptic population. The Constitution declares Egypt to be an Islamic state. Such a statement only emphasizes the old traditional methods of dividing the community according to religious groups, the Ottoman millet system. Yet, in the elective system, there is no recognition of this basis: the elections are held on a geographical and not sectarian basis. Since the spatial distribution of Copts throughout the country is dependent on class-orientation rather than on religious affiliation, it is clear that it is only in rare spots that a Copt can actually win. It is no wonder that the numbers of Copts sitting in the National Assembly do not reflect the actual percentage of Copts in the population of Egypt.[14]

Revival of the Church

As this paper tries to show, the explanation of the phenomenon of religious revivalism in Egypt involves analyzing the structure of the political system, social and economic inequalities, class conflict, the hardships of everyday life, and the inability of the government to come to grips with the various problems facing it. Coptic political activities and Islamic activism have a lot in common, including their involvement in a power struggle with the State. One big difference between the two, however, is that the official Muslim clergy, while promoting Islamization, are not involved in a power struggle with the government; rather they are its partners. The Coptic Church, on the other hand, has become the leader in a struggle between Church and State. In this way, the Coptic Church has played a parallel role to the radical Islamic groups and has ceased to be an instrument of the regime, as it has traditionally been.

Since the independence of Egypt, Copts have been divided into two groups, one that saw the future of the Coptic community as an integral part of Egypt, and therefore gave priority to national unity over Coptic needs,[15] and another which called for a revival of the Copts as a nation. Members of the first group consisted of the wealthy upper classes of Egyptian society, who participated in Egypt's nationalist struggle against the British and held high government posts, including that of prime minister. Their political role deteriorated after the 1952 Revolution, when their wealth was confiscated and the multi-party system that had been their avenue for political participation was abolished. The revival of political parties, as well as the restoration of some of the expropriated land to its original owners by the Sadat regime, has allowed this class of Copts to reappear among the ruling elite.

The second group represents the Coptic middle classes. Today, largely urbanized, yet closely connected with rural areas and towns, particularly Upper Egypt, they have not participated in either the power or the wealth of the country. Education gave them the awareness and the need to be involved, and to promote their own interests and the good of the country. That proved difficult, particularly after the 1952 Nasserist revolution's abolition of political parties. The armed forces and government service were then the best avenues of social mobility. A very small percentage of the army were Copts, and the 1952 Revolutionary Council did not include a single Coptic member. At the same time, there was a clear discrimination in the hiring practices for higher governmental positions.

The large majority faced the same social and economic deprivations as their Muslim counterparts. As the latter began to turn to Islamic revivalism, and some to political radicalism, so too did the Copts. A number turned to Marxism or became quite active in the Arab Socialist Union. Others immigrated to North America or Australia in search of better opportunity. This latter group has provided the main support to the Coptic Church in its struggle with the state. This support involves holding conferences,[16] pressuring the Egyptian government, and demonstrating against the visits of presidents, such as that of Sadat to the US in 1981 (when the Coptic community took out a one-page ad in the *Washington Post* attacking his treatment of Copts). Since the immigrants are of the same social background as Pope Shenouda and the new leadership of the Church, they identify with his ideals and have organized themselves in his support. After the Nasser Revolution, thousands of Copts left Egypt. The rich among them went to Switzerland, Paris, or other capitals of Europe where they could live in the same cultural environment they were used to. The middle classes immigrated to places where there would be an opportunity to build a future, and from their new locations have supported the Church and helped contribute towards its political actions.

Just as is the case with Islamic revivalism, the origins of Coptic revivalism can be dated back to the beginning of the century. The Pan-Islamism of Afghani and his disciples, and the Islamic nature of Mustafa Kamel's Nationalist Party, stimulated similar feelings amongst the Copts. However, it was not the Church that responded to this call, nor the Coptic upper classes. Both were involved in an internal struggle over who should control Coptic *waqf* property, the Church or the *Majlis al-Milli* dominated by Coptic political leaders. It was a young accountant by the name of Habib Girgis who began the call for the regeneration of the "Coptic Nation," the first time that such a term was used. His plans included the awakening of the Coptic community and reformation of the Church, which he saw as a weak, inactive body that needed to be infused with new leadership and awakened to a new role. The awakening of Coptic culture and language would be achieved through a reformed educational system that would include Sunday Schools for young Copts and a theological seminary to educate the clergy beyond their traditional training in monasteries. It was through his efforts that *al-Kulliya al-Iklirkiyya,* the theological school, was established in 1910.[17]

The Coptic community seemed to be ready for this revivalism which was soon to bear fruit. In 1945 a group of young men led by a lawyer named Ibrahim Fahmy Hillal formed an organization in Cairo that they named *Jama'at al-'Umma al-Qibtiya,* the Society of the Coptic Nation, which soon had many branches and a membership of 92,000.[18] While it represented itself as an agent for social services, its true political nature was exposed in 1952 when six of its members broke into the Papal residence and forced Pope Yosab II to sign documents declaring his resignation and calling for an immediate conference of the bishops, together with leaders of the Coptic community, to review Church election laws and allow for a wider participation by the lay membership in Church matters.

This was clearly a desperate attempt that had no chance of success. The radicalism of the *'Umma al-Qibtiya* evolved from the reforms introduced by Girgis calling for regeneration of the Church and the Coptic community. Thus, one of its earliest activities was to open schools throughout Egypt where the Coptic language was taught free of charge. In these schools young Copts, graduates of Girgis's Sunday School movement, taught with what has been described by a Muslim critic as "the fiery enthusiasm of prejudice [which caused them to] refuse [to use] the word Egyptian, but [they] were careful and insistent on using the word Copt."[19]

Other developments had a direct impact on the direction Coptic activism was taking. The increasing importance of the Muslim Brotherhood as well as the appearance of its vocally anti-Coptic outgrowth, the *Jama'at Shabab Muhammad* in 1940, were a source of anger and distress to the Coptic community.[20] One of the characteristics of Coptic activism is that while originating from similar political, social, and economic conditions that have stimulated Islamic radicalism, Coptic activism has been very sensitive to the evolution of its Islamic counterpart. When Islamic political activity increased, so did Coptic. The motto chosen for the *'Umma al-Qibtiya* tells us of this connection. "The Bible is our Constitution, Coptic our language, and death for the sake of Christ our greatest hope," seems to echo the Muslim Brotherhood's, "The Quran is our constitution, Arabic our language, and death in the way of God our greatest hope."[21]

Yosab II was an elderly man, typical of the old school which acquiesced to the demands of the State and the dictates of national unity. The new generation was impatient with this policy and saw national unity as costly to the Copts, for they were asked for unique concessions to achieve it.[22] They could see the growth of Islamization and found little possibility of inclusion in the political process that would counteract the activities of the Islamic groups and achieve the social demands of the Coptic community. Furthermore, since members of the 1952 Revolutionary Council had what appeared to be strong relationships with the Muslim Brotherhood, the future appeared to be quite grim. One unified stand had to be taken which would include an active stand by the Church, the recognized representative of the Copts.

The contemporary political activism of the Coptic Church is part of the continued evolution of the ideology launched by Girgis. Pope Shenouda III, who is a central figure in this drama, took the tradition begun by Girgis to its logical conclusion by bringing the power of the Church into the same reformist tradition. No longer would it be the acquiescent Church that the State had used to justify its rule in much the same manner as the official Azhari hierarchy. Rather, it would be the political instrument by which the Coptic community would achieve equal rights and opportunities, as well as become an active participant in determining the future of the nation. The Church was the only route open for this, and this activism headed in the direction of "the establishment of a Coptic Nation independent of the centralized Egyptian state."[23]

Originally from the vicinity of the city of Assiut in Upper Egypt, where he must have experienced sectarian conflicts first hand, Shenouda is the first pope to have received the education designed by Girgis. After graduating in 1947 from Cairo University's Faculty of Arts, department of history, he opted to enter religious orders, then enrolled in the *al-Kulliya al-Iklirkiyya*. He was an activist long before he became the head of the Church, donating his time to teaching in the Sunday Schools, and working as a journalist for its press, where he wrote fiery criticisms of the government and its treatment of Copts.[24] Later, as director of the educational programs of the Church he was known to deliver fiery speeches weekly, reminiscent of those of Hassan al-Banna. His popularity was proof of his charisma as well as of the agreement of the Coptic community with the grievances he voiced against the government and his political agenda for the future.

In May 1981, President Sadat attacked the Pope publicly, blaming him for trying to create a state within a state. This clash between President Sadat and Pope Shenouda was bound to happen given the changed nature of the Church's leadership and Sadat's autocracy. To be faced with an opposition in the form of an intransigent Church must have been a shock to the president, who probably had not even taken Copts into account when drawing up his plans for controlling the state after Nasser's death. His conservative religious outlook, old ties with the Brotherhood and use of Islamic groups to combat socialists on university campuses all opened the way for a confrontation. Thus, after he came to power, the Muslim Brotherhood, once pushed underground by Nasser, became openly active, opening the way to the more radical anti-Coptic groups, such as the *Takfir wal-Hijra* and the *Jihad* cells. When the *Jihad* cells began to attack Coptic merchants and rob their stores in Assiut, and when churches were attacked (as in April 1978 in Minufiya and Alexandria in 1980), or a Coptic priest was murdered (as in Minya in 1978),[25] the government was slow to act.

The response of the Copts was to take things into their own hands. There was a flood of pamphlets and books attacking Islam and the Quran, the authors of which used pseudonyms.[26] Their associations began to multiply all over the country, and the missionary activities of the Church both within and outside of Egypt increased perceptibly. Publications of Christian associations abroad supported the stand of the Church, the Congress of the United States held a hearing about human rights infringements against the Copts, and the pope himself travelled to the United States, where he was given an honorary doctorate from the University of Bloomfield in New Jersey in 1977.[27] When President Sadat travelled to the US on a state visit in 1980, the Copts demonstrated in front of the White House, took out ads attacking him in the *Washington Post,* and thoroughly embarrassed him.

Furthermore, seeing that the government was unwilling to change the laws limiting the building of churches, some of which dated back to Ottoman days, the Church decided to go around them. In fact, one of the main reasons that there were so many church-burnings was the building of Coptic churches without permission. In 1934 new regulations by the Egyptian government had set ten conditions for the approval of building churches. These included the need and the location of the church, how far it was to be from the nearest mosque, whether it was located among the houses of Muslims, how close it was to town and other churches, how many Christians lived in the particular area, as well as the need to receive government approval before building could begin.[28] Because the government bureaucracy could stall the building of churches long enough to allow for the building of a mosque too close to where the church would have been built, and since there was no permit necessary for the building of mosques, only a limited number of churches could be built with permission. To build a church, therefore, the Copts would create an association, and some time later would celebrate mass in its premises, turning it into a church. No permit had been asked for or received — a challenge to the government and a total disregard for its authority.[29]

One much-publicized case of sectarian violence was that of the burning of the building of a Coptic association in Khanka, one of the suburbs of Cairo, which had been turned into a church without government authorization. The following Sunday saw a congregation of priests and Coptic citizens arriving at the spot of the burned church for prayers, with the approval of the Church authorities.[30] The Church had decided to take a public stand against such burnings and to challenge the government's power to question its right to build churches. Furthermore, the Pope publicly attacked government discriminatory policies that required permission for building churches when no such requirements existed for the building of mosques. He demanded that the laws pertaining to the building of houses of worship be revised to allow for freedom of worship.[31]

Potentially the most important source of sectarian problems for Egypt has to do with establishing the Islamic *shari'a* as the law for all citizens, Muslims and Christians alike. The establishment of the *shari'a* would make the Copts second-class citizens, moving them even further away from political participation. It would also affect the powers of the Church, which explains the centrality of the *shari'a* issue to the clash between the Church and the government. Most laws in the country are applicable to both communities, i.e., the criminal law, civil law, administrative laws, as well as political rights and duties are all shared by the communities equally. Only personal laws are different in both communities because they are based on religion, and it is the clergy that has the power to interpret these laws. Herein lies the power of the Church over the lives of the Copts: if its control over family and marriage law is taken away, so are its most important powers. It is an interesting situation, because while the Islamic clergy and radical groups are trying to establish the *shari'a* as a means of controlling Egyptian society by making themselves the only arbiters of personal law, the Church, which already has such a power, is trying to stop itself from losing it.

The question of *shari'a* involves more than a simple refusal to allow Islamic laws to be applied to Christians, for there are cases where the *shari'a* already applies to Copts and there is no complaint. One example is the question of inheritance. Inheritance laws stemming from the *shari'a* apply to both communities; thus it is not only amongst Muslims that the son inherits double the share of the daughter, but amongst Copts as well.[32] However, we do not hear of complaints regarding such issues. Nor do we hear much about the application of *shari'a* law to matters of banking, commerce, or finance. In such cases the Copts use the civil law to redress any harm that befalls them. A case in point is the decision taken last year by the governor of Bani Sweif to forbid the selling of alcohol in the governerate. This meant that all shops selling alcohol were forced to close. The matter affected about fourteen Copts, who have taken the matter to court. The Church is probably supporting their action, but the recourse was to the civil court system.[33] The question of *shari'a* law, therefore, has to do with the powers of the Church.

On January 17, 1977, the Egyptian Coptic Church held a high ecclesiastical conference at Alexandria which was attended by its bishops, the *Majlis al-Milli,* and "representatives of the Coptic people." The decisions that came out of this meeting were directed toward the question of making the *shari'a* the source of law for both Muslims and Copts, the cancellation of the old Ottoman laws that control the building of churches, the demand for true equality regarding government employment on all levels, freedom of religion, equality of political rights, and freedom of publication.[34] All were long-standing Coptic grievances that the government needed to address. The advancement of Coptic goals may be measured in terms of the government's attitude to the Coptic position on each of these issues. At present, the Coptic Church seems to have achieved a truce and is adopting a wait-and-see attitude. Discussions of the application of the *shari'a* have been stalled, and new legal codes are being drawn up. The Church, therefore, sees itself as in a sort of alliance with Mubarak's government because the government has put the *shari'a* question in a temporary freezer, does not interfere with the Coptic freedom of the press, and has made hunting down Muslim extremists its priority. Moreover, Mubarak himself has emphasized the point that "there should be no connection between extremism and religion."[35]

Notwithstanding the aggressive actions taken against radical Islamic groups by the government, or the use of the official clergy to counter them, their radical activities have continued and their numbers are not diminishing. Thus, in the case of the attack on the *Faniyya 'Askariyya* in 1974 there were 91 defendants; in the *al-Takfir wa al-Hijra* trial in 1977 there were 258 defendants; in the affair of the *Jihad* movement and the assassination of President Sadat, there were 578; and in the attempt to kill Abu Basha and Nabawi Ismail, those arrested numbered 519.[36] Another radical group, *al-Najun min al-Nar,* was caught in January 1988 in the act of trying to blow up one of the casinos in Giza. December 1988 saw the capture of about 200 young men belonging to another *Jihad* cell. Investigations regarding this last cell are still underway.[37]

Clearly, as long as Egypt's government refuses to address the basic problems that have caused the rise of these radical groups, and fails to open the political system and allow for participation in the wealth and power of the country, such religious strife will continue. Paradoxically, while political Christianity is alive and watching over events, radical Islam has entered a new phase which pits the police against rapidly growing numbers of the country's youth. The outcome could be traumatic and the results potentially cataclysmic.

Bibliography

'Abd al-Fattah, Nabil. *al-Mushaf wa al-Sayf.* Cairo: Maktabat Madbuli, 1984.

al-Ahram, December 8, 1987; February 9, 1988; December 6, 1987; January 23, 1988.

Antoun, Richard and Hegland, Mary Elaine, eds. *Religious Resurgence: Contemporary Cases in Islam, Christianity and Judaism.* Syracuse: Syracuse University Press, 1987.

Badawi, Jamal. *al-Fitna al-Ta'ifiyya fi Misr.* Cairo: 1980.

Bahr, Samira. *al-Aqbat fi al-Haya al-Siyasiyya al-Misriyya.* Cairo: Anglo-Egyptian Bookshop, 1984.

al-Bishri, Tariq. *al-Muslimun wa al-Aqbat fi Itar al-Jama'a al-Wataniyya.* Cairo: Dar Al-Shuruq, 1988.

Chitham, E. J. *The Coptic Community in Egypt: Spatial and Social Change*. University of Durham: Center of Middle Eastern and Islamic Studies, 1986.

al-Fiqi, Mustafa. *al-Aqbat fi al-Siyasa al-Misriyya*. Cairo: Dar al-Shuruq, 1985.

Girgis, Girgis Guda. *al-Sadat . . . wa al-aqbat*. Beverly Hills, California: American Coptic Association, 1982.

Hanna, Milad. *Na'am . . . Aqbat wa Lakin Misriyyun*. Cairo: Maktabat Madbuli, 1980.

Heikal, Mohamed. *Autumn of Fury*. New York: Random House, 1983.

Mirel, Pierre. *L'Egypte des ruptures*. Paris: Sindbad, 1982.

al-Nur, February 17, 1988, p. 3.

al-Qaradawi, Youssef. *Ghayr al-Muslimin fi al-Mujtama' al-Islami*. Cairo: Maktabat Wahba, 1984.

Sonbol, Amira El-Azhary. "Egypt." *The Politics of Islamic Revivalism*. Indiana University Press, 1988.

Springborg, Robert. *Family, Power, and Politics in Egypt*. Philadelphia: University of Pennsylvania, 1982.

U.S. Congress. House of Representatives. Committee On Foreign Affairs and its Subcommittee on Human Rights and International Organizations. Religious Persecution: A Violation of Human Rights. Washington: 1983.

al-Wafd, December 22, 1988.

Notes

1. *al-Ahram,* December 8, 1987, p. 1.
2. E. J. Chitham, *The Coptic Community in Egypt: Spatial and Social Change* (University of Durham, Center of Middle Eastern and Islamic Studies, 1986),p. 106.
3. The case of Ahmad Sobhi Mansur who was fired from his job at the Azhar for having questioned the validity of the *sunna,* is a good example.
4. Robert Springborg, *Family, Power, and Politics in Egypt* (Philadelphia: University of Pennsylvania, 1982).
5. Of Egypt's 52 million people today, 40 percent are under the age of fifteen.
6. Mohamed Heikal, *Autumn of Fury* (New York: Random House, 1983),p. 158.
7. 100,000 graduates enter the job market from trade schools. *Al-Ahram,* February 9, 1988, p. 3.
8. *al-Ahram,* December 28, 1988, p. 1.
9. *al-Ahram,* December 19, 1988, p. 8.
10. *al-Ahram,* December 23, 1988, p. 7.
11. *al-Wafd,* December 22, 1988, p. 7.
12. *al-Ahram,* December 23, 1988, p. 3.
13. "We refuse to accept the *Majlis al-Sha'ab* as a spokesman for Islam on all

accounts . . . it is a *Majlis* created to serve the interests of one party . . . the party system in Egypt has proven to be a disaster because he who was generous enough to have granted it . . . put a governmental committee in control of creating a new party and (created a system) in which all the success and gains would go to the government party." Interview with Umar Abd al-Rahman, *al-Nur,* February 17, 1988, p. 3.

14. Copts constitute about 8 percent of Egypt's population, yet government surveys, primarily because of inefficiency in census gathering, have shown Copts to have a population as low as 2,316,000, or 6.32 percent in 1976. Meanwhile, Copts insisted that the number of Copts was then nearly 5 million, i.e., about 13 percent of the population and certain Copts insist that the true number is nearer to 20 percent.

15. Girgis Guda Girgis, *al-Sadat . . . wa al-Aqbat* (Beverly Hills, California: American Coptic Association, 1982), p. 17, tells one story in which members of the Coptic Nation approached Ibrahim Farag Pasha on the occasion of the burning of a church in Suez in January 1952. The breach between the groups was clear when the Pasha could not understand the complaint of the younger Copts. He went to the point of demanding "for whom do you work. The problem is ended . . . you are threatening national unity." Girgis describes this as the "scandal" of a Coptic minister.

When the 1923 Constitution was being written and the idea of including a description of Egypt as an Islamic country came up, Makram Ebeid Pasha is said to have found nothing wrong with the idea, saying, "I am a Christian by religion and a Muslim by nation." *Ibid.,* p. 46.

16. Jamal Badawi, *Al-Fitna al-Ta'ifiya fi Misr* (Cairo, 1980), pp. 88-90. Examples include the Coptic conferences held in Melbourne and Sydney in June and July 1977; the many letters presented by Coptic immigrants in the US and Canada; a journal that appeared in France named "The Coptic World;" and the establishment of the American Coptic Association, which the Coptic Church has declared does not represent its point of view.

17. Heikal, *Autumn of Fury,* p. 152.

18. Badawi, *al-Fitna al-Ta'ifiyya fi Misr,* p. 64.

19. *Ibid.,* p. 67.

20. Nabil Abd al-Fattah, *al-Mushaf wa al-Sayf* (The Quran and the Sword), (Cairo: Maktabat Madbuli, 1984), p. 127.

21. *Ibid.,* p. 79.

22. Girgis, *al-Sadat . . . wa al-Aqbat,* p. 17.

23. Badawi, *al-Fitna al-Ta'ifiya,* p. 64.

24. Girgis, *al-Sadat . . . wa al-Aqbat,* p. 12.

25. Chitham, *The Coptic Community in Egypt,* p. 104.

26. Badawi, *al-Fitna al-Ta'ifiya,* p.72.

27. Girgis, *al-Sadat . . . wa al-Aqbat,* p. 67.

28. Badawi, *al-Fitna al-Ta'ifiya,* pp. 73-74.

29. Samira Bahr, *al-Aqbat fi al-Haya al-Siyasiyya al-Misriyya* (Cairo: Anglo-Egyptian Bookshop, 1984), p. 155.

30. *Ibid.,* p. 154.

31. Bahr, *al-Aqbat fi al-Haya al-Siyasiyya al-Misriyya,* p. 155.

32. Hanna, *Na'am . . . ,* p. 39.

33. *al-Nur,* 7 December, 1988, p. 1.

34. *Ibid.,* p. 156

35. *al-Ahram,* December 6, 1987, p. 3.

36. *al-Ahram,* December 6, 1978, p. 3.

37. *al-Ahram,* January 23, 1988, p. 1.

14 DEMOCRATIZATION IN EGYPT

Afaf Lutfi al-Sayyid Marsot

During the 1980s, Egypt witnessed a trend toward greater political liberalization. It remains an open question whether this process was a profound one, justifying a favorable prognosis for a future stable democracy, or whether the democratization process is likely to fall victim to the many serious problems faced by the country.

The increased liberalization in the country was reflected in a number of important developments: greater press freedom, the willingness of the judiciary to assert its independence of the government, and an upsurge of political party activity. On the other hand, Egyptian politics were characterized by low electoral turnouts, and by a parliament with weak powers vis-a-vis a president who had been the sole candidate in the presidential election. The political system had still to prove capable of reforms that would convince the mass of the population that politics was more than a means for the rich and powerful to promote their interests, and that the political arena was a forum for the resolution of pressing issues, and not merely for the airing of disagreements among the elite.

Western and Islamic Political Thought

Discussions of liberalization and democratization often draw on an intellectual tradition derived from seventeenth-century English political thought and the challenge by Locke to the Hobbesian advocacy of the absolute power of the sovereign. Hobbes had expressed a philosophy of power. Claiming that human beings were basically equal, he asserted that they had a natural right to self-protection, and that they would do what was in their perceived best interest. Since the personal rights of one person might conflict with those of others, a state of war was the norm in societies without government. According to Hobbes, to avoid a state of permanent belligerency, the masses created a social contract among themselves (not between the population and the ruler(s)) which transferred power to a sovereign. The sovereign, not being party to that contract, could not be accused of having breached it or broken it, for his action was law. Sovereign power is "incommunicable and inseparable,"[1] and the state is the guardian of the sum total of private interests.

Such an absolutist form of government was made inevitable, Hobbes believed, by the basically egotistical nature of human beings. It was an enlightened form of egotism, in that people chose the lesser evil to a continuous state of war. Under such a government the population was expected to offer unqualified obedience, and could not challenge the sovereign's wisdom or the legality of his actions. Thus, the Hobbesian concept of a reified government could not accommodate democratization.

In contrast, Locke argued that the executive power of the government was subordinate to that of the legislature. He affirmed that the laws of nature, which governed human beings in a state of nature, taught them that they were equal and independent and should not harm the health, liberty, and possessions of others.[2] Since fear was not a sufficient restraint, people had to be guided by reason. Frequently, however, they were biased, and the injured were not strong enough to execute the sentence of the law. An organized society was therefore established in order "to maintain law and order [and] to create predictable laws and impartial institutions." Hence, the legislature became the supreme power, with an executive subordinate to it. Above both lay "the people," who had rights and who had set up the government as a trust.[3] Hence, law preceded the state. The principal purpose of government was the mutual preservation of lives, liberties and estates, described by the general name "property."[4]

Locke believed that four limitations must be placed on the legislature. First, the law must apply equally to rich and poor. Second, the law must not be arbitrary or oppressive, and third, taxes must not be raised without the consent of the people or their representatives. Finally, the legislature must not transfer its power to any other body. State and society are distinct, and society is entitled to overthrow the state when it acts contrary to the interests of the public. There thus exists a right to civil disobedience and rebellion. Obedience to government on the one hand is balanced by the right to disobey certain kinds of rulers on the other.

These two seventeenth-century theories still influence the Western debate about political rights, even in discussions about non-Western societies. While the theories of Hobbes and Locke have become part of Western democratic culture, the Arab world has inherited the different theoretical tradition of Islamic thought.

The historical tradition of Muslim thought reiterated the inseparability of religion (*din*) and the world (*dunya*). Muslim government was predicated on the *shari'a,* and concerned with a just, as well as a religious society. The rights of an individual were not as important as those of the community (the *umma*) and the group (the *jama'a*). The happiness (*sa'ada*) of people was derived from actions being directed toward God. Moral education taught people to submit to God's laws, and government was necessary in order for human beings to reach ethical perfection. Humans are viewed as rational, religious creatures, living within a religious society and state. God rules the universe and demands from humans obedience to His laws, which are designed to guarantee happiness in this world and salvation in the afterlife. As in Locke's theory, in Muslim thought the law predates the state. The law is to be applied equally to rich and poor, and it cannot be arbitrary or oppressive because it is the will of God.

But how does mankind know God's laws? First, there is the Quran, the major source of the law, followed by the *sunna,* the sayings and actions of the Prophet Muhammad. Next, in the early ages of Islam, the learned established the *shari'a,* which is regarded by many Muslims, quite erroneously, as sacred law. The *shari'a* is, however, the outcome of human attempts at codifying or deriving laws from a system of moral and religious injunctions found in the Quran. Therefore, while some part of the *shari'a* is based on the Quran, the rest is based on the *hadith* and *sunna* of the prophet, on analogy (*qiyas*), on consensus (*ijma'*), and even on customary behavior (*'urf* and *'adat*). Some Muslims question the authenticity of the *hadith* and *sunna,* while others claim that *ijma'* is too vague a term. Of whom, and at what time does it represent a consensus? Or is it the *ijma'* of the learned of every generation? Thus, the *shari'a* is, at best, man's interpretation of the Quran, based on the human under-standing of the time. There is nothing sacred or immutable about it, and it changes, or should change, with changing circumstances. In spite of this fact, Muslims and hence Egyptians have a deep theoretical respect for the law. However, this respect is frequently retracted when the law is assumed to derive from alien legal systems, i.e., those which are not based on the *shari'a.*

Second, there is the belief that an individual is expected to obey God's commands, and that true happiness lies therein. Government is, in theory, below the law; but the ruler has a wide range of powers so long as he does not openly contravene the obvious dictates of the *shari'a,* that is, so long as he epitomizes the upright man (*al-rajul al-salih*). The function of the masses is to obey, and that of the learned is summarized in preaching (*wa'z*) and offering the ruler advice (*nasiha*) pointing out the path of righteousness. Going far beyond Locke, it is the theoretical duty of each Muslim to be responsible for the wrong-doing of every other Muslim, as manifested in the *hisba*, "to order good and set aside evil," (*al-amr bi al-ma'ruf wa al-nahy 'an al-munkar*). In contrast to Locke's political philosophy, the notion of a contract is one between humanity and the Maker, and like Hobbes, between humanity and itself. It should be noted that the individual, while expected to obey the ruler, may, and on occasion must, disobey certain kinds of rulers when they depart from religious injunctions.

Put together, the different concepts sustain the right to civil disobedience or, at least, to forming a "loyal opposition." They include the liberal principle of preservation of property (not only in the strictly economic sense, but in the general sense that Locke used to designate the means of labor); and the right of humans to see that justice is done and the path followed is one leading to happiness (in the religious sense). Muslims are entitled to work and to earn a living, and are instructed to prevent evil-doing whenever possible. There are no other forms of duty.

The early corpus of *'ulama*, who were created as a government institution in the ninth century (unlike their predecessors, who were simply learned men), taught the population to obey the ruler no matter how evil he was. Chaos and sedition (*fitna*) were seen as greater sins than obeying an unjust ruler, even though obedience to an unjust or illegitimate ruler was one of the major sins (*min al-kabair*). The *'ulama* also taught that a person's reward was received in heaven; and when humans suffered under an unjust ruler, it was punishment for their sins. The Quran states the opposite. It requires human beings to see that justice is done, and it informs us that we are entitled to happiness on earth as well as to salvation in the afterlife. Later, the *'ulama* taught that the right of civil disobedience was built into the Muslim system, and that activism was a basic element in Islam, as in the *ayat* that say, "God does not change anything in a people until they change what is in themselves."[5]

The Ottomans, with their usual bent toward institutions, summarized the essence of government and the relationship of subjects to the state in a circular fashion, showing the interconnected nature of the elements within society. Society was described as a garden, its walls being the state. The foundation of the state was the *shari'a*. There could be no support for the *shari'a* without royal authority, and no royal authority without the military. There could be no military without wealth, which was produced by the subjects. The sultan protected the subjects by making justice reign. Justice required harmony in society. If we substituted the concept of "government" for "royal authority," the Ottoman view would hold good in general Muslim terms. Nevertheless, a wide range of political positions can be rationalized in Islamic terms.

Egypt's Recent Political Experience

During the period of the liberal experiment in Egypt before the Nasserist revolution of 1952, the theory of democracy was used by the ruling elite as a weapon against the colonial power. There was, in fact, some degree of democracy among the ruling elite (i.e., the wealthy landowners and professionals), but the masses did not share in the governing process. When the political party system became discredited and the monarchy was overthrown, the word "democracy" was the catchword of the new ruling elite, but here it meant something slightly different. A new elite of military men and their supporters came to power, displacing the old elite and its multi-party system. The new elite tried to sway the masses in support of the new regime by raising their standard of living, but it was afraid that the masses would challenge governmental authority. True democratization thus was aborted in favor of a one-party system that ratified the actions of the elite, without criticism or amendment. The new system resembled the old one in that both governed through elites, albeit different ones; both distrusted the masses, while claiming to rule for them; and each asserted that it was democratic. The major difference was that the masses adulated Nasser, while they had grown to despise the king.

At the time, decolonization in the world had produced a new set of heroes and new perceptions. The new heroes had successfully fought colonial powers. Nevertheless, they were not accustomed to holding power, and they felt continually threatened and believed they needed to fight internal sedition, i.e., the *ancien regime*. A new system of power carefully weeded out those who were allegedly seditious, and it set up a repressive system that was more authoritarian than the previous one. After the British, French, and Israeli invasion of 1956, the population accepted the arguments which justified repression, fearing weakness of the state and its vulnerability to foreign interference. Under the monarchy, riots and demonstrations were a common response to any attempt at repression by the government, while under Nasser the public remained quiescent. As the government advanced socialist theories, it even became possible to use religious arguments in support of socialism. Intellectuals began to produce books equating socialism with Islam. By then, the religious institutions were thoroughly cowed, and the rest of the population muzzled.

The Sadat regime came to power at a time when perceptions had changed once again. Decolonization no longer interested the masses, and the new regimes were no longer threatened. Sadat believed that socialism had reached a dead end; in order to induce a change in Egypt's troubled economic situation, he moved to the right. For both political and economic reasons, he decided to begin a limited process of democratization, while simultaneously discrediting the theories of the previous regime. To support his new line of action, he had to induce the religious institutions and movements to support him. Socialism, etatism, and the intellectuals who supported these theories now came under attack. Moreover, circumstances had forced Egypt to reconsider its alliances, and the US displaced the USSR in its role as ally and mentor. The government in Washington was delighted by the new rising religious current, since it seemed to be a perfect weapon against communism.

Circumstances changed with the advent of the Mubarak era. Inflation, the consequences of oil riches, the rise of an affluent new elite, and the radical actions of some of the Muslim organizations, all led to a different political climate with a greater degree of liberalization. Fearing extremism among the religious groupings, the government turned to the more moderate religious organizations, such as the Muslim Brotherhood. The government has made it possible for them to join political parties and be elected to the Assembly, where they can act as spokesmen for a more restrained religious voice.

Political liberalization is widely viewed as the path leading toward democratization, i.e., fair and open elections, a mass participation in the political process, freedom of political parties and political representation, freedom of speech, and the rule of law. Muslim tradition does not necessarily oppose this view since humanity is seen as subject to the laws of God, and *shura,* consultation, is advised. Political parties and the holding of elections may be seen as a logical consequence of *shura.* However, they also could be regarded from a different Islamic perspective as irrelevant, since the ruler can make do with a privy council. Thus, liberalization would be limited to the rule of law and to a process of consultation.

Economic liberalization, in the western sense, is centered on the *laissez faire* system of a free market place, limited by a minimum of laws, and guided by the laws of supply and demand. Above all, it means the protection of property, through the imposition of law and order and the state's control of the power of sanction. Islamic law protects private property and the accumulation of wealth, in addition to stressing the right of the individual to earn a living and the duty of the community to ensure that right for its members. Through the imposition of law and order, the state sees that justice is carried out and makes it possible for people to follow a Muslim way of life.

Democracy, on the other hand, is predicated on mass participation. However, in order for there to be mass participation, the population must detect some benefit for itself in the political system. In rich countries experiencing economic growth, the population feels that its condition is improving, even if the powerful become richer, because the size of the pie is big enough to be distributed. This perception leads to widespread acquiescence in the system, and it makes democracy easier for countries which enjoy economic growth. In poor countries the pie is much smaller, and little is left for the population after the ruling elite has taken its share. Thus, the masses feel that they have no stake in the system. Nonetheless, when the majority of the population feels that it has no property to protect, how then does it participate in the political process? Government by and for elites may have been acceptable in the past, but widespread mass communication has alerted even the most uninformed to the fact that there are alternatives to suffering a government or submitting to it. The ordinary person can see popular revolutions breaking out regularly on television, and thus it is almost impossible to convince people that they have to put up with a miserable life. The inexorable conclusion is that people can and do change their circumstances through activism of some kind.

In short, even if political participation in elections is low, political thought and thinking can be widespread among the population. If there are constant reminders of the Muslim ideal that government must ensure that people are able to earn a living, and acquire a stake in the pie, and that living under an illegitimate government—one which does not follow Islamic dictates—is a major sin, we see a clear justification for the overthrowing of unsatisfactory governments.

This brings us back to the first question regarding the extent to which democratization has occurred in Egypt. The answer is a qualified yes. When compared to earlier periods under Nasser or Sadat, there has been a relative degree of democratization under Mubarak, particularly for the propertied classes. The press also is relatively freer, and anyone, even the president, can be criticized, depending on the manner in which it is done. The cabinet and the bureaucrats have all been openly and severely criticized and, even more significant, satirized. The army is seldom attacked, but politicians are constantly lampooned and lambasted by both the ruling party and opposition press. In contrast to the Sadat era, the opposition press is seldom censored, and it is quite outspoken. Additionally, the *'ulama,* the fundamentalists, and the secularists all receive criticism from different organs.

People have a choice of political parties, which now function openly. Although anyone can run for office, elections are not necessarily free. Despite the fact that mass arrests are no longer the norm as they were under Nasser and Sadat, there have been arrests of members of organizations (*jama'at*) said to be planning violence or sedition.

Meanwhile, the power of the judiciary has been enhanced. It asserted power through its willingness to declare the elections of 1984 unconstitutional because independent candidates were not allowed to stand. This verdict prompted new elections.

A freer press and the presence of a multi-party system have brought the government under greater scrutiny than in the past. Incidents are openly discussed in the media rather than whispered about in salons or coffee houses. In spite of the existence of political parties and the relative fairness of the recent elections, parties, by and large, neither represent mass interests nor are they even truly representative. The government, particularly the ruling elite, has deliberately attempted political demobilization, fearing the possibility of mass opposition.

Nasser attempted a limited mobilization of the masses in his support, while Sadat tried to mobilize religious support for his policies. In contrast, the present government is not committed to mobilize anyone. The political parties, by and large, also are content to act on their own without the extra burden of a questioning constituency. Thus, democratization and liberalization largely seem to be limited to the elite. Political activity has been concentrated in the hands of the urban, the educated, and the wealthy.

As in other countries, the poor in Egypt seldom vote. While some countries, such as the United States, have a system of lobbies, some of which cater to minorities, lobbying is unknown in Egypt outside the elite. Democratization merely has meant that a greater number of people with vested interests have been allowed to speak and to run for office. Although the candidates claim to represent the interests of the people, the populace, through its notable absence from the polls, has shown that it takes such assertions with a grain of salt. Egypt's political process can change and true democracy can emerge only when a greater proportion of the population participates in political activity.

This leads us to the question: what, then, is the significance of elections? When people believe that a change of cabinet or of an assembly is a purely cosmetic function and real power resides elsewhere, they do not bother to vote. In such behavior, there may be an element of passive resistance, a vote with the feet. It also could represent a streak of cynicism or a true belief in the lack of effectiveness of the present system of government. In the elections of 1987, those who voted were the older and the educated. The young and the bulk of the population stayed away. This distribution signifies a high degree of alienation on the part of the population, as well as a loss of faith in the value of the system. Hence, there has been a continued rise in activist movements. Should an elected assembly show its teeth, then more faith in elections and political parties might be expected; but should it simply be used by the administration as a rubber stamp, the alienation will grow rather than diminish. On the other hand, should Mubarak use the assembly as a means of passing resolutions such as higher taxation on the rich and powerful, or as a means of enacting general reforms of the system, then there will slowly develop a respect for democratic procedures.

It also must be questioned whether the various parties within parliament will be able to show their mettle. In other words, will the opposition develop into a "loyal opposition" which has the interests of the population at heart, or will it consistently push for narrow vested interests? Past parliaments were discredited because they espoused high-sounding declarations that did not have the slightest chance of becoming reality. Dominated by landowners, no parliament during the monarchy passed a law in favor of the *fallah*. Nor, for that matter, were laws passed in favor of workers until the mid-thirties.

Admittedly, landowners today no longer have the same degree of power, and wealth is diffused among a variety of sources, increasing the chances of passing effective laws to help the majority. However, if parliament becomes the stronghold of the new entrepreneurial/ compradorial middle class, then the same deadlock that occurred in earlier parliaments will recur in this one. The assembly will continue to reflect the ideology of the state, which means that the religious idiom will continue for some time to take center stage. As Professor Galal Amin has pointed out, the cultural basis of the new bourgeoisie is Islamic thought. Its milieu anchors its ethics in religious teachings and does not believe that religion and the temporal world are different spheres.

Among those who use the religious discourse, there is a wide spectrum of political attitudes, ranging from those who wish to overthrow the entire value system in favor of "Islamic government," to those who simply wish to reform what is wrong in society, believing that ethics and morality can only be revived and sustained through religious discourse. Thus, the opposition to the government is neither unified nor clear as to its position or its direction. There is a strong chance that the opposition will snipe at the government and its actions rather than offer constructive options that would help the country at large. In brief, opposition could become an end in itself rather than a means of swaying ideas and shaping legislation.

The limited legal rights of the new Assembly exacerbate the current situation. For example, in most countries, parliament has the right to present a vote of no-confidence, which automatically results in the fall of a cabinet. It is also common for the head of the majority party to form a cabinet and to be responsible to parliament. This form of organization is not present in Egypt. Instead, Egypt has an amalgam between the presidential and the parliamentary systems in which the president has the final say. The Egyptian president can veto laws, rule by decree, or even suspend laws for a period of time. He cannot be overruled. He is not accountable to parliament, and he can act over its head. These powers represent one of the basic weaknesses in the system. They mean that the head of state generally is held responsible for everything that happens. There is no one else to blame. Furthermore, there is only one candidate for the presidency, so that instead of an elected president, it is more appropriate to speak of a president who received an acclamation (*bay'a*) from the electorate. Past history offers a precedent: the king was entitled to prorogue parliament and rule by decree, parliaments rarely fell from a vote of no confidence, and the average session lasted no more than 18 months as a result of decisions by the king.

The principal challenge faced by Egypt's present political system comes from the fundamentalist *jama'at* and their sympathizers, who have questioned the very value system of the government and of the assembly. This opposition poses a potential danger to the stability, and even the legitimacy of institutions in general.

The current political system draws support, on the other hand, from a situation in which a combination of different institutions support it. One institution which the government repeatedly favors is the army. Since every family in Egypt has a member in the army, benefits for the army are not as greatly resented as those for any other group. The army also is given a greater share of the pie with the intention of keeping it quiescent and under control. It is widely believed that the top-ranking officers in the army are satisfied with the system; and as long as they are able to offer material satisfactions to their men, they are content to leave the government alone. On the other hand, the younger officers and the enlisted men are regularly rumored to be dissatisfied with conditions, and a number are allegedly involved overtly or covertly in *jama'at* of various kinds. Disgruntled soldiers are a potential threat to the government. After all, the Free Officers were all younger members of the army.

The officer corps may be seen as representing the new bourgeoisie, which is closely involved with the transactions of multinational corporations. Former generals act as consultants and sit on the boards of these companies. Meanwhile, the army is almost a third sector between the private and the public: it bids on civil contracts, produces for the consumer market (selling bread from its bakeries, chicken from its hatcheries, and other consumer products from factories manned by the conscripted soldiers). Whatever profits result and wherever the capital to set up such enterprises comes from, are not publicly known; but the assumption is that the army has become a self-sufficient, if not an income-producing, sector of the state.

Does the army control the government? Although the army has an input into government policies, and could potentially, as in any other country, destroy the government, the answer is negative. Egypt's case is not similar to that of Turkey. The army in Turkey habitually and regularly takes over the government at times when the civilian politicians are considered to have failed and returns government to civilian hands in due course. By contrast, in Egypt, when the army took over, it became civilianized. The army has consistently refused to interfere directly in internal matters. Because it is an amalgam of all classes and all interests, it may become the vehicle for popular or general discontent; but, on the other hand, it also could become a tool used by government to suppress discontent. The army mirrors the political currents that exist throughout the country.

The relationship of other major institutions to the process of democratization is mixed. Foremost among those that provide an institutional basis for democratization in Egypt is the judiciary, which historically has been the bastion of democratic principles. In Muslim tradition, judges, or at least the *qadis* and the *'ulama* in alliance, have opposed tyrannical rulers. Although the judiciary is appointed by the government, its members have maintained something of their reputation for uprightness and respect for legal procedure. It is likely that the government, which depends on law and order for its survival, cannot afford to undermine legality too blatantly. The judiciary applies the law, but does not make it. Thus, it appears as an impartial arbiter, even though the government can use it as a weapon. There have been clashes between the judiciary and the government, but it is difficult for the government to go against the Conseil d'Etat or the Cour de Cassation, the highest courts in the country. These actions would signify the government's contempt for its own laws, hence undermining its own legitimacy.

Another institution clearly in favor of democratization is the People's Assembly. It can promote such democratization effectively if it represents the electorate as a whole rather than just the vested interests of a few. The Egyptian press continues to be dominated by the government and is liable to censorship, but it is growing stronger and more outspoken. Thus, it is pushing for a greater degree of democratization and an end to government supervision. Since the opposition press is becoming responsible in its criticisms, great strides are being made in that direction.

Another effective set of institutions working for a greater degree of liberalization and democratization are the professional organizations. The syndicates of judges, lawyers, doctors, engineers, etc. have, at times, conflicted with the government over issues of professional practice and of principles. As they grow stronger, their push for democratization will also grow stronger since they will demand a greater measure of independent action and decision-making. They also are likely to find themselves weakened should the trend for liberalization come to a halt. Traditionally, Egyptian labor unions and trade unions have been weak. Nasser further defused them, and no succeeding government has allowed them to hold any significant amount of power. As institutions, they may push for liberalization, but thus far they have had little influence.

Intellectuals are another social group which could develop into an effective basis of support for liberalization and democratization. They must, however, regain lost ground. During the period of Nasser and Sadat, intellectuals served the state (or were silenced by it) and thus lost their position as intermediaries between government and people. By simply transmitting theories which pleased the state, many intellectuals lost their audience and became limited to communicating with each other. As Antonio Gramsci has pointed out, governments try to impose a hegemonic ideology on the masses through their use of intellectuals. However, if an elite is attuned to western notions of government, seeks to impose western notions of culture on a non-western population, and is more interested in talking to its western counterparts than in addressing its countrymen, this elite will become irrelevant to the man in the street. Although the ideal function of a liberal society is to allow a forum for different voices, in the world's truly liberal societies there tends to be a consensus on the processes and structure of government. This agreement does not yet exist in Egypt.

In the future, there is hope that intellectuals might play a role as intermediaries between the population and the government, rather than simple government mouthpieces. Among the younger intellectuals and older intellectuals, there is a tendency to move away from being government stalwarts toward an interpretation of the common man and his needs. This group could highlight reforms which are necessary and urgent, in addition to predicting the outcome should such reforms not be carried out, thus ensuring a greater degree of democracy.

Two institutions which may obstruct democratization and liberalization are the unwieldy bureaucracy and the reactionary religious establishment. The former is large and unproductive, while the latter is scared of losing more ground than it already has. The greatest danger, however, arises from the more extremist *jama'at*, which seek to tear society asunder and build it anew, according to their own notions of what is "Islamic."

The Egyptian population differs widely on what it considers to be "Islamic" forms and institutions. Most Muslims over the past centuries have adopted a "live and let live" attitude. Modern extremist *jama'at* follow the lines adopted by revolutionary groups in the past, such as the *khawarij*. The revolutionaries believe that those who do not accept their interpretations are miscreants who no longer form a part of the Muslim *'umma* and can be killed with impunity. Such groups do not favor a democratic form of government. They have a rigid hierarchical system, in which total obedience is expected by the hierarchical superiors. Such groups represent a small, extreme minority; but should they grow, or should they acquire a greater degree of power, they will certainly put an end to whatever liberalization and democratization processes exist.

Is the government more stable and more legitimate than before? Since the assembly is the result of general elections, which are considered to have been fair despite a poor voter turnout, it is certainly more legitimate. If the government shows signs of initiative, then this legitimacy is likely to extend further. Will this lead to stability? The stability of a government is predicated on a number of issues. First, there is the apparent control of the power of sanction. Stability tends to be shaken when the government becomes incapable of controlling its own forces, i.e., the army and the police. The police riots of 1987 showed a crack in the facade of control, but they antedated the elections and may be overlooked. Any time that government forces fail to control a demonstration, it signals the vulnerability of the government. A second important consideration is the government's ability to supply economic well-being to the country. Past governments have subsidized foodstuffs to keep the urban masses content. It should not be forgotten, however, that the affluent also benefit from subsidized foods, such as inexpensive cooking fuel, sugar, petrol, etc. People do not necessarily revolt because the price of living has gone up. Disbanding the food subsidies need not necessarily lead to civil unrest. The manner in which such subsidies are ended is far more important. In other words, would it appear to be an act of greater oppression of the poor, or a necessary adjunct to a general belt-tightening, beginning with the top levels of society? The only way that food subsidies can be disbanded will be for the People's Assembly to present a means by which the poor can be subsidized, but not the rich.

As E.P. Thompson's brilliant study of the English working class has shown, it is not how much is taken away that matters, but how much remains in a person's hands. The Egyptian government appears to have learned this lesson. It has changed the policy of buying staples from the peasantry at fixed prices, by opening the market up to a system wherein the farmer can earn a fair share for his produce.

The government's ability to be responsive to ordinary people will be extremely important for its stability. Building freeways and helping the traffic in Cairo is a positive step. However, most of the population does not own cars. Affordable housing, clothing, and food are more important to them than improved traffic flow. In the realm of foreign relations, the government will be judged by whether it projects an image of an independent government or that of a satellite of a foreign power. In other words, is Egypt willing to accept insults from Israel and the United States in return for subsidies?

Bureaucratic inertia is a continuing bane for Egypt. In the past, inactivity might have been seen as a form of passive resistance toward the colonizer, whether that was the Ottoman government or the British in Egypt. Today it has become an incubus stifling the government. The Mubarak regime has earned its share of public contempt precisely for that very trait, although more recently the regime has shaken its passivity and taken some decisive steps.

Egyptians distinguish between the head of state and the government, and much of the odium is directed toward the latter rather than the former. Nevertheless, the head of state bears the ultimate responsibility for the actions of his government, and what it does reflects on his ability to govern. If jokes are regarded as an indication of popular attitudes toward a ruler, we find that jokes about Nasser generally represented him as a hero; even when he was the butt of the joke, he was still larger than life. Jokes about Sadat, during his later years, portrayed him as a wily individual, who manipulated events and people. Mubarak, on the other hand, has been depicted as a simple and honest man, neither particularly active nor gifted, a man of average talent. Lacking the charisma of his predecessors, Mubarak is more dependent on the legitimacy obtained by his system. This legitimacy depends upon his government abiding by the law, which increasingly means parts of the *shari'a* and ensuring justice for the poor as well as the rich. Finally, his government must demonstrate an independent foreign policy. Recently, President Mubarak has shown initiative in foreign affairs by trying to act as an intermediary between the PLO and the US, and calling for an international conference to settle the Middle East conflict.

Liberalization is only a transitional period. If the final goal is democratization, then it can only be attained by increased economic growth in Egypt. Such growth would enable each group in society to feel that it has a stake in the whole.

If economic hardship is all that Egyptians have to look forward to, then they are not likely to be supportive of the state or the government, and they are more likely to listen closely to talk of revolution and change. Let us not forget that revolutions are begotten in periods of rising expectations.

The safeguards that would be needed to lead Egypt toward liberalization and eventual democratization are both economic and political. Egypt's first imperative is a more healthy economy, which means a massive dose of financing, the equivalent of a financial blood transfusion. Second, the major conflict in the Middle East must be solved before a healthier political climate can come into existence. Egypt's peace treaty with Israel is of little consequence if the other Arab states are at war with Israel and the Palestinians remain oppressed. The political health of the region depends on a settlement of this conflict.

Notes

1. William Ebenstein, *Great Political Thinkers* (New York: Holt, Rinehart & Winston, 1965), p. 361.

2. *Ibid.*, p. 387.

3. *Ibid.*, p. 389.

4. *Ibid.*

5. The Quran, Sura 13:11.

15 EGYPT, ISRAEL AND THE PALESTINIANS

Ibrahim Ibrahim

In any attempt to address the relationship among Egypt, Israel and the Palestinians, three important factors must be noted. The first is Egypt's renewed relationship with the Arab world after the interruption of Camp David; the second is the continuing centrality of the Palestine question to the entire Middle East, including Egypt and Israel; and the third, the fact that the effects of the Palestinian uprising are felt far beyond Palestinian territory. Indeed, the final act in the long drama involving the return of Egypt to the Arab fold coincided with the *intifada*. Egypt's formal resumption of diplomatic relations with most Arab states has provided a backdrop — inadvertently, of course — for the most serious Palestinian challenge to the status quo in recent memory. That coincidence of recent history — on the one hand, a long-planned, carefully measured diplomatic initiative, and on the other, a spontaneous, unplanned but deep-seated popular rebellion — should be borne in mind today.

A brief comparison between the *intifada* and the 1936-39 rebellion will be instructive. There is one important point of contrast and one similarity. First, unlike the rebellion of half a century ago, which was carried out by Palestinian peasants and led by one faction of Palestinian notables, today's *intifada* is a grass-roots revolt. It involves the whole litany of society: villagers and town-dwellers, men and women, the young and the old, fathers and sons, mothers and daughters, professional classes and working men and women.

Second, as was the case during the peasant rebellion from 1936 to 1939, the current uprising is bound to draw Egypt into the very heart of the Palestine question once again, just as Egypt's entry into the affairs of the Arab East took place against the backdrop of the rebellion of the 1930s. This is a development that bodes well for both Egypt and the Palestinians, as will be discussed later.

Prior to 1936, Egypt was preoccupied with its own problem, namely, the British occupation. Thus, Egypt was not allowed to nor could it devise its own Arab policy. But the rebellion of that time coincided with the conclusion of the Anglo-Egyptian Treaty in 1936. This meant that Egypt was now free to conduct an Egyptian policy in the Arab East, and Palestine was the crucial test. Palestinian armed resistance to Great Britain was supported enthusiastically by the masses of Egyptians, and by Muslim groups who mobilized support through demonstrations, meetings and parliamentary campaigns. Their collective efforts convinced the hesitant Wafd Party that Egyptian support and perhaps even leadership of the Arab East would be welcomed by the average Egyptian. Much of the popular support was drawn from students and youths, although the growing intellectual elite, including the Muslim Brotherhood, demanded deepened Egyptian involvement in pan-Arab issues.[1] This concern found fruition under Nasser, whose stand on the Palestine issue expressed the sentiments of the majority of Egyptians, as did his pan-Arabism.

This historical precedent is relevant to the present situation. It is highly likely that Egypt's successes in the regional diplomatic arena will again be an important motivating factor in pushing, although perhaps slowly, for a resolution of the Arab-Israeli conflict. Let me turn now to Egypt's role, and attempt to answer some questions regarding its policies toward Israel and the Palestinians.

The Summit Conference in Amman of November 1987 shortly before the outbreak of the *intifada* was important for Egypt and the Palestinians. First, it allowed the individual Arab states to renew ties with Egypt; and second, it propelled the Iran-Iraq war to center stage. At the same time, it marked a departure with the past that may have been misunderstood, for in Amman the Arab-Israeli conflict and the Israeli occupation of the West Bank and Gaza Strip were relegated to the back burner. This stemmed in part from the urgency of the threat of an Iranian victory, but it was also part of a deliberate collective effort to signal Arab readiness for a peaceful, diplomatic solution of the Palestine problem.

Ironically, whether in response to the summit stand on the Palestine problem or not, the *da'wa* came now not from the PLO but from Palestinians under occupation. The uprising began in the West Bank and Gaza only three weeks after the summit. It is almost an understatement to say the *intifada* caught Israel, Egypt, Jordan, the PLO and Arab leaders by surprise. It has subsequently set off political and diplomatic shock waves throughout the Middle East that have not yet subsided. Israel itself has been most directly affected and challenged by the uprising.

What is the impact of the *intifada* on Egyptian policies, and in particular on public opinion and prospects for internal stability? The Camp David accords, which resulted in the Egyptian-Israeli peace treaty, have been unpopular with the Egyptian public and continue to be so; three of Sadat's close advisers (including two ministers for foreign affairs), Isma'il Fahmi, Muhammad Ibrahim Kamel, and Muhammad Riyadh saw it as an Israeli *diktat,* engineered by Begin and sanctioned by the US.[2] Opposition continues to be expressed publicly, almost ten years after the fact.

This tension between the government and the public is exacerbated by Egyptian dependence on the US. This relationship lessens Egypt's maneuverability and limits its options, as does Israel's intransigence on the question of peace. It is now part of the historical record that Begin reneged on the second part of the accords, namely, autonomy for the Palestinians in the West Bank and Gaza. Today, Shamir preaches a new and radical interpretation of UN Security Council Resolution 242. According to the Israeli prime minister and his Likud bloc, Israel has already "complied" with Resolution 242 by returning Sinai to Egypt. In his view, the West Bank, East Jerusalem, the Gaza Strip and the Golan Heights are not Arab but biblical lands that have been restored to Eretz Israel. This intransigence was frustrating for Sadat and is still dangerous for Mubarak. As a result, since 1985 Mubarak has been pleading the case with the Reagan administration for the absolute urgency and necessity of resolving the Palestine-Israeli problem. During his 1988 visit, he publicly warned his hosts: "What is taking place in the occupied territories—the West Bank and Gaza—is contagious."

Mubarak was correct in his assessment. The Palestinian uprising is potentially lethal for Jordan, Egypt, and even Israel itself. Protests and civil turmoil sparked by the uprising have already taken place, with serious consequences. The likely repercussions of this "new stone age" are of special import to Arab governments whose state structures are weak and vulnerable. For the most part, the modern Arab state does not reflect "civil society" or public opinion, nor does it embody the popular will; and this lack of legitimacy invites serious challenges to stability.

As observed by Muhammad Hassanayn Haykal, ". . . the Arab people have reached a level of equilibrium with their governments whereby they can confront the regimes. This is clearer in Egypt than in any other country in the Arab world. In Egypt, there is some democracy, but not true democracy. The regime knows that it cannot adopt oppressive measures against its people because the sum total of the popular forces is equivalent to the power of the regime."[3]

The challenge of the *intifada* to Arab regimes and Israel provoked an American initiative, known as the Shultz Plan. Notwithstanding

Shamir's rejection, the plan was new wine in an old bottle, the Rogers Plan plus Camp David and the Reagan Plan. The gist of the matter was "land for peace," based on all the provisions and principles of 242. In specific terms, the plan involved a two-stage interlocked set of negotiations designed to produce rapid and fundamental change in the way Arabs and Israelis related to each other, all to take place within the framework of an international conference.

The US had vetoed an earlier UN Security Council resolution that called upon the Secretary General to convene an international conference—one which would have an authoritative role or plenipotentiary powers. According to the Shultz Plan, the international conference now proposed would be specifically enjoined from intruding in the negotiations, imposing solutions or vetoing what had been agreed upon bilaterally. Shamir reiterated his opposition to the Plan: the only word he agreed with was Shultz's "signature."[4]

By contrast, Egypt gave the plan its firm and public support. This support stemmed more from the lack of a better alternative than from the conviction that it could lead to a lasting and comprehensive settlement of the Arab-Israeli dispute. Egypt's interest was to reactivate US involvement in resolving the conflict, for Egypt was increasingly desperate for a comprehensive settlement to the entire Arab-Israeli conflict. Pressing economic problems, underlined by the deadlock in negotiations between Cairo and the IMF, were and are a major threat to stability in Egypt. It would not take much to spark off a serious round of destabilizing unrest. The uprising has already provoked anti-government demonstrations in Cairo.

Public support for the *intifada* has been widely expressed in Egypt. A committee of solidarity has been formed, "with members representing all political parties, while the Egyptian government used the occasion to improve its diplomatic leverage with Israel and the United States to *consolidate its legitimacy at home.*"[5] [Italics added] Another support organization is the Egyptian National Committee in Support of the Palestinian Uprising. Formed by the well-known writer, Lutfi al-Khuli, a prominent figure of al-Tajammu' party, the organization was endorsed by four opposition party leaders, such as Fuad Sirag al-Din of the Wafd party, Khalid Muhyi al-Din of al-Tajammu', Mustafa Kamil Murad of the Socialist Liberal Party and Ibrahim Shukri of the Socialist Labor Party.[6]

Just as Egypt needs to keep the US actively involved in the search for a peaceful settlement, the US too views Egypt's role as a core state in the Arab East as crucial in helping to implement any solution.

As always, however, power can never be equally shared between the metropolis and a client state. Despite its important assets—its geostrategic position, its human endowment, its demographic size and its leadership role in a growing and potentially rich and powerful Arab world—Egypt today is dependent on the US; and therein lies its weakness.

Of course, Israel too is a client state of the US, but the "special relationship" between the two makes the difference, despite the fact that this very special relationship makes Israel much more dependent on Washington than is the case with Egypt. Therefore, despite the peace treaty, Egypt's influence on Israel is non-existent; and if Cairo's voice is to be heard at all, it has to be channeled through Washington.

Paradoxically, part of Egypt's strength today, as was the case during Nasser's time, is derived from Arab division and weakness. Egypt's return to the Arab fold was hastened by the Iran-Iraq War and by the dispersal of the PLO from Beirut in 1982. It was significant that the first Arab capital Arafat chose to visit afterwards was Cairo, at a time when Egypt was still ostracized by most Arab governments. When almost all Arab ambassadors left Egypt in protest at the peace agreement with Israel two close aides of Arafat; Nabil Sha'ath and Sa'id Kamil, stayed put. The PLO and Egypt have been in close consultation on matters for many years, despite Egypt's formal exclusion from the Arab ranks.

Of course, there were and still are many problems between Egypt and the PLO: the exclusion of self-determination from the accords signed at Camp David; and the fact that American plans exclude the PLO from negotiations. Nevertheless, Egypt's insistence on transcending the Camp David formula by convening an authoritative international conference with the participation of the PLO is a step in the right direction.

By now it has become evident that the resolution of the Palestine question and its derivative, the Arab-Israeli conflict, cannot be achieved by Israel and Egypt with the help of the US alone. What was achieved at Camp David resulted in a separate peace, which is a precarious and frozen one. Subsequent American plans have been another variation on the theme of Camp David, in that they refuse to accept the PLO as the authorized representative of the Palestinian people in the process of Arab-Israeli negotiations.

The American policy of exclusion of the PLO continues even though the whole Arab world, including Egypt and Jordan, recognizes the PLO as the legitimate representative of the Palestinian people. In contrast, the European Community, whose countries include America's most faithful allies, endorsed the right of the Palestinian people "to exercise fully its right to self-determination" in Venice in 1980, and further called for the PLO "to be associated with the negotiations." The Arab world, Europe, the Third World, the Soviet bloc, China and Japan, and a growing body of opinion inside Israel itself call for negotiations with the PLO as a principal participant.

Encouraged by its return to the Arab fold in 1988 and by Europe's support, Egypt continued its diplomatic efforts toward the establishment of a dialogue between the US and the PLO. Just a couple of months before the Reagan-Shultz exit from the White House, Egypt succeeded in moving the PLO toward the acceptance of the principle of two states in Palestine at the meetings of the Palestine National Council in Algiers in November 1988.

Two historic documents emerged from the Algiers meetings: The Declaration of Independence and the Political Statement. As stipulated in the Declaration, the Palestinian state will be "committed to peaceful coexistence and will act with all other states and peoples to establish permanent peace based on justice. . . ."[7]

After Arafat's renunciation of terrorism and his declarations in Stockholm and Geneva in which he expressed his willingness to recognize the State of Israel within pre-1967 boundaries, the Bush-Baker administration began its efforts to reactivate the "peace process" in the Middle East. The continuation of the *intifada* in the West Bank and Gaza, and Arafat's public recognition of the State of Israel within the pre-1967 war borders, accelerated the need for movement. Shamir's initiative of May 14, 1989 urging the holding of elections in the West Bank and Gaza Strip was a by-product of domestic Israeli pressure, and Egyptian, European, and US displeasure with his government's intransigence. Nevertheless, under attacks from his right-wing Likud members, Shamir reneged on his own initiative, which was reduced to a set of diplomatic maneuvers designed to make Israel look cooperative.

It was at this juncture that Mubarak—with the encouragement and active diplomacy of James Baker—produced a ten-point plan to help restart the old "peace process" and move Shamir's own initiative along. Both Baker's five points and Mubarak's ten points were more favorable to the Israeli position than to that of Arafat, neither the PLO as the recognized leadership of the Palestinian people, nor the notion of self-determination, appeared in the language of the Egyptian plan.

This absence of the PLO from the Egyptian proposal suggested a return to the earlier futile Egyptian-American efforts to revive the "peace process." Since the days of Kissinger, US officials had been obsessed with the notion that Jordan was the representative of the Palestinians, even though King Hussein of Jordan had recognized the PLO as the sole and legitimate representative of the Palestinian people. Since the king legally and formally severed Jordan from the West Bank, the United States has asked Egypt to step in; today it appears that the "Jordanian option" is being superseded by the "Egyptian option." This is similar to the situation in 1979 during the period of the Camp David accords, when Egyptian president Sadat, Israeli prime minister Begin, and president Carter of the United States called on King Hussein but not the PLO to join in. Baker and Mubarak are currently trying to convene a meeting between US, Egyptian, and Israeli officials to discuss the list of Palestinians who could meet with the Israeli delegation in negotiations in Cairo. Arafat and the PLO have been asked "to confer privately with Egyptian officials on the composition of a Palestinian delegation, say nothing in public about the delegations and assume no visible role after that. . . ." Arafat most fittingly told a European diplomat, ". . . he had once read a book called *The Invisible Man,* 'I never thought I'd be one'."[8]

The essence of the Arab-Israeli conflict was and still is a Palestinian-Israeli conflict: it started in the late 1890s and is still going on as evidenced by the *intifada.* From the time of Johnson's administration until the present, the US government has treated the PLO and the Palestinian people as irrelevant. A problem involving the right of a people to self-determination cannot be resolved by manifestations of the arrogance of power, a cold war mentality, non-concern for Third World peoples, and disrespect for the inalienable rights of people to self-determination.

Predictably, not much progress has been made toward the Egyptian aim of convening a meeting between Israel and the PLO in Cairo under the sponsorship of the US and Egypt. Neither Baker nor Mubarak have been able to move Shamir away from his stand on the PLO which is based on keeping the PLO out of negotiations so as to delegitimize and rule out the idea of creating a Palestinian state. Shamir even requested the US to "back whatever actions Israel deems necessary if the talks [between Israelis and Palestinians] break off. Israel asks for this 'assurance' in writing . . . and says it won't consider the Baker proposal further without it." The *Washington Post* called this request a "blank check."[9]

But, despite "the timid passivity of Bush and Baker,"[10] and Mubarak's helplessness as a bridge-builder between Israel and the Palestinians, the status quo can no longer be preserved. First, the *intifada,* now in its third year, is challenging the status quo and Mubarak's acquiescence with Israeli-US policies. Second, the *intifada* has opened the eyes of world public opinion to Israeli machinations and state brutality. On December 8, 1987 the world came to witness not just a Palestinian event, but as Sari Nuseibeh eloquently put it, "a landmark in the universal annals of national liberation movements. Indeed, the *intifada* is not just a Palestinian story. It is a human story. It is a lesson in the strength of the human will, the strength of the national will, and the strength and value of the call for freedom." The *intifada* is "a great and spontaneous popular explosion, manifesting itself in the furious out-pouring of the unarmed masses into the streets, . . . *brazen defiance of death itself.*"[11] [Italics added]

Another movement that is in support of efforts to change the status quo and end Israel's occupation of the West Bank and Gaza Strip is the Israeli "Peace Now" movement. Since the Israeli invasion of Lebanon in 1982 and the massacres of Sabra and Shatila during that invasion, a sizable number of Israeli citizens have started to question the wisdom of their leadership and the utility of Israel's policy in the occupied Palestinian and Arab lands. Apart from the demonstrations that took place in Tel Aviv over Sabra and Shatila in 1982, one of the largest demonstrations for Palestinian rights ever staged in Israel was the "human chain" around Jerusalem's walled Old City on December 29, 1989. In this demonstration of Israeli peace activists and Palestinians demanding negotiations and an end to the occupation, it is interesting that both Israeli and Arab participants joined hands with about 1,300 demonstrators from Italy, Britain, West Germany and other West European countries. According to the *Washington Post,* the Israeli police estimated that a crowd of 15,000 to 25,000 people, "more than two-thirds of them Israelis, turned out."[12] Many American Jewish organizations are also disturbed by the brutality of the attempt by the Israeli government to suppress the *intifada*. The American-Israeli Public Affairs Committee sent Tom Dine and Robert H. Asher—two key members of the Israel lobby—on a top-secret mission to Israel to warn Shamir "that Israel and the Palestinians must be brought to a dialogue, the sooner the better, and that a fair election must be held."[13]

Shamir's plan to hold elections in the West Bank and Gaza, Mubarak's ten-point plan and Baker's five-point plan are doomed to failure. The Palestine question has moved no closer to a resolution as a result of any of them. Its continuation remains a major threat to peaceful relations between Egypt and Israel, and to the United States policy which depends upon maintaining both Egypt and Israel as allies. Egypt's long-term interest in peace can only be maintained by a breakthrough involving a shift in the official Israeli position toward talks with the PLO about the conditions in which Palestinian self-determination could be exercised as part of an overall Arab-Israeli peace agreement.

Notes

1. See Anis Sayigh, *Al-Fikra al-Arabiya fi Misr* (Beirut, 1959) pp. 142, 202; also, J.W.D. Gray, "Arab Nationalism, Abdin Against the Wafd," *The Middle East Forum,* Vol. 38, No. 2 (February 1962), pp. 17-18.

2. Ismail Fahmi, *Negotiating for Peace in the Middle East* (Baltimore: The Johns Hopkins University Press, 1983), pp. 309-21.

3. *Journal of Palestine Studies,* Vol. 18, No. 1 (Autumn 1988), p. 119; see also "Hawajiz Mustaqbaliya" in *al-Muntada,* No. 28 (January 1988), pp. 8-9.

4. Peretz Kidron, "Picking up the Gauntlet," *Middle East International,* No. 326 [or 321], March 19, 1988, p. 5.

5. Mustafa K. al-Sayyed, "Egyptian Popular Attitudes Toward the Palestinians Since 1977," in *Journal of Palestine Studies,* Vol. 18, No. 4 (Summer 1989), p. 43.

6. *Op. cit.* p. 46.

7. For an excellent interpretation of the Declaration and Political Statement see Walid Khalidi, *At a Critical Juncture: The United States and the Palestinian People* (Washington, D.C.: Georgetown University Center for Contemporary Arab Studies, 1989).

8. Cited in *Washington Post,* December 4, 1989.

9. Cited in *Washington Post,* November 7, 1989.

10. Nasser Aruri, *Middle East International,* No. 363, November 17, 1989, pp. 16-17.

11. "A True Popular Revolution," *Middle East International,* No. 365 (December 15, 1989), p. 16.

12. *Washington Post,* December 31, 1989.

13. *Washington Post,* November 15, 1989.

PART 3: EPILOGUE

LOOKING TOWARD THE FUTURE

16 A Look Ahead—Problems and Prospects

Ashraf Ghorbal

The Egyptian dream of building a new society is being frustrated. It faces three possible principal obstacles: the population dilemma, the production dilemma, and that of the bureaucracy.

With reference to the population dilemma, numbers speak louder than words. By 1986 the natural increase of the Egyptians amounted to 4,166 persons daily—a rate of increase of 125,000 per month or 1,500,000 per annum. It is estimated that the total population will reach 70 million by the year 2000. As a result of such an uncontrolled increase, the burden on the state or on the market to fulfill the rising expectations of the population threatens to become unmanageable. By the year 2000, Egypt will need 4,902,000 dwelling units in the cities and 2,952,000 in the rural areas. In other words, the Egyptian government will be required to construct about 1,000 dwelling units every working day until the beginning of the twenty-first century. Similarly spectacular achievements will be required to meet the parallel needs in food, clothing, transportation, health care, education, and other human services.

These figures reflect one of the main underlying problems of contemporary Egypt, the limitations of state capabilities. These limitations are particularly acute in the face of the growing disparity between supply and demand in the areas of basic needs. According to official Egyptian figures, the rate of population increase has vastly outpaced the rate of expansion of the cultivated land. Since the beginning of the century, cultivated land has expanded only by 25 percent while the population increased by 380 percent.

The population dilemma is more than a problem of birth control. It involves the impact of the dislocation of population on socioeconomic and political structures. Population distribution is at the heart of the dilemma. Two instances of national demographic dislocation during the last twenty years have been particularly significant. The first experience came after the war in 1967. As a result of that war and its subsequent war of attrition, there was an exodus by the inhabitants of the Canal cities to the Nile Valley. The second experience, still unfolding, is internal labor migration. In both cases, the socio-economic and political systems have had to deal with unprecedented problems.

The dislocation of population has produced grave side effects such as increased crime and an abnormal birth rate, as well as broader problems of values, such as an attachment to superficial consumerism.

The problem of demographic dislocation poses its own challenge: that of finding solutions. One possible solution is an emphasis on building and expanding self-reliant new communities outside the Nile Valley. This process has already begun but is moving at a slower pace than anticipated. It should be accelerated. Another possibility is a radical scheme for decentralization. The third solution is offering income incentives to those who maintain a family size, residence, and work place that conform to Egypt's social needs.

The second dilemma is that of production, and the challenge of increasing labor productivity and managerial rationality. One of the major findings of a study by the World Bank on labor productivity in Egyptian industry was that it was far lower than the standards of industrial countries. This reflects a reality in Third World countries in general to which Egypt is no exception. The study described the Egyptian labor market as characterized by inadaptability. In essence, there is a discrepancy in Egypt between labor and market conditions. There is a lack of skilled labor, particularly in the construction sector; a surplus of labor in the informal urban sector, public sector and small farms; and a lack of training. In other words, the gap between the demands for development and the market supply of labor plagues every facet of Egyptian life. As for managerial rationality, the aforementioned study emphasized the administrative and organizational aspects of the production dilemma. It concluded that in the public economic sector, the rise of productivity required a separation between ownership and management, the disengagement of ministers from daily managerial work, a reduction in the number of decision-making channels, and strict adherence to criteria of efficiency in management.

Although the margin of freedom for private business is now wider than during the sixties, the corporate structure that organizes the norms, finances and methods of production is statist in nature. The state sector in the economy, despite changes during the last ten years, still shapes and influences the conduct of private business in production. The government is anxious to ameliorate this problem, but progress has been slow here, too.

The third dilemma facing Egypt is the bureaucratic one. An enormous number of decrees are not implemented, or else are implemented in a way that does not fulfill their intended purposes.

There are three probable reasons for this problem. The first is that the decrees and decisions are made without taking their applicability into consideration. The second is that the apparatus for decision making is not coherently linked to that for implementation. The third is that the personnel who are charged with implementation have different views and ideologies from those responsible for making decisions. In short the philosophy of the state as policy, represented in laws and regulations, does not seem in many instances to filter down to policy-targeted groups.

As Egypt charts its course toward the twenty-first century and toward democracy, those dilemmas pose potential constraints. Democracy invites more freedom and makes the political authority more accountable to the public. The preparation for the twenty-first century also requires more innovation and efficiency. But centralization of the Egyptian state makes the transition to real democracy and preparation for the coming century very difficult.

It is also important to highlight the achievements. Egypt has, during the past decade, overhauled its infrastructure; from water to waste water; from electricity to communications; from roads to overpasses. Cairo is a different city. Though twelve million inhabitants overcrowd Cairo, it is not as claustrophobic as it was in the past. Construction abounds, carried out more by private companies rather than by the government. Stark desert in the areas between Cairo and Alexandria is now lush with greenery. Egypt is exporting more, although it is also consuming more. The drought in the African Plateau has resulted in a low level of Nile water. This problem has forced Egyptians to economize on water. Even the subsidies for food, energy, and other goods are gradually being eliminated, although the IMF would prefer a faster growth rate. There is a new realism supported by a determination to face up to problems. Maybe the difference between Egypt and the IMF is not one about measures, but about the pace of development. Tourism has become a shining example of achievement for Egypt. Production for export is next, and self-sufficiency in food production is on everyone's mind. But to do all that, favorable conditions are needed, Egypt needs help, and it definitely needs peace in the region.

It is important to remember that in this part of the world democracy and prosperity would have little chance of flourishing unless peace and order prevail. But peace and order in the Middle East are certainly not forthcoming with the persistent Israeli denial of the Palestinian right to self-determination. Furthermore, preventing Soviet participation in the peace process is both unwise and counterproductive.

Egypt has a special relationship with the United States, which is not likely to change in the near future. Egyptian-American relations have some unhealthy ingredients. At present there is a high degree of Egyptian economic dependence on the US. The continuation of this dependence is not in the interest of either party. It breeds an expectation in each of taking the other for granted. This is indeed unhealthy.

One way to effect change is for the US to invest more in Egypt in a manner which ultimately strengthens the Egyptian private sector. The Private Investment Encouragement Fund (the PIE Fund) is a good beginning but is not enough. A partnership based on investment is more durable than dependency on government aid. But aid should not be reduced until we are sure that a high degree of US investment is in place.

The introduction of US investment in Egypt has contributed significantly to a rise of technological standards in addition to to a strong emphasis on the work ethic. The American investments that have come to Egypt have been a shining example of success. Examples of this are General Motors Truck Plant, the Union Carbide Batteries Plant, Ideal Standard, and the Coca Cola Concentration Plant, not to mention the many consumer industries. All are advertisements of the opportunities that exist in Egypt for economic achievement. Although all investors have the right, under Law 43, to repatriate their profits (even the capital), many have recycled their profits into further expansion. It is noteworthy that US and other investors speak highly of the Egyptian worker, of his efficiency, discipline and commitment to a quality of product. Egyptian managers have also demonstrated first-rate abilities to manage and direct complex productive activities.

One way to increase US investment would be for the US government to establish an Independent Fund for Overseas Investment. The Fund could invest in different projects in Egypt as well as other Third World countries. The US could entrust the Fund's management to an autonomous body comprising a group of well-known and respected American private sector businessmen, leaders in their fields. Once the projects are successful, then Washington could sell its shares to the US private sector. However, the US government contribution should come from a fund different from AID appropriations or supplementing it. One way of approaching capital funds for the projects would be to recycle Egypt's payments of its military debts to the US as the US capital investment in these joint ventures. The US would be able to sell its share to the private sector once the projects are viable, thus realizing a profit and recovering its loans simultaneously.

Peace in the Middle East has recently gained new grounds through the resumption of diplomatic relations between Egypt and the Arab states. The new Egyptian-Arab conduct confirms Egypt's Arab identity and its role as the center of Arab gravity. After estrangement of a decade, the Arab countries have, by resuming relations with Egypt, certified that to face the challenges of the present and the responsibilities of the future, Egypt has to be in their midst. Egypt can now influence the drive for peace.

Peace with Israel is here to stay. The main obstacle to further progress does not come from the Egyptian corner. We are a nation that respects its commitments. Rather, lack of progress comes from the Israeli corner. It is by now common knowledge that Israel is a split nation over the issue of peace. The Likud, allied with the religious and rightist political forces, stands against exchanging land for peace. On the other side, Shimon Peres and the moderates in the political arena see benefits for Israel making such an exchange.

Prime Minister Shamir's objection to an international peace conference has not been based, as some have argued, on his opposition to Soviet participation. His objection derives from his reluctance to face a situation in which he might have to relinquish land. When the PLO accepted all the necessary peace prerequisites—Resolutions 242 and 338, recognition, and direct negotiations—Shamir found another excuse not to go to the negotiating table. Israel has started to taste the bitter fruits of lost opportunities. Occupation is anathema to human dignity. The current Palestinian *intifada* drives the point home. Its message is that the Palestinians are a nation that refuses second-class treatment. Even though Palestinians may work in the Israeli economy, this does not mean they are not willing and ready to sacrifice their means of livelihood to regain their lost land. When politicians and statesmen fail to accept people's legitimate aspirations and rights, the people take the issue to the streets.

It seems that Israel is unable to learn from past mistakes. In Lebanon, Israel had to pay a heavy price in human casualties for its mistake in invading the country. The Lebanese tragedy is still unfolding. Does Israel have to go through the same ordeal in the West Bank and Gaza Strip to learn that freedom is everyone's right? The true friends of Israel should have dissuaded her from invading Lebanon. Her true friends should now dissuade her from her present repressive policies.

APPENDIX

SELECTED STATISTICS ON EGYPTIAN
SOCIAL AND ECONOMIC DEVELOPMENT

Compiled by Julia Devlin

TABLE 1

Gross Domestic Product and Gross National Product, 1965, 1987

	1965	1987
1. GDP[a] (U.S.$ million)	4,550	34,470
2. Distribution of GDP (%)		
a. Agriculture	29	21
b. Industry	27	25
. Manufacturing	n.a.	14
c. Services, etc.	45	54
3. GNP per capita (1987 U.S.$)	170	730

Source: World Bank, *Social Indicators of Development, 1987*
       World Development Report, 1989

[a]The figures for the GDP are dollar values converted from domestic currencies using single-year official exchange rates.

TABLE 2

Economic Growth Rates, 1965-1987

Average Annual Growth	1965-80	1980-87
1. Average Annual Growth Rate (%)		
a. GDP	6.8	6.3
b. Agriculture	2.7	2.7
c. Industry	6.9	5.5
d. Manufacturing	n.a.	6.1
e. Services, etc.	9.4	8.1
2. Average Annual Rate of Inflation (%)	7.3	9.2
3. Consumption & Investment Average Annual Growth Rate (%)	1965-80	1980-87
a. General Government Consumption	n.a.	5.3
b. Private Consumption	5.5	5.0
c. Gross Domestic Investment	11.3	2.7

Source: World Bank, *World Development Report, 1989*

TABLE 3

Balance of Payments, 1970, 1987

Current Account Balance (U.S.$ million)	1970	1987
1. Before Official Transfers	−452	−3,757[a]
2. After Official Transfers	−148	−2,705[a]
3. New Workers' Remittances	29	2,845[a]
4. Net Direct Private Investments	—	869[a]
5. Gross International Reserves	165	2,556

Source: World Bank, *World Development Report,* 1989
[a]World Bank estimates

TABLE 4

Government Finance, 1987

Central Government Current Revenue	1987
1. Tax Revenue (percentage of total current revenue)	
a. Taxes on Income, Profit and Capital Gain	15.2
b. Social Security Contributions	14.6
c. Domestic Taxes on Goods & Services	12.0
d. Taxes on International Trade & Transactions	13.4
e. Other Taxes	7.8
2. Non-tax Revenue	37.0
3. Total Current Revenue (percentage of GNP)	39.0

Central Government Expenditure	
1. Percentage of Total Expenditure	
a. Defense	19.5
b. Education	12.0
c. Health	2.5
d. Housing Amenities, Social Security & Welfare	16.0
e. Economic Services	10.0
f. Other	40.1
2. Total Expenditure (percentage of GNP)	45.5
3. Overall Surplus/Deficit (percentage of GNP)	−6.6

Source: World Bank, *World Development Report,* 1989

TABLE 5

Debt and Assistance, 1970, 1987

External Debt (U.S.$ million)	1970	1987
1. External Public Debt, Outstanding & Disbursed (U.S.$ million)	1,713	34,515
As Percentage of GNP	22.5	105.4
2. Interest Payments on External Public Debt (U.S.$ million)	56	716
3. Debt Service as Percentage of GNP	4.8	4.6
4. Use of IMF Credit (U.S.$ million)	49	182
5. Flow of Public and Private External Capital		
a. Public and publicly guaranteed	397	1,219
b. Private non-guaranteed	—	245

U.S. Aid to Egypt (U.S.$ thousands)	1977	1988
1. Grants Disbursed by the U.S. to Egypt (Total)	52,920	1,504,702
PL-480[a]	15,073	1,377
FAA-ML[b]	1,200	866,995
FAA-OT[c]	36,647	636,330
2. Credits (Loans) Disbursed by U.S. to Egypt (Total)	429,175	2,071,098
CCC[d]	—	230,841
EIB[e]	10,140	15,127
PL-480	185,296	296,342
FAA-ML	—	1,431,159
FAA-OT	233,739	97,629
3. Credit (Loan) Repayments Received by U.S. from Egypt (Total)	47,278	95,584
CCC	11,077	3,926
EIB	9,032	24,981
PL-480	18,302	50,643
FAA-ML	—	—
FAA-OT	8,867	16,034
	1974/5	1986/7
4. Food Aid in Cereals (thousands of metric tons)	610	1,977

Source: United States Department of Commerce, Bureau of Economic Analysis, November 1989

[a]Under Agricultural Trade Development and Assistance Act (PL 83-480).
[b]Under Foreign Assistance Act of 1961 (as amended) and related programs for grants of military goods and services, and for grants and credits financing military purchases.
[c]Under Foreign Assistance Act of 1961 (as amended) and related programs other than military.
[d]Under Commodity Credit Corporation Charter Act.
[e]Under Export-Import Bank Act.

TABLE 6

Foreign Trade, 1965, 1987

Merchandise Trade (U.S.$ million)	1965	1987
1. Percentage Share of Merchandise Exports (%)		
a. Fuels, minerals, metals	8	69
b. Other primary commodities	72	12
c. Machinery & transport equipment	0	0
d. Other manufactures	20	19
Textiles & clothing	5	12
2. Percentage Share of Merchandise Imports (%)		
a. Food	26	24
b. Fuels	7	2
c. Other primary commodities	12	7
d. Machinery & transport equipment	23	28
e. Other manufactures	31	39
3. Average Annual Growth Rate (%)	1965-80	1980-87
a. Exports	2.7	8.4
b. Imports	6.0	2.8

Source: World Bank, *World Development Report,* 1989

TABLE 7

Population, 1950-2000 (est.)

					Year			
Population (in thousands)	1950	1960	1970	1980	1990[a]	2000[a]		
1. Total	20,330	25,922	33,053	41,520	54,059	66,710		
2. Sex Ratio (males per 100 females)	98.9	101.2	102.5	103.0	103.1	103.3		
3. Functional Age Group (%)								
a. Young child (0-4 yrs.)	16.2	17.1	15.2	16.1	15.2	11.9		
b. Child (5-14 yrs.)	23.5	25.4	26.2	23.9	25.7	23.9		
c. Youth (15-24 yrs.)	19.3	17.3	19.6	20.1	18.0	20.6		
d. Elderly (60+ yrs.)	5.1	5.5	6.7	6.3	6.1	6.3		
e. Elderly (65+ yrs.)	3.0	3.3	4.3	4.1	3.9	4.2		
f. Women (15-49 yrs.)	24.5	22.7	22.6	23.4	23.1	25.2		
4. Median Age	20.0	19.1	18.9	19.8	19.9	21.6		
5. Dependency Ratios[b]								
a. Total	74.4	84.3	84.2	78.8	81.0	66.7		
b. Aged 0-14 yrs.	69.2	78.3	76.2	71.5	74.0	59.7		
c. Aged 65+ yrs.	5.2	6.0	8.0	7.3	7.0	7.0		

TABLE 7 (continued)

Year

	1950/5	1960/5	1970/5	1980/5	1990/5[a]	2000/5[a]
Annual Population Growth Rate (%)						
a. Total	2.46	2.51	1.87	2.72	2.24	1.71
b. Urban	4.20	3.95	2.45	3.51	3.35	2.95
c. Rural	1.59	1.58	1.43	2.07	1.12	0.09
1. Crude Birth Rate (per 1000 pop.)	48.6	45.4	38.4	39.7	30.9	23.5
2. Crude Death Rate (per 1000 pop.)	24.0	20.4	16.3	11.9	8.4	6.4
3. Total Fertility Rate (per woman)[c]	6.56	7.07	5.53	5.27	4.20	2.99
4. Gross Reproduction Rate (per woman)	3.20	3.45	2.70	2.57	2.05	1.46
5. Net Reproduction Rate (per woman)[d]	2.07	2.35	2.00	2.09	1.78	1.34
6. Infant Mortality Rate (per 1000 Births)	200	175	150	100	71	46
7. Life Expectancy at Birth (years)						
a. Males	41.2	46.2	50.8	56.8	61.8	66.1
b. Females	43.6	48.6	53.4	59.5	64.5	69.3
c. Both sexes	42.4	47.4	52.1	58.1	63.1	67.7

Source: United Nations: *World Population Prospects*, 1988.

[a]Projected estimates
[b]Dependents per 100 persons of working age (15-64 yrs.)
[c]The total fertility rate is the average number of children that would be born by a group of women in the child-bearing ages if they experienced no mortality. This is usually defined as the replacement-level fertility.
[d]Included in the preparation of fertility assumptions is the fertility level that produces the net reproduction rate when it is combined with the mortality schedule prevailing in the period. Essentially the net reproduction rate is a combination of fertility and mortality.

TABLE 8

Employment, 1960, 1983

Economically Active Population* by Major Divisions of Economic Activity (in thousands)	1960	%	1983	%
Economic Sectors				
1. Agriculture, Forestry, Fishing	4,405.2	56.6	4,722.0	40.7
2. Mining, Quarrying	20.9	0.3	32.9	0.3
3. Manufacturing	704.3	9.0	1,697.4	14.6
4. Electricity, Gas, Water	157.7	2.0	100.4	0.9
5. Construction	36.3	0.5	619.4	5.3
6. Trade, Restaurants, Hotels	630.3	8.1	1,019.6	8.8
7. Transport, Storage, Communication	256.7	3.3	571.0	4.9
8. Services	1,348.8	17.3	2,578.0	22.2
9. Not Adequately Defined	221.9	2.9	260.7	2.2
Occupations	1960	%	1983	%
1. Professional, Technical & Related Workers	214.9	3.1	1,270.5	11.1
2. Administrative & Managerial Workers	74.5	1.1	236.4	2.0
3. Clerical & Related Workers	249.0	3.6	985.1	8.5
4. Sales Workers	552.1	8.0	747.4	6.4
5. General Service Workers	638.6	9.3	933.5	8.0
6. Agriculture, Animal Husbandry & Forestry Workers, Fishermen & Hunters	3,671.3	53.5	4,642.0	40.0
7. Production & Related Workers, Transport Equipment Operators & Laborers	1,315.2	19.2	2,760.9	23.8
8. Not Adequately Defined	151.6	2.2	25.6	0.2

Source: International Labor Office, *Yearbook of Labor Statistics,* 1970, 1987.
*Excluding persons seeking employment for the first time.

TABLE 9

Health Statistics, 1965, 1987

Nutrition	1965	1987
1. Daily calorie supply per capita	2,435	3,275
2. Daily protein supply per capita (grams)	69	82
3. Life Expectancy at birth	49	61
4. Index of Food Production per Capita		
(1979-81 = 100)	103	106
5. Child Death Rate per thousand	21	11

Health Services (in thousands)	1973	1988
1. Population per Physician	1.9	0.8
2. Population per Nurse	2.3	0.8
3. Population per Hospital Bed	0.5	0.5
4. Access to Safe Water (% Population)		
a. Total	66	90
b. Urban	88	93
c. Rural	50	61
5. Family Planning		
a. Acceptors (annually)	150	357
b. Users (% of married women)	21	32
6. Centers for Maternity & Infant Care	2,112	3,000
7. Treatment Units in Towns		
a. General & District Hospitals	189	335
b. Endemic Diseases Hospitals	162	161
c. Dental Units	948	1,347
d. School Health Units	218	313
e. Psychiatry Clinics	35	29
f. Rural Area Units	2,068	2,740

Sources: Central Agency for Public Mobilization and Statistics, *Statistical Yearbook,* 1973, 1988.
World Bank, *World Development Report,* 1971, 1989.

TABLE 10

Primary and Secondary Education Statistics, 1965, 1988

Percentage of Age Group Enrolled in
Education

	1965	1988
1. Primary		
a. Total	75	85
b. Male	90	94
c. Female	60	76
2. Secondary		
a. Total	26	62
b. Male	37	73
c. Female	15	52
3. Pupil/Teacher Ratio		
a. Primary	39	32
b. Secondary	20	23
Literacy Rate (%)	20	44

Sources: Central Agency for Public Mobilization and Statistics, *Statistical Yearbook,* 1973, 1988.
World Bank, *World Development Report,* 1971, 1989

TABLE 11

University Students, 1986

Number of Students at the University
or University-Equivalent Level

Field of Study	Total Students	Female Students
1. All Fields	592,256	203,115
2. Education	85,196	40,951
3. Humanities, Religion & Theology	83,581	39,794
4. Fine and Applied Arts	7,904	3,607
5. Law	88,282	18,397
6. Social and Behavioral Sciences	5,830	2,373
7. Commercial & Business Administration	137,782	42,532
8. Mass Communication & Documentation	1,692	912
9. Home Economics	2,024	1,566
10. Service Trades	1,192	759
11. Natural Science	25,371	9,387
12. Mathematics & Computer Science	2,536	580
13. Medical Science & Health-Related	50,245	19,780
14. Engineering	52,363	6,772
15. Agriculture, Forestry & Fishery	39,565	12,555
16. Other	8,693	3,150

Source: United Nations Educational, Scientific and Cultural Organization, *Statistical Yearbook,* 1989.

TABLE 12

Urbanization & Housing, 1960, 1987

Urbanization

	1960	1987
1. Urban Population as Percentage of Total Population	37.9	48.0
2. Percentage of Population in Largest City	38	39 (1980)
3. Average Annual Growth Rate of Urban Population		
1965-1980 2.9		
1980-1987 3.7		

Housing	1960	1986
1. Total Number of Housing Units	1,638,858	5,858,971
2. Number of Households	1,992,491	9,732,728
3. Average Size of Household	4.8	4.9
4. Percentage of Dwellings with Electricity	46 (1973)	60 (1983)[a]

Sources: Central Agency for Public Mobilization and Statistics, *Statistical Yearbook,* 1973
United Nations, *Statistical Yearbook,* 1965
World Bank, *Social Indicators of Development,* 1987
World Resources Institute, *World Resources,* 1987
[a]Euromonitor, *International Marketing Data and Statistics,* 1988-89

CONTRIBUTORS

Robert Bianchi is an associate professor of political science at the University of Chicago, where he completed his doctoral degree. Dr. Bianchi has lectured and published widely on politics and political development in the Middle East. His works include: *Interest Groups and Development in Turkey* and *Unruly Corporatism: Associational Life in Twentieth-Century Egypt*.

Julia Devlin compiled the statistical appendix to this volume while a graduate student at the Center for Contemporary Arab Studies, Georgetown University, where she received her M.A. in Arab Studies. She is currently a Ph.D. candidate in Economics at the University of Virginia.

Ashraf Ghorbal was the Egyptian ambassador to the United States from 1973-1984. Dr. Ghorbal has also served as deputy advisor on national security affairs and press advisor to President Anwar Sadat. He was a party to both the Camp David accords and the peace negotiations with Israel. Dr. Ghorbal received his Ph.D. in political science from Harvard University and is presently a consultant in Cairo.

Heba Ahmad Handoussa is a professor of economics at the American University in Cairo, an economic advisor to the Egyptian ministers of economy and industry, and a consultant to the World Bank and to the Egyptian Foreign Investment Authority. Among her published works are *Employment Opportunities and Equity in Egypt,* "Productivity and Change in Egyptian Public Sector Industries After the Opening, 1973-1979" (co-author), and "Conflicting Objectives of the American-Egyptian Aid Relationship."

Enid Hill is a professor of political science at the American University of Cairo, where she has taught for over twenty years. Dr. Hill earned her Ph.D. in political science at the University of Chicago. Her

327

publications include *Al-Sanhuri and Islamic Law,* and *Mahkama! Studies in the Egyptian Legal System.*

Raymond A. Hinnebusch is an associate professor of political science and chairman of the department at the College of St. Catherine. Dr. Hinnebusch received his Ph.D. in political science from the University of Pittsburgh. Among his published works are *Egyptian Politics Under Sadat: The Post-Populist Transformation of an Authoritarian-Modernizing State, Peasant and Bureaucracy in Ba'thist Syria* and "Egypt, Syria, and the Arab State System."

Ibrahim Ibrahim is Acting Director of the Center for Contemporary Arab Studies. He received his M.A. from the University of Heidelberg and his D.Phil. from Oxford University. Prior to joining the Georgetown University faculty, Dr. Ibrahim was Advisor to the Ministry of Foreign Affairs in the United Arab Emirates. He has also taught at Warwick University and the American University of Beirut. His publications include *Arab Resources: The Transformation of a Society* (editor and contributor), and many articles on the recent history and current political developments of the Middle East.

Charles Issawi is Bayard Dodge Professor Emeritus of Near Eastern Studies at Princeton University. Educated at Magdalen College, Oxford, he has taught at Columbia, Harvard, the Johns Hopkins School of Advanced International Studies, American University of Beirut, New York University and the Ecole des Hautes Etudes (Paris). He has also held positions at the Egyptian Ministry of Finance, the National Bank of Egypt, and the United Nations. His numerous publications include *The Fertile Crescent 1800-1914, The Economic History of the Middle East and North Africa, The Arab Legacy,* and *Issawi's Laws of Social Motion.*

Ann Mosley Lesch received her Ph.D. in political science from Columbia University and is currently an associate professor of political science at Villanova University. Dr. Lesch has published many works on the Arab-Israeli conflict, Egypt and the Sudan, including *The Politics of Palestinian Nationalism* (co-author), "Egyptian Labor Migration: Economic Trends and Government Policies," and "The Impact of Labor Migration on Urban and Rural Egypt."

Afaf Lutfi Al-Sayyid Marsot received a D.Phil. in Oriental Studies from Oxford University. She is currently a professor of Near and

Middle East history at the University of California at Los Angeles, where she has taught for the past twenty years. She is a former president of the Middle East Studies Association and editor of the *International Journal of Middle East Studies*. Dr. Marsot has written several books and articles dealing with Islamic resurgence, the *ulama*, women in the Muslim world, and the politics of the Arab world.

Said El-Naggar, a former director at the World Bank, also served as director of the UN Economic and Social Office in the Middle East, deputy director of research at the UN Council on Trade and Development, and professor of economics at Cairo University. Dr. El-Naggar received a doctorate in economics at Cairo University and has published extensively on international economics, microeconomics, the history of economic thought, and economic development.

Ibrahim M. Oweiss earned a doctorate in economics from the University of Minnesota and is currently an associate professor of economics at Georgetown University. Dr. Oweiss served for one year as first undersecretary of state for economic affairs in Egypt and has also been chief of the Egyptian Economic Mission to the United States. His numerous publications include *Arab Civilization* (co-editor), *The Dynamics of US-Arab Economic Relations in the 1970s* (editor and contributor), "Petrodollars and Regional Economic Development," and "Pricing of Oil in World Trade."

Delwin A. Roy is president of the Hitachi Foundation, Washington, DC. He has worked with USAID and several international trade and finance organizations. He has also served with the Ford Foundation in the Middle East, consulting on government projects with Egypt, Jordan, Saudi Arabia, and the Sudan. Dr. Roy is the author of numerous articles, monographs, and reports on management development, labor migration, economic liberalization, and economic policy planning in the Middle East.

Mustapha Kamel El-Sayed is an associate professor of political science at Cairo University and the American University in Cairo. Dr. El Sayed's publications include *Society and Politics in Egypt,* and *Issues of Political Change in Three Continents* (both in Arabic), and "Interest Groups in Sadat's Egypt" (forthcoming).

Amira El Azhary Sonbol received her Ph.D. in history from Georgetown University, where she is a visiting assistant professor.

Her main areas of expertise include the role of women in Egypt, Islamic revivalism, and the Egyptian educational system. Among Dr. Sonbol's published works are "The Role of Islam in Egypt Today" and "Doing Right by a Troubled Friend."

Denis J. Sullivan is an assistant professor of political science at Northeastern University. This article is part of a wider study in progress on bureaucracy and foreign aid in Egypt. Dr. Sullivan, who received his Ph.D. from the University of Michigan at Ann Arbor, has written extensively on the state systems and economic policies of a number of Arab countries.

Fuad Sultan is currently Egypt's minister of tourism and civil aviation. His previous posts have included appointments as chairman and managing director of Misr Iran Development Bank (Cairo), acting general manager of the Arab International Bank (Cairo), and advisor to the International Monetary Fund. His post-graduate studies were conducted in economics at Cairo University. He spent one year at the International Monetary Fund Institute.

INDEX

332   *Index*

Fund, Investment, Labor, Military, Oil, Peasants, Population, Privatization, Private Sector, Productivity, Public Sector, Rent, Rentalism, *Riba,* Savings, Suez Canal, Tariffs, Taxation, Textiles, Tourism, Transportation, Unemployment, World Bank

politics
see al-Azhar, Bourgeoisie, Bureaucracy, Copts, Foreign Relations, Islam, Israel, Labor, Military, Muslim Brotherhood, National Democratic Party, New Wafd Party, Palestinians, Peasants, Personal Status Law, Politics, *Sharia,* State Formation, *Ulama,* Union of Soviet Socialist Republics, United States, Wafd

Energy 4, 62, 70, 117, 121
see Oil Exports, export sector 5, 63-64, 71, 119, 140, 179

Fahmi, Ismail 300
Farid, Muhammad 222
Feige, E.L. 13
Food industry 66-67, 140-141, 179
Foreign aid 22, 26, 109-24, 113, 116, 125-60
misconceptions 110
politics of 171-72
size of 126-29
Foreign relations 206-208, 299
Gulf states, oil-producing states 26
see Israel, Palestinians, US, USSR
Foreign trade 80-81, 118-20, 127
international competitiveness 10, 34, 64-68
foreign exchange earnings 10, 18-19, 52, 64, 80, 128
removal of restrictions 73-74, 118-20
protectionism 64-65, 118-20

GDP 9, 109, 116-17, 127
GNP 34, 71
al-Gabali, Mustafa 7
Ganzouri, Kamal 142, 146
al-Gazzali 178
Gershuny, J.I. 13
Girgis, Habib 274
al-Graitli, Ali 7, 8, 23, 35, 46
Gramsci, Antonio 294
Gutmann, P.M. 14, 15

Hansen, Bent 11, 13
Hansen, N. 13
Heikal, Muhammad Hassanein 197, 300
Henry, S. 13
Hilal, Ibrahim Fahmy 274

Hobbes, Thomas 282-86
Housing 29-32
Hussein, Fuad Kamil 7
Hussein, King 304

Ibrahim, Saad Eddin 225, 227
al-Imari, Abdul-Galil 6, 7, 8, 23, 35, 46
Imports 64,71, 99, 113
Industry 4, 9, 66, 71, 117, 180, 182, 184-85
see economic policy-import substitution; public sector-investment
Inflation 5, 20-22, 25, 61, 69, 79, 83, 99
Interest rates 13-18, 25-26, 61
International Monetary Fund (IMF) 21, 26, 35, 52, 64, 118, 121-22, 150-51, 166, 205, 311
Investment 5, 26-29, 33, 65, 67, 71, 100, 116-18
rate of return 60-62
Islam 222-39, 240-64, 265-81
and government 283-85
Islamicist parties 198-204, 216, 270-71, 274-79, 289-91, 294
Jama'at al-Islamiya 203, 217, 225-26, 228
see Muslim Brotherhood, *Shari'a*
Islamic investment companies 16-17, 26, 43-44, 224, 231-32, 253-56
Israel 206-207, 298-306, 313
Camp David 37, 114-15, 148, 171, 192, 267, 298-302
relations with US 191, 302
Issawi, Charles 38

Johnson, Lyndon 304

Kamel, Muhammad Ibrahim 300
Kamil, Mustafa 222, 273
Kamil, Said 302
Kaufman, Robert 154
Khater, Suleiman 207
al-Khuli, Lutfi 301
Kimball, Frank 142, 152
Kissinger, Henry 304
Korayem, Karim 125

Labor 35
emigration 31, 90-108
labor unions 214, 233-34, 293
remittances 17, 18-19, 25, 52, 90-91, 99-100, 104, 116, 129
Locke, John 282-86